# Continuous Learning in Organizations

*Individual, Group, and Organizational Perspectives*

# Continuous Learning in Organizations

*Individual, Group, and Organizational Perspectives*

VALERIE I. SESSA
*Montclair State University*

MANUEL LONDON
*State University of New York at Stony Brook*

LEA LAWRENCE ERLBAUM ASSOCIATES, PUBLISHERS
2006 Mahwah, New Jersey London

Lawrence Erlbaum Associates, Inc., Publishers
10 Industrial Avenue
Mahwah, New Jersey 07430
www.erlbaum.com

Cover design by Tomai Maridou

CIP information for this book can be obtained by contacting the Library of Congress

ISBN 0-8058-5017-1 (cloth : alk. paper)
ISBN 0-8058-5018-X (pbk. : alk. paper)

Books published by Lawrence Erlbaum Associates are printed on acid-free paper, and their bindings are chosen for strength and durability.

Printed in the United States of America
10 9 8 7 6 5 4 3 2 1

*For Joseph and Marilyn*

# Contents

# Preface

Learning is needed more than ever in today's complex world. You know the litany: Globalization, changing economies, new technology, increased competition, new products and services, and emerging and interacting disciplines all impose pressures to adapt. These changes raise the potential of rewards for those with foresight. Individuals, groups, and organizations need to learn continuously to be ready for these changes and create a world that maximizes their chances for success.

What do we mean by learning and continuous learning and how does this apply to individuals, groups, and organizations? We think of people learning, but groups and organizations learn too. *Learning* is the process of acquiring new skills, knowledge, and worldviews. At the individual level, learning is manifest in new behaviors. At the team level, learning is evident in changing communications between team members, standard operating procedures, and behavioral routines. At the organizational level, learning is demonstrated through changes in such areas as vision, strategy, policies, regulations, structure, and products or services. *Continuous learning* is regularly and purposefully acquiring ever deeper and broader knowledge and skills and applying them to new behaviors. At the individual level, this includes learning new disciplines, expanding one's knowledge and expertise, and reconstructing one's self-concept. At the group and organizational levels, continuous learning is manifested in the form of restructuring to meet changing conditions, adding new skills and knowledge, and creating increasingly sophisticated systems through reflection on processes and outcomes. Continuous learning is a mentality and behavioral routine that reflects a belief and dedication to learning and change.

Learning and continuous learning are vital in today's complex, ambiguous, and constantly changing world. Individuals, groups, and organizations need to take control of their own learning. They need to acquire the skills and knowledge to do their work better and be ready for future challenges. They cannot wait to be told what to learn because such instructions may never be forthcoming. Those who learn only in response to changing conditions may be too late. Those who seek feedback and are hungry for new ideas, methods, and processes are likely to protect themselves against unforeseen barriers. They are ready to "turn around on a dime." They are flexible and responsive in the face of new demands, and they create conditions that allow them to control their environment.

In a nutshell, individuals need continuous learning to do their jobs well today and tomorrow and to increase their chances for advancement and professional growth under changing conditions. Groups need continuous learning to meet their goals and be ready to accept new goals as the situation changes. Organizations need continuous learning to form achievable missions and master uncertain and ambiguous environments.

Learning is already big business. According to the American Society for Training and Development, 79% of employees in the United States received some sort of training in 2002. Across the world, this ranges from 59% in Japan to 90% in Australia/New Zealand and Africa. U.S. organizations spent an average of 2.2% of payroll on training in 2002, which, along with Japan, was the lowest. Africa spent the highest percentage of payroll on training (5.9%) (American Society for Training and Development [ASTD], 2003). But these percentages underestimate learning expenses. They do not take into account adults returning to college, taking classes, reading books, or researching online on their own time. They do not take into account adults learning in organizations by joining interest groups and professional societies and by just helping each other. And they do not take into account resources spent on consultants who help organizations bring about change.

Given this investment in learning, what is to be done to use our resources as wisely as possible to improve learning? Our view is that learning takes place within a system of individuals, groups, and organizations all interacting in a complex environment. This book integrates learning theories and concepts across multiple levels—individuals, groups, and organizations. This allows us to broaden and simplify what we know about learning and continuous learning. Our approach is grounded in current theory, research, and practice, and draws from a multitude of learning disciplines. We describe the triggers and resources needed for meaningful and ongoing learning within individual, group, and organizational systems to make the most of our learning investment.

This book focuses on "knowing about" rather than "knowing how." In other words, this is not a "how to" book. Our purpose is to communicate the meaning and value of continuous learning to individuals, groups, and organizations. The book is for students and practitioners in the fields of human resource development, training, management and executive education, coaching, and organizational change and development. It is also for executives who establish directions for learning and need to convince others that continuous learning is key to the ongoing success of their enterprise. Professionals and students of organization development and change will benefit from understanding how people learn, the different ways that learning occurs, and the link between individual learning and organization success. Trainers will benefit from recognizing individuals' readiness for learning and how curricula and instructional design meet organizational needs. Coaches will benefit from seeing how they can enhance their contribution as guides, role models, and corporate educators for targeted behavior change. Human resource professionals will learn how to integrate training and development within a cohesive set of interrelated human resource processes that directly support business objectives. Top-level executives will see how human resource development is a continuous process that rests on, and contributes to, their vision for corporate success. All readers will benefit from contemporary directions for leadership and management training, and our emphasis on assessing learning needs and outcomes.

The book is divided into nine chapters. In chapter 1, we describe what we mean by continuous learning at the individual, group, and organizational level, and present a systems model of adaptive, generative, and transformative learning. The next three chapters focus on individual continuous learning (chap. 2), individual characteristics affecting learning (chap. 3), and environmental conditions that support learning (chap. 4). Chapters 5 and 6 examine the meaning of group learning and ways to support it, and chapters 7 and 8 examine organizational learning and ways to support it. The final chapter considers future directions for continuous learning processes and methods for development across levels.

Throughout the book we highlight several themes. We apply adaptive, generative, and transformative learning to individual, group, and organizational levels of analysis. Conditions establish demands for different types of learning, and individual, group, and organizations are systems that may vary in their readiness for different types of learning. Hence, we have a contingency model suggesting that interventions for facilitating learning depend on the match between interconnected systems at different levels and between the environment or task and a given system. Assessment of learning outcomes is key to understanding and tracking the accomplishment of learning goals, and we discuss assessment at each level of analysis.

Writing a book is often a collaborative effort, not just between authors but also with the assistance of many others. One of the ways that we tried to embrace continuous learning is by involving others who are knowledgeable in this area. We conducted an online "Delphi" discussion on current practices and future directions for continuous learning in organizations and invited academic researchers, practitioners, and executives whom we believe are opinion leaders and experts to participate. First, we needed to learn how to "get" a group online, and we thank Joseph Fung for his valuable assistance. Then, we posed sets of questions during the course of 10 weeks to engender discussion with our participants. The first set of questions focused on the meaning of learning:

- What is individual learning? . . . group learning? . . . organizational learning?
- How do organizations make decisions based on continuing input of information?
- How can we tell that learning has occurred at each level?
- How is learning similar or different at the individual, group, and organizational levels?
- What is continuous learning and why is it more important today than ever before?
- How is learning similar to or different from development at the individual, group, and organizational levels? How does development impact learning and vice-versa?

The second set examined systems and/or cultures for individual, group, and organization learning, and their interplay:

- How can learning and development at each level—individual, group, and organization—enhance or detract from learning and development at other levels?
- What are examples of organizational systems and/or cultures currently used in organizations that enhance or are detrimental to individual, group, and organizational learning and development?
- What key questions or issues for research and practice are you struggling with?

The third set of question examined future directions for continuous learning:

- What are pressures, trends, and opportunities in learning and development at all levels?
- What conditions influence learning and development (e.g., cultural, economic, systemic, biological, technological, others) and how are these evolving to influence learning and development in the future? What are alternative futures for research and practice.

We are especially grateful for the insightful contributions of William Byham, David Day, Phillip Doesschate, Susan Jackson, Cynthia McCauley, Robert Mintz, and Michael West for participating actively in this online discussion. We draw on their comments throughout the book to enrich our ideas and commentary on the literature.

In addition, we asked our participants and other personal acquaintances for personal reflections about the meaning of continuous learning. In particular, we wondered:

- What does continuous learning mean to you?
- Do you consider yourself to be a continuous learner?
- What is the importance of continuous learning in your life?
- How have you helped others to become continuous learners?

We wish to thank Brother Clark Berge, Dr. Richard Bronson, Professor Richard Gerrig, Ann Helfgott, Sister Margaret Ann Landry, Stella Lee, Allen Sachs, and Professor Gerrit Wolf as well as our online participants for their insights about what continuous learning means to them.

Finally, we used a classroom of graduate students at Montclair State University to participate in a learning community with us. As individuals, they read our original drafts and added additional references, tried out our ideas, critiqued them, and provided ideas and examples. We thank Adam Barbaris, Lori Anne Caserta, Erin Edler, Rose Flores, Mark Halliday, and Irina Melnichuk for being open to a cutting-edge classroom experience based on learning principles that allowed them to take control of their own learning experiences, and to be teachers, students, facilitators, questioners, individual learners, group learners, and organization learners at the same time.

We dedicate this book to our spouses, who make continuous learning a necessity and pleasure.

# About the Authors

*Valerie I. Sessa* is Assistant Professor of Industrial and Organizational Psychology at Montclair State University in New Jersey. Previously, she was a research scientist at the Center for Creative Leadership in Greensboro, North Carolina. During her tenure at CCL as the director of executive selection, she managed the start-up operation designed to provide cutting-edge research and knowledge on executive selection to the academic and business communities. In this role, she served as the company expert and spokesperson to clients, professional audiences, and the press. Later as director of new initiatives, she directed, designed, and implemented ongoing innovative business initiatives that supported long-term business goals. Valerie has also worked as a consultant in a variety of areas, most recently assessing middle and high-potential managers using instruments, behavioral-assessment centers, and feedback. Valerie has presented and published extensively on such topics as executive selection, e-leadership, and teams. She has written a book with Dr. J. Taylor, *Executive Selection: Strategies for Success* (Jossey Bass, 2000). Valerie holds her M.A. and Ph.D. in Industrial and Organizational Psychology from New York University. She is an active member of the APA, SIOP, Academy of Management, and Metropolitan New York Association of Applied Psychology.

*Manuel London* is professor and director of the Center for Human Resource Management in the Harriman School for Management at the State University of New York at Stony Brook. He previously taught at the University of Illinois at Champaign and was a researcher and human resource manager at AT&T. He received his Ph.D. in industrial and organizational psychology from the Ohio State University. His books include *Self and Interpersonal Insight: How People Learn About Themselves and Others in Organizations* (Oxford University Press, 1995), *Leadership Development: Paths to Self-Insight and Professional Growth* (Lawrence

Erlbaum Associates, 2002), and *Job Feedback: Giving, Seeking, and Using Feedback for Performance Improvement* (Lawrence Erlbaum Associates, 2nd edition, 2004). He consults with business and government organizations on competency modeling, performance evaluation, employee attitude surveys, and management and career development programs.

CHAPTER

# 1

# The Meaning of Continuous Learning

Continuous learning is risky. It is risky for people. It is risky for organizations. We know this is an odd way to start a book on continuous learning, but we want to address these risks outright. What we are presenting is not simple. We have no silver bullet. We have no magic solution. Organizations and the people in them who want to embrace continuous learning—who truly see the need for it—are not in for an easy time.

Why is continuous learning risky for individuals? If you need to learn, that means you have to admit that you do not know something. If you need to learn, you need to stop doing what you have been doing and do something different. If you need to learn, you might look bad as you stumble trying something new. If you need to learn, you might fail. Such risks may be okay occasionally, but continuously . . . ?

Continuous learning for organizations is even more risky. Do top managers really want employees who have been trained to think critically, question the status quo, come up with better ways of doing things, and expect their managers to make decisions effectively (Albrecht, 2003)? Frederick Herzberg, the noted motivation theorist, contended that most executives want workers who are "housebroken." They say they want highly motivated employees who can add value, but when it comes right down to it, they really want obedience, and they are threatened by bright subordinates (as cited in Albrecht, 2003).

Even worse, once an organization begins to encourage continuous learning, there is no going back. Because if continuous learning is no longer supported, executives now have an organization full of employees who think critically, question the status quo, come up with better ways of doing things, expect their managers to make decisions effectively, *and* are angry because they are no longer being treated like the adults they have been encouraged to become.

## THE NEED FOR CONTINUOUS LEARNING

Despite these risks, there is a growing need for continuous learning at the individual, team, and organization levels in today's organizations, be they large or small, for profit or not-for-profit, private or public, corporate, governmental or nongovernmental. We are seeing a rapid pace of change in business, an intensely competitive global environment, greater demands placed on organizations, an increasing dissatisfaction of managers and employees with the traditional, hierarchical, command-and-control management model, and the realization that knowledge is a competitive advantage.

Groups at any organizational level need continuous learning. Increasingly groups are being called on to make important decisions in and for the organization. People are not inherently equipped to work in groups. Group members need to learn to be a group—that is, move from a collective of individuals to a cohesive unit focused on the same goals and understanding the methods of achieving those goals. The group needs to learn how to structure itself, communicate, conduct work processes, make decisions, and put these decisions into action. As the organizational context shifts, groups must be fluid enough to shift with them—restructuring themselves, adapting decisions, and updating plans. Groups and the individuals who make up the groups need to learn continuously or they will find themselves standing still in a continuously changing environment.

Organizations need continuous learning for at least four reasons:

1. They are dealing with the increasing complexity of managing in multicultural and multinational environments and uncertain economic climates.
2. Ambiguity is often high because complex systems such as organizations are not predictable and thus not controllable.
3. Ways of working are becoming more fluid with the advent of electronic communications technologies, allowing, for instance, geographically dispersed teams and labor markets in different parts of the world.
4. They have moved from a heavily manufacturing age to a service age and are now moving to a knowledge age, and creating knowledge requires continuous learning.

To address these issues, organizations are paradoxically being called on to be aligned and change at the same time. They need to recognize and adapt to current conditions while they generate new models of operating and possibly transform themselves entirely. This means that they need to learn continuously, and they need to encourage the learning of the groups and individuals who make up the organization. If they don't, they will not be able to keep pace with their competitors.

The average individual, at any organizational level, is not equipped to handle the complexity, ambiguity, and fluidity of today's organizations. Individuals must learn and develop continuously in order to perform well in their *current* jobs, support their employment security as conditions change, and promote their career advancement. When organizations provide their employees with training, they train employees on the skills that the organization deems necessary. Employees' traits and attitudes that are unnecessary or that seem to impede work (such as cognitive and emotional development that lead people in new directions—see risks discussed earlier) may be unused, suppressed, and perhaps even thwarted, and gradually weaken. As a consequence, employees may work harder and longer to succeed, but may feel detached, bored, angry, empty, and out of control (LaBier, 1986). They may increasingly feel alienated but don't know why. If they do not see the need for continuous learning and take control of their own learning, they will be left out in the cold by the very organizations they work for and the society in which they live.

## TOWARD A MULTILEVEL CONTINGENCY THEORY OF CONTINUOUS LEARNING

Continuous learning may be risky, but it is necessary and, as we argue, actually a natural characteristic of individuals, groups, and organizations. As systems, they have internal learning mechanisms that can be activated or triggered and supported or stymied and thwarted. In this book, we wanted a way to get our arms around the vast and divergent field of learning and both broaden and simplify it—thereby making the knowledge that we have about learning more useful. We propose a model of continuous learning that argues the following:

1. Individuals, groups, and organizations are nested living systems. The term *system* implies input, throughput or process, output, and feedback over time (e.g., output affects later input). Living systems have three additional characteristics. First, they are self-organizing through their interactions with the environment. That is, living systems maintain and renew themselves using energy and resources from the environment. Second, living systems are both closed and open. That is, they have forms or structures that remain stable as information, materials, or other matter are transformed as they flow through. Third, living systems have an organizing activity or process involved in the continual embodiment of the system's pattern of organization and structure (Capra, 1997). A simple system is depicted in Fig. 1.1. A system that learns monitors and collects information from the environment (input), translates that information to see if it is consistent with prior experiences (throughput), and if different, engages in a new behavior (output) and formulates knowledge about the relationships between own actions and environmental reactions (feedback).

2. Individuals, groups, and organizations are engaged in intention-bound work. Learning is a by-product of this work. Goals and obstacles in the environment establish the need for learning. The need may arise from any trigger or

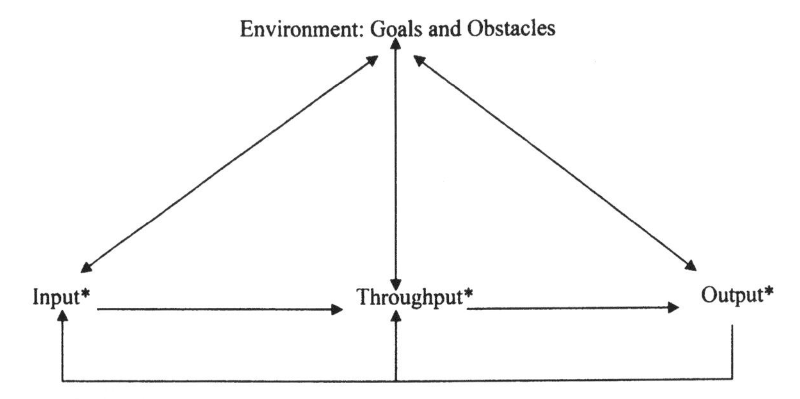


FIG 1.1. A simple open-systems model. Adaptive, generative, and transformative learning are possible within each asterisked (*) element. This system can be an individual, group, or organization.

disturbance in the environment, which could include such things as a new competitor, a change in the task because of a new technology, or a new idea that needs to be brought into fruition such as developing a new product or creating a new market.

3. Learning at the individual, group, and organization level can be adaptive, generative, and/or transformative. Adaptive learning is reacting to a change in the environment. Generative learning (Senge, 1990) is generating new knowledge and conditions. Transformative learning (Mezirow, 1990, 1991, 1994) is creating and applying frame-breaking ideas and bringing about radically new conditions.

4. Fit is the match between (a) environmental demands for learning and (b) the capability or readiness of the individual, group, or organization to alter components of themselves. The system–environment interaction is a two-way street. Goals and obstacles in the environment impose the need for change and learning. Conversely, individuals, groups, and organizations may initiate change and learning that affects the goal, obstacle, or environment.

5. This systemic, contingency model of continuous learning suggests barriers to continuous learning and interventions to support continuous learning. These are discussed throughout the book.

6. Feedback and assessment are needed to determine the need and readiness for learning and the match between need and readiness, evaluate the effectiveness of different learning methods for achieving learning goals (i.e., meeting the need), and recalibrate learning methods for ongoing improvement in meeting goals—the essence of continuous learning.

7. All of the preceding elements are a fluid process that occurs over time, with ebb and flow, give and take, and positive and negative experiences and outcomes.

### A Systems Approach to Individual, Group, and Organization Learning

A way to broaden and simplify learning is to approach it from a systems perspective. Systems theory, often applied in organizational sciences, is the science of "wholeness" and was first established by Ludwig von Bertalanffy in his 1968 book *General System Theory* (Von Bertalanffy, 1976). Bertalanffy's vision of a "general science of wholeness" was based on his observation that systemic concepts and principles could be applied in many different fields of study. He believed that general principles apply to systems irrespective of their nature as the theory is concerned with problems of relationships, of structure, and of interdependence rather than with the constant attributes of objects. Whereas Bertalanffy was concerned with open systems in general, our interest is specifically with living systems—individuals, groups, and organizations.

A key characteristic of systems is that they are integrated wholes whose properties cannot be reduced to those of smaller parts (Capra, 1997). Their essential or "systemic" properties are properties of the whole, which none of the parts have. These properties arise from the organizing relations of the parts. Individuals are wholes that cannot be reduced to their parts. Groups are wholes that cannot be reduced to their parts. We can talk about the individuals who compose the groups, but what makes them a group is something more and different, over and above the individuals in the group. Similarly, organizations need to be understood as wholes that cannot be reduced to their parts.

A key characteristic of living systems is that, although they do not exist to learn, they have learning mechanisms built into their very being. At their core they are engaged in intention-bound work (Jaques, 2001). That is, they are engaged in selecting goals, choosing how to achieve them, overcoming obstacles on the way, and evaluating the outcomes of their work. Systems learn in the process of work or trying to achieve valued goals. Systems find themselves in situations in which they wish to attain something. For instance, individuals may seek to do work that they find fulfilling, or they may want to look good to those higher in the organization. Groups may have a product to produce with quality and efficiency. Organizations may have a vision to fulfill and bottom-line goals, but are not sure how to go about it. So the system explores and experiments, and if it is successful, learning occurs and goals are achieved. Thus, learning is a by-product of intention-bound work; it is not an end in itself and happens only when there is a need. Living systems, triggered by a goal, obstacle, or disturbance in the environment, experiment and practice, and in the process, set goals, try new behaviors, seek feedback, and find ways of interacting that work best for them. Sometimes they change the environment in the process, making it more welcoming and beneficent—a greater source of enrichment and support (Jaques, 2001). All living systems are continuously engaged in this testing and learning—in judging, choosing, deciding, in order to establish goals and in order to overcome obstacles or uncertainties encountered while engaging in goal-directed work. However, as we describe in later chapters, learning at the individual, group, and organizational levels may not be in line with what the organization (or top management) needs or expects.

Living systems maintain themselves in a changing environment (Capra, 1997; Laszlo, 1996). Because of constant fluxes in the environment, systems must adapt, change, develop, and evolve, as they select and achieve goals and new goals, overcome obstacles, and evaluate outcomes of their work, or they die—they can never be "still." At work, individuals may be fired or derailed, groups may be disbanded, and organizations may fail if they do not adapt, change, develop, or evolve. Systems thrive in constantly changing environments by re-creating themselves. They don't just respond to change and adapt. They can also explore new forms and behaviors and change the world in which they operate.

Because living systems span such a wide range of phenomena, involving individual organisms, social systems, and ecosystems, Bertalanffy believed that a general systems theory would offer an ideal conceptual framework for unifying various scientific disciplines that had become isolated and fragmented. In terms of understanding continuous learning at the individual, group, and organizational levels, a systems approach has three advantages:

First, it affords us the capability of integrating and simplifying several fields of learning across many disciplines including developmental psychology, educational psychology, education and adult education in particular, group theories and research, and organizational learning theories and research. Although we found that there is little crossover between these fields (written materials are not cross-cited) and different vocabularies are often used, many concepts and ideas can be applied across fields.

Second, our analysis shows the relationships between levels of analysis. Though individuals are whole systems in and of themselves (and see the group and the organization as environment), they are a part of other wholes—groups and organizations—that themselves need to be understood as whole systems. Similarly, groups are systems in and of themselves (and "see" the individual members as parts and the organization as environment), yet they are part of organizations, which are also whole systems. This forms an increasingly complex hierarchy of intertwined systems. Thus we must think in a nested and iterative fashion. Figure 1.2 depicts this nested quality. Organizational learning builds upon group learning, which is dependent on individual learning. Yet group learning is more than the learning of the individuals in the group, and organizational learning is more than the patterns of behavior established by groups within the organization. Finally, organizations and groups are environments that impact individual learning (see, e.g., Kozlowski & Salas, 1997).

Third, approaching learning from a systems perspective encourages us to understand simultaneously the individual and the collective (groups and organizations), and the internal and external processes associated with each of them (Wilbur, 2001a, 2001b). To fully understand learning, we must study how people

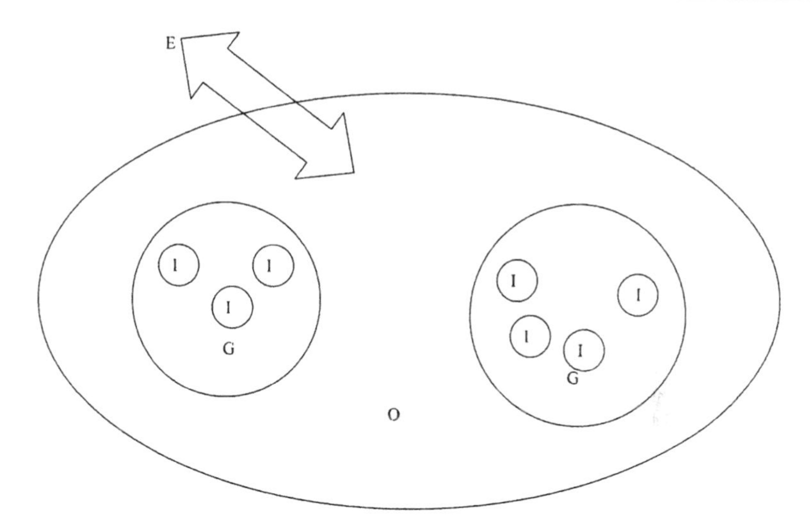


FIG. 1.2. Nested individual (I), group (G), and organization (O) systems and environment (E).

make sense of the situations they face and how they feel about them (their cognitions and emotions) as well as their readily observable behaviors and decisions. Similarly, we must understand the internal workings of groups—their culture and values—as well as the patterns of behavior. We must understand the exterior of the group—practices, procedures, policies, structures, strategies, and visions. Finally, we must understand the internal and external workings of the organization. Each of these is related to and affects the other. If we do not take into account all pieces and their relationships, vital information is lost in our understanding of learning at each level.

### Permeability Between Levels

As noted previously, the nested-systems concept implies causal interrelationships between levels. Systems develop networks of relationships—interconnected social relationships that offer opportunities for, and place constraints on, behavior (Brass, Galaskiewicz, Greve, & Tsai, 2004). Individual, group, and organizational learning contribute to each other in multiple ways. For instance, consider the following:

Individual to group:

- Group members' knowing about others' experiences and expertise helps them understand who can contribute to different elements of the group's task. This leads to patterns of behavior that become enmeshed in group operations—that is, "how we do things."

- New group members may disrupt group routines and lead to new ways of doing things.
- Motivated individuals can energize the group.
- Individuals' work patterns and preferences affect how they interact with others.

Group to individual:

- Individuals teach each other.
- Group members spark ideas.
- Group members inspire/motivate each other.
- Group members may be role models for learning.

Individual to organization:

- Individuals request attention to, and resources for, career development.
- Individuals in key positions serve as role models, champions, and sources of resources for learning.
- Individuals create communication patterns and work structures that become routine in the organization.
- Individuals use their knowledge of systems and processes to suggest ideas for continuous improvement.
- Individual job satisfaction affects organizational climate.

Organization to individual:

- Learning is a value promulgated by the organization; top executives are champions and role models for continuous learning.
- The organization provides training, job assignments, and other learning opportunities and resources.
- The organization evaluates and rewards learning and development (development as an important part of performance goal setting and performance appraisal); human resource development clearly is tied to the organization's competitiveness for the best talent and hence to bottom-line objectives.
- Job requirements affect who is hired.
- The organizational climate affects individual work satisfaction.

Group to organization:

- Intergroup perceptions, work relationships, and communication patterns affect organization effectiveness (e.g., means of working out intergroup conflicts; "us vs. them" relationships affect organizational performance).
- Team spirit, friendships, and interpersonal feeling affect organizational climate (feelings about the organization).

Organization to group:

- The organization creates work groups—permanent or temporary; part of the organizational hierarchy or ad hoc.
- The organization establishes cross-function and within-function structures and hierarchies.
- The organizational culture (characteristics of the organization that affect standards and work relationships) affects team culture and morale as well as individual feelings and job satisfaction.

### Adaptive, Generative, and Transformative Learning

Outside forces disturb the system's status quo and thereby trigger lerarning. At its simplest level, learning is *adaptive.* It is an unconscious behavior change where the system reacts to a new stimulus—an obstacle or uncertainty that is getting in the way of goal attainment. In addressing this often unwanted or unexpected stimulus, the system may try an already familiar solution, modify a familiar solution, or maybe try a new behavior, using trial and error. Systems pick up information from their environment on how they should act, and they change their behavior accordingly—but this learning is not conscious or reflective. A simple example of adaptive learning is a young child learning the language that is spoken to him or her.

However, people are endowed with reflective consciousness—the capacity to know and monitor one's own mental events (Laszlo, 1996). Thus humans, and systems made of humans, can engage in a second kind of learning—*generative* learning, which is purposefully adding new knowledge and skills in the expectation that the new knowledge or skill will aid in goal attainment. A simple example of generative learning is an adult deliberately learning a new language—through courses, studying, listening to tapes, reading, speaking, practicing, immersion, and so on.

Finally, systems can undergo a dramatic and fundamental shift in the way that they interact with the environment in order to achieve their goal—*transformative* learning. All living systems may be able to do this, but they don't do so as a matter of course. Some people have a proclivity or talent for transformation. Others are resistant. After all, sticking with the status quo or making minor adaptations is easier and more comfortable. Sometimes, systems (individuals, groups, or organizations) are forced into transformational change, or at least trying to transform, due to dire circumstances. They must re-create themselves or die. They develop a new understanding of themselves through reflective practice and experiential learning. A simple example of this is a person developing a new understanding of themselves through conversation (language) with others.

Learning is self-determined. An outsider can never direct a living system to learn, they can only disturb and support it. It is like the old adage, "You can lead a horse to water, but you can't make him drink." The living system not only specifies which disturbances from the environment trigger it but also specifies its changes (Capra, 2002). Individuals, groups, and organizations will learn only what they need or want to learn, and will use that learning only if they perceive they need it. Teachers, consultants, facilitators, mentors, and so on, can provide triggers, needed resources, and encouragement in the direction the organization needs, but they can't make learning occur, or predict what will be learned (if anything) from a trigger, or make the system use its learnings.

A final characteristic of living systems is that as the system learns, it is also changing as a learner. As it explores and experiments, it learns more about what it takes to explore and experiment. In essence, learning begets more learning in a continuous cycle. The system, when effective, learns how to learn continuously.

In summary, individuals, groups, and organizations need to be and are by their nature continuous learners. However, this is risky business in today's business organizations because continuous learners take responsibility for their learning, upsetting the status quo, thinking for themselves, setting new directions and strategies to get there, and changing their environment. Individuals, groups, and organizations are interrelated systems. They are stimulated by environmental changes and the effects of their own behavior, and they learn from each other over time. They adapt to changes, initiate learning, and sometimes transform themselves and the environments in which they operate.

### Match Between the Need to Learn and the Capability and Readiness to Learn

Environments may be internal (e.g., the task) or external (e.g., a competitive force) to an individual, group, or organizational system. Environments impose demands and set conditions in which the system operates. Of course, these demands and conditions are in constant flux—sometimes in foreseeable ways, but often not. Similarly, the system itself may impose pressures on the environment to change as it engages in intention-bound work. Sometimes, the two mesh nicely. The environment requires an adaptation, and the system is "triggered" by the change and ready to adapt. Other times, the environment changes but the system does not learn—perhaps due to attention to a different goal or obstacle. Alternatively, the system may attempt a transformation that the environment is not ready to accommodate (e.g., the picture phone in the late 1970s has now become commonplace in the early 2000s with the more convenient and affordable cell phone technology). A mismatch in need and readiness to change in either direction (system to environment or vice versa) is likely to cause a collision and the collapse, or at least weakening, of the system.

The mismatch between learning needs and readiness is a barrier to continuous learning in today's organizations. It may thwart learning altogether or may bring about learning, but learning the hard way—that is, learning from failure, which can

System's Readiness for Change

| Environment's Need for Change | Not ready | Ready |
|---|---|---|
| Low | A<br>Status Quo | B<br>Frustration, Disappointment, Struggle; Persistence leads to success |
| High | C<br>Learning failure beyond adaptation | D<br>Continuous learning |

FIG. 1.3. Match between system's readiness for change and environment's demand or need for change.

be costly in time, energy, and financial resources. Facilitating factors can promote learning readiness and generate an environment that encourages learning.

The boxes in Fig. 1.3 suggest what happens when there is a match or mismatch in the type of learning (adaptive, generative, or transformative) between a system's readiness to change, whether the system is an individual, group, or organization, and the demands or needs of another system, the task, or the environment. The system will be stable or at equilibrium if there is no need for change and the system is not triggered or ready to change (Box A). If change is not needed but the system is somehow triggered (via attention to another goal or obstacle not readily apparent) and is ready and in fact anxious to generate a new idea or transform in some way, for instance, to implement an exciting new idea, the system may be in for disappointment (an idea before its time) or may become the pioneer in a new field (the next Xerox, Microsoft, or Apple) (Box B). If the system is not ready (not triggered) and the need is high, the system is likely to fail or at least not learn beyond adaptation (Box C). Methods to help trigger the need for a change or lack of preparedness may be helpful, for instance, ways of demonstrating how other systems changed successfully (role models) or establishing recognition of the need to change through discussion. Learning is likely to occur without much prompting or aid if the need matches readiness (Box D).

What is not represented in this simple model is the interrelationships between the nested systems. At the individual level, the group and the organization are part of the environment. At the group level, the organization is part of the environment. But what happens when individuals (who are parts of groups and organizations) are ready to change, but the group or the organization is not? And how do need for change and readiness for change interact between levels?

This analysis suggests a contingency model of interventions to enhance learning depending on the condition. Let's consider a couple of scenarios:

1. A new technology imposes a radical transformation on the way a group processes work, for example, a computer-assisted design and prototype application to product development in a research-and-development (R&D) team. Two members of the team may be experts at producing customized drawings and hand-crafted prototypes. They may not see the need to adopt the new technology, which may be faster but far more expensive and not as high quality. Moreover, they may not feel that they have the time to learn. Perhaps they are ready to adapt by using computer-aided design, but they aren't willing to examine new prototype development methods. Are they holding the team back? Are they still needed on the team? Is the team risking their high-quality prototype design for rapid trial of new ideas? Can the team adopt both approaches—computer design and production for early prototypes and hand-crafted methods for final designs?
2. A new chief executive officer (CEO) has a vision for transforming around a low-growth, regional retail chain into a worldwide, online business. Buyers need to understand new markets, advertising, and pricing strategies. A new head buyer is hired who generates innovative processes for tracking sales and linking sales to orders from factories abroad. Buyers need to focus on sales trends and sales volumes by region and relying on the new automatic, just-in-time ordering and distribution system instead of monitoring inventories and placing orders one season in advance. They need to experiment with styles and observe what catches on in different markets rather than employ a follow-the-leader mentality that requires commitment to one make-it-or-break-it fashion line. Can the buyers be generative learners, trying new ideas? Can they become transformative learners, going beyond the example set by the CEO and head buyer by creating new roles for themselves and contributing to the evolution of new directions for the business? Suppose the CEO and head buyer are ready to make the transformation but the organization isn't? Suppose its people and systems don't have the capability and financial resources to make the change? Suppose the market is not ready to respond to what seems to be a good idea? Will this lead to a slow start? Will the CEO be able to maintain a steady course for the new business in hopes that persistence will pay off (as it did for Amazon.com) or will it lead to bankruptcy? Do the leaders of this new business model recognize the resistance they may encounter, and do they have strategies to overcome these barriers to change?

### Feedback and Assessment

Finally, *feedback* is a critical systems component. Feedback allows the system to recognize the effects of its actions and choices and to change them over time to have a more positive effect. *Assessment,* or measurement, is one basis for feedback. Of course, assessment is not perfect. It may be subjective, in which case, it may be biased or one-sided. It may be faulty in other ways, for instance, inconsistent measurement (i.e., unreliable), or it may not measure what it is supposed to (i.e., invalid). Careful delineation of objectives and development of reliable and valid measures of learning need, readiness, and outcome are essential to guide continuous learning over time.

***Defining Assessment.*** Learning may be slow and incremental or rapid and transformational. We need some way to determine whether learning has occurred, and whether continuous-learning behaviors and actions have had a positive effect. As we argue through the course of this book, feedback is crucial to learning, and assessment is a type of feedback. Individuals and groups need feedback on the value of their continuous-learning efforts so they can change their behaviors and spend their time more wisely. Organizations need to know whether the resources they devote to employee training, group development, and organization change efforts are cost-effective. They also need to evaluate whether the organization itself is developing and whether minor or major changes are making a difference to the bottom line or the organization's long-term viability.

In addition to determining whether learning efforts have been worth the investment, assessment is a way to identify learning gaps and provide directions for future learning. Borrowing a medical model, assessment at any given time is a way to diagnose current conditions and prescribe treatments. Assessment pinpoints problem areas that can be fixed. It also raises opportunities—new and previously unrecognized directions for learning. It is an exploration process that focuses on the target of assessment (the individual, group, or organization) and the environment.

In a nutshell, *assessment is a process by which information about the individual's, group's, or organization's current state is identified and made available to help direct learning decisions.* Assessments are an important step in recognizing the gap between where the individual, group, or organization currently is and where it needs to be, thereby clarifying learning that needs to take place. Later in the learning process, (re)assessment(s) determine what has changed and what needs to be learned next. Assessment is not a one-time event, but rather, as a part of learning, it is a continuous process. Our goal throughout this book is to explain what we know about assessment so that students of learning can get their arms around this complicated topic and so practitioners of learning can evaluate the resources that exist and decide what is needed in their organization.

Assessment of continuous learning tracks growth as it is accumulated, integrated, and used over time by individuals, groups, or organizations. We need to track what is happening to make learning occur, and what is being learned. The question for assessment is how to measure and evaluate learning at any one point in time, and continuous learning over time, at the individual, group, and organizational levels. We say more about assessment of learning outcomes in subsequent chapters.

## EXPERT VIEWS: THE DISCUSSION BEGINS

As we mentioned in the Preface, we elicited experts' opinions about the meaning and effects of continuous learning. The names and backgrounds of the professionals who participated in our 10-week online discussion are included in Appendix A along with excerpts from these conversations. In the chapters, we synthesize their perspectives to help inform our presentation. Readers can delve into their attitudes more deeply by reading the excerpts in Appendix A.

We began our online discussion by asking our experts to define individual, group, organization, and continuous learning and how they could tell whether learning has happened at each level. Did they feel that learning is similar at each level or different? Is learning different from development? Also, we wanted to know whether they believed that continuous learning is as, or more, important today than ever before.

Robert Mintz, an organization human resource executive, argued that we form our beliefs early in life and that discontinuities in the environment that threaten these beliefs provoke learning. Teachers or coaches help validate the need for learning and provide directions for learning. People who learn on their own are likely to change more readily.

Cindy McCauley, a researcher at the Center for Creative Leadership in Greensboro, North Carolina, suggested that learning by definition is continuous and so learning doesn't need "continuous" as a modifier.

Bill Byham, the founder and director of an international human resource consulting firm, distinguished between learning and its application. He believes that the world is changing and business and job requirements are changing—all requiring people to adapt. "Organizations that are not filled with continuous learners will inevitably fall behind." He warned that the world of work is full of examples of organizations that may teach one skill but reinforce another. Bill emphasized that learning alone is not really important unless it is put to some use. Realization of learning—for instance, employees using knowledge and skills they acquired in training—is key. "Realization is a sustainable, positive change in people's performance that dramatically increases the ability of an enterprise to achieve its business goals." He described the need to coordinate the acquisition of skills at various levels (individual, group, and organization) so that an initiative can be implemented.

Phil Doesschate, a systems analyst, offered models of individual, group, and organizational learning and development, providing examples at different levels of depth and complexity and highlighting the cumulative or evolutionary nature of learning. He distinguished between rote learning, application of learning, independent thought, and achieving major breakthroughs as the stages of learning, and moving from a basic connection to one's environment to mastering one's environment and enlightenment as stages of development.

In summary, our experts, whose opinions are outlined more fully in Appendix A, emphasized that learning is developmentally linked based on "life scripts imparted at the earliest of ages." They suggested that learning often happens when a person faces a disruption—a life change or transition—that creates the need and motivation for new ways of doing things. Such disruptions happen more frequently now than in the past, due to globalization and technology, creating the press for continuous learning and ongoing sense making of the world around us. Learning is a way to respond in an individual way—to transform ourselves in relation to the needs of our changing situations. Learning builds self-sufficiency and gives us a sense of power and autonomy.

## CONCLUSION

We argued that there is a growing need for continuous learning at all levels of analysis. The systems perspective gives us a framework for understanding how individual, group, and organizational systems operate and interrelate in a continuously changing world. The systems approach allows us to integrate fields of learning across disciplines, shows relationships between levels of analysis, and allows us to understand internal and external processes of the individual and the collective. Adaptive learning is basically an unconscious or mindless response to changes in the environment. Generative learning is proactive, anticipating change and establishing readiness to face unexpected situations. Transformative learning is self-reinvention, sometimes even altering the environment to make it more supportive of systems growth.

## QUESTIONS FOR THOUGHT AND DISCUSSION

1. When you think about yourself and your future and the need to be a continuous learner, how does that make you feel? Do you feel anxious about it? . . . fearful? . . . excited? Are you up to the task?
2. How are people learning systems? Think about yourself. What is the input, throughput, and output of your learning? What environmental factors influence your learning?
3. Select an organization you know well. How do the members of the organization comprise groups? Is each person a member of one group or several groups? How do the groups interrelate? When people in a group change (say, they suddenly behave differently), how does the group react? When a group changes (say, the members make changes in how a product is produced), how does the organization react?

4. Describe a case when you or a group tried to adapt to a situational change when a more major, transformational change would have been more successful.
5. In your view, is continuous learning a habit that people acquire early in life? For people who are not continuous learners, how can they be encouraged to participate more actively in developmental activities?
6. Do people learn most when they experience a new experience than when they are engaged in routine tasks? Does learning require a traumatic event or a rude awakening to startle us into changing our routine behaviors?
7. Does the term *continuous learning* seem redundant to you? Do you understand the distinction between learning and continuous learning?

## TOPICS FOR RESEARCH

1. Identify examples of adaptive, generative, and transformative learning at each system level.
2. Determine ways individuals, groups, and organizations are triggered to learn. Are there some triggers that are more powerful or noticeable than others? What happens if triggers send mixed messages?
3. How can a system's readiness to learn be stimulated or enhanced?
4. How do systems at one level trigger learning and change in systems at another level?
5. Determine the match between levels (e.g., individual and group, group and organization) and needs or demands of the environment or task. Test the model in Fig. 1.3. What changes and learning occur when there are different types of matches and mismatches between need and readiness—particularly between levels? What different strategies are needed for different contingencies (e.g., team members are adaptive but not transformative learners, but transformative learning is needed)?
6. Identify barriers to learning in cases of mismatches. Experiment with ways to overcome these barriers and support learning. Measure the effects of these interventions.

CHAPTER

# 2

# Understanding Individual Continuous Learning

In this chapter, we summarize different ways that individual learning and continuous learning occur in organizations. We begin by considering the meaning of continuous learning. We then describe the difference between "learning about" and "learning how." Next, we present three ways individuals learn: adaptation, generation, and transformation. Finally, we consider the feedback portion of the learning process, without which learning cannot occur.

## DEFINING CONTINUOUS LEARNING

We asked our participants in the online discussion to define continuous learning. These definitions are presented in Appendix A. We also asked other people whom we happened to know who seemed to us to be continuous learners. Their reflections on the meaning of continuous learning are in Appendix B. Several themes emerge from their input. One theme that each person touched on is that learning is transformational. For example, one person said, "I think that man was placed on earth to figure out why we are here and to figure out life's mysteries. There are many mysteries. When you think you've gotten a handle on something, it unveils itself to show you something different. If there is a God, he placed us here just to understand those things." Another theme is that continuous learning satisfies passion, compulsivity, or drive as well as a tendency to be curious that transcends job requirements. As one person said, "Continuous Learning means . . . to me . . . to be AWAKE! To have the humility to recognize that something or someone who is right around the corner could change your life totally." Continuous learning means "trying something new" and "experiencing something old in a new way."

Another respondent reflected on the paradox that continuous learning is both fun and, occasionally, anxiety provoking in adding to work load. Several respondents felt that they inculcated continuous learning in their students and family members, and noted that their own continuous learning stemmed from their parents.

Continuous learning implies progression or growth as the result of learning experiences or events that continue to deepen and broaden as additional learning takes place. In general, as we described in chapter 1, all humans and systems made up of humans have the potential to be continuous learners. Individuals, groups, and organizations often find themselves in situations in which they wish to attain a goal, but are not sure how to go about it. So they explore and experiment. If they are successful, learning as well as goal attainment occurs. As the individual or the group or the organization learns, they are also changing as a learner. If they are successful as they explore and experiment, not only is the goal attained, but the individual, the group, or the organization learns more about what it takes to explore and experiment. In essence, learning begets more learning in a continuous cycle. Learners learn to be continuous learners. Thus the key to continuous learning at all levels is to provide the direction, resources, and supportive environment for continuous learning to take place guided throughout by assessment.

*Continuous learning at the individual level is regularly changing behavior based on a deepening and broadening of one's skills, knowledge, and worldview.* This may entail figuring out how to act in a new situation, learning new disciplines, expanding one's knowledge and skills in areas in which one is already expert, and reconstructing how one interprets and uses one's skills and knowledge. Individuals who are purposefully engaged in continuous learning assess what they are learning and pay attention to learning opportunities.

However, learning can go awry. For a literary example, consider Jack London's *Martin Eden,* a sailor and laborer who educates himself believing that high thinking and education will earn him the respectability of the wealthy bourgeoisie and win the love of a college-educated society girl. In doing so, he loses touch with his own class and finds that the new (and hollow) class shuns him and that his sweetheart's love is false; it ends in Eden tragically taking his own life. In a more real-world example, an individual may be led to believe that in order to advance to the next level, she needs to learn a particular skill only to be passed over for promotion. Was she misled? Was the skill she learned valuable anyway? Or, perhaps she enjoyed the process of learning or learned something about herself and the organization in the process. Maybe she will benefit in unforeseen ways in the future. Would more deliberate assessment up front have been more beneficial in directing her learning?

Learning at the individual level takes time and effort; this is compounded in complexity at the group level, and even more so at the organization level. Although this chapter is about the individual, consider briefly at this point how our definition of individual continuous learning can be extended to definitions at the team and organizational levels, because these levels are, after all, made up of individuals. *Continuous learning at the team level is a deepening and broadening of the group's capabilities in (re)structuring to meet changing conditions, adding new skills and knowledge, and (re)creating into a more and more sophisticated system through reflection on actions and consequences.* Groups that are engaged in continuous learning in organizations use the work they must accomplish to reach a desired goal as a learning opportunity, as well as participate in a variety of formal and informal learning events and activities. For example, a group may reflect, at various times during a particular project, on "how are we doing as a group?" and "what have we learned that we should make sure we take forward (or not)."

*Continuous learning at the organizational level, similar to the team level, is a deepening and broadening of organizational capabilities in (re)structuring to meet changing conditions, adding new skills and knowledge, and (re)creating into a more and more sophisticated system through reflection on its own actions and consequences.* Organizations that are engaged in continuous learning are characterized by the sharing and adopting of systems and processes that allow the acquisition, sharing, and use of new information, knowledge, and capabilities. Similarly, departments and organizations can be open to new work structures and adopting models that work in other parts of the organization or in other organizations entirely. They need to know what is working and communicate this knowledge, and so assessment is vital to the organization learning process.

## HOW INDIVIDUALS LEARN

From the systems point of view, human beings, adults in particular, are unique because we are the only living "system" that possesses a reflective consciousness (Laszlo, 1996). Not only are we, like many other biological systems, aware of our experience of sensations, but also we are aware that we are having these sensations. We see, hear, smell, taste, feel, *and* know that we are doing so. Moreover, we can manipulate the stimuli we are exposed to. As individuals at work are confronted with goals that require them to learn in order to reach their goals or overcome obstacles, we can choose to learn about something, we can learn how to do something, or we can learn both. Academic learning tends to focus on "learning about." This occurs through teaching and the development of cognitive skills. Educators provide students with knowledge, theories, concepts, information, and tools relevant to understanding and conceptualizing a particular topic or discipline. Workplace learning is often centered on practices in the organization and focuses on "learning how" to do something. Learning is not just acquiring technical skills but also reflecting and learning from experience. Students are provided with experiences to conduct routine tasks effectively and to recognize and deal with unpredictable situation through mentoring, modeling, and practice. Learning stems from action and problem solving in the course of carrying out projects and facing challenges. This is *action learning*—learning by addressing and solving real problems (Revans, 1980).

Workplace learning requires employees to exhibit contradictory characteristics: (a) the ability to comply with organizational requirements and the ability to act autonomously with initiative and entrepreneurial spirit, (b) extrinsic rewards and intrinsic satisfaction that motivate behavior, and (c) dependable, consistent behaviors and a willingness to be flexible and adapt (Tosey & McNair, 2001). Elements of each of these dichotomies are important.

Corporate universities often try to combine "learning how" with "learning about." They offer employees a competency-based training curriculum specific to organizational and job requirements, provide employees with a common vision of the firm, and offer a learning laboratory for trying new approaches—for employees to experiment and practice. Training centers use instructional technologies to explore new ways of designing and delivering learning initiatives (Meister, 1994, as cited in Jarvis & Tosey, 2001). Training focuses on such competencies as communication, collaboration, creative thinking, problem solving, technological literacy, global business literacy, leadership, career self-management, and learning to learn (Meister, 1998, as cited in Jarvis & Tosey, 2001). Other, more general competencies are corporate citizenship (understanding how the organization works and how to contribute to it and its members) and contextual framework—the firm's customers, competitors, and best practices (Jarvis & Tosey, 2001).

In addition to learning about and learning how, there are three ways individuals acquire the behaviors, skills, and knowledge that they need to achieve their goal. These are *adaptation,* which emphasizes the often unconscious behavior changes of individuals as they react to a stimulus in their environment; *generation,* which emphasizes purposefully seeking out and adding what is needed; and *transformation,* which brings about a fundamental shift through behavioral and cognitive means as individuals learn from others, reflect on their environment, and experiment with new behaviors.

### Adaptive Learning

At the simplest level, a person demonstrates a relatively permanent change in behavior in reaction to a stimulus in the external environment. (This type of learning is exemplified in the behaviorist tradition of learning theorists such as Guthrie, 1940, 1952, Pavlov, 1927, Skinner, 1971, Thorndike, 1932, Tolman, 1932, and Watson, 1924.) Individuals pick up information from their environment on how they should act and change their behavior accordingly—without necessarily being aware that they are doing so. Indeed, the resulting knowledge may be difficult to express (Berry & Dienes, 1993; Reber, 1993). Individuals in organizations pick up clues from their organizational environment—clues about the organization's climate, culture, norms, policies, procedures, and rules that inform employees about how they should act and, often, how they should change their behavior to fit in.

Examples of this type of unintentional and unintended, yet powerful, learning were captured clearly in Steve Kerr's (1975/1997) classic article, "On the Folly of Rewarding A, While Hoping for B." For instance, managers may say that they want employees to make suggestions for quality improvement and enhance the quality of products or services produced, but the company reward system may be based on the number of units produced. Or commissions may be paid on sales volume, not retention of clients, even though executives give lip service to the importance of building long-lasting customer relationships. Employees quickly learn that what managers say may not be what is rewarded.

This learning is automatic, unconscious, and powerful. It could occur for many different phenomena, including how team members typically behave, elements of organizational culture (e.g., dress and mannerisms, greetings, telephone and e-mail etiquette, etc.), problem-solving strategies (e.g., when and how to search for information, what sources to approach, who to ask), methods for collaboration (frequency of meetings, integration of disciplines), and decision making (e.g., when and to what degree to involve subordinates) (Kelly, Burton, Kato, & Akamatsu, 2001; Mathews et al., 1989). People may even pick up functional knowledge adaptively as they collaborate with people of different disciplines.

Learning of this type can be made intentional (though still adaptive) by deliberately arranging the environment or designing the larger system to elicit the desired response. For example, in a large pharmaceutical company, strategy called for more cross-fertilization of district managers across regions. To make this happen, regional managers could not receive their full bonus unless they moved either a district manager or a sales representative to a district manager position in another region. It worked; the regional managers "learned" to transfer district managers across regions rather than within regions.

However, to date, little has been done to take advantage of the adaptive learning of individuals in organizations. The key to capitalizing on this type of learning for organizations is to understand what sort of adaptations the organization is currently asking individuals to make and then to determine if these adaptations are in line with the company mission, values, strategy, practices, and procedures. And if not, to shift organizational conditions in such a way that individuals adapt automatically to new conditions.

### Generative Learning

Generative learning is purposefully adding and using new behaviors, knowledge, and skills. There are several generative models of learning available in the literature, each addressing different aspects of learning. All have merit in understanding the nature of generative learning at the individual level.

The first generative model emphasizes that the human mind is more than an unconscious adaptive learning system. Rather, the thinking or cognitive person interprets incoming information and gives meaning to that information. (Learning theorists associated with this cognitive orientation include Ausubel, 1968, Bruner, 1960, Gagné, 1978, Koffka, 1924, and Kohler, 1947.) The generative learning process is based on internal mental processes (including insight, information processing, memory, and perception) and their (re)structuring.

A manifestation of this type of learning in organizations is intelligence and memory as a function of age. Research on older adults suggests that mental faculties decline with age. However, some recent research is much more optimistic. Specifically, research in the area of adult intellect suggests that there are two types of intelligence (based on perspectives of Hebb, 1941, and Cattell, 1943; see Ackerman, 1996, for a review). One type is physiologically based and is more "academically focused," including perceptual speed, spatial orientation, and abstract reasoning. Another type of intelligence is educationally and experientially based and is more "practically focused." It includes acculturated or tacit knowledge based on such things as occupational and avocational experience as well as interest. Reviews of the literature suggest that whereas physiological intelligence naturally peaks in early adulthood and then declines over time, the educationally and experientially based intelligence increases across the life span (Ackerman, 1996; Ackerman & Rolfhus, 1999; Reeve & Hakel, 2000; Schaie, 1994; Tennant & Pogson, 1995; Torff & Sternberg, 1998). However, there is some evidence that with the proper environment, stimulation, and training, adults can and do learn and develop *both* kinds of intelligences across their entire life span. Even skills associated with the physiologically based intelligence that have been found to decline over time (possibly due to disuse rather than some sort of detriment in human brain functioning) can be improved with training (Schaie, 1994).

For most individuals in organizations, educationally and experientially based intelligence is more important. Organization changes in performance requirements as jobs, roles, and technologies evolve present adults with an ever-changing set of skills to learn. Thus the specific content of knowledge and the skills often needed in the past become less important. Instead there is a need for continuous learning and relearning of knowledge and skills.

Another related example is the concept of *emotional intelligence* in adults. Emotional intelligence stems from E. L. Thorndike's concept of "social intelligence" in the 1920s. Gardner (1993) coined the term "interpersonal intelligence" as the ability to understand other people—understanding what motivates them and how to work cooperatively with them. Salovey and Mayer (1990) outlined five domains of emotional intelligence: (a) self-awareness: observing oneself and recognizing one's feelings for what they are; (b) managing emotions: realizing what is behind one's emotions; discovering how to handle fears and anxieties; (c) motivating oneself: self-regulation, channeling emotions to accomplish goals; (d) empathy: being sensitive to others' feelings and appreciating their unique value; and (e) human relationships: social competence and social skills. Although emotional intelligence is presumed to be learned adaptively in children, adults may purposefully learn to be more emotionally intelligent—similar to educationally and experientially based intelligence.

Our understanding of emotional intelligence and the influence of emotional intelligence on work-related issues is nascent, but preliminary research suggests that emotional intelligence is linked to job-related issues (Matthews, Zeidner, & Roberts, 2003). For example, emotional intelligence has been linked to change management, decisiveness, persevering in the face of obstacles, straightforwardness and composure, participative management, building and mending relationships, putting people at ease, dealing with problem employees, and balancing work and personal life (Ruderman, Hannum, Leslie, & Steed, 2001).

The second generative learning model focuses on the fact that people learn by observing others. This is called *social learning.* (Social-learning theorists include Bandura, 1986, and Rotter, 1966.) Social learning proposes that learning is an interaction of person, behavior, and environment. The purpose of education is to demonstrate new roles and behavior. The teacher's role is to model and guide new roles and behavior. A manifestation in adult learning is modeling—observing and copying others, retaining that behavior, and then reproducing it in other contexts. Modeling is an extremely pervasive technique, especially when an individual is not sure how to behave or fit in. For example, new employees watch more veteran employees and emulate them in terms of when they arrive at work, when they leave, and how long they take for lunch (and where), how closely they follow formal policies and procedures, and even how they should feel and talk about their job and their company.

A third generative model is based on the belief that humans can control their own destiny and are free to choose and act—thus learning is self-determined. (Theorists representative of this humanist tradition include Maslow, 1970, and Rogers, 1969.) This model emphasizes human nature, human potential, and human emotions. Behavior is the consequence of human choice. The purpose of education is to become self-actualized and autonomous, with the role of the teacher to facilitate this process.

A label for adult learning based on this model is *andragogy* (Knowles, 1975). This concept is based on the following assumptions:

1. Adults' self-concept is one of being responsible for their own decisions and lives. They do not like other people's wills imposed upon them.
2. Adults are life/task/problem centered.
3. Adults become ready to learn those things they need to know and are able to do in order to cope effectively with their real life.
4. So, adults need to know why they need to learn something before undertaking to learn it.
5. Adults already have a large volume and quality of experience. Although they can provide rich experience and learn from each other, on the

downside, they have mental habits, biases, and presuppositions that guide, and sometimes limit, learning.

6. Although adults can respond to external motivation, the most potent motivators of learning are internal.

Generative learning is purposeful. When they have a goal or see the need, adults in organizations attend training programs, earn degrees, and observe others to keep their behaviors, knowledge, and skills up-to-date with what is needed in their job (or next job), their organization, their profession, or even their life. Adults control what they learn generatively across their life span in a variety of different ways.

More attention has been paid to generative learning in organizations than the other two types of learning, with the assumption that individuals can and should take charge of their own learning. For example, London and Mone (1999) viewed continuous learning, in the generative sense, as *the process of acquiring knowledge, skills, and abilities throughout one's career in reaction to, or in anticipation of, shifting performance expectations.* The need for learning may be related to such goals as doing one's current job better, preparing for upcoming changes that will affect one's job, and/or positioning oneself for new job opportunities inside or outside the organization as a means of advancing one's career or protecting one's employment security.

Furthermore, *career-related continuous learning* is ". . . an individual-level process characterized by a self-initiated, discretionary, planned, and proactive pattern of formal and informal activities that are sustained over time for the purpose of applying or transporting knowledge for career development" (London & Smither, 1999a, p. 81). This can be exemplified in three stages that include (a) *prelearning*—recognizing the need for continuous learning, (b) *learning about*—actually acquiring new behaviors, skills, and knowledge generatively and monitoring that learning, and (c) *learning how to*—using, evaluating, and reaping the benefits of learning. The stages hold that people recognize the need for learning and begin to set learning goals when they are prompted to do so by environmental and organizational factors such as technological change, global expansion, deregulation, job insecurity from restructuring and downsizing, mergers and acquisitions, corporate decentralization, quality improvement efforts, and management strategies that empower employees to make decisions on their own.

Organizations need to measure and track career-related continuous learning behaviors (London & Smither, 1999a). Employees' feedback seeking is a function of the extent to which they initiate constructive discussions with supervisors and other coworkers about their performance and seek advice about how to perform more effectively. Frequency of participation in development should be tracked, including initiating a career-planning discussion with a supervisor or mentor, reading books or articles to help develop skills or expand business knowledge, attending training programs or workshops, using computer-based training software or videos, asking for new assignments to develop skills (e.g., assignment to a committee or task force), and setting learning goals and making commitments to improve specific skills. The effects of career-related continuous-learning behaviors and improvements in performance should be evaluated (London & Smither, 1999a). This also includes continuing to participate in learning, adapting new knowledge to different sorts of problems, increasing in self-confidence, displaying a new habit of asking for feedback, and developing innovative solutions to problems.

### Transformative Learning

When individuals engage in transformational learning, they undergo a dramatic and fundamental change in the way they see themselves and the world in which they live (Mezirow, 1990, 1991, 1994). During the transformational learning process individuals (re)construct meaning and reality from experience. (This constructivist tradition is based on theorists such as Dewey, 1900, 1933/1986, Lave [cf. Cole, Sharp, & Lave, 1976], Piaget, 1952, Rogoff, 1990, von Glaserfeld, 1996, and Vygotsky, 1978.)

One of our learning experts, Bob Mintz, gave his definition of transformative learning:

> It is my current belief that individual learning is developmentally linked based on life scripts imparted at the earliest of ages. These "truths," socially constructed by the birth family get tested as one begins to experience other "truths." Thus, if one spends most of one's life in a rural, remote farming town, one is less likely to experience any narrative disruptions that challenge the "truths" proffered by those in their lives. The child of an international relocating executive will have quite a different experience as they will constantly be confronting "truths" that are different from theirs. It is my contention that learning (and, therefore development) occurs when there is sufficient narrative disruption that creates enough internal conflict for the individual that they must face the "new truth," try it on (so to speak) and then decide if it has a place in their belief system. At the same time, the individual must revisit "old truths" and decide what no longer holds for them. These narrative disruptions are occurring in people's lives much more frequently than in the past due to globalization and technology advances. This leaves the individual with three choices: hunker down and hold onto current beliefs despite the discomfort, seek comfort in some form of fundamentalism, or reshape their belief system through introspection, expanding one's network, etc. I do believe that people have a need to continually make coherent sense of their life stories and thus, are prompted to conduct these reviews fairly frequently. Often, this requires validation from a new "scripter" or mentors/teachers who support the new world view [*sic*].

***Tranformative Learning Through Others.*** Bob's definition describes transformative learning about oneself through others. People develop a new understanding of themselves through conversation (language) with others. This is echoed in Gergen's (1991) relational theory. There is a growing understanding or belief that whereas earlier generations tended to see language as describing the real world, people today are realizing that language creates the real world (Anderson, 1997). We rely heavily on language to make sense of ourselves, others, and the world. That is, reality is constructed and agreed upon through our conversations with others rather than as a result of some objective reality.

In addition, this language is built into a growing number and variety of patterns of relationships. Whereas our conversations were once limited to those we saw regularly and face-to-face, in today's world, we encounter and exchange with an almost limitless variety of people from all over the world with wholly different beliefs and even language (words) about life and truth, from our own. This is causing a major transformation in our understanding of self and others and our lives. In this era, selves no longer possess "real and identifiable" characteristics. We are *protean* (able to change) and may appear different to different people. Thus, although we experience ourselves as a single "I" and can summon up memories to support that "I," the "I" may feel, think, or act differently at different times, without knowing it (literally a different "I" with a different re-creation of memories). As we become aware that each "truth" about ourselves is a construction that may be true only for a given time or within certain relationships—that we are in fact multiple and disparate beings possessing many voices—then the whole concept of "objective truth" is put into doubt. Truth, in the moment, is determined through our conversations with others. As an example, Gergen (1991) suggested that on a single day, a heartfelt conversation with a colleague leads to an obvious conclusion, which later makes little sense when discussed with a spouse, and has no meaning at all when we talk to an old friend later in the evening.

Manifestations of transformation in adult learning include *reflective practice* and *experiential learning*. We discuss each next.

***Transformative Learning Through Reflective Practice.*** Transformative learning is based on critical reflection (Mezirow, 1990). Reflection is an assessment of how or why we have perceived, thought, felt, or acted. Critical reflection is challenging the validity of our presuppositions in prior learning—not just adding to, but fundamentally evolving our underlying premises and assessments. As we engage in instrumental learning (learning how to do something for a specific purpose or outcome), we consider whether our actions are consistent with our values, whether we are being objective, how well we are doing in relation to our goals, and whether our interpretation of our results is convincing. As we engage in communicative learning (learning the meaning of what others are trying to communicate), we consider their and our own values, ideals, feelings, and moral decisions. Transformative learning occurs when we change our previous assumptions as well as the content of what we know—typically becoming more inclusive (open to new ideas), discriminating (able to understand fine points), and integrative (able to see interactions and linkages).

***Transformative Learning Through Experiences.*** Learning from experience, or learning on the job, is one of the most powerful ways for individuals to learn, especially when it involves new challenges. In a landmark study from the Center for Creative Leadership on learning from experience, researchers asked successful and high-potential upper-level executives to describe key events in their careers (events that led to lasting change in them as managers) and what exactly they learned from those events (Lindsey, Homes, & McCall, 1987). Executives indicated that they learned from specific assignments, including start-ups, turnarounds, changes in job scope, switches from line to staff, and participating in cross-functional teams. They also learned from other people, particularly superiors who exhibited exceptional skills or faults. Executives also learned from hardships, such as business failures and mistakes, demotions, missed promotions, lousy jobs, and personnel problems. For instance, executives learned the hard way (i.e., through a negative experience) how to confront a subordinate who has a performance problem, cope with situations beyond their control, and manage people who used to be their peers or supervisors.

In a similar study, personal accounts and stories were collected from a senior group of 37 thought leaders in the field of management and organizational development (Goldsmith, Beverly, & Shelton, 2003). Many of them indicated that they were continuously learning from life's experiences. Lessons these leaders described included seeing yourself as others see you, developing self-knowledge, unlearning what you thought was so, and learning from hardship.

However, experience alone does not lead to learning (Levine, 2002). Learning from experience needs the following conditions: *time* (there is a time lag between an experience and learning from it), *maturity* (the ability to be critical of yourself and acknowledge weaknesses or failure), and *interaction with others* (lessons are socially constructed and people need interaction with others to reflect on their experience) (Baker, Jensen, & Kolb, 2002). It also needs the following process: *narrativizing* the experience (talking about it in interactions with others), *emotional aspects* (the emotions accompanying the experience led learners to get insights into their own practice), and *disequilibrium* or *reframing* (things that "stuck out" or were unaccounted for in people's grasp of the situation) (Ben-Peretz, 2002).

Individuals in organizations make powerful and lasting changes based on what they have learned in their job and their life experiences. Transformative learning can happen unintentionally when one's truths get tested through conversations with others or through experiences that force one to see things a different way. Or transformative learning can be aided through purposeful reflection.

In many of today's organizations, transformative learning is given short shrift. Many people feel they are barely keeping their heads above water. They rarely have the time to think about what they are learning. Their supervisors do not encourage them or give them the resources to advance their learning in this manner. Organizations fail to recognize and capitalize on this type of learning when it does occur.

To give transformation learning more of a focus, it is useful to change perspectives and view one's career from the point of view of a *learning career*—one in which all job experiences are described in terms of their relationship to learning (Hodkinson & Bloomer, 2002). New phases of a learning career evolve from earlier phases in a continuous process of change. These transformations are affected by employees' sense of identity shaped by habits and dispositions and the social, cultural, and economic contexts of the organization and people's lives.

### Combining Adaptive, Generative, and Transformative Learning

These theories and the evidence that supports them suggests that individuals can and do learn adaptively, generatively, and transformatively in organizations. Developing learning that lasts in practice combines "learning about" and the "learning how" with adaptive, generative, and transformational learning, which together allow individuals to learn by continually broadening and deepening their understanding (Guile & Griffiths, 2001; Mentkowski & Associates, 2000).

In terms of deepening understanding, individuals build on, expand, and transform their behaviors, knowledge, and skills. Some of this learning may be adaptive—individuals may receive rewards and recognition for delegating and empowering subordinates. Learning may be generative such as when the individual seeks information on how to delegate better and tries different methods. Also, learning may be transformative as the individual is stretched and finds that the only way to get the job done is through delegation and empowerment of subordinates.

In terms of the broadening, individuals learn to apply their learning to an increasing variety of contexts, for example, moving learning from a training program to the workplace, from role to role, from organization to organization, from nonwork experiences to work experiences, and so on. This broadening can best be conceptualized as a sort of learning across boundaries such that individuals become "polytextually" skilled (Guile & Griffiths, 2001). And again, the learning can be adaptative (using the same behavior in a new situation), generative (purposefully trying a behavior learned in a training situation back on the job), and transformative (realizing why a certain behavior, knowledge, or skill works across situations and deliberatively using that realization in a variety of novel ways).

Three things can be said for certain (or at least have a solid research base) regarding how individuals broaden and deepen their learning (Bransford, Brown, & Cocking, 2000). First, individuals come to each learning experience with preconceptions about how the world works, and they act on this initial understanding. If this initial understanding is not understood and engaged, new concepts and information may not make sense to the learner and thus they may fail to grasp them as expected. They may actually learn something other than expected, or they may "learn" for the purposes of getting by in the learning experience and revert back to their preconceptions "back in the real world."

Second, to develop competence in an area, individuals must have a deep foundation of factual knowledge; they must understand or know facts and ideas in the context of some sort of framework that helps them make sense of the facts. Also, they must organize the knowledge in ways that facilitate retrieval and application in a different context in which the individual originally learned it.

Third, a *metacognitive* approach to instruction can help students learn to take control of their own learning by defining learning goals and monitoring their progress in achieving them. Metacognition refers to people's abilities to predict their performance on various tasks and to monitor their current levels of mastery and understanding. Teaching practices congruent with a metacognitive approach to learning include those that focus on sense making, self-assessment, and reflection on what worked and what needs improving.

***Expertise.*** An example of broadening and deepening skills and knowledge is in the understanding of how expertise develops and how experts differ from novices (Miller, 1978; National Research Council, 1999). Experts acquire substantial content knowledge that is organized in a manner that reflects deep understanding—core concepts and "big ideas" that guide their thinking, such as principles or values that suggest how to approach a problem, not just a list of facts and formulas. Experts notice features and meaningful patterns of information. For instance, chess masters chunk together several chess pieces in a configuration in reference to a strategy for the game. Novices do not have the hierarchical, organized structure of knowledge to do this.

Experts also recognize contexts and nuances, not just isolated facts. They don't have to search through all their knowledge for every task, but can retrieve just what they need. Their knowledge is "conditionalized" in the sense that they can draw on their knowledge relative to the context in which it is needed at the time. They know the conditions under which they can use their knowledge; they know how and when to use it. Experts retrieve key aspects of their knowledge with little attentional effort. This doesn't mean that they will solve problems faster than novices. They may take more time, especially because they don't just do solutions but take time to think through the issues and alternative solution strategies. They can determine what aspects of the task require more of their attention than others, and so they use their limited time and processing capacity better than novices. They are fluent at recognizing problem types and the principles and appropriate solutions that apply to them.

In addition, experts vary in their flexibility in approaching new situations. Some experts are good at following prescribed recipes or paths (the London cabbie who has internalized "the knowledge" of the London streets to identify the shortest route between destinations instantly). Others are able to adapt recipes to fit the situation (the "Iron Chef"). One is routinized expertise and the other is flexible. "Artisan experts" accept problems as presented to them. New problems are chances to apply their existing expertise to do familiar tasks better or more efficiently. Virtuoso experts, on the other hand, treat problems as points of departure and exploration.

Experts may have trouble teaching novices because they approach problems differently. Experts retrieve sets of interconnected information and principles, whereas novices examine components in serial fashion without seeing the connections up front. Recognizing this, experts who teach other experts can continually challenge them until ideas begin to make sense, whereas when teaching novices, they may not recognize the difficulties novices face in not understanding the underlying connections right away.

In summary, individuals learn adaptively, generatively, and transformatively. Together, as individuals learn through reflection and experience, they broaden and deepen their knowledge. Ultimately, they become experts who are striving continuously to expand their knowledge and ability.

Next, we turn to the feedback and assessment portion of the learning process. We describe how feedback works and consider how people process feedback and the extent to which they welcome and learn from feedback. Then we discuss the first of the individual characteristics that we believe impacts an individual's readiness to learn—their feedback orientation. Others are discussed in the next chapter.

## HOW FEEDBACK WORKS

Feedback may be the most important part of the learning process. However, it is the part that is also most fraught with difficulty for adults both at work and during life in general. Feedback is part of an ongoing cycle of information about our behaviors and their outcomes (Aronson, 1999). Without feedback of some sort, individuals are unable to learn. Feedback helps us keep our actions goal directed; it directs our behavior toward the goal and keeps us on track. We use feedback to set future goals as we consider gaps in our performance (how well we are doing relative to our goals). Also, feedback gives us information about what elements of performance are important in the organization, thereby setting standards against which we evaluate our performance in the future. Interestingly, feedback goes beyond merely giving us information about our behavior for learning purposes. Feedback can also motivate and reward performance (cf. London, 2003b, pp. 14–15). For example, it provides positive reinforcement (when the feedback is positive) and thereby increases our motivation for goal accomplishment. It helps us discover errors in our performance and directions for improvement, and it focuses our attention on what is important in the organization (see reviews by Ilgen, Fisher, & Taylor, 1979; Larson, 1984; London, 2003b; Nadler, 1979). Ill-used, feedback can just as easily do the opposite—denigrate, de-motivate, and punish.

We receive feedback in a variety of ways, for example, from ourselves in terms of how we feel, from others about their perceptions (person-to-person feedback), by observing how others react to our behavior, by noting whether rewards and promotion are forthcoming, and by tracking objective indicators of performance (e.g., a salesperson monitoring weekly sales figures). Here, we concentrate on feedback individuals receive directly from other people, either verbally or through written reports. Person-to-person feedback is a common, yet paradoxically complex, form of feedback because the feedback occurs in a relational sense and encompasses things other than the behavior or performance. It also involves the characteristics of the person giving the feedback, the relationship between the feedback giver and the receiver, and the environment.

Supervisors are supposed to give feedback as part of formal performance appraisal processes and good ones know to give feedback on a regular basis. Yet people tend to shy away from being honest and open with each other, especially when it comes to something as sensitive as job performance. Supervisors often feel uncomfortable giving subordinates their annual appraisal and talking about it with them. Also, the appraisal process is used for more than goal-directed behavior. It is also used for making administrative decisions, such as salary increases (or decreases) and promotions (or demotions), not to mention lay-offs.

### When Person-to-Person Feedback Works

As we suggested earlier, feedback can be motivating by helping people clarify their goals and understanding what behaviors are needed to achieve these goals. Feedback can increase the recipient's and sender's sense of self-control. The recipient recognizes what behaviors (or even perceptions) are needed to influence valued outcomes, and senders feel they can help their coworkers (subordinates and peers) improve their performance and contribute to departmental goals. Positive feedback from a respected feedback giver can be a reward in and of itself, enhancing the recipient's sense of self-worth.

There are three stages in the process of receiving and using feedback (London & Smither, 2002):

Stage 1: Anticipating the feedback, receiving it, and initial emotions and thoughts about the feedback.

Stage 2: Processing the feedback mindfully—seeing it as part of a bigger picture, interpreting it, understanding its meaning and value, dealing with emotions, and believing or discounting the feedback in terms of messages received from other feedback mechanisms.

Stage 3: Using the feedback from a variety of sources to (re)set goals and track progress.

These three stages lead to positive outcomes, such as learning and behavior change, better performance, and increased self-awareness and self-confidence. Critical events may trigger asking for feedback, for instance, events that are unfamiliar, have important consequences, and do not have obvious responses (i.e., where there is uncertainty about what to do). The three stages of feedback will be stronger and have a more positive outcome when the individual welcomes feedback (has a sufficiently high self-concept not to be threatened by feedback) and when the organization has a supportive feedback culture (managers are expected to provide employees with feedback, multisource feedback surveys are used annually, and there is a general atmosphere that promotes discussions of performance; see chap. 4).

### When Person-to-Person Feedback Doesn't Work

Consider this conversation, which actually occurred almost verbatim:

*Valerie to her Administrative Assistant (AA):* Let's set some time up to go over the feedback from your performance appraisal. Hey, let's do it over lunch.

*AA:* Performance appraisal? Do we have to? I think I'm going to be sick.

*Valerie:* Hmm. There are no surprises here. You know I think you are great and any feedback I have for you, I give you right away.

*AA:* To be honest, I hate feedback.

*Valerie:* As your boss, I need to do this as a formal procedure. And you already know what's on here! It's really no big deal!

*AA:* I'm going to be sick.

Feedback is supposed to lead to learning that can be challenging and exciting, yet it is threatening, and some people avoid it like the plague. Another anecdote:

> I had been excited when my new project leader had invited me to breakfast. This was a cutting-edge project and the diverse team was full of promise. But now my breakfast was sticking in my throat. The project leader had just said that he wanted to give me feedback that he was hearing from other "people." "They" had told him that I was untrustworthy, noncollaborative, and did not give credit where credit was due. Furthermore, there was no way "they" would ever work with me. My new boss, who apparently saw no reason to doubt this "they" (who remained anonymous to me) and their feedback, could give me no examples of behaviors, situations, or anything that could demonstrate how I could be perceived in this way by other person(s). So there was no way for me to reflect, understand how I could be perceived this way, and correspondingly change my behavior in some way. This was not feedback, and this wasn't about learning. This was a deliberate attempt to malign my character under the rubric of "feedback."

Unfortunately, person-to-person feedback can be and is used for purposes other than helping individuals learn. Drawing on the general feedback literature, perhaps the first comprehensive review that questioned the value of feedback interventions was Kluger and DeNisi's (1996, 1998; DeNisi & Kluger, 2000) meta-analysis (summary of research findings across many existing studies).

They discovered that person-to-person feedback is not necessarily effective. It may even be detrimental if not given in a manner that protects the recipient's self-concept and focuses on behaviors that can be changed (Kluger & DeNisi, 1996). Atwater, Waldman, Atwater, and Cartier (2000) found that improvement following an upward feedback intervention resulted for only 50% of the supervisors who received it. Many factors may intervene to cause the feedback to backfire—including the sender's biases, lack of support for development in the organization, and the recipient's sense of self-worth.

### Feedback Orientation

Individuals differ in their readiness to pursue and accept feedback and do something about it. Individuals have a *feedback orientation,* which is their overall receptivity to feedback, including: comfort with feedback, tendency to seek feedback and process it mindfully, and the likelihood of acting on the feedback to guide behavior change and performance management" (London & Smither, 2002, p. 81).

Some people have a high feedback orientation. They seek feedback for a variety of reasons: to reduce uncertainty, see what others think about what aspects of performance are important, gain a feeling of competence and control, calibrate their own self-evaluations, and manage the impressions others have of them. People who are high in self-confidence, sense of internal control, and self-efficacy are more likely to have a feedback orientation that allows them to make more accurate attributions about the reasons for feedback they receive, accept the information, adjust their views about their own strengths and weaknesses, and use the information to clarify their role and/or improve their performance (Brown, Ganesan, & Challagalla, 2001).

Continuous learners may be high in feedback orientation, but not necessarily. Some may be motivated to learn about their professions, technology, and interests of all sorts (London & Diamante, 2002). This does not mean they want feedback about their behavior and performance. They may feel threatened about what others think, or, on the other hand, may not care. Other continuous learners may be more internally focused, driven to increase their self-awareness. Some expansive individuals are motivated to learn about both the world around them and their behavior. They seek and welcome feedback from others, and so are receptive to multisource feedback.

Many people view feedback selectively in ways that protect their self-image (London, 2003b). Multisource feedback encourages making feedback a normal part of the performance management process, but feedback—when it indicates directions for change—may jolt recipients from their comfortable, taken-for-granted self-concepts. Feedback requires deconstructing the self—tearing down preestablished self-perceptions/schemas and building a new reality. It also requires recognizing the self as part of a relational world—a potentially discomforting process of de-individualization and externalization.

Some people simply try to avoid feedback altogether. Most individuals are more sensitive about feedback—they are more likely to avoid it than seek it. Feedback is viewed as threatening by many people, especially those who are already low in self-esteem. In addition, people may fear that asking one's supervisor for feedback risks criticism, feeling incompetent, having to spend the time and effort to do something about the feedback, and embarrassing themselves or others (Fedor, Rensvold, & Adams, 1992).

Those who receive negative feedback and are low in self-confidence and want to protect their ego are likely to deny or misattribute the feedback in some way. For instance, they may attribute the feedback to the sender (e.g., "She never liked me!" or "My supervisor is not around enough to know what's going on."). They may deny the feedback altogether (e.g., "This isn't what happened." or "This is incorrect."). They may look elsewhere for feedback, asking others until they are told what they want to hear.

In summary, feedback is necessary for learning. Without feedback individuals are unable to evaluate whether their behavior and changes in behavior are effective and worth repeating, modifying, or changing completely. However, one popular form of feedback, person-to-person feedback, is difficult for both parties to it—those giving it and those receiving it. Thus, whereas some people actively seek feedback, including feedback from others, others would rather avoid it if at all possible. But when feedback works, individuals do more than learn. Feedback can be motivational and rewarding.

## CONCLUSION

In this chapter, we begin to describe our nested and iterative systems model of learning by concentrating on how learning occurs in individuals—the basic building block of our model upon which learning at the group and at the organization occurs. Humans are unique living systems because they possess a reflective consciousness. They are both aware of their sensations and aware that they are aware; other systems (including "groups" and "organizations") are not.

This chapter focused on the human capacity to learn continuously and purposefully. We defined continuous learning at the individual level as regularly changing behavior based on a deepening and broadening of one's skills, knowledge, and worldview. Individuals can learn about and learn how to do something. This learning occurs adaptively, generatively, or transformatively. Adaptive learning is a powerful yet often unconscious type of learning that occurs when a relatively permanent change in behavior results as a reaction to a stimulus in the external environment. Generative learning occurs through purposeful thought, observing others, and taking self-control over learning. Transformative learning is a fundamental shift in understanding that occurs through learning from others, reflections, and experiences. However, we point out that organizations often recognize and capitalize on learning only in the generative sense.

People deepen their knowledge and skills in particular disciplines or areas of expertise and apply these new knowledge and skills to new contexts. In addition, they expand their knowledge and skill base to new disciplines or areas of expertise as needed to fulfill their goals and deal with obstacles during their work. Thus, learning is built into the very being of individuals and people learn continuously throughout their lives, although it might not be recognized as what was expected or needed to be learned as defined by the organization.

And all learning can occur only when the learning cycle is completed through some sort of feedback mechanism that individuals use to determine if their behavior moved them closer to their goals. However, we pointed out that feedback, particularly person-to-person feedback, is fraught with difficulties, making it the "weakest link" in the learning process. Also, we examined the extent to which people welcome and use feedback, their feedback orientation, as a way of evaluating their goal accomplishment and calibrating their achievement along the way.

In the next chapter, we explore other internal individual characteristics that influence whether, what, and how people learn. Some people are natural and active continuous learners and are ready to learn with ease. But not everyone is like this. We cover factors that distinguish natural learners from those who are not. These factors include development level or stage, personality, ability to learn, motivation to learn, and learning styles and tactics.

## QUESTIONS FOR THOUGHT AND DISCUSSION

1. What is your definition of continuous learning?
2. Do you have friends who are continuous learners (think beyond your friends that use schooling as a way of learning)? Is their continuous learning broad (covers a lot of territory), deep (concentrates on specific areas or disciplines), or both? Does their continuous learning include hobbies and interests as well as work-related areas?
3. Do you see yourself as a continuous learner? If no, what is stopping you? What support do you need and how can you get it? If yes, what factors contribute to your continuous learning—your own personality and motivation, the way you were raised, the expectations in your environment? How has the continuous-learning habit helped you?
4. What are examples of adaptive, generative, and transformative learning in your own life, or the life of someone you have observed? What led up to it, and what was the result?
5. Are you becoming an expert in an area or discipline? Think of experts you have known. How did you know they were experts . . . by reputation? . . . by

seeing an example of their knowledge? What contributed to their expertise? Were they able to maintain it?

6. Do you ask others for feedback about your performance? Who do you ask? When do you ask? When do you know you have done well? When do you know that your performance could have been better?
7. Do you shy away from feedback? If so, why? What are you afraid of (rejection?, calling attention to your faults?, giving the impression that you are begging for praise?).
8. In evaluating yourself, do you tend to be critical or lenient? How about evaluating others—do you tend to be critical or lenient? What could you do to be more objective or honest?
9. Is performance a topic of conversation in your department among peers and between you and your supervisor and you and your subordinates? Do you feel comfortable talking about your own and your work group's performance?

## TOPICS FOR RESEARCH

1. Measure continuous-learning behavior and attitudes toward continuous learning. Are continuous learners more successful in their careers and/or more satisfied with their lives than those who are not continuous learners? . . . or are continuous learners more frustrated and dissatisfied because they are always searching to go beyond the status quo?
2. Explore the relationship between adaptive, generative, and transformative learning and learning outcomes. Are adaptive learners more productive in relatively stable organizations, whereas generative and transformative learners are more productive in unstable, changing organizations?
3. Start a longitudinal study of the effects of continuous learning, and interventions to enhance continuous learning, on career and life behaviors and attitudes.
4. Study the relationship between feedback orientation and seeking feedback. Furthermore, how does feedback seeking relate to attitudes about learning?
5. Examine whether low feedback and learning orientation, that is, avoiding feedback and low motivation to learn for the sake of development, are a barrier to professional growth. How can this be overcome?
6. Study the relationship between setting learning goals and feedback. Do people alter their goals or their goal-directed behavior after receiving feedback?

CHAPTER

# 3

# Individual Characteristics Affecting Continuous Learning

In this chapter, we focus on individual characteristics that affect individual continuous learning. Despite the fact that we argue that humans are by nature learners, many individuals are not active continuous learners *at work*. Beyond adapting, people often seem to prefer to stay with the behaviors that have made them successful, even when the conditions change and past behaviors do not work as well or may not even be appropriate. Most people learn easily within their comfort zone but find it difficult to learn when the circumstances change. That is, most people do not *actively pursue* learning at work and require considerable support for their learning to occur (Bunker & Webb, 1992).

Some of the reasons some individuals do not engage in active continuous learning at work whereas others actively pursue learning may be due to their development level, their personality, and their motivation and readiness to learn, which we discuss in this chapter. Another reason, which we discuss in the next chapter, has to do with the organization itself. Some people are naturally active and continuous learners and do so with ease at work. They have the personal resources to learn easily by virtue of their personalities or early life experiences. The ability and motivation to learn involve being able to recognize when a current behavior is not working and when new behaviors, skills, or attitudes are necessary. This requires taking advantage of, and engaging in, a variety of experiences to learn new skills or test skills that were previously untested, and try new approaches or reframe points of view (as opposed to avoiding the situation or denying the need—which, in reality, can also be seen as "learning," but perhaps not the most productive for work purposes). Also it may require developing and using a variety of learning tactics or styles (Thornton, 2003; Van Velsor & Guthrie, 1998).

Unfortunately, failure to learn and change is a primary reason why executives derail (McCall & Lombardo, 1983). In an effort to understand the ability and motivation to learn from experience, McCall (1994) interviewed 46 experienced corporate executives who had been involved in identifying people with international executive potential, promoting them into positions of higher responsibility, and tracking their careers. The executives interviewed indicated that in seeking managers with top-management potential, they looked for signs of openness to learning and learning from mistakes among other characteristics. Managers who are *open to learning* reflect on their experiences, ask themselves why events happen and why they respond the way they do, seek and react to feedback, know their strengths and weaknesses, learn quickly from their experiences, are not afraid to ask others what they think, ask clarifying questions, are willing to discuss most anything, think about how they can do things differently, and are able to change. Those who *learn from their mistakes* recognize the mistakes, accept them, try to resolve them directly, don't blame others, and consider what they learned from making and correcting the mistakes. More specifically, McCall identified characteristics of talented managers who are able to learn from experience: They (a) show curiosity about how things work, (b) have a sense of adventure, and (c) accept responsibility for learning and change. As a result, they have more learning opportunities than others. They (d) respect differences, (e) seek and use feedback, and (f) are biased toward action while carefully observing the impact of those actions. As a result, they generate more learning in the opportunities they have. Moreover, they (g) are hardy (i.e., open to feedback and not threatened by criticism) and (h) grow consistently—act like a person who wants to learn. As a result, they seem to benefit more from learning than others.

In this chapter, we cover factors that distinguish continuous learners from those who need to be encouraged to learn. One factor is *psychological development* level or stage. A second factor is *personality,* including characteristics that demonstrate a readiness for learning, such as beliefs about the self, openness to experience, conscientiousness, and a learning/mastery orientation. A third factor is an individual's *motivation and readiness* to learn. A fourth is *learning styles and tactics.* Together, these four interrelated factors determine what people will do when placed in a situation that requires them to learn and apply new behaviors.

## ADULT PSYCHOLOGICAL DEVELOPMENT AND CONTINUOUS LEARNING

To fully understand learning, we must understand how people make sense of the situation they face and how they feel about that situation, because this influences readiness to learn and what people think they need to learn. One way people may vary in readiness to learn and interpretations of what to learn is their level or stage of development.

Consider some basic questions about adult development: What is adult development? Do all people develop continuously? Does development occur mainly at major transitions in life that pose challenges, or does it happen slowly and incrementally so you can barely perceive it is happening? If people don't develop, is that bad for them or their employer? If they do develop, is that necessarily good? Of course, there are no easy or simple answers to these questions. Development is not an all-or-nothing event. Still, development is clearly important in all our lives.

Consider some case examples:

George is a 30-year old programmer who was just promoted to his first supervisory position. He is struggling with how to give assignments to the members of his work team. They were his former peers, and he considered many to be friends. He views himself differently, and the team members view him differently. He needs to change, and he is changing, but he hasn't yet figured it all out. He is pleased with his promotion, but the anxiety won't go away.

Mary devoted herself to her career since graduating from college. She is a successful attorney who is about to make partner. Her boyfriend of 8 years wants to get married. She does, too, and she wants a family. She wonders what she will give up and what types of transitions she will face.

Sheri is 50 years old. She attended a leadership workshop for top executives. The workshop included receiving the results of a performance review completed by her supervisor, peers, subordinates, and customers called 360-degree feedback. A coach helped her interpret the results and consider their implications. She began to see her strengths in new light and had trouble admitting several glaring weaknesses. The coach eased the process and led her to consider new ways of behaving she should try. The workshop would give her a chance to try these new behaviors.

John was just fired after 32 years with the same company. Actually, he was downsized and given a golden parachute. The money helped, but he was at a loss. What should he do now?

Shirona is an architect for a major university. She has worked in the field for 20 years now. Most of her projects are renovations of office, laboratory, and classroom space. The work requires good relationships with her clients (usually faculty and administrators), attention to detail, and close monitoring of construction. Her favorite part of the work is the initial design phase where she can mesh her creative talents and knowledge of the latest building materials and methods with an understanding of her clients' goals. She attends all the conferences she can, and she reads avidly in her field. She has developed a reputation for being a delight to work with. She has been assigned to increasingly larger projects, and just recently was asked to work with an outside firm on the design of a major new research building.

Kerry lives for soccer. He follows international teams and frequently can be found in a downtown bar late at night with his cronies watching the latest

European tournament. He can tell you anything you might want to know about any team or player. At 42, he is an account representative for a hospital supply firm. He has a wife and two children who also love to watch sports with him. His kids play soccer on local teams. He has been in the job for 12 years now. His territory has expanded somewhat, and his income has kept pace with inflation—but just barely. He is disappointed that he has not been promoted to district manager, especially because his boss tells him he continues to do a fine job. Yet others who have been in similar jobs for far less time have been promoted. One person in his company who was hired only 2 years ago as a new college graduate has already been promoted ahead of him. When he thinks about it, life isn't too bad, but somehow he wants more.

Development can be viewed as moving through discrete stages in life. Each transition is a chance for a major jump in learning. Alternatively, development can be viewed as a continuous process of deepening our sense of our world and how we respond to it. As we do so, we become increasingly able to deal with the complexities we face. In our examples, George is early in his career, and faces a transition and supervisory challenge as he begins to move up in the business. Mary wants it all—a career and family. Sheri, in midcareer, is encouraged to recognize and overcome some behavioral weaknesses. John has to make a major, unanticipated career adjustment late in life. Shirona is a continuous learner but wonders whether she is ready for the challenge of a sizable project. Kerry has a wonderful family and an interest in sports, but wishes he could get ahead faster.

In the following sections, we explore the meaning of development and, more basically, why, when, in what directions, and how individuals develop. Being an "adult" in today's society is defined by our culture (Anderson, 1997; Csikszentmihalyi & Rathunde, 1998; Gergen, 1991; Tennant & Pogson, 1995). Universally, the common picture of ideal adults (or older people) is of people who are fit in body and mind, curious and interested in life, and in pursuit of a vocation with vigor; they are close to family and friends, are helpful and involved in the community, and concerned with making sense of the world. They find meaning and enjoyment in all these endeavors. They have the ability to develop and use a full range of potential, and they recognize and value this ability (Csikszentmihalyi & Rathunde, 1998). They have a capacity to think of alternative solutions to problems, group unlike objects in creative new ways, be more autonomous, resolve childhood conflicts and anxieties, and be intimate without a loss of personal identity (Tennant & Pogson, 1995). Development occurs when there is growth in those qualities. Therefore development is growth toward and capability in handling increasing complexity in one's life.

Whereas there is a relationship between developmental level and age in children, this does not continue through adulthood. There is no clear-cut relationship between development and age. Other factors such as cognitive and personality variables, role-taking skills, family climate, education, and sensitivity to age changes all play a role (see, e.g., Labouvie-Vief, Chiodo, Goguen, Diehl, & Orwell, 1995; Labouvie-Vief & Diehl, 2000; Pratt, Diessner, Hunsberger, Pancer, & Savoy, 1991).

One often ignored area in adult development is the active and purposeful role of the individual in helping to shape his or her own development. To develop, a person has to *want* to develop. But why would a person *want* to become a more complex person? What motivates them to develop? One viewpoint is that development occurs when individuals attempt to escape boredom by raising challenges and overcome anxiety by raising skills (Csikszentmihalyi & Rathunde, 1998). If life is not stimulating enough, people become bored. If life is too overwhelming, they become anxious. People like being in a situation where their skills fit with the challenges in the environment and seek to find that fit. Challenges increase arousal whereas skills decrease arousal at the same time, permitting deep involvement in the present activity. Csikszentmihalyi called this *flow*—the balance between arousal-increasing and arousal-decreasing processes.

At least seven bipolar dimensions of complexity create flow in adulthood (Csikszentmihalyi & Rathunde, 1998). These are (a) a drive toward independence and interdependence (agency and communion—an example would be speaking and listening), (b) passionate investment and detached objectivity (e.g., being carried away and excited at the same time one is making sure that one's enthusiasm fits reality), (c) divergent and convergent thinking (e.g., problem solving and problem finding), (d) playfulness and discipline (combining a sense of play with hard work), (e) extroversion and introversion (enjoying both the company of other people and solitude), (f) energy and quietude (interweaving activity and rest), and (g) iconoclastic and traditional (blazing new trails while preserving the integrity of the previous). Agency, passion, divergent thinking, playfulness, extroversion, energy, and iconoclasm are all associated with escaping boredom. Communion, detachment, convergent thinking, discipline, introversion, quietude, and tradition are all associated with overcoming anxiety.

## STAGES OF DEVELOPMENT

Development can occur in a series of relatively fixed stages based on age throughout adulthood. Years of theory and research have established that adulthood is a period of active change based on a combination of internal factors and life events combined with sociocultural expectations. Factors such as race, gender, social-class membership, and even social events also affect life changes. The world looks different to a young adult embarking on life than to a middle-aged adult reviewing their life so far and making changes moving forward or to an older adult coming to terms with the life they have lived. "Life stage" theorists have dealt with various aspects of these stages of adult development.

For example, Levinson formulated age-related stages of development from interviews with men (1978) and women (1996). Somewhat different from the aforementioned formulation, Levinson distinguished between nine stages:

Early-Adult Transition—Leaving the Family (17–22)
Entering the Adult World (22–28)
Age-30 Transition (28–33)
Settling Down (33–40)
Becoming One's Own Person (later phase of 33–40)
Midlife Transition (40–45)
Entering Middle Adulthood—Restabilization (45–50)
Age-50 Transition (50–55)
Culmination of Middle Adulthood (55–60)
Late Adult Transition (60–65)

Levinson recognized that a person's life structure is influenced by the environment, particularly other people who play a significant role in the individual's life. Yet, he argued that life stages are very specific and follow chronological age closely for almost everyone.

A more general model of developmental stages that integrates Levinson's work with other theorists is summarized in Table 3.1 (based on Wortley & Amatea, 1982, and Jackson, 1996).

People tend to leave home and enter the adult world between the ages of 20 and 30. They explore job alternatives, find a first job, complete their formal training, and establish a commitment to a specific profession or job. Internally, they form a core identity and commit to accomplishing certain goals for advancement and accomplishment. They develop a sense of themselves as an adult, including feelings of autonomy and competence. They gain a sense of self-worth as they deepen their relationships with significant others. They detach from their parents and may begin their own family. In the process, they establish a personal worldview with a set of values, beliefs, priorities, and goals.

Between the ages of 30 and 40 people build on this foundation. They strive to achieve their career goals. Women, especially, may enter, leave, and reenter the career world as they have children. Some men may do the same, taking on child-care responsibilities as their wives continue their career. Individuals in this stage of early adulthood may readjust their career goals in line with changing expectations they have for themselves and that significant others have for them. They seek mastery in their profession along with recognition for their early achievements. Some commit to continuous learning and/or to increased productivity as they struggle to balance the complexities of work and family life. Sometimes, they find they have to adjust their goals in light of the demands of their profession, finding that life is not exactly what they expected or that they don't have the energy or know-how to accomplish all they hoped. Alternatively, they may seek new vistas, perhaps changing jobs or moving to new areas to enhance their opportunities for career growth.

Midlife (roughly ages 40–50) is when people focus on making their mark and establishing their legacy. Building on their previous stage, they enter a period of peak work commitment, achievement, and recognition. They may develop as supervisors, managers, and executives. They may also become mentors to younger people entering the profession. Corporate politics may seem less important. Their values may change from valuing the outward signs of success to valuing continued learning and accomplishment. They may redirect their career in substantial ways, sometimes forced to do so by company downsizing. Internally, they redefine their work roles and goals in light of changing values, priorities, and opportunities. They begin a review of their lives so far, recognizing contradictions and making adjustments in their values as they look back on the past and forward to the future.

Ages 50–60 is a stabilization phase as the individual's career begins to culminate. People may gain enjoyment and a sense of accomplishment from being an adviser or mentor to others. They evaluate how secure they can be in retirement and determine if and how soon they want to retire. They may face age-related employment problems. For instance, older individuals who lose their jobs are likely to have more trouble finding employment than those who are younger and have the time and luxury to retrain (having few family responsibilities and the availability of education loans and the time to pay them off). The 50- to 60-year-old begins to disengage from work, or may postpone retirement and even avoid planning for it. Internally, they begin to recognize their mortality and vulnerability. They may restabilize their support system, valuing relationships at work and outside of work. Of course, they are likely to have to deal more deliberately with aging parents as well as their own aging.

Late maturity and retirement usually occur between the ages of 60 and 70. This is when people reflect on the meaning of their lives. They are likely to detach from a formal work role and develop interests in hobbies. They value learning for learning's sake. They engage in more volunteer work. Their personal identify is less and less associated with job, employer, and profession. They adapt to an increasing distance from being in the mainstream. They need to conserve their energy and deal with decreasing vigor.

The final stage of life is a time for review and cultivation of leisure activities. People over 70 fulfill honorific and sage roles. They don't seek recognition. They enjoy reminiscing as a way to confirm to themselves that their life was meaningful. They may find themselves accepting aid from their children as they deal with being alone. Independent and assisted-living facilities may provide needed resources but also the loss of privacy and individuality.

Stage theories are descriptive of life's cycle of events and the feelings and accomplishments that relate to them. The stages help us understand how events

TABLE 3.1
Adult Development Through Life Stages as Related to Career and Inner Life

| | *20–30* | *30–40* | *40–50* | *50–60* | *60–70* | *70-Death* |
|---|---|---|---|---|---|---|
| | *Leave Home and Enter the Adult World* | *Develop and Extend Roots* | *Midlife* | *Stabilization* | *Late Maturity and Retirement* | *Life Review and Termination Issues* |
| | Identify self as an adult | Become an adult | | | Reflect on adulthood | |
| Career: External | Find a job and begin paying own bills.<br>Job exploration, training/education, and trial entry.<br>Commit to specific work area or continue career exploration. | Commit to set career pattern and strive for vertical movement (play the corporate game).<br>Commit to a function or profession.<br>Enter or leave due to children (women especially). | Focus on making one's mark, legacy.<br>Enter period of peak work commitment, achievement, and recognition.<br>Take on supervisory, managing, and mentoring responsibilities.<br>Feel that corporate games are less important than they were.<br>Possibly face midlife career change to meet changing values or changing opportunities—e.g., lose corporate job in downsizing and start own business. | Culminate career.<br>Act as mentor/adviser.<br>Evaluate retirement security.<br>Face increasing age-related employment problems (unskilled especially). | Retire from full-time work.<br>Detach from formal work role.<br>Become interested in hobbies again and learn for learning's sake instead of learning on the job.<br>Increase community service.<br>Fulfill honorific and sage roles. | Cultivate leisure activities and new outlets for skill development and use.<br>Continue fulfillment of honorific and sage roles (though may be quietly amused at any recognition received). |

| | | | | | | |
|---|---|---|---|---|---|---|
| Internal | Establish specific work identity.<br>Commit to generativity (ongoing learning and professional and personal growth) or productivity with push toward a "dream." | Readjust career goals to realign with changing expectations of self and significant other.<br>Seeking mastery, promotion, recognition, credentials, and confidence. | Redefine work roles/goals in light of changing values, priorities, and possibilities. | Begin to disengage, or postpone and ignore upcoming retirement.<br>Evaluate and review work accomplishments. | Redirect energy into "nonwork" activities and life maintenance routines. | |
| Inner life | Establish self as an adult.<br>Develop autonomy and competence.<br>Develop sense of personal worth and identity.<br>Establish and commit to primary relationships.<br>Increase self-knowledge.<br>Establish personal worldview, values, beliefs, priorities, and goals.<br>Detach from parents and siblings; start own family. | Commit to generativity and striving for productivity.<br>Integrate and prioritize multiple commitments and responsibilities to work, family, mate, friends, community.<br>Compromise and adjust goals to reality—life's demands.<br>Begin to feel concern about own and parents' aging. | Begin midlife review—face contradictions, and adjust.<br>Feel midlife shift in time perspective (look forward and backward). | Increase personalization of death and consciousness of own vulnerability.<br>Stabilize support systems again.<br>Consolidate resources in response to recognition of increasing vulnerability.<br>Deal with aging parents/death of parents. | Detach personal identity from work role.<br>Develop leisure orientation and life enrichment.<br>Adapt to increased distance from mainstream—accept "subculture" status.<br>Adapt to decreasing vigor.<br>Begin to conserve one's energy. | Conduct life review and reminisce.<br>Consolidate symbolic belief system.<br>Feel that one's life had meaning and was well spent.<br>Accept aid from children.<br>Face increasing social separation—bury friends and family.<br>Deal with physical frailty.<br>Deal with aloneness or loss of privacy. |

*Note.* From Wortley and Amatea (1982) and and Jackson (1996).

fit within the cycle of life. They suggest a development sequence that builds on each previous stage and includes increasing reflection and self-understanding as we age. Of course, people vary in their life structure due to many factors—early success, illness, and family circumstances not to mention motivation and ability. Some people may age but not change much at all, at least in terms of their values and cognitive development. We have to look more deeply to understand how self-perceptions, feelings, attitudes, and abilities intertwine with life events and evolve over time to different degrees.

## DEVELOPMENT AS A PROGRESSION OF INCREASING COMPLEXITY: KEGAN'S FIVE ORDERS OF CONSCIOUSNESS

Another way to look at development is to determine how people create meaning from the events that happen to them. Kegan (1982) held that people may evolve through as many as five orders of consciousness. These are not really stages, but progression markers. This is based on progressively more complex understanding of what is "self" and what is "other" (that is, subject–object relations). When people are "subject" to something, they *are* that something and cannot see it.

In the "zero" order of consciousness, the "incorporative stage," babies are unable to separate themselves at all—everything is a part of them, and they are a part of everything. Babies are their reflexes.

In the first order of consciousness, the "impulsive stage" (2–6 years), children are able to recognize that objects and people exist independent of their own sensing of them (object permanence), and they can distinguish between inner sensation and outer stimulation. But they cannot distinguish their own perception of an object from the properties of the object, construct a cause–effect relationship, recognize that other people have their own purposes independent of them, or distinguish their own impulses from themselves. In this order of consciousness, children are subject to their own impulses and perceptions. The way they see the world is the way the world is, and they have no idea that others may perceive the world differently. Alternatively, if their perception changes, so does the world. However, they understand that they have reflexes such as sensing and moving.

In the second order of consciousness, the "imperial stage" (6 years to teens), children are subject to their needs, interests, and wishes. In this order of consciousness, children have durable categories. They can understand that objects have properties separate from their own perceptions and that both they and other people can have differing points of view and can drive, regulate, or organize their impulses (e.g., to delay immediate gratification). They cannot reason abstractly or make hypotheses, take their own and another's point of view simultaneously, or distinguish their own needs from themselves. They attempt to control or at least predict the world. However, they understand that they have impulses and perceptions. What makes this stage "imperial" is the sense of the absence of a shared reality (what a kid wants vs. what a parent wants).

In the third order of consciousness, the "interpersonal stage" (teenage years and beyond), people are subject to their interpersonal relationships. That is, they are defined by their relationships. There is no "self" independent of "other people." However, people at this order of consciousness understand that they have needs, interests, and wishes and that others have needs, interests, and wishes as well. They are aware of shared feelings, agreements, and expectations. They internalize others' points of view, and coordinate more than one point of view. Yet their self-concept is inextricably tied to relationships they have with others. Regarding their jobs, they see work as owned and created by their employer. That is, they expect that their supervisor and others in higher levels of management will create visions, frame problems, initiate adjustment, and determine whether things are going well. Their role is to follow orders of those above them.

In the fourth order of consciousness, the "institutional stage," people can stand alone. They are their "own organization" and have "a mind of their own." They recognize the relationships they have with others, but they don't define themselves in terms of these relationships. Those who reach this order of consciousness invent or own their work. They are self-initiating, self-correcting, and self-evaluating rather than dependent on others to frame problems, initiate adjustments, or determine whether things are going acceptably well. They are guided by their own visions, take responsibility for what happens to them at work, and expect to be accomplished masters of their own work, roles, jobs, or careers. But they don't yet see themselves as part of a larger more complex system until the final order of consciousness.

Individuals who make it to the fifth order of consciousness, the "interindividual stage," can now see themselves both as an individual person and as a partner in interrelations—part of a much larger, interconnected system. They recognize how they can influence their environment and relationships and are influenced by them. But they are neither defined by these relationships nor isolated from them. They comprehend how they fit into the larger system of interrelationships and organizational structures and processes.

People evolve very slowly and constantly, taking years to achieve an order of consciousness, at which point they are still evolving toward the next. And they must evolve through each in order. They cannot skip a level. However, they don't necessarily reach the fifth level, and may not reach the fourth.

## HOW LEARNING AND DEVELOPMENT ARE RELATED

There are actually two developmental levels active in an adult at one time (Vgotsky, 1978). The first is the actual development level. The second is the *zone of proximal development*. This is the distance between the actual development and the level of potential development. The zone of proximal development defines those functions that are not yet mature but are in the process of maturation. The essential feature of learning is that it creates the zone of proximal development. It awakens a variety of internal development processes that are able to operate only with a more capable person or peers. Once these processes are internalized, they become developed. Properly organized learning results in mental development and sets in motion a variety of developmental processes that would be impossible apart from learning. Adults may not continue to develop into the more advanced stages of cognitive complexity unless they have exposure to more complex ways of thinking and learning.

Social interaction creates, extends, and utilizes zones to foster skills and capacities. The learner observes others, then emulates them with support (e.g., a coach), then finally internalizes learned behaviors as part of their own repertoire of skills for independent use. Learning assistance, a broad domain of "cognitive apprenticeship," can occur in a number of different ways. These include modeling, coaching, scaffolding, questioning, exploration, reflection, structuring, and instruction. For example, scaffolding provides the learner with support and assistance to complete a task or solve a problem that couldn't have been mastered without help through such methods as hinting, elaborating, leading, linking, requesting, reworking, suggesting, commenting, prompting, probing, simplifying, and providing emotional support. Modeling provides the learner with a prime example of appropriate or desired behavior then gradually gives control of the situation to the learner (Bonk & Kim, 1998).

Tools and artifacts in the environment can also assist learners—either intentionally or unintentionally. These include announcements, memos, bulletin boards, Post-it® notes, illustrations (flipcharts, whiteboards, slide presentations, etc.), office mail, brochures, journals, newsletters, and technology (phones, voice mail, fax machines, Internet pages and chat rooms, blogs, e-mail, workstations, collaboration tools, help screens, instant messages, and even manuals). Supportive learning settings, institutions, and environments to consider are lounges, conference rooms, lunchrooms, boardrooms, laboratories, libraries, associations, memberships, committees, conferences, retreats, vendor training, training institutions, workshops, and distance education centers (Bonk & Kim, 1998).

## TAKING DEVELOPMENT INTO ACCOUNT IN CONTINUOUS LEARNING

Being in "flow" is most likely to be experienced when an individual is fully functioning relative to the developmental opportunities that a given "stage" provides (Csikzentmihalyi & Rathunde, 1998). Developmental level, both in terms of life stage and in terms of how individuals make meaning, guides what motivates people to learn, what kinds of learning are attractive to them, what they are capable of learning, and the kinds of transformations that they might make.

### Learning Throughout All Stages of Life

Consider learning through the life stages. When entering the adult world, individuals are interested in learning about a variety of career choices, learning about different departments in organizations and what they do, and learning about themselves before committing to a desired career path. Once in the career path, they are interested in learning about it in more depth. The emphasis here is on skill-building competence toward one's desired career "dream" and learning for and about one's self. However, learning such things as "coaching" or "mentoring" may not make much sense to people in this stage of life unless that's what they want to do in their career.

As individuals become rooted in their career, they are interested in learning whatever it takes to move ahead in their chosen career path. This includes continued skill development for increased productivity, mastery, and credentials as well as learning the "right stuff" to play the corporate game for promotion and recognition purposes. Individuals may be less interested in learning more about themselves, particularly if they have had to compromise and adjust their goals, values, and assumptions to meet the demands of what they perceive is needed for success in the real world. The first author once attended a weeklong training program where one of the participants was teased because he had all the correct "training program" attire—golf shirts with collar turned up "just so" wearing khakis and loafers—whereas the rest of the attendants wore a motley assortment of clothes that looked as if they had dug through their entire wardrobe to find a week's worth of "casual clothing." The participant admitted that every year he attended the "right" off-site training program.

During the midlife period, individuals may be less interested in deepening skills—unless they are women reentering the workforce and are still closely aligned with the rooting and extending stage. Individuals are interested in broadening skills as they move up in the organization, start their own organization, or change careers. Self-assessment becomes important once again as individuals struggle with realigning their values with their work—possibly leading to career changes based on a combination of their current skills and a reemergence of important values. Individuals in this stage are more interested in learning about managing, leading, and empowering others. Though individuals still want to achieve and receive recognition for their accomplishments, they are less inclined to play corporate games. Training in such areas as team development and diversity is more powerful now as individuals are less focused on themselves. In this stage, individuals also switch from being in the learner role to being in the teacher role with a burgeoning interest in coaching, mentoring, and advising.

During the stabilization stage, learning in the areas of managing, leading, and empowering remains though it may weaken somewhat as mentoring, coaching, and advising grow in importance as individuals continue to be less and less interested in "doing" and more and more interested in molding the next generation and creating their legacy. However, some individuals may find themselves forced back into learning new skills as they struggle to remain in the workforce despite age-related forced terminations.

During the late maturity/retirement and life review/termination stages, individuals switch from learning career-oriented knowledge and skills to more self-oriented knowledge and skills as they once again become interested in hobbies and avocational/leisure activities. There may be a desire for wholly new career-related skills. Individuals may need these skills for community-based activities (e.g., accomplishing the lifelong dream of becoming a lawyer and using their legal skills and knowledge in defending a local not-for-profit as it negotiates the use of community space). Or they may just want to learn for learning's sake. Generally individuals at this stage approach learning in terms of life mission and how one's life mission relates to the skills and knowledge acquired (see, e.g., Kroth & Boverie, 2000). Motivation is a function of not just the immediate need for the learning but the deeper force that drives the learner to discover and enact the existential questions, "Who and why am I?"

A word about life mission: Learning is enhanced when learners see the link learning and their life mission. Learning deepens the understanding and meaningfulness of one's life or purpose. However, people do not normally focus on their life mission. Indeed, they may not even know they have one until they reflect on it later in life. This recognition may not occur earlier unless the individual is faced with a disorienting dilemma. This may be an adult education experience or a new role in life. It could be work related, for example, a new job, or nonwork related, for example, the birth of one's first child. Life mission, whether clearly explicated or implicit/not self-articulated, provides a source of self-direction of learning choices and motivation. The disquiet or uncertainty of facing a dilemma presents a source of desire to move beyond the satisfaction of self-identity and self-awareness.

### Learning Through Orders of Consciousness

Where people "are" in terms of their ability to construct meaning influences how they see and experience the world. As a concrete example, leadership may have wholly different meanings for people in different orders of consciousness. For an adult in the interpersonal stage, it might be: "I am the follower and she or he is the leader—whatever she or he does is leadership and whatever I do is not. So I do not need to learn how to be a leader until I take on such a role." For an adult in the institutional stage, it might be: "I show elements of both leader and follower, sometimes even in the same situation. And my boss shows elements of leader and follower and lets me influence him or her. I need to learn about both leadership and followership to really be competent in this role." For an adult in the inter-individual stage it might be: "Leadership is defined and enacted by myself and the people I interact with. There really is no 'leader' and no 'follower' unless we make it so. I and others need to learn a variety of things about leadership so that we can start with those options and work from there."

Consider how learning occurs through orders of consciousness. (We concentrate on typical levels of healthy adults.) In the interpersonal stage, adults define themselves through their relationships with others. They are attracted to learning what is expected in their current or desired future role and in learning job-related skills in more depth, that is, how to do their job better. They like to be seen as "competent," as skilled, or as an expert by others. However, they do not tend to take initiative and instead wait to be told what to learn because they do not see it as within their role to take an active role yet. As a consequence, they may be seen by others as needing to learn such skills as assertiveness and confidence so that they *can* take control of their own work. In addition, certain "standard" learning may be beyond their scope. That is, they may not "get" such concepts as big-picture orientation, perspective taking, taking initiative, self-management, double-loop learning, empowerment, followership, and dialogue.

During the institutional stage, individuals define themselves by their work and employer—work role, career, duties, position, and so forth. They define what is important to learn. And they may be attracted to learning that exposes them to a bigger picture of the organization, perspectives of others, taking different perspectives and examining alternatives from those perspectives, empowerment, creativity, taking initiative, self-management, and dialogue.

In the interindividual stage the learner realizes that they are not their work roles, career, or duties. They have these roles, careers, and duties, but they are not them. Here, the learner's goals are to help the organization and develop themselves simultaneously. They realize that what they and others choose to learn creates the situation and not the other way around.

### Lack of Fit between Environmental Demands and Capacity to Learn

Currently, there is a lack of fit between what the culture demands of adults' minds and their mental capacity to meet these demands. A majority of adults have not yet reached the fourth order of consciousness but are at or above level three (Kegan, 1982, 1994). However, the environment, at least in the United States and other Western nations, is calling for a fourth order of consciousness with some needs in the fifth order. The fourth order of consciousness expects intimate relationships, dealing with diversity, and continuous learning. Organizations expect people to resolve conflicts openly and give each other honest and direct feedback. They expect leaders to convey new ideas and communicate a vision that transforms the organization quickly in relation to environmental changes. They expect employees to not only learn to do better today and prepare for tomorrow but also to generate new knowledge and ideas that disrupt the status quo and create new modes of operating and new products and services. Many large organizations use competency models that indicate dimensions and level of performance that are expected for success in the organization. These may include general areas that can be learned such as business acumen, financial analysis and understanding, and industry and technical knowledge. Some dimensions such as people management, teamwork, and big-picture orientation are, in part, related to an individual's development.

People's order of consciousness may determine how they interpret competencies, their motivation to learn, and their capability to learn. This is little understood as all competencies are considered to be "learnable." Unfortunately, organizations often expect individuals to interpret the meaning of these elements of performance for themselves and determine how their own performance contributes to the organization's and their department's goals. Sometimes people are left to their own devices to evaluate and track their performance, perhaps with the exception of a formal performance review once a year. So we shouldn't be surprised when employees have trouble calibrating how they are doing and making adjustments. The organization may help by offering performance feedback in different forms (informal performance discussions from peers and supervisors; performance ratings from peers, subordinates, supervisors, and/or customers; objective data such as sales performance or production; as well as annual performance reviews from the supervisor). The individual needs the capacity to understand and accept this information, which may be unfavorable at times. Moreover, the individual needs to integrate and comprehend the various elements of performance, and relate the feedback to changes they can make in their behavior to enhance their strengths and overcome weaknesses in technical and interpersonal areas.

In addition, organizational priorities are likely to change, sometimes very quickly. An organization may move into new product lines, enter new markets around the world, merge with or be purchased by another company, spin off a segment of the business, and reorganize or restructure to form new reporting relationships and new work teams with broader (or narrower) spans of control and opportunities for individual decisions before being evaluated. Keeping up with these changes, maintaining high performance, and making a significant contribution to the organization is a never-ending, complex, and often stressful process.

Most people are "in over their heads" in today's world. A performance deficit or learning need may in fact be a need for a higher order or a new way of making meaning. To develop a person to a higher order takes many years and requires safety and support along the way.

Kegan and Lahey (2001) developed such a learning technology using a series of questions to help people do this. The questions give individuals a process for how to transform subject to object. Step-by-step, an individual is led through a series of questions asking them to identify things in their work setting that, if there were more of them (or less), would be supportive of their own development at work. Next they are asked to analyze this situation and specify what they are committed to ("I am committed to the value or importance of . . ."). Then they are asked to determine what they are doing (or not doing) themselves that is keeping their commitment from being more fully realized (asking them to take responsibility). As a next step, they are asked to determine competing commit-

TABLE 3.2
Examples of Kegan and Lahey's (2001) Learning Technology

| *Commitment* | *What I'm Doing or Not Doing That Prevents My Commitment From Being Fully Realized* | *Competing Commitment* | *Big Assumption* |
|---|---|---|---|
| I am committed to the value or importance of: | | I may also be committed to: | I assume that if: |
| Getting the resources and support I need to succeed and thrive (rather than barely survive) in my job and life. | I try to do too much and everything at once in order to be successful. I'm trying to be a well-regarded teacher, a top-notch researcher, a respected I/O professional, and a good spouse, parent, and community member all at once. | Not failing at what I do. Being successful in all parts of my life. | I fail then I will be fired, unhirable, broke, unloved, and out on the street. |
| More open and direct at work. | I don't speak up when people are violating the norm I value. Silently, I collude in it being OK to talk behind one another's back. | Not being seen as the brave crusader, or holier than thou. Having people comfortable with me. | People did see me that way, then I would eventually be shunned, have no real connections in my office other than the most formal and functional, and work would be a nightmare. |

*Note.* Updated from Kegan and Lahey (2001). Adapted by permission. The table is based on this sample question followed by two exampes of possible responses: **Question:** What sort of things—if they were to happen more frequently in your work setting—would you experience as being more supportive of your own ongoing development at work? **Example 1:** If I had more time. It all comes down to that. I'm expected to carry a full teaching load, counsel students, do research, participate in committees, contribute to my profession, and have a life outside of work. **Example 2:** No one talks to each other at work; people talk about each other behind their backs rather than going to the person we have an issue with.

ments that keep them from this commitment. The final step is to surface the "big assumption" (that which the individual is subject to). Individuals are asked that if they are seen as failing in their competing commitment, then how they would feel. This surfaces what they are subject to and helps them focus on it. Does this work? Research is needed to test the theory and method. See Table 3.2 for examples.

A second way to help adults develop and think beyond their current state is to apply techniques based on Vygotsky's *zone of proximal development.* Individuals operating at lower orders of consciousness are paired with mentors, coaches, managers, and peers operating at higher orders of consciousness. This requires a long-term commitment on the part of the organization (as development cannot be rushed). Also, the developmental level of all parties must be known to the organization with a deliberate pairing of individuals at lower orders of consciousness with those at higher orders. This requires that those at higher orders of consciousness be equal to or higher in the organizational hierarchy to those in lower orders of consciousness, and that they learn, use, and be rewarded for using appropriate techniques to provide learning assistance such as modeling. However, people at higher levels of the organization are not necessarily at higher orders of consciousness than those at lower organizational levels—and may, in fact, be at lower orders of consciousness!

Third, the policies, procedures, practices, structure, and culture in an organization can be designed to provide a safe holding and development environment—both providing support and development toward a higher order of consciousness. Because our environment in general is calling for a higher order of thinking, and because everyone develops through every order of consciousness, there will always be a range of orders in any work environment. Most adult employees are operating at or between the interpersonal stage and the institutional stage. Thus, the organization can be designed with a long-term commitment to development. In earlier societies, including in the United States, the societies themselves provided "pacers of transformation" or higher order structure and direction through such mechanisms as the Constitution of the United States of America and religion (Kegan, 1994; Wilbur, 2000a). Organizations provide the same support with policies and processes that clearly communicate sets of values.

## OTHER INDIVIDUAL CHARACTERISTICS THAT SUPPORT CONTINUOUS LEARNING

In addition to developmental stage or level, which centers on how people make sense of the world and what they may be open to learning, there are characteristics that distinguish those who learn from those who appear more reticent to learn at work. Active continuous learners at work have different beliefs about themselves and their learning than those who need to be encouraged to learn. They believe that the responsibility for growth and development rests within themselves and not the organization (self-direction). They believe that they can set and achieve their own learning goals (self-efficacy and self-esteem). They believe that they have a choice regarding what they need to learn (self-determination), and that they are in control of their learning goals, strategies, and experiences (self-regulation). As we noted earlier in this chapter, an individual's emphasis on the self and their realization that learning is up to them may also be a reflection of how they have learned to make meaning about the world and thus may be related to their stage of development. Thus these characteristics should not be construed as mutually exclusive.

### Self-Efficacy and Self-Esteem

People who are high in self-efficacy believe that they can set and achieve their own learning goals. Self-esteem refers to how positive a person feels about him or herself. People who are high in self-esteem tend to be adaptable and resilient in the face of barriers. Self-esteem is part of a general construct called core self-evaluation (Judge, Erez, Bono, & Thoresen, 2002; Judge, Locke, Durham, & Kluger, 1998). People who are high in self-evaluation are high in self-worth, believe they are able to perform well across a variety of situations, tend to be positive or optimistic, and believe that they can bring about positive outcomes.

Phil Doesschate, a systems development executive and one of our continuous learners, exemplified this when wrote about his enjoyment of continuous learning in our online discussion:

> I think that continuous learners enjoy trying something new, experiencing something old in a new way, identifying and fully experiencing the unexpected. It's diving in headfirst and experiencing and knowing things fully. To me, it is delving into something at considerable depth, turning something over, looking at it a new way, and coming up with a new perspective and a new foundation with which to step into a new level of experience and sometimes a new level of development.

### Self-Direction and Self-Regulation

Organizations often establish activities to support formal learning, such as goal setting, the availability of courses, assigning challenging job responsibilities, and providing assessments and feedback. Organizations also help informal learning by encouraging leaders and coworkers to be supportive, assignments to new projects, and providing on-the-spot feedback (Noe, 1999; Simmering, Colquitt, Noe, & Porter, 2003). But organizations cannot *make* an individual learn, they can only provide them with the triggers to let them know that learning is needed. Nor can organizations predict what an individual will learn from those triggers. But the organization can provide the resources and support for individuals to take advantage of, and that may guide learning in the needed organizational direction. Ultimately, the extent to which employees participate and learn from provided activities is up to them. Individuals high in self-direction realize this. They figure out what they need to know and use organizational resources to gain this knowledge. They realize that the responsibility for learning rests with themselves. They see the organization's role in learning as providing guidance and resources that enable their learning. Of course, some organizations may do a better job of this than others. Clearly this involves a fairly high order of consciousness.

Self-directed learners look for guidance from their organizations in terms of what competencies are desired, the level of performance that is expected and will be rewarded, and the opportunities and resources that are available. They want their supervisors to be coaches and mentors, helping to guide them to enhance their insight about themselves and the organization. Supervisors and other co-workers can be expected to support and reinforce their learning and development by using tools provided in the organization's performance management system (appraisal, feedback, goal setting, training). Organizational resources that enable self-directed individuals include people to access, software, courses, workshops, tuition dollars, job experiences, and time to reflect.

Stella Lee, a web designer and one of our continuous learners, showed self-direction when she wrote, "I think I just have this urge to learn; I'm just very curious about things I don't know and also to keep up with professional knowledge."

Individuals are active in satisfying their own needs for learning when they perceive that they have a choice. When they are confronted with a problem that they cannot easily ignore and that requires action with no solution immediately evident, they are more likely to learn if they feel in control (Sims & McAuley, 1995). Also, they are more likely to learn when the actions that they take are personally meaningful and based on nonthreatening feedback that acknowledges their feelings and perspectives (e.g., the manager empathetically suggests that "learning this behavior will enhance your performance; you will find it challenging but do-able") (cf. Deci, Egharari, Patrick, & Leone, 1994; Deci & Ryan, 1991).

Self-regulated learners feel in control of the learning situation. They are self-initiators who apply personal choice and control of learning goals and methods. That is, they generate and direct their own learning experiences rather than react to external controls. They are purposeful and strategic in what they learn and are persistent in pursuing learning. They are able to evaluate their own progress in relation to the goals they have set and to adjust subsequent behavior in light of those self-evaluations (Purdie, Hattie, & Douglas, 1996).

Self-regulated learners structure their environmental to be conducive to learning, set goals and plans, seek needed information, organize and transform the information, rehearse and memorize, keep records of their performance, and monitor others' reactions to them. Self-monitoring is an element of self-regulation. People who are high in self-monitoring are sensitive to the situation and to different people, and respond differently depending on the situation as compared to those who are low in self-monitoring who don't bother to understand others' needs and reaction to them (Snyder, 1974). Self-monitors are sensitive to feedback and willing to use it to improve their performance. They seek assistance from others (instructors, peers, family), evaluate themselves, and give themselves consequences for achieving a learning goal or failing to achieve a learning goal (Zimmerman & Martinez-Ponz, 1986, as cited in Purdie et al., 1996, p. 88).

Sister Margaret Ann Landry, RSHM, Chaplain of a Catholic campus ministry/interfaith center and one of our continuous learners, naturally incorporates these learning strategies into her life. She wrote:

> I graduated from college with a major in Philosophy and a minor in French, then pursued an M.A. in History. Throughout my life I have studied theology, spiritual-

ity and worship, economics, Latin and Chinese history. Beyond these formal educational experiences, I have had the opportunity to learn by my experiences in travel throughout the United States, Europe and Africa. One cannot help but learn through these experiences about diverse cultures, traditions, languages and religions. I believe in the importance of athletics in my life and their importance in the lives of others. Through sports we learn about the "game" of life . . . how to be a leader, a team player and a good sportsman (woman). Another important learning experience is that of realizing the significance of transferable skills.

### Conscientiousness and Openness to Experience

Active continuous learners may also differ on other personality traits from those who need encouragement to learn. During the past quarter century, the views of many personality psychologists have converged around the idea that there are five domains of personality: extraversion/intraversion, emotional stability, agreeableness, conscientiousness, and openness to experience (McCrae & Costa, 1987). Openness to experience and conscientiousness may be particularly related to learning.

Openness to experience is being imaginative, cultured, curious, broad-minded, original, artistically sensitive, and intelligent—generally the types of attributes we would expect to be associated with positive attitudes toward learning (Barrick & Mount, 1991). Although there has not been a lot of research on openness to experience and learning, per se, those who are more open to experience have been found to be more able to successfully utilize effective strategies when coping with stressful life events (obstacles) and organizational change (Judge, Thoreson, Pucik, & Welbourne, 1999; McCrae & Costa, 1986). In addition, openness to experience is also related to such things as identity flexibility both at work and in life in general (Whitbourne, 1986). Given the tendencies of individuals who are high in openness to experience to be tolerant of and inquisitive about new situations (and in fact, seek out such situations), we may also expect them to have positive attitudes toward learning in new situations at work.

Conscientiousness is the tendency to be reliable, hardworking, self-disciplined, and persevering (McCrae & Costa, 1987). Individuals who are conscientious are well organized, efficient, goal oriented, and persistent (Barrick & Mount, 1991). Conscientiousness is related to commitment to goals, motivation to learn, and actually participating in learning activities (e.g., Colquitt & Simmering, 1998). However, overly conscientiousness individuals may deceive themselves that they are doing better than they really are (Martocchio & Judge, 1997) and may apply what they learn too exactly, causing lower performance when the situation calls for flexibility (LePine, Colquitt, & Erez, 2000). Conscientiousness may provide the personal resourcefulness and perseverance for learning as long as employees who are conscientious perceive a need for learning (Simmering et al., 2003). Need may be evident if the job provides more or less autonomy than the employee wants. Autonomy is important to feeling challenged (Kulik, Oldham, & Hackman,

1987), and learning can be an important way to gain more autonomy, if the person desires more (Noe, Wilk, Mullen, & Wanek, 1997). Learning can also be a way to live up to expectations if the job requires being more autonomous than the individual wants. Research by Simmering et al., based on managers in an executive master's of business administration (MBA) program, revealed that conscientious managers were more likely to participate in learning activities when they felt that their jobs were not meeting their autonomy needs. Conscientiousness was strongly related to learning when managers possessed too little autonomy, suggesting that the desire for more autonomy causes managers to try to acquire the skills and confidence they need to accept more autonomy and presumably demonstrate to themselves and others that they are ready to be more autonomous. Conscientiousness was also related to learning when managers possessed too much autonomy. Learning may be a way for these managers to demonstrate to themselves that they can handle being autonomous. Ironically, as these managers participate in learning, their supervisors may given them more autonomy, creating an increased person–environment misfit.

## Goal Orientation

Active learners may differ from those who need encouragement to learn in terms of their goal orientation as well. Those who need encouragement and support to learn may believe that their ability is a fixed, uncontrollable, personal attribute whereas active learners may believe that their ability is a malleable attribute that can be developed through experience and effort. Type of goal orientation is related to an individual's implicit theory of ability as being either fixed or malleable (Button, Mathieu, & Zajac, 1996; Dweck & Leggett, 1988), and thus has an impact on learning. A *learning* goal orientation is the desire to increase one's competence by developing new skills and mastering new situations, whereas a *performance* goal orientation is a desire to demonstrate one's competence to others and to be positively evaluated by others (Bell & Kozlowski, 2002; Dweck, 1986, 1989; Farr, Hofmann, & Ringenbach, 1993). Measures of learning and performance goal orientation tend to be unrelated to each other, meaning they are independent constructs that may have different effects on behavior and performance (cf. Bell & Kozlowski, 2002; VandeWalle & Cummings, 1997).

Individuals with a strong performance goal orientation tend to believe that their ability is a fixed, uncontrollable personable attribute. There are two types of performance goals: a *prove* goal orientation, which focuses on demonstrating one's competence and receiving favorable reactions from others, and an *avoid* goal orientation, which focuses on avoiding failure (negating one's existing competence) and negative reactions from others (VandeWalle, 1997). If those with a prove or avoid performance orientation perceive they lack the ability to perform a task, they are not likely to try because they don't feel that effort would improve their ability and increase their chances of accomplishing the task. They are likely to demonstrate a *maladaptive response pattern* by withdrawing from tasks, especially in the face of failure, showing less interest in difficult tasks, and seeking less challenging tasks, which they are likely to be able to perform well with their current level of ability. People who are high in performance goal orientation respond positively to survey items such as "I feel smart when I do something without making any mistakes" and "The opinions others have about how well I can do certain things are important to me" (Bell & Kozlowski, 2002; Button et al., 1996).

Individuals with a strong learning or *mastery* goal orientation tend to believe that their ability is a malleable attribute that can be learned with through experience and effort. Individuals with this belief view effort as a way to develop the ability they need for mastering the task, and they are likely to exert effort to learn especially if they think they currently lack the ability needed to perform the task. They are likely to demonstrate an *adaptive response pattern* by persisting in the face of failure, pursuing more complex learning strategies, and pursuing difficult and challenging tasks (Bell & Kozlowski, 2002). People who are high in learning goal orientation respond positively to survey items such as "The opportunity to learn new things is important to me" and "I prefer to work on tasks that force me to learn new things" (Bell & Kozlowski, 2002; Button et al., 1996).

In general, a learning goal orientation is likely to lead to positive outcomes, especially for able individuals, whereas a performance goal orientation is likely to hurt performance for able individuals. In a study of 125 undergraduate college students performing a version of a tactical navy decision-making task, Bell and Kozlowski (2002) found that learning goal orientation was significantly and positively related to individuals' self-efficacy (confidence) in being able to perform elements of the task, knowledge of the task, and task performance, however performance goal orientation was related negatively to individuals' performance. This suggested the adaptive nature of learning orientation and the maladaptive nature of performance orientation. Learning orientation was especially adaptive for individuals with high cognitive ability. Bell and Kozlowski argued that high-ability people are more likely to pursue more challenging tasks and use more complex learning strategies than are people of lower ability. However, high levels of learning orientation were nonadaptive for low-ability individuals, in that learning orientation tended to be negatively related to performance for these students. Furthermore, performance orientation was positively related to performance for low-ability individuals but negatively related to performance for high-ability individuals. This is consistent with the idea that performance-oriented individuals tend to pursue less challenging tasks and use less complex learning strategies.

Other research found that people who are high in learning goal orientation seek feedback whereas those who are high in performance goal orientation do not (VandeWalle & Cummings, 1997). Those high in performance orientation are likely to view seeking feedback as of limited value and potentially costly in terms risking negative feedback or calling attention to one's failures or limitations. Those high in learning orientation are likely to view feedback as useful, and they are not likely to be worried about receiving a negative viewpoint or causing others to think less of them. Individuals with a performance orientation tend to overestimate their instances of failures after they encounter setbacks, whereas those with a learning orientation tend to more accurately estimate their degree of failure (Diener & Dweck, 1980). Feedback facilitates later performance for those with a learning goal orientation, however, it diminishes performance for those with a prove performance goal orientation (performance is lower for those with an avoid goal orientation regardless of feedback) (VandeWalle, Cron, & Slocum, 2001).

### Summary

So far we have examined development, which helps explain how people make sense of the world and what they might be open to learning as well as personality characteristics that support continuous learning. These include self-esteem and self-efficacy, self-direction and self-regulation, conscientiousness and openness to experience, and learning goal orientation. People who are high in these characteristics are likely to be poised to learn, and indeed are likely to learn on their own. However, unless individuals know what they are supposed to learn and agree with that assessment, learning, or at least the learning wanted by the organization, will not occur. Next, we consider when people are ready to change and open to learning.

## OPENNESS TO CHANGE

As we suggested in the previous section, some individuals, due to personality and early life experiences, are more poised to learn and are more likely to start the learning process on their own. What we have not yet discussed is what makes a person ready to learn what an organization needs them to learn. Studies of change within individuals have found that people move through a series of five stages of readiness to learn and change:

1. In *precontemplation,* people are unaware or underaware that their goals are not being reached or that there are obstacles in their way. This may occur for several reasons. For example, there may be a mismatch between the goals and obstacles that the individual is aware of and interested in and the goals the organization is interested in the individual pursuing.
2. In *contemplation,* individuals are aware that goals are not being met and that obstacles are in their way, but they have not yet made a commitment to take action to make the change.
3. In *preparation,* individuals have begun to make small behavioral changes and intend to take on a larger effort soon.

4. In the *action* stage, individuals are modifying their behavior, experiences, and environment to overcome obstacles and reach their goals.
5. Finally, in the *maintenance* stage, individuals work to maintain changes made over a period of time.

These five stages, and the theory behind these stages (transtheoretical model of change), have been shown to be remarkably robust in their ability to explain behavior change (learning) across a broad range of behaviors, from addictions to professional practices (Prochaska, DiClemente & Norcross, 1992; Prochaska, Prochaska, & Levesque, 2001).

Research comparing stage distributions across a range of behaviors and populations found that about 40% of "preaction" individuals are in the precontemplation stage, 40% are in the contemplation stage, and only 20% are in the preparation stage (Laforge, Velicer, Richmond, & Owen, 1999; Velicer, Fava, Prochaska, Abrams, Emmons, & Pierce, 1995). People in precontemplation and contemplation who are required to participate in some sort of learning situation to alter their behavior are likely to see change as imposed on them. They can become resistant and defensive if forced to take action before they are ready. This has implications for both group and organizational learning as well. It demonstrates that individuals, groups, and organizations need to be open and ready for change (the preparation and action stages) in order for the learning needed by the organization to have a chance to occur!

### Motivation to Learn

Individuals can be motivated to learn only what is needed in certain stages of readiness. That is, they must be in at least the preparation stage where they are aware that they need to work on certain goals and obstacles at work and are ready to do so. In general, all adults want to make sense of their world, find meaning, and be effective at what they value (Wlodkowski, 1998). This is what fuels an individual's motivation to learn, and when there is a match between an individual's interests and stage of readiness, then motivation to learn will be heightened in that direction. The key here is triggering the needed learning to be in line with what is needed at work—and remember, the organization cannot force learning, it can only trigger it, support it, and provide resources to encourage a certain direction. Motivation to learn is a person's tendency to find the learning activities meaningful and of benefit to them. People with a strong motivation to learn find provided learning activities meaningful and of benefit to them and actively pursue such activities.

There are several related disciplines that have targeted motivation to learn in one form or another. First, Wlodkowski (1998) concentrated on four work conditions that can substantially enhance an adult's motivation to learn: (a) *attitude,* (b) *competence,* (c) *meaning,* and (d) *inclusion.* Attitude, which we have already touched on in several forms in this chapter, is a predisposition to respond favorably (or unfavorably) toward learning. Competence is a person's natural striving for effective interactions in their world—it is the desire to be effective at what that person values. Assuming that the individual values what he or she is doing at work, he or she will want to be effective and will want to learn what is needed. Meaning is stimulated by value, interest, and need in the work that the individual is doing—its opposite is boredom. The extent to which an individual finds the work he or she does interesting, the more likely he or she will want to learn. If, however, a person is bored with what they do at work, there is little motivation to learn. Inclusion is the awareness by learners that they are part of an environment in which they and their instructor are respected by and connected to one another. The extent to which a person feels included and has a say in his or her work and setting his or her own learning goals, the more likely he or she will be motivated to learn.

***Pretraining and Training Motivation.*** A second way that motivation to learn has been addressed is in focusing specifically on training activities. Here, the emphasis is on understanding whether an individual is motivated to attend training and motivated to learn while there. Individuals enter training programs with differing levels of motivation. *Pretraining* motivation is the degree of perceived value or benefit that an employee thinks is likely to result from the particular training program—that is, expecting valued outcomes from training before attending. People who are high in pretraining motivation enter into the training with heightened attention and increased receptivity to new ideas—they are primed and ready to learn (Mathieu & Martineau, 1997). Similarly, *training* motivation is the direction, intensity, and persistence of learning-directed behavior during training contexts (Colquitt, LePine, & Noe, 2000). People who are high in training motivation are more likely to learn the contents and principles of the program better than less motivated participants (Mathieu & Matineau, 1997). In a meta-analysis determining the antecedents and consequences of training motivation, Colquitt and colleagues determined that personality characteristics similar to the ones we have already discussed (in their case: locus of control, conscientiousness, anxiety, age, cognitive ability, self-efficacy, valence, job involvement) influence training motivation, which, in turn, was related to such things as transfer of training (what we called "polytextually skilled" in chap. 2) and job performance.

***Career Motivation.*** Also related to learning motivation is career motivation. Career motivation is the desire to exert effort to enhance career goals. People with higher career motivation may be more likely to have a better match between the goals and obstacles they work on and what is needed by the organization because their interest are more closely tied to the organization than someone who has lower career motivation. There are three elements to career motivation: (a) *insight*—how well individuals know their strengths and weaknesses and how these match with the demands and opportunities in their organization, (b) *identity*—what they want to accomplish, such as a drive to be a leader, and (c) *resilience*—the ability to overcome career barriers (cf. London, 1983, 1985; London & Noe, 1997). Insight is the spark that ignites motivation. Identity is the direction of motivation—that is, what people want to accomplish. Resilience helps them persist even in the face of barriers to goal accomplishment.

Each component consists of multiple dimensions, some of which are easier to change than others. For instance, resilience includes personality characteristics such as self-esteem and internal control (the feeling that one can affect one's environment positively). These characteristics are generally established by the time an individual reaches early adulthood, but they can be strengthened or weakened by job experiences. For instance, training and positive reinforcement for performance improvement can enhance employees' self-evaluation. This, in turn, will increase their ability to overcome career barriers. Insight entails individuals' awareness of their strengths and weaknesses and opportunities in their organization or profession. Identity includes such personal characteristics as need for achievement and desire to be a leader.

Unlike resilience, which is hard to change and shifts only over long periods of time, insight and identity can change as a result of information processing. A supervisor can affect employees' career insight by providing feedback about their performance and information about career opportunities. If the feedback is presented in a constructive way—focusing on behaviors and what can be done to change them to improve job performance—then an individual is likely to listen, become more self-aware, and use the feedback to set goals for learning and behavior change. Similarly, if a supervisor tells an individual about anticipated organizational changes and resulting career opportunities in the firm, they may alter their career goals, perhaps realizing that promotion is indeed possible or recognizing that there will be few opportunities for advancement and that they will need to look elsewhere for promotional opportunities.

All three components of career motivation—resilience, insight, and identity—are necessary to understand dynamics that drive the desire to acquire knowledge about oneself, information about one's environment, and skills and knowledge that an individual can use for performance improvement or to open up new job challenges. However, resilience is critical to motivation in that it is the foundation that allows people to be open to developing meaningful insight about themselves and their environment and an identity that is achievable. People who are low in resilience are not likely to be open to information about themselves. They are more concerned with protecting their self-image, even if it is low, than they are in expanding the worldview and being more able to set and accomplish challenging goals. They are likely to deny negative feedback, give up in when the going gets tough, and avoid challenges that may lead to failure. Their low resilience prevents forming an accurate self-view and leads to weak self-identity or an identity that is inappropriate, for instance, striving for an outcome that is very unlikely. In contrast, individuals who have a solid foundation of resilience are likely to be open to information about themselves and their environment. They are likely to have the confidence to use this information to their advantage. Also, they are likely to be flexible to changing direction as new opportunities and interests emerge. For them, resilience leads to increased insight, which in turn enhances their sense of self-identity.

### Summary

People need to be ready to change to engage in learning. Organizational leaders who try to impose change before people are ready are likely to be frustrated. Some employees may welcome the change. Others are likely to resist it because they do not have enough time to contemplate the meaning and value of the change and their ability to be successful. If people are ready for change, then motivation for learning entails an individual being aware that certain learning is important in their environment, that learning is a favorable, meaningful, and stimulating activity, and that learning enhances their competence in achieving their goals and overcoming their obstacles. Going into and during a learning experience, people need to feel that that they can indeed learn and apply new behaviors and knowledge and that doing so will result in valued outcomes. Career motivation is another way to think about learning motivation. People who are high in resilience are likely to be open to information about themselves in the environment and able to use that information to form a professional identity and career goals that can be accomplished.

## LEARNING STYLES AND TACTICS

Developmental level or stage, personality variables, learning motivation, and readiness to change determine whether and what someone is interested in and capable of learning when opportunities arise. Another set of individual differences—learning styles and tactics—influence how they learn.

### Learning Modes for Understanding and Transforming Experience

Kolb (1984) suggested that learning styles derive from four basic learning modes: two modes of grasping experience and two modes of transforming experience.

***Modes of Experience.*** There are two modes of grasping or taking in experience. An *apprehension* orientation toward concrete experiences focuses on being involved in "real" experiences, relying on senses, and dealing with immediate human situations in a personal way to digest information. It emphasizes feeling and sensing as opposed to thinking, a concern with uniqueness and complexity rather than theories and generalizations, and an intuitive "artistic" approach rather than a systematic approach. People with this mode relate well with others. They are intuitive decision makers and do well in unstructured situations. They are open-minded.

A *comprehension* orientation toward abstract conceptualization focuses on using logic, ideas, and concepts and emphasizes thinking rather than feeling to take in information. It emphasizes building general theories rather than understanding the uniqueness of each situation and a scientific rather than artistic approach to problems. A person with this orientation enjoys systematic planning, manipulation of abstract symbols, and quantitative analysis. Such an individual values precision, rigor, and the discipline of analyzing ideas and the aesthetic quality of a neat conceptual system.

***Modes of Transforming Experience.*** Then there are two modes of transforming experiences. An *intension* orientation toward reflective observation focuses on understanding the meaning of ideas and situations by carefully observing and then impartially describing them. The emphasis is on understanding rather than practical application, a concern with what is true or how things happen as opposed to what will work, and an emphasis on reflection rather than action. Those with this orientation like to intuit the meaning of situations and ideas and understanding their implications. They look at things from a variety of perspectives though they value their own thoughts and opinions. They value patience, impartiality, and considered thoughtful judgment.

An *extension* orientation toward active experimentation focuses on jumping right in and starting to do things—actively influencing people and changing situations. It emphasizes practical applications as opposed to reflective understanding, a pragmatic concern with what works as opposed to what is absolute truth, and an emphasis on doing rather than observing. People with this orientation enjoy and are good at getting things accomplished. They take risks to achieve their objectives. They like to influence the environment and get results.

### Learning Styles

People vary in their tendency to grasp information, some preferring to focus on concrete experiences (apprehension) and others on abstract conceptualization (comprehension). Also, people vary in how they transform information, some preferring to focus on reflective observation (intension) and others on experimentation (extension). Combinations of these orientations toward experience and transforming experience result in the following learning styles:

*Convergent*—abstract conceptualization and active experimentation. The greatest strength of those with the convergent learning style lies in problem solving, decision making, and the practical application of ideas. People with this sort of learning style organize information through hypothetical-deductive reasoning; they prefer dealing with tasks and problems rather than social and interpersonal issues.

*Divergent*—concrete experience and reflective observation. The greatest strength of those with the divergent learning style lies in imaginative ability and the awareness of meaning and values. People with this sort of learning style see things from different perspectives and organize them into a whole "gestalt"; they generate alternative ideas and implications. They tend to be imaginative and interested in people.

*Assimilation*—abstract conceptualization and reflective observation. The greatest strength of those with the assimilation learning style lies in inductive reasoning and the ability to create theoretical models—in assimilating disparate observations into an integrated explanation. People with this sort of learning style are more concerned with ideas and abstract concepts than people. It is more important that the theory be sound and precise rather than practical.

*Accommodation*—concrete experience and active experimentation. The greatest strength of those with the accommodative learning style lies in doing things, carrying out plans and tasks, and getting involved in new experiences. It is best suited for situations where one must adapt oneself to changing immediate circumstances. People with this orientation solve problems in an intuitive trial-and-error manner, relying heavily on other people for information rather than on their own abilities. They are at ease with other people but may seem impatient or pushy.

Individuals are typically drawn to, or prefer, one learning style although they may use all four during the learning process.

### Learning Tactics

Another taxonomy of learning focuses on learning tactics. Van Velsor and Guthrie (1998) distinguished between four types of tactics:

1. *Thinking tactics* are solitary, cognitive activities. They include recalling the past to search for similar or contrasting events; imagining the future through such activities as visualization; or accessing knowledge, facts, and wisdom through sources such as the library or the Internet.
2. *Action-oriented tactics* comprise behaviors that have to do with direct, hands-on experimentation, jumping in with little hesitation to learn in the moment, and learning by doing.
3. *Accessing others' tactics* involves seeking advice and support, identifying role models and coaches, and seeking their help.
4. *Feeling tactics* are those activities and strategies that allow people to manage the anxiety associated with trying something new so that they

can take advantage of an opportunity to learn. Rather than being paralyzed by fear of failure, an individual might talk through their fear with a trusted peer (or write about it in a journal) before moving to a new and challenging assignment.

When individuals approach an opportunity for learning, people not only use a preferred style or tactic but also tend to move in a pattern, beginning with their most preferred style or tactic, shifting to another only if the first doesn't work—regardless of whether this makes sense or not. People often stick to one style or tactic or one sequence over and over, even if it is not working. "Blocked" learners try harder and harder without changing their approach (Bunker & Webb, 1992). Effective learners are more facile in their use of styles and tactics. The key point for organizations to keep in mind is that learning experiences should make use of a variety of learning styles and tactics to accommodate individual learners and their preferences. Also, the extent to which individuals engage in a variety of learning styles and tactics via learning situations will make them more able to utilize all four learning styles and less dependent on a preferred one (learn to learn).

### Summary

Preferred learning styles vary in how people deal with experiences (abstract conceptualization or concrete experience) and process these experiences (reflective observation or active experimentation). Also, people use different tactics to help them learn (thinking, taking action, relying on others, and feeling). People may use a combination of these styles and tactics or rely on one that they prefer—sometimes even when the preferred learning style doesn't work very well in the situation. Individual characteristics and situational conditions both affect learning. Some people are able to vary their learning style depending on the requirements of the situation—for instance, relying on abstract conceptualization and reflective observation to process complex information under risky circumstances and relying on concrete experience and active experimentation when there is plenty of time to try new behaviors and other people support this experimentation by providing feedback and coaching.

## JOINT EFFECTS OF INDIVIDUAL CHARACTERISTICS ON LEARNING

Maurer, Weiss, and Barbeite (2003) examined how a variety of individual characteristics similar to those discussed in this chapter that affect learning motivation work together to affect participation in developmental activities. Specifically, they conducted a longitudinal study of the effects of age, individual attitudes, and situational support on participation in learning activities. They first measured attitudes and situational support in a sample of 800 working adults (54% female) and then related these variables to participation in development 1 year later. They discovered that people who participated in learning activities were likely to have been involved in learning previously, believed in the need for learning, felt they had the capacity to learn, received intrinsic benefits from participating, had social support at work and home for learning, were involved in their job, and had career insight (an awareness of their strengths and weaknesses and thoughts about career plans).

These results indicated that participation in learning is a function of both individual and situational conditions organized into eight sets of variables:

1. The employee's age—chronological age and perceptions of the person's age relative to others in his or her work group.
2. Situational support for development, which includes support from the organization and people at work, such as supervisors, coworkers, and subordinates, and support from family, friends, and others outside work who encourage work-related development. Age influences situational support by possibly discouraging or preventing older employees from participating in development.
3. Individual learning preparedness, which includes (a) prior participation in learning, (b) learning anxiety, (c) perceiving oneself to be intelligent, (d) perceiving oneself to possess qualities needed for learning and development, (e) beliefs about how sound one's mental function is, and (f) belief in one's capacity to function effectively in different domains of life—general self-efficacy.
4. Career motivation variables, which include career insight (awareness of one's strengths and weaknesses and thoughts about career plans), perceived need for improvement through learning, and job involvement.
5. Self-efficacy for learning—the belief that one is capable of improving his or her career-related competencies. There are two types of self-efficacy for learning. Absolute self-efficacy for learning is the belief that one can improve competencies in comparison with where they currently are. Relative self-efficacy for learning is the belief that one can improve skills relative to other people. Both types of self-efficacy may be affected positively by individual learning preparedness and career motivation.
6. Perceived benefits for learning may be intrinsic (feelings of self-worth, more interesting work, more enjoyment from learning and work) and extrinsic (pay, promotions, job security). These benefits may be affected positively by individual learning preparedness, career motivation, and situational support for learning.
7. Developmental attitudes—feeling favorably toward and having high interest in development. These attitudes may be positively affected by

self-efficacy for development and perceptions of the benefits accruing from development.

8. Intentions to participate in development, which may be positively affected by attitudes toward development and lead to actual participation.

Maurer et al.'s (2003) research suggested that these variables work in the following causal sequence: Employee age determines the salience of individual characteristics related to learning. Individual characteristics combined with situational conditions that support learning lead the individual to perceive the potential benefits of learning and feel a sense of self-efficacy for development (the belief that development is indeed possible). These perceptions contribute to a favorable attitude about learning, which in turn leads to intentions to engage in learning activities and actual participation in learning programs. We say more about situational conditions that support learning in the next chapter.

## CONCLUSION

This chapter addressed individual characteristics that affect learning behavior, readiness to change, motivation to learn, and learning styles and tactics.

Development is the continuous growth toward greater complexity. Individuals do not merely move from issue to issue, stage to stage, or ways of making meaning to a wholly new way of making meaning. Instead, each new step builds upon the past way of thinking in such a way as to embrace it and move beyond it. Development does not occur through aging alone. It requires a supportive and safe holding environment that is rich in opportunities and interaction with others different from oneself. In this sort of environment, individuals are motivated to change themselves to fit their environment better. They escape boredom by trying out new behaviors and overcome anxiety by learning new skills.

In this chapter, we concentrated on development from two perspectives. From the life stage perspective, individuals deal with issues in a fairly predictable sequence. Each stage builds on the previous stage. From the meaning-making perspective, individuals continuously grow in their understanding of the world. They continuously confront new situations for which the way they make meaning no longer seems to work. This forces them to develop more complex ways of understanding. This development cannot be rushed. Steps cannot be skipped. Individuals must be allowed to work through issues at their own pace.

Learning and development are intertwined, and to understand continuous learning at the individual level it is also necessary to understand individual development. Individuals are at a particular developmental level, and they have a more complex developmental level to which they can aspire and achieve with the proper support. This zone of proximal development, between current and potential development, is where learning occurs.

Finally, we suggest that in the current environment, the world is calling for and expecting a greater complexity of development than that embodied in the average adult. Many people are in over their heads. Continuous learning, which leads to more complex levels of making meaning, is no longer a luxury, but a necessity.

Next, personality may predispose some people to seek, enjoy, and benefit from learning activities more so than others. However, all individuals can and do learn. When they learn successfully, they are learning how to learn. They discover what it takes to learn and become aware of their own abilities, styles, and tactics that help them regulate their learning. They increase their learning self-esteem, self-efficacy, and self-determination. They become more open to experience and conscientious about learning. They learn how to ask for feedback. They learn that their abilities are not fixed, and they can learn about how to prepare themselves for learning. Moreover, they become motivated to start the learning cycle again. In short, they become continuous learners.

In the next chapter, we change our focus to the organizational environment and how it supports or discourages learning directly and indirectly. All organizations are learning environments (whether this is intentional or not); they continuously send messages about appropriate ways for employees to behave. We need to understand the environment and the various messages it sends in order to recognize what is triggering learning in, what they are learning, and why they are behaving the way they do.

## QUESTIONS FOR THOUGHT AND DISCUSSION

1. Does thinking about learning from a developmental perspective makes sense to you? That is, do you believe that people's learning is guided by their developmental stage? How does this apply to you?
2. Compare yourself to the life stages development model. Where are you? Do you agree with what it says about your interests in learning?
3. Compare yourself to the order of consciousness model. What order of consciousness do you think applies to you? What does this mean for how you learn?
4. Think about a training program you recently attended. Can you determine the order of consciousness that the training program was aimed at? (Most are at the third order of consciousness.)
5. How has your job changed and what changes do you anticipate during the next year or several years? Are these changes influenced by the industry you are in, the organization, your department and the people who manage it, or other factors? Are the changes fast and furious? Are the expectations higher than you would like? Are you having trouble keeping up with all the changes and meeting expectations? Do you need to learn more and learn continu-

ously? What do you need to learn? How? What support would help you in this learning process?

6. What is your attitude about learning? In particular, do you have confidence in your ability to learn? Do you learn on your own? Do you seek opportunities for learning? Are you open to new experiences? When confronted by new technology, or knowledge of any type, are you conscientious in finding out everything you can about it? Are you energized by opportunities to learn new things? Do you want to generate new knowledge? Do you seek ways to apply what you learn? Do you learn for learning's sake, or more for what you can do with what you learn?
7. Are you open to information about yourself? Do you seek information about career opportunities? When you are faced with information you didn't expect (e.g., negative feedback about your performance, barriers to achieving a career goal), do you accept the information, deny it, or ignore it? If you accept it, you are high in career insight, a component of career motivation.
8. Are your career goals realistic? Do you have a plan to achieve them? Does your plan include short-term actions (what you will do this week) and long-term strategies (what you will do this year and in the next 5 years)? Answering yes to these questions indicates you are high in career insight.
9. When you learn that your organization is about to undergo a major change (e.g., a merger or reorganization is in the offing), are you excited or anxious? When your boss asks you to work on a task you have never seen before, are you fearful? Do you look for excuses or jump right in with enthusiasm? In other words, are you ready for change? If so, you are probably high in career resilience.
10. Think of a time that you were particularly motivated in engaging in a learning experience. Why were you motivated? Think of a time when you were not so motivated to engage in a particular learning experience. Why were you not interested? Was there a misalignment in your own goals and the organization's? Where were you in terms of readiness to change?
11. How do you like to learn—by doing, thinking, or both? Do you prefer being in a classroom in which the instructor reads a detailed lecture allowing you to take copious notes, or do you prefer to watch a demonstration and then try the behavior yourself?
12. When you have signed up for a training program or volunteered for a new work assignment, think about what motivated you. Was your decision driven by your desire to learn for learning's sake and/or for the career opportunities it may afford? Was it motivated by the support from your supervisor or coworkers? Did you recognize benefits from participating? Were you ready to learn? Were you looking forward to the learning experience? How successful was the experience? Did it motivate you to look forward to more learning opportunities?

## TOPICS FOR RESEARCH

1. Identify people at different life stages of development and study people who are continuous learners at each stage. What is their focus of learning? How does learning contribute to their quality of life?
2. Within each life stage, explore the relationship between level of maturity and participation in continuous learning in terms of the nature or focus of learning and the time and energy spent learning.
3. Measure how learning sparks potential for further growth. Conduct longitudinal research on how learning contributes to maturity. Does learning increase the capacity of the individual for even deeper and more expansive learning?
4. Relate the individual characteristics that we suggested to readiness to learn at work. Are these the key variables, as we suggested? Do these characteristics explain enough variance in readiness to learn to be useful?
5. Replicate and extend Maurer, Weiss, and Barbeite's (2003) study of the effects of age, attitudes, personality, and situational support on participation in learning activities. They predicted participation in development after a year. Study the process of how people identify the need for learning and react to learning opportunities over time. Include a broader range of behavioral measures of participation in learning and development and examine how participation affects later attitudes about learning and subsequent participation over a longer period of time.

CHAPTER

# 4

# Facilitating Individual Continuous Learning

In previous chapters, we argued that individuals, by their nature, are continuous learners, whether organizations realize and capitalize on this or not. Some individuals are better at this than others, purposely seeking new knowledge and skills or attempting to transform themselves. In this chapter, we change our focus from the individual learner to the learning environment (the group and the organization) that the individual is in and begin to describe the connections between our nested systems. As we stated in chapter 1, although groups and organizations are systems in their own right, they are learning environments from the point of view of the individual. Here we argue that all organizations are learning environments, whether this is intentional or not. Some organizations do a better job of providing a supportive and encouraging learning environment than others, purposely encouraging employees' continuous learning in line with the organization's goals, or at least not standing in their way. Some organizations may actually thwart needed learning, by, for instance, withholding resources. Employees may learn in spite of this. Or they may learn *not* to learn. Of course, in the process, all employees learn about the organization and how to adapt their work lives to the environment. To fully understand individual continuous learning, we must understand how the environment supports and encourages learning directly or indirectly. Some aspects of the work environment are clear and observable, such as company policies and practices. Others are less obvious and cannot be seen or measured directly, such as organizational culture.

As continuous learners, individuals regularly interact with their environment. With every interaction with the organization and with the various teams the individual is a part of, individuals receive messages about appropriate ways to behave and modify their behaviors accordingly. We need to understand the environment and the messages it is sending in order to recognize what individuals are learning and why they are behaving the way they do. What individuals learn from their environment is often subtle, not expected, and not well understood. And what people learn in organizations may not be compatible with organizational goals.

By better understanding the environment, we can understand what individuals are learning, why they are learning it, and even design the environment that supports learning that is wanted or needed by the organization. Often learning is adaptive, as people learn to work within the parameters (goals, strategies, and expectations) set by the organization and the environment beyond it. The learning may also be generative and transformative, as people grow professionally, apply what they learn in new contexts, and behave differently.

In the first part of this chapter, we give examples about how individuals learn from how work is done in the organization, the structure of the organization (e.g., its management roles, functions, and hierarchy), the communities within the organization that the individual comes in contact with, and the broader environment (e.g., the industry, economic conditions, advancing technology). This learning may be unexpected, unintentional, and sometimes even conflicting, such as when employees receive messages to act one way from one aspect of the environment and another way from another aspect. In the second part of the chapter, we discuss how various aspects of the organization's culture affect learning. We consider whether employees know what they are supposed to be doing and whether they are held responsible for doing that work. We consider the important role that supervisors and others play in the process of creating environments that are conducive to learning. Such environments can empower employees and managers to take responsibility for their own learning, help them to diagnose their strengths and weaknesses in line with organizational needs, and provide learning resources. Also, we consider how organizations establish cultures that support giving feedback to employees, for instance, through the use of multisource feedback surveys, the results of which help employees recognize their learning gaps, acquire new skills and knowledge, and apply them to further organizational goals. We show how learning opportunities can transform an organization from a structured, bureaucratic monolith that discourages change to a flexible, collaborative engine for creative problem solving and growth. Then we turn to assessment of learning capacity and learning outcomes, including a discussion of measurement issues. Finally, we consider experiential methods that inculcate learning that lasts and ways to assess the continued value of these learning experiences.

## THE LEARNING ENVIRONMENT

The organization's environment can be viewed on several levels. There are the activities, roles, and interpersonal relationships in an individual's immediate environment, such as conversations between the boss and subordinate or a group meeting, that occur during the daily course of work. The next level is the full spectrum of these daily events taken together. This would include all the various settings experienced at work and outside of work. Also, there are the settings that do not involve the person as an active participant, but in which events occur that affect, or are affected by, the individual. For example, some employees may never visit corporate headquarters, but they are nonetheless influenced by the decisions made in the various departments such as finance, human resources, marketing, and so forth. Finally, there is the whole set of environments along with the belief systems and ideologies that underlie the systems—what we call organizational culture (Bronfenbrenner, 1979). Some of these aspects of the environment are "knowable" and observable, such as policies, practices, task and group structures, and information. Others cannot be seen or measured directly, such as culture, interpersonal pressure, and leadership. All of these settings, from the most micro to the most macro—from the closest to the individual to the farthest away—influence what people learn at work.

Consider the effects of different elements of the environment: the structure of work itself, the communities in which work is conducted, the structure of the organization (levels and functions), management policies and programs, and the external environment.

### The Structure of Work

The nature of a person's work, including task requirements and changes in these requirements over time, affects what employees need to know and learn to do their jobs (Evans, Hodkinson, & Unwin, 2002). For example, such things as work overload and job stress (due to downsizing/right sizing, mergers and acquisitions, emphasis on short-term goals, the current economy, etc.) may inhibit learning beyond adaptation as the pressure to produce may increase a person's resistance to changing work methods.

As another example, consider the complexity of the work. Jobs with a variety of tasks, increasing skill levels, and rapidly advancing technology require continuous learning. The employee in this situation needs to seek out new knowledge and acquire new skills, not just adapt to shifting situations but anticipate and be on the forefront of change (generative learning). When risks are encouraged and mistakes less often punished, individuals learn to think beyond the normal way of doing things (transformative learning). In contrast, routine work, though saving time and energy (perhaps a good thing from the organization's point of view), does not necessitate, or even permit, reassessment of new situations. More than likely, such work does not provide sufficient challenge to think beyond the immediate requirements of the job, thereby inhibiting learning beyond the adaptive level (Karakowsky & McBey, 1999).

Third, the surrounding conditions also affect what needs to be learned. For instance, the organization may be faced with increasing competition, which in turn drives the need to keep operational costs as low as possible. In manufacturing plants, this leads to standardized work processes, structured jobs, and little room for individual input and creativity (Evans & Rainbird, 2002; Keep & Rainbird, 2000, p. 190). Employees learn the one way to do things as determined by task analysts and industrial engineers. In other circumstances, for instance, making handcrafted products, production may be influenced by demand for high quality, which in turn drives the need for artisanship in some cases regardless of the cost. This condition leads to customization and little tolerance for sameness. Employees learn by experimenting with different production methods and materials, and indeed each product may be unique.

In the case of standardized tasks and products, learning is a one-time event structured by the organization, and the goal is to maintain behavioral consistency. In the case of customized tasks and products, learning is an ongoing process guided by the learner, and the goal is continuous improvement and variation. However, learning may be hindered by the ambiguity and variability of quality (in the eye of the beholder), the pain of criticism (dependent on the whims of society), and the need for self-reliance.

Of course, most jobs are a middle ground between these two extremes. Main elements of a job may be standardized and must be learned, but they change over time as technology changes or the design of products or method of delivering service change. Also, there is room for individual input, and employees can make suggestions for better work methods, learn new tasks, and take part in different elements of the production process.

## Communities of Practice

Actually engaging in work with others is a fundamental process by which individuals learn (Wenger, 1999). Typically, we think of jobs in individual terms. For example, in job analyses and resulting job descriptions, jobs are analyzed and described job-by-job—from an individual, asocial, and linear viewpoint, which is then reflected in policies, procedures, metrics, training programs, and so forth. In reality, individuals work with their immediate colleagues and customers to get the job done. No matter what the official job description might say, employees together create a practice to do what needs to be done (Wenger, 1998). Although workers may be employed by a larger organization, in day-to-day practice they work with and "for" a smaller set of people.

As an example, claims processors make their jobs possible by working *together* to invent and maintain ways of solving organizational demands, although they may appear to work individually. Their community of practice: (a) provides resolutions to institutionally generated conflicts between measures and real work—such as processing claims and time on the phone; (b) supports a communal memory that allows individuals to do their work without needing to know everything—that is, they can go to colleagues for assistance; and (c) helps newcomers "join the community" by participating in its practice and thereby learning (Wenger, 1998).

### Organization Structure and Systems

Organization structure and systems refer to the roles and activities that tie people to the organization and define the working relationships between them. These structures and systems include human resource responsibilities (such as recruitment, selection, training, performance appraisals, and rewarding or sanctioning employees), communication, knowledge management, and information technology systems. For instance, research has found that firm performance is influenced by the set of human resource management practices a firm has in place (see, e.g., Huselid, Jackson, & Schuler, 1997). These structures and systems can also affect individual learning that is taking place in the organization. For example, roles are constructed to achieve certainty and consistency in organizational behavior; they promote stability rather than change. When individuals "get into their roles," they define themselves in terms of their roles. They may carry out duties without thinking about whether they should change or whether there might be new ways of viewing themselves in relation to the organization (Karakowsky & McBey, 1999). Encouraging and rewarding employees to carry out their roles without considering the appropriateness of these duties inhibits learning and development (LaBier, 1986). The traits, skills, and attitudes that are useful to work and the role are stimulated and reinforced as the person receives more recognition and rewards. Traits, skills, and attitudes that are unnecessary or that impede work are not recognized and rewarded and as a result are eventually suppressed, unused, and weakened.

***Training.*** Training programs are, of course, an important organizational system affecting learning. Most training and organizational development efforts are aimed at teaching workers new knowledge and skills that enable them to function better in their current developmental level. This works most of the time because most adults are between Kegan's third and fourth levels of consciousness, and they are good at single-loop learning or detecting and correcting errors within the framework of existing organizational policies, procedures, structures, and practices (Fisher, Rooke, & Torbert, 2000). However, different learning goals need different learning methods, and individuals vary in their abilities and motivation to learn (National Research Council, 1999).

Learners draw on their current knowledge to construct new knowledge. Their current knowledge and beliefs affect how they interpret new information in training sessions. The extent to which the training draws on what learners bring to their learning determines whether learning is facilitated or inhibited. *Learner-centered environments* help people connect their previously learned knowledge to their current learning and give them feedback to reflect on the meaning of what they are learning and how they can improve. This promotes integrated and comprehensive learning with understanding rather than acquisition of disconnected facts and skills.

Assessments (tests) during and after training further people's understanding of their newly acquired behaviors and gives them a chance to improve the quality of their performance. The resources devoted to learning in the organization and expectations for participation in developmental activities convey the value of learning. When employees share norms that value learning and high standards, they are likely to respond positively to change, give and accept feedback, and learn. Most learning environments combine these different components to varying degrees. Consider the following example of an electronic learning environment.

The first author participated in a distance-learning class offered by the University of Pennsylvania. The course consisted of an in-depth syllabus that included numerous hyperlinks to online readings and videotaped minilectures, a running discussion thread where the professor posed broad questions to stimulate discussion, regular office hours via chat room, and three "live" classes that included the option to be present in the classroom or be present via streaming video joined with a discussion board and two phone lines for live chatting. Students could access the material any time of day or night, and students participated actively. (Woe to anyone who "stepped out" for a day or two; they would have hundreds of e-mails from the discussion board.) The professor, and soon the students, developed norms and gave feedback to each other, thereby pushing the participants to explore their opinions and reactions to the material. Discussions and assignments were directed toward reasoning rather than stating facts. The message is that the learning environment must recognize employees' current knowledge, help employees understand how to use what is taught, reward learning, and provide feedback on performance improvement.

Training must recognize three key variables in the process of retention and use of knowledge and skills: (a) acquisition of information or skills, (b) retrieval of the learned information or skill stored in memory, and (c) performance of the skill demonstrating "positive transfer" (Cochran, Lammelin, Logan, & Bennett, 2003). Retention is a function of ability, prior knowledge, and motivation. The individual needs to be motivated to both acquire the new skill or information and use it. Motivation to learn is positively associated with job involvement, the decision to participate in training, and the receipt of extrinsic rewards. Of course, other variables affect retention, such as, the complexity of the task to be learned and retained, the instructional strategies used during the acquisition period, the retention interval, and aspects of the retention situation. As such, although the training system is a key aspect of the organizational environment that affects learning, many other factors must be considered to understand the effects of training. These include learner characteristics, job conditions, and the organization itself.

***Performance Appraisal and Reward Systems.*** Competencies and performance dimensions for appraisal spell out what managers and employees need to know and the level of performance expected of them. For instance, sales organizations may measure sales staff's clarity of communications, powers of persuasiveness, and persistence as key elements of performance. The process provides the staff with information about performance expectations. Feedback about their performance on these dimensions guides their learning. Employees will concentrate their learning on areas that are emphasized. If the focus is bottom-line results and sales revenue, employees may ignore building lasting customer relationships. When holding a performance appraisal discussion with a subordinate, a supervisor will often discuss areas for improvement and available development opportunities. Performance appraisal forms often include a place to specify directions for development.

Rewards and sanctions for learning and performance improvement include tangible outcomes, such as salary, raises, bonuses, and special job assignments. They also include intangible or less obvious outcomes, such as being given an assignment that is important to the organization. Rewards and sanctions communicate organizational values, beliefs, and opinions about what is important and what is not.

### Management

The management environment is concerned with predicting, ordering, controlling, coordinating, and directing the other activities in the organization so that the total organization continuously adjusts to its environment. Activities are concerned with such things as the formulation of rules and procedures and policy and structure development. Hierarchical management structures and systems may emphasize control and surveillance and maintain decision making at high levels in the organization. This enhances the organization's stability and predictability. However, it limits discovery, flow, and flexibility—all needed for generative and reflective learning. Instead, employees become strong adaptive learners as they comply with the latest edict.

In contrast, in flexible organizations that foster employee involvement in management, employees create their own learning environments. Moreover, they communicate what they learn to others in the organization, promoting the growth of the entire enterprise. They create and extend their skills and capacities by learning from their colleagues. They observe, emulate, and then internalize what they see others doing as part of their own repertoire of behaviors.

Even when managers promote employee participation, new ways of doing things can become institutionalized as employees teach each other. Institutionalization is the degree to which shared beliefs take on a rulelike status (and is akin to organizational learning; see chap. 7). Individuals create a shared definition of what is appropriate or meaningful. Organizations that incorporate these rationalized elements into their formal structures maximize the legitimacy of these routines. Once adopted, these routines are not likely to be questioned (Karakowsky & McBey, 1999). Employees form roles for themselves and carry out their duties without necessarily considering the appropriateness of their behaviors to new situations. They see themselves and the situation in one way, and have trouble changing when the situation changes (Karakowsky & McBey, 1999). This natural organizational drive toward institutionalization thereby has a tendency to inhibit more learning at the individual level.

Executives and managers who want to foster change need to be particularly conscientious and persistent in shaking up routines. This is not necessarily a comfortable situation because everyone throughout all levels of the organization ends up living with more uncertainty. Moreover, organizational systems must be integrated to maintain a learning environment. For example, in poorly integrated organizations, top-level executives may affirm that they want to drive decision making down to the lowest possible level of the organization. Yet they may have no learning or training in place for those lower in the organization to attain or develop skills and knowledge they need to make decisions, no rewards for either making decisions or allowing decision making to take place at low levels, and no allowances in the work arena or technologies for the decisions to have an effect. In this case, employees at lower levels will probably neither learn to make decisions nor make them.

### Information Technology

Another aspect of the organization's environment that is critical to learning is the use of information technology. New information technologies not only provide access to a wide array of information, they also provide connections to other people who provide information, feedback, and inspiration. Also, use of interactive technologies creates environments in which people collaborate across disciplines and organizations, learn by doing, give and receive feedback, and continually refine their understanding and generate new knowledge. Consider a recent technology that has become a rich, online learning environment—Weblogs.

Weblogs are personal, diary-like Web sites that are updated frequently and can be made available to anyone through Web feeds. They provide readers with automatic updates as the "blog" author writes them. Increasingly, professionals use them as repositories of personal knowledge. Essentially, they are learning journals. They are also a means for social networking and collaboration as blog writers link their blogs with others. Weblogs meet the needs of knowledge workers for flexible and dynamic learning environments. They allow authors to express their interests, communicate with others, and record their thoughts. They are a chance for readers to benefit from access to emerging ideas and the development of loosely coupled learning networks (Efimova & Fiedler, 2004). Readers often respond to the blogs with their own information and opinions. This technology offers a particularly appropriate environment for knowledge workers because it allows individualization and recognizes the situational specificity of learning needed for knowledge-based work. Weblogs provide access to new ideas and tools that reach beyond conventional methods of central planning bodies such as human resource departments (Fiedler, 2003). They become "flexible, bottom-up, and somewhat dynamic learning environments" that promote professional growth and personal learning (Efimova & Fiedler, 2004).

In an online survey of 62 bloggers and 20 nonbloggers, Efimova (2003) examined the motivation to have a Weblog and the factors in the environment that support it. The respondents indicated that they started Weblogs to organize ideas, notes, and sources and that the process of creating such records and receiving feedback from interested parties enhances their own thinking and learning. Once started, the process of contributing to the ongoing Weblog improves the author's knowledge and skills in such areas as the latest technology, writing, organization of ideas, and the ability to pose questions and articulate concepts. New ideas emerge from the serendipity, feedback, and dialogues in contributing to the Weblog. Also, authors noted the social effects of discovering people with similar interests and building communities.

Further benefits of participating as a creator of, or contributor to, a Weblog include (from Efimova & Fiedler, 2004): (a) learning from multiple perspectives, (b) gaining from the synergies of organizing material and creating the community of learning, (c) learning from experts who are "thinking in public" and thereby serve as role models who cross geographical and disciplinary boundaries, and (d) supporting the development of *meta-learning skills*—making reflective thinking public encouraging better skills for self-observational and intentional change.

### The External Environment

Finally, the external environment influences learning within the organization. The external environment includes the economy, competition, technology, and the labor market. These elements vary in their stability (or volatility) and the extent to which change is understood and predictable. Some environments change slowly. Others are turbulent, for instance, with a rapid rate of change in customer preferences and competitive intensity.

Contexts that are well understood and stable promote single-loop learning, meaning that the organization can concentrate on refining existing methods of production, making small improvements in efficiency, and introducing newcomers to standard operating procedures that have served the organization well. For example, in a sales milieu, this would include teaching newcomers how to complete expense reports, deliver a canned sales presentation, and grant discounts to prospects (Chonko, Jones, Roberts, & Dubinsky, 2002). Turbulent environments promote double-loop learning, meaning that the organization needs to transform itself by entering new markets, creating new work methods, and changing the way the company is organized. Learning takes the form of experimenting and giving people a chance to develop their own ideas and run with them, letting others benefit from the experience, whether it is a success or a failure. Instead of informing newcomers of standard operating procedures, newcomers have a chance to participate in different parts of the business and may be asked to participate in a cross-functional problem-solving or product development team. People with a high tolerance of uncertainty and a desire to learn rather than avoid failure are likely to do well in such an environment.

So far in this chapter we have examined how different elements of the environment affect learning. We reviewed how the structure of work itself, organizational systems and practices, such as training, performance appraisal, and management styles and methods, information technology, and the external environment determine learning opportunities and requirements. Next, we consider how learning is infused within the culture of the organization.

## ORGANIZATIONAL CULTURES

Organizational culture is actually a multifaceted concept. Here we focus on three aspects of organizational culture that are closely tied to learning: the performance culture, the self-learning culture, and the feedback culture. We also discuss methods that support the development of these cultures, such as multi-source feedback.

### Performance Culture

An organization's performance culture is the degree to which an organization specifies the results it wants from employees and provides the means for employees to reach these goals. An organization with a vague or nonexistent performance culture might encourage employees to arrive at work at 9 A.M., spend the day emulating a mushroom, leave at 5 P.M., and expect the usual 3% raise at the end of the year. No performance and certainly no learning (beyond how to emulate a mushroom) is required. Alternatively, an organization with a high-performance culture has effective performance management and reward systems in place including the following:

- The performance appraisal program establishes processes and procedures for planning, monitoring, developing, appraising, and rewarding employee performance.
- Employee performance plans are aligned with organization goals and so are rewards.
- Employees understand how their jobs support the mission and goals of the organization.

- Standards in employee performance plans are measurable and credible. Performance of those standards is observable and verifiable.
- Supervisors and managers are accountable in their own performance plans for completing performance management responsibilities.
- The organization develops its supervisors' and managers' performance management competencies.
- The appraisal program addresses and improves poor performance; supervisors and managers are encouraged to address poor performance.
- Supervisors are held accountable when they do not address poor performance; employees are as well.
- Results are rewards as are top performers; employees with poor performance do not advance, whereas employees with good performance do.
- Employees feel valued for their good performance.

If a performance culture stresses pressure to produce (and thus promotes a performance orientation in individuals rather than a learning or mastery orientation), learning beyond adaptation may not be encouraged. To promote learning, the performance culture must allow some at least some room for exploration, trying things out, risk, and the potential of failure.

### Self-Learning Culture

The degree to which an organizational environment empowers learning in individuals is based on the extent to which the organization provides employees with learning resources and encourages them to take advantage of these resources on their own. In cultures that promote self-learning, employees determine what they need to know and when in the course of doing their jobs. This may mean that individuals need to keep up with changing technology or changes in industry standards as they engage in solving problems, improving work processes, or creating new products and services. Continuous learning is the foundation in all these cases. In cultures that do not promote self-learning, employees either are informed what training they need and when, or are given few opportunities, resources, or encouragement to learn.

There are several ingredients for increasing the empowered self-learning culture (based on London & Smither, 1999b, p. 13). *In an empowering learning environment, the organization/supervisor provides employees with:*

- A selection process that identifies candidates that are continuous learners—people who are open to experience, conscientious, and have a sense that they can make positive things happen (i.e., they are high in self-efficacy).
- Insight into organizational goals, likely organizational directions, and implications for future performance requirements.

- Skill-based pay plans.
- Behavioral choices (i.e., employees are not pressured to think and behave in certain ways) with clear consequences.
- The authority to make decisions that affect important outcomes.
- Requests that minimize pressure and convey autonomy.
- Informational (nonthreatening, noncontrolling) feedback that focuses employee attention on the task and highlights specific behaviors that need to be done differently.
- 360-degree/multisource feedback (feedback from one's supervisor, peers, and subordinates) or assessment center feedback (results from participating in a set of behavioral exercises that reflect management ability or potential and that are observed and rated by trained assessors).
- Resources (including training) to enable development.
- Self-management training (using self-dialogue, mental imagery, and positive patterns of thought).
- A tool kit of self-paced methods (for development planning).

*In an empowering learning environment, the organization/supervisor creates a climate where:*

- Employees can interact directly with everyone else (regardless of level, function, or department).
- Objectives are set by those who must make them happen.
- Individual employees and teams are accountable for decisions.
- Managers are expected to be coaches, advocates, and developers.
- Use of new skills and knowledge on the job is rewarded.
- Managers and employees are held accountable for continuous learning (measured on and rewarded for learning).

*In an empowering learning environment, employees:*

- Are ultimately responsible for recognizing their own developmental needs.
- Assume responsibility for their own learning.
- Actively seek performance feedback.
- Compare their self-assessments to current and future skill requirements.
- Investigate opportunities for development.
- Set development goals, evaluate their progress, and adjust their goals.

### Support for Self-Learning

Organizations provide structures and direction that encourage individuals to engage in learning. Of course, some people are more receptive to this than others.

Those who are more receptive will be people who have achieved a higher complexity of development, have the personal traits, and have the motivation and readiness to learn (as we discussed in chap. 3).

Consider several examples of how organizations support self-learning. Boeing's Waypoint Project, started in 2000, brings together volunteers from all levels of management in the company for a joint exploration of their job challenges (Gary, 2003). An interactive Web site allows participants to take assessment tests, formulate learning plans, and identify training and stretch assignments. The site is a support tool for self-directed learning. Rather than place managers into training programs, the managers use these tools on their own as they establish their own directions for training and development. For instance, a first-level manager may become certified as an instructor of a course on lean management principles, take a 200-hour university-based course on program management, or take a 2-week course on strategic leadership.

Gary (2003) provided the following recommendations for manager who are plotting their own career growth and guiding that of their direct reports:

1. *Focus on the job, not the classroom*—managers need to reflect on what they are learning as they work on and accomplish business goals.
2. *Look for the overlap between individual interest and the company's strategic needs*—there is no point in taking part in programs in which the individual has no interest or that have little value to the company.
3. *Remember that companies are dynamic and so are the leadership skills they require*—learning processes should not be rigid; they need to evolve as the business changes.
4. *Know when to reach out*—there are times when the company should provide training programs and insist that managers participate, for instance, when managers are promoted from one organizational level to another or across functions or just after a merger when the company is trying to combine disparate corporate cultures.
5. *Now more than ever, take responsibility for your own learning*—managers realize they must direct their own learning (given rapidly changing corporate priorities and less than secure positions) and should take every opportunity to experiment with new learning opportunities.

Another example of a corporate environment that empowers learning is General Electric. When Jack Welch took over as CEO of GE, it was a bureaucratic company in which employees and managers operated in insulated environments with hierarchical boundaries and departmental walls separating them. This environment discouraged initiative and feedback (Kotelnikov, 2004; Ulrich, Kerr, & Ashkenas, 2002). Welch felt that in the knowledge-driven economy, the company needed to create an open, collaborative environment in which everybody contributed. The *Work-Out* process was developed to build trust, empower employees, continuously reinvent increasingly better ways of doing business, eliminate unnecessary work, and develop boundaryless organizations that encouraged employees to identify problems and develop solutions. Employees closest to a problem, regardless of their organizational level or function, were invited to work as a group to solve the problem during the course of 1 to 3 days. These workshops were focused on solving real company problems while the participants learned to work with each other in a collaborative, nonevaluative mode that respected each person's contribution. The program communicated the sense of urgency to change, helped participants see the whole picture, and created a culture in which ideas were translated into actions and results. The groups brainstormed ideas, selected the best ones, developed recommendations and action plans, and then presented them to top management. Participants represented different functions and levels. They were engaged because they could see progress quickly and understood that their individual contributions and joint collaboration were valued by the company. In the process, they acquired new knowledge and skills from each other as they learned new work behaviors they could later apply on the job. The Work-Out sessions, combined with a change acceleration program throughout the organization and articulation of corporate values, essentially changed the culture of GE into a highly charged, learning organization that was unconstrained by organizational structures and boundaries.

A number of organizations have borrowed the GE effort, establishing a corporate culture of continuous learning, collaboration, and process improvement. An example of a different type of organization that embarked on this effort in the early 2000s is the North Shore-Long Island Jewish Health System. This health delivery system consists of three tertiary-care hospitals, two specialty-care hospitals, nine community hospitals, and other health care facilities employing more 30,500 people (Gallo, 2004). The comprehensive change effort was driven by a number of forces, such as a revolution in medical technology, changes in medical-delivery models, and a consumer-driven marketplace. The leadership of the system recognized a need for professional staff members who are able to adapt to the accelerating pace of change. A "Leadership Institute" was established by the CEO in 2001 to develop leaders at all levels. Professional staff volunteered to attend the institute, where they participated in team-based learning experiences that focused on real problems and opportunities for improvement. Similarly to GE, this effort "changed the DNA" of the organization, breaking down barriers between levels and functions, increasing collaboration, and establishing an environment for continuous improvement based on continuous learning. We say more about learning organizations in chapters 7 and 8.

### Feedback Culture

As we argued in chapter 3, feedback is an important element of learning that is difficult to enact. Some organizations are better at providing and encouraging feedback about performance than others. The degree to which an organization has a feedback culture is based on the number of performance discussions that are frequent and occur soon after critical events. For example, in a high-feedback culture, supervisors don't wait for the annual review but give subordinates feedback on their performance as events occur. Moreover, they present the feedback in a way that doesn't attack the person but focuses on behaviors that need to change. London and Smither (2002) described the organization's feedback culture or support for feedback as including the extent to the organization or supervisors provide "nonthreatening, behaviorally focused feedback, coaching to help interpret and use feedback, and a strong link between performance improvement and valued outcomes" (p. 81).

Steelman, Levy, and Snell (2004) developed the Feedback Environment Scale (FES) to measure employees' perceptions of the feedback they receive from their supervisor and coworkers. Specifically, the scale measures the following seven dimensions of feedback, with examples of items reflecting each source (pp. 180–182):

1. *Source credibility:* "My supervisor is generally familiar with my performance on the job." "In general, I respect my coworkers' opinions about my job performance."
2. *Feedback quality:* "I value the feedback I receive from my supervisor." "The feedback I receive from my coworkers helps me do my job."
3. *Feedback delivery:* "My supervisor is tactful when giving me performance feedback." "When my coworkers give me performance feedback, they are usually considerate of my feelings."
4. *Favorable feedback:* "When I do a good job at work, my supervisor praises my performance." "I frequently receive positive feedback from my coworkers."
5. *Unfavorable feedback:* "When I don't meet deadlines, my supervisor lets me know." "On those occasions when I make a mistake at work, my coworkers tell me."
6. *Feedback availability:* "My supervisor is usually available when I want performance informatioin." "I interact with my coworkers on a daily basis."
7. *Promotes feedback seeking:* "I feel comfortable asking my supervisor for feedback about my work performance." "My coworkers encourage me to ask for feedback whenever I am uncertain about my job performance."

London and Smither (2002, p. 85) offered the following organizational practices and interventions that create a high level of feedback culture:

Ways to enhance the *quality of feedback.*

- Creating clear standards concerning valued behaviors that are relevant to organizational goals.

- Providing clear performance measurements.
- Providing reports tying individual performance to bottom-line departmental or organizational (e.g., financial or operational) indexes.
- Training for supervisors and others about how to provide useful feedback.
- Providing time to review and clarify feedback results with others, such as one's supervisor.

Ways to emphasize the *importance of feedback in the organization.*

- Expecting top-level managers to serve as role models about how to seek, receive, and use feedback.
- Ensuring that everyone receives feedback (i.e., it's not voluntary) and uses feedback to guide development.
- Encouraging the importance of information (or "in the moment") feedback.
- Involving employees in the development of behavior/performance standards.
- Ensuring that performance improvements following feedback are recognized and rewarded.

Ways to provide *support for using feedback.*

- Providing skilled facilitators to help recipients interpret formal feedback (e.g., multisource) feedback, set goals, and track progress.
- Training and rewarding supervisors for coaching.
- Encouraging feedback recipients to discuss their feedback with raters and other colleagues to help clarify the feedback and reach a shared agreement concerning behavior expectations and changes.
- Providing feedback recipients with freedom concerning how they will act on the feedback (giving them a sense of self-control).
- Providing opportunities to learn.

### Multisource Feedback Surveys

Organizations can foster an environment that supports feedback by administering multisource (360-degree feedback) surveys. These surveys collect performance ratings from supervisors, subordinates, peers, and customers along with self- ratings. These have become highly popular (3-D Group, 2003). The method can be part of a process that involves employees in collecting performance data, providing feedback (sometimes with the support of a coach), using the results to set development goals, and tracking performance improvement over time.

Multisource or 360-degree feedback can be useful for identifying learning gaps and setting goals for learning. The essence of multisource feedback is helping individuals understand how others perceive them and how they perceive themselves. The feedback receiver obtains a written report showing comparisons between the different groups and generally noting discrepancies, strengths, and developmental areas. A coach may deliver the results, or the results may be distributed in a workshop during which the recipients are guided in how to interpret the results. The idea is to enhance self-awareness. The opinions from multiple sources, usually based on average responses within each source group (i.e., the average of peer ratings, the average of subordinate ratings) and individual ratings from the supervisor can help individuals learn how others "see" them and use this information to learn and ultimately change their own behavior and improve their own performance (assuming that the feedback is linked to critical goals and other organizational systems). Individuals evaluate the gap between self-ratings and ratings by others, their ratings in comparison to company or industry norms, and changes in their performance over time. This information can be used to set goals for learning, career development, and performance improvement.

Multisource feedback may be a one-time event: The survey is developed and administered, and reports are distributed. The recipients may digest the information or discard it. For those who take the feedback seriously, this is a learning event. They evaluate the meaning of the feedback in relation to the source, what they know about themselves, and the demands of their jobs. They may learn something new about themselves (e.g., "My subordinates feel I'm not paying adequate attention to their career development."). Or the information may confirm what they already thought was the case ("Some of my coworkers feel I don't communicate clearly. I thought this was the case. It might be due to their lack of expertise, but this tells me I need to be more patient in explaining what I mean."). Some recipients may be shocked at some of the results, and agreement between rater sources may make the feedback hard to deny ("I didn't know my supervisor and subordinates felt so strongly that I am unorganized."). The results may prompt recipients to alter their behavior, possibly making a minor change, simply adapting to the conditions at hand, or to make a major change, transforming the way they make decisions or interact with others.

Multisource feedback can be more than a one-time learning event. It can be part of a continuous learning *process*. This occurs when the results are used to set development goals, which in turn drive participation in development activities and eventually changes in behavior and performance. Later multisource feedback provides evidence of these changes and suggests directions for further learning, refining, or redirecting one's behavior.

Human resource practitioners recommend that the process be used solely for learning purposes and not be used to make organizational decisions about the employees rated. Raters also prefer that their ratings be used for development and not be used to make decisions about the ratee's pay. Raters also want to remain anonymous, and those who sign their names provide higher ratings than those who are anonymous. But raters also want ratees to be accountable for using their feedback. Ratees appreciate receiving detailed written feedback along with the ratings (Antonioni, 1996; London & Smither, 1995). Multisource feedback programs are continuously evolving. They have moved from department-wide or corporate-wide, development-focused tools to customized, just-in-time, online methods for seeking and receiving feedback.

A review of the literature on multisource feedback found that feedback ratings are related to other measures of leadership effectiveness; however, improvement in ratings over time is generally small (Smither, London, & Reilly, 2005). Improvement was most likely to happen when recipients had a positive feedback orientation, they realized that the feedback pointed to needed changes, they reacted positively to the feedback and believed that change was feasible, they set appropriate goals to regulate their behavior, and they took actions that lead to skill and performance improvement.

***Challenges for Multisource Feedback.*** Ultimately, the value of multisource feedback depends on feedback recipients using the information to change their behavior and improve their performance. Although the outcome depends on the recipient's self-regulation, organizations clearly have expectations that the information will be used to improve performance. Whereas in theory, multisource feedback has much to offer, it is also often associated with confusion and disappointment as well as discouraging evidence regarding its effectiveness as a tool in bringing about individual learning and performance improvement through behavior change. Consider the following challenges to the effective use of this learning support tool:

1. Performance evaluation processes assume that there is an objective/accurate indication of behavior and performance that can be captured by the ratings. However, the ratings themselves, the opportunities to change, and the perceptions of change depend on relationships with other people. Ratings are not objective indicators but are inextricably wrapped up in issues of power, legitimacy, and impression management. The very method is politically charged. (Just try to implement a multisource feedback process.) The wording of the items conveys meaning in ways that organizes thought and experience, deliberately or otherwise. The ratings themselves (the translation of perceptions and reflections into numbers and averaging these numbers across dimensions and/or raters) are not concrete substances that exist in their own right as accurate, objective reflections of reality. Raters' viewpoints are not independent of their context, personal background, and individual proclivities. Raters have unique perspectives and systematic biases that affect their ratings (e.g., leniency or harshness). In addition, raters may disagree with each other because ratees behave differently with different people and in different situations. Ratees' reactions to feedback are not independent of context and the social situation. Their emotional as well as verbal and behavioral reactions may be influenced by what they believe others think. Self-

perceptions may be a reflected viewpoint (e.g., people seeing themselves as they believe others see them or as they would like others to see them). In the end, the assumption behind multisource feedback is that it reflects the dominant behavioral tendencies.

2. Multisource feedback can be confusing and chaotic. Feedback from multiple sources and multiple levels tends to be abundant in breadth and depth. More information from different groups of people does not necessarily generate better feedback because raters may vary in how they see the ratee's role. Rater disagreement may be rampant and difficult to understand. Ratees differ in their ability and willingness to cope with this divergent data. Without facilitation and coaching, feedback recipients may miss or purposefully ignore some information, fail to see trends, and see what they want to see (i.e., results that match their self-image) while avoiding contradictory information.

3. Individuals do not necessarily learn from the feedback. Longitudinal research on multisource feedback indicates that feedback survey results often lead to small performance improvements, especially for people who are not cynical, set goals for improvement, discuss the feedback with others, and are initially rated poorly (or overrate their own performance) (London, Smither, & Reilly, 2003). The value of the feedback to an individual depends on the needs of the organization. If development occurs, is it in the direction needed by the organization (Goodstone & Diamante, 1998)?

4. The costs of time and money spent on the entire process are high. Consider the sources of cost: developing the instrument itself, time spent on filling out the instrument, preparing the feedback report, training feedback givers, giving the feedback to the manager, digesting the feedback, preparing the manager to give feedback to their constituents, and so on.

5. Multisource feedback is not necessarily more objective and accurate than traditional top-down performance appraisals, and it is subject to rating errors and distortions unless it is developed to be psychometrically sound and valid (Fletcher, Baldry, & Cunningham-Snell, 1998). The use of predesigned items that are easy to understand, score, and disseminate may not be relevant to a particular workplace. A customized, context-specific instrument takes considerable time, money, and effort to develop. Also, the quantitative results may be less meaningful than qualitative comments. However, asking for open-ended responses is more difficult to quantify and may also cause raters to be very careful what they say.

6. Relationships are based on the concept of reciprocity. If multisource feedback is used for making administrative decisions, people may collude to obtain reciprocity ("tit-for-tat"). The agreement to cooperate by giving each other positive ratings may be explicit or, more likely, implicit. Essentially, managers try to game the system, recognizing their mutual dependence. Multisource feedback surveys make this likely because the surveys are repeated over time, giving managers a chance to rate each other multiple times. As a result, they can infer how they

evaluate each other and the effects of these evaluations. The need for cooperation wins over the desire for objective information. Organizations may try to reduce collusion by randomly assigning raters rather than giving ratees the freedom to select their own raters. However, the value of feedback may be in asking people who know you well to rate you. Organizations may administer the survey less often as a way to reduce collusion; however, follow-up surveys are important if the results are to be valuable for development (Toegel & Conger, 2003).

7. Cultural differences are an issue of concern in multisource intruments. Cultural patterns affect multisource ratings (e.g., Leslie, Gryskiewicz, & Dalton, 1998). For example, whereas collectivist cultures, for instance, in Taiwan or Korea, view the use of extreme scores as boisterous and in bad taste (Hui & Triandis, 1989), Hispanics often use extreme ratings to express their feelings (Marin, Gamba, & Marin, 1992) (see Walker, Wang, & Lodato, 2003). Additionally, Taiwanese college students perceived that seeking feedback incurred greater effort and face loss costs than American college students (Kung & Steelman, 2003). The researchers explained that the communication pattern in Taiwan, which is a high-context collectivistic culture, may induce more psychological costs in general and may not be an environment that supports feedback seeking. In contrast, the United States is a low-context individualistic culture. U.S. students were more likely to inquire directly about their performance than Taiwanese students. U.S. students involved in frequent teamwork are more likely to seek feedback. Taiwanese students with more frequent supervisory interaction are more likely to seek feedback. U.S. students may be more influenced by teamwork values than Taiwanese students who take collectivistic work structures for granted. However, Taiwanese students may overcome high-power distance by working more closely with their supervisors. More research of this nature is needed.

Despite these challenges, multisource data offer a number of possibilities for organizations beyond traditional feedback mechanisms that may make resources spent sensible. They can be used to link individual with organizational change, map the impact of the multisource feedback on the organization, and tie multisource feedback to other policies, practices, and tools in the organization (such as competency models, succession planning, management development programs, performance management tools, and coaching).

Organizations must establish clear rules for using the feedback results. Ratings collected for learning purposes should be the property of the recipient. Ratings collected for administrative purposes, such as appraisal decisions, are the property of the organization. If multisource feedback ratings are used for administrative purposes, recipients may be wary of the motives of the raters and they may be concerned about who will have access to the results. They won't necessarily feel that they "own" their evaluations, as they would if the data were collected for development alone and they were the only ones who had access to the results. If the ratings are used for administration, recipients will be looking for ways to enhance their self-image, denying or rationalizing negative results and not seeing them as constructive suggestions for performance improvement (Baumeister, 1998).

### Summary

Organizations can create environments that encourage and support performance management, self-directed learning, and feedback. Many factors develop a culture that fosters learning. Training programs, feedback surveys, and coaching are examples of methods to highlight the value of continuous learning. Multisource feedback occurs within a political, economic, cultural, and organization context involving cognitive, emotional, and social dynamics of raters and recipients. Multisource feedback is relational and subjective, drawn from people's implicit theories about jobs and work behavior. Challenges abound. The potential value of multisource feedback stems from calling attention to performance management and opportunities for learning and self-direction, having confidence in the process, and expecting positive outcomes. However, improvement is not inevitable, and feedback alone does not produce behavior change or learning. Given these challenges, multisource feedback is in danger of losing its effectiveness as a way to provide honest and constructive feedback.

In general, a key question in understanding factors that support learning is the extent to which these support mechanisms and interventions are effective. This requires assessment.

## ASSESSING CONTINUOUS LEARNING

Learning is a continuous process and so is assessment of learning. Essentially, we are proposing continuously learning about continuous learning! After all, we've made a strong argument that individuals need to be continuous learners to be successful in today's rapidly changing world. Similarly, as we show in forthcoming chapters, group learning is a continuous process—that groups need to adjust and sometimes radically transform working relationships as goals and task demands change and as group members come and go. Also, organizations need to be continuous learners, continuously fine-tuning and sometimes reinventing structures, processes, policies, strategies, communications mechanisms, and other aspects of operations and culture. And so, too, we need to learn continuously about how to foster continuous learning.

In this next section, we introduce and broadly discuss assessment at all three levels—including individuals, groups, and organizations as assessment of nested and iterative systems is itself nested and iterative. We begin by discussing assessment in general, then we outline the beginning state or what we term "capacity to learn" and the ongoing state or whether, what kind, and how much learning has occurred.

### Measurement Issues

In the assessment of learning, measures need to be both reliable and valid. Reliability is the degree to which the measure is dependable and produces the same results consistently. Validity is the degree to which an index measures what it says it measures. Assessment measures are like rulers—you want to be able to measure something three times and get similar if not identical results (reliability) and you want to be sure that you are measuring what you think you are measuring (validity), before you encourage the individual, group, or organization to change in some way!

There is a range of measurement methods. Measurements can be obtrusive (evident that measurement is occurring) and/or unobtrusive (not evident, such as an automatic counter to record behaviors). They can be objective and/or subjective. Also, standardized methods may be used—that is, measures that have been tested in large samples that provide normative data for comparison to results from any one organization. Measures need to be taken at several points in time in order to see the "value added" from learning and demonstrate the continuous nature of learning. Self-assessments, though subjective, allow learners to compare themselves to the past, to others (norms), and to organization expectations. This enhances understanding and can lead to setting goals for improvement. The assessment needs to consider how people reaction to measurement. Indeed, the measurement may be a source of learning.

Assessments need to be realistically "doable" in an organization. We, ourselves, have done many different kinds of assessments in organizations (including assessing potential with paper-and-pencil instruments and behavioral exercises in assessment centers; using multisource feedback instruments for individuals and groups; designing organizational attitude surveys about management, culture, and change; and developing performance measures that link individual outcomes to organizational goals). We know how tedious and time consuming assessment can be. Meaningful assessments use the best measures that the organization can provide from different perspectives and seek to capture breadth and depth, in other words, details about a broad range of issues. An organization that is new to assessment may elect to use a few simple measures and add additional measures over time. Organizations that regularly do assessments can handle more sophisticated measures by modifying or adding to their current assessments to take learning into account. Assessments may be able to be used in multiple ways. For example, multisource feedback can be viewed at the individual, group, and organizational levels, each level used to assess something quite different (how individuals are performing, average performance of work groups, and capabilities within the organization). Questions about learning environments may be included in attitude surveys, organizational culture surveys, or any other large-scale organizational assessments rather than being done separately.

### Assessing Capacity to Learn

Assessment of a learning opportunity and continuous learning behaviors over time may start by assessing capacity to learn. Some of the variables that reflect capacity assessment measures at the individual, group, and organization level are presented in Table 4.1.

The most important characteristic for facilitating continuous learning is the presence of goals that require the individual, group, or organization to stretch in some way in order to accomplish their goal. As we stated in the first chapter, individuals, groups, and organizations are engaged in goal-directed, intention-bound work. In striving to reach a goal, learning occurs. Because learning is self-directed (individuals, groups, and organizations cannot be forced to learn), a difficult goal provides the trigger for learning to occur. In addition, learning begets learning. Individuals, groups, and organizations learn in the process of trying to reach goals. But as they learn, they also change as a learner. They draw on their prior learning experiences—both successful and unsuccessful—to use in current and future learning experiences.

Past experience with learning will affect participation in later learning. Employees who have been thwarted in their attempts to learn (e.g., denied permission by a supervisor to attend a short course on company time) will be less likely to try again. On the other hand, if their prior experiences have been supported and rewarded and they have attained their goals, then they are more likely to seek learning opportunities in the future. Questions to assess the extent to which individuals are continuously learning and the organization supports continuous learning would include: Is it common for employees in the organization to spend time and resources on learning activities? Do they reflect on what they are learning and how it can be used? Within teams, do members take time out for reflecting on what they learned while carrying out a group task? Does the organization offer learning resources, such as training software and executive coaches, and does it provide resources for assessing learning needs?

The *desire* to learn, or motivation, is an important component of capacity as we discussed in the previous chapter. Attitude surveys and interviews may be administered to inquire about motivation, for instance, asking directly, "How willing are you to register for this workshop?" Other measures of employee motivation to learn may be records of the number of requests for information about training programs, the number of hits to a Web site, books sold, or how quickly a course is filled to capacity. At the team level, motivation may be reflected in members asking each other about their skills and discussing gaps between perceived needs and actual knowledge or skills in the group. At the organization level, learning motivation may be evident in meetings requested to seek information and ideas, the purchase of new equipment or materials and the adoption of new work methods and operations, and/or some other major change that introduces the need to behave and work in different ways.

TABLE 4.1
Assessment Criteria for Learning Capacity

| *Assessment Category* | *Definition* | *Individuals* | *Teams* | *Organizations* |
|---|---|---|---|---|
| Goal setting | Goals are set for performance. | Individuals have "stretch" performance goals that require them to learn in order to perform those goals. | Teams have performance goals or work in changing situations that require them to learn in order to accomplish goals. | Organizations have performance goals or work in changing situations that require them to learn in order to accomplish goals. |
| Prior learning experiences | History of learning and change experiences—successful and unsuccessful. | Perceptions of the extent to which prior experiences are recalled, valued, and deemed relevant to future learning experiences. | Group members have worked together in the past, or worked with others, on change efforts; resistance to change was low or easily overcome; conflicts were resolved quickly. | Organization has changed structure and/or processes in the past with low cost in dollars and time and little to no negative effect on morale. |
| Participation in learning | Extent to which people spend time on learning activities, take stock of what they have learned and how it can be applied, and actually use new skills and knowledge. | Individuals devote time and energy to learning activities, seek learning activities on their own, and recognize what they have learned from formal and informal (incidental) learning. | Members assess learning required for improved team performance and spend time on learning as a group or as individuals. | Organization provides learning resources (courses, coaches, online training) and assesses learning utilization and application at all levels. |
| Desire, or motivation, to learn. | Positive feelings for participating in learning. | Attitude surveys and interviews ask, "How willing are you to register for this workshop?"; employees seek information about learning opportunities and register; employees volunteer for new job assignments. | Group members share information about their skills and abilities and how they can contribute to the group effort; members participate actively and show enthusiasm; gaps between perceived need and actual knowledge or skills are identified; feedback is sought from fellow group members. | Meetings held to collect information and prepare; employees involved in formulating new work processes and structures; new equipment and materials are ordered. |

| | | | | |
|---|---|---|---|---|
| Readiness to learn | Recognizing the need for learning; being ready to take action. | Measuring reactions to impending change; observing reactions and performance during sample learning exercises; observing participation in learning events. | Team members discuss problems and need for change; voice recognition of the need for change; propose alternative actions and suggested changes; little readiness would be demonstrated if group members derided or discouraged a member who suggested change. | Attitude survey measures regarding leaders' change initiatives; volunteers to serve on design and implementation committees. |
| Potential or aptitude to learn | Underlying foundation for successful learning is present (e.g., basic skills, abilities, prior experiences, interests, attention span, perseverance). | Measurement of foundation knowledge or skills, physical condition; determination of prior success in learning and experiences that help understanding need for new information, skills, abilities; role models, facilitators, and/or coaches are present. | Team has demonstrated responsiveness and change in the past; leader champions change; facilitator is available to support change. | Organization has a fluid structure—has been changed quickly and has demonstrated responsiveness to shifting conditions in the past; leader expresses clear vision for change; managers voice support for the change. |
| Development level | Growth in becoming a more complex and sophisticated system. | (a) Growth along fixed stages based on age that build upon previous stages throughout life; or (b) Growth along orders of consciousness toward increasing complexity. | The group increasingly moves from a collection of individuals into a well-ordered system. They pass through periods of focusing more on the group itself or more on the task at hand. | Organization development may be thought of as (a) an orderly process through a series of predetermined stages, (b) goal directed and purposeful, (c) an ongoing struggle for scarce resources, or (d) a continuous give and take between entities within the organization and with other organizations. |
| Expectation for generating new knowledge | Creating and applying new knowledge and discoveries. | Involvement in research; experimentation with new ways of doing things; expressed desire for feedback, feedback obtained and used. | Team tries new modes of communication and production; members discuss group process and invent and try new ways of interacting. | Organization provides resources for research and creative activity; invents new ways of responding to changing environment; adopts new modes of communication through advanced technology. |

*(Continued)*

TABLE 4.1 *(continued)*

| *Assessment Category* | *Definition* | *Individuals* | *Teams* | *Organizations* |
|---|---|---|---|---|
| Use of feedback | Information about performance and capabilities is available and used to guide development. | Individuals seek, think about, and use feedback to set development goals and guide their participation in learning and development activities. | Team members provide each other with feedback about their individual performance and discuss the team's performance and how group members can enhance it. | Organization encourages feedback; builds feedback into performance management programs; requires participation in multisource feedback surveys; uses survey results for development, not administrative decisions. |
| Agreement in how others perceive a person | People see each other similarly and see themselves in the same way others see them. | Individuals recognize their skills/competencies and deficiencies and performance gaps; self-perceptions match perceptions of others. | Newly formed teams begin with members describing their strengths and weaknesses, backgrounds, and capabilities; group members draw on this information to involve each other in accomplishing the group task. | Assessments are provided to individuals and teams; Normative data and clear descriptions of desired competencies are well-known; employees evaluate themselves against organizational standards. |
| Social, interpersonal, and collaborative skills | People work together cooperatively; when conflicts arise, they are recognized and dealt with directly. | Individuals have strong interpersonal skills (verbal and written communication skills; conflict resolution skills) and personality characteristics that are conducive to effective work relationship. | Team members demonstrate effective interpersonal skills; work is tightly integrated for interdependent tasks; any conflicts are resolved expeditiously. | Organizational and systems structures and policies facilitate open communication; lines of communication are clear and utilized; support is available to promote effective interactions within and between units. |
| What is to be learned | Specific skills, areas of knowledge, concepts and ideas, behaviors, etc. | Tests of information recall and demonstration of newly acquired skills, knowledge, and abilities (measures collected online or by paper-and-pencil or by oral exam); behaviors exhibited under controlled conditions, such as business simulations (assessment centers). | Records of team interactions demonstrate new patterns; new responses are enacted when relevant situations arise (e.g., learned ways of resolving conflicts). | New structures and work processes are put in place; new positions are created and filled |

*Readiness* to learn includes recognizing the need for learning and being ready to take action as we discussed in both chapter 1 and chapter 3. People in a training program or part of an organization change effort may be at different stages in their recognition of the need for learning, their acceptance of this need, and their readiness to do something about it (see Levesque, J. M. Prochaska, & J. O. Prochaska, 1999; Prochaska, Prochaska & Levessque, 2001). Some people resist the learning or participate in learning in a passive way—for example, being present at a mandated training program but not internalizing the learning (e.g., understanding and using whatever is taught). Others may actively seek the learning, experiment by applying it in different ways in a variety of contexts and conveying the knowledge to others. Readiness may be assessed, and affected by, informing people of the learning/change opportunity and asking their opinion about its potential value, having people participate in sample learning experiences and observing their reactions and performance, and involving them in the change effort and observing their degree of participation.

The *potential* to learn, or aptitude, may be reflected in tests of foundation knowledge or skills, physical condition (if what is learned is a physical skill of some kind), prior success in learning, experiences that help understanding of new information/skills/abilities, and the opportunity to observe others who serve as role models. AT&T pioneered management assessment centers for this purpose, and they are used widely in many organizations throughout the world. The design of such an assessment center for entry-level managers begins with identifying the dimensions of effective managerial performance at middle levels of management, such as decision making, organizing, leadership, oral and written communications skills, self-awareness, and self-objectivity. Business games and exercises are created to give participants a chance to demonstrate their ability on these performance dimensions. For instance, participants may be asked to review material and then develop and give a presentation arguing for a specific viewpoint. Another exercise, called an "in-basket," provides participants with memos, reports, phone messages, and other pieces of information in a typical in-basket and asks them to deal with them. An interviewer will later review the extent to which the participant reviewed and prioritized the information and responded to requests. The assessment center usually takes place during the course of 2 or 3 days. In addition to the behavioral exercises, it likely includes a detailed background interview and various cognitive and personality tests. Trained assessors, usually people with substantial management experience, observe participants as they participate in the behavioral exercises. They rate and write reports about participants' performance following each exercise. After the participants have left, the staff holds an integration session during which reports on each participant are read aloud and the assessors rate the participant on the performance dimensions. This information is later fed back to the participant manager as a guide for learning.

A variant of the assessment center is a 6-hour business simulation during which participants interact as they would in an office. They are given roles, desks, and a host of information about a fictitious company. Assessors observe how they interact with colleagues as they acquire information and make decisions during the course of the 6 hours. The Center for Creative Leadership calls their simulation of this type, "Looking Glass," because it provides participants with a mirror image of their performance (i.e., feedback), which in turn is the basis for learning activities.

Some organizations use this information solely to help managers learn about themselves, rather than for making decisions about the managers. (AT&T called their developmental assessment center, "Insight.") This is fairly rare, however, because of the expense of the center. Most organizations use the assessment information both for learning and to place managers into management development programs that lead to promotion opportunities.

Development level of the individual, group, or organization influences what the system is capable of learning. Development is movement from simplicity toward complexity. As discussed in chapter 3, at the individual level, development can be construed as growth along fixed stages based on age that build upon prior stages throughout life. Alternatively, development can be seen cognitively as growth toward more complex orders of consciousness. Groups and organizations also move toward more complexity. They can be seen as moving from a collection of individuals into a well-ordered and synergistic system.

Another element of learning capacity that may affect motivation and enthusiasm for the process is the extent to which participants expect to generate new knowledge. Expansive learners are avid not only about acquiring knowledge but also about creating and applying it. This would be evident from their involvement in research, experimentation with new ways of doing things, and desire for feedback.

As discussed in chapter 2, use of *feedback* for performance improvement and learning also indicate learning capacity. Feedback can be assessed by examining the availability of information about performance and capabilities. Do individuals seek, think about, and use feedback to set learning goals and guide their participation in learning activities? Do team members provide each other with feedback about their performance and ways to improve it? Does the organization encourage feedback by administering feedback surveys for learning purposes or designing performance appraisal processes that expect supervisors to provide subordinates with feedback? Goal setting can be assessed by examining whether employees periodically review their learning accomplishments and organizational needs and set goals for learning that are realistic, clear, challenging, and achievable. Assessment of teams can evaluate whether they discuss and reach consensus about learning goals for the team as a whole. At the organizational level, assessment can examine whether performance management systems encourage goal setting for career development and whether supervisors or other sources provide information about organizational strategies and the environment that will guide goal setting.

Agreement in *how others perceive a person* may be important to the extent to which people feel that their skills and abilities as well as their deficiencies are recognized. This should affect the extent to which others rely on them for tasks they are able to contribute to and also the extent to which supervisors and group leaders provide resources for skills development. Assessment of learning capacity can measure the extent to which individuals recognize their skills/competencies and deficiencies and performance gaps and the extent to which self-perceptions match perceptions of others. Team learning capacity can be assessed on the extent to which members describe their strengths and weaknesses, backgrounds, and capabilities and the extent to which group members use this information to involve each other in the group's work. At the organizational level, assessment can include data on competencies averaged across individuals in the organization that people can use to calibrate the adequacy of their abilities and their competitiveness in the organization. Another organizational indicator of learning capacity may be the clarity of competencies needed by the organization so that employees have a firm understanding of performance and learning expectations.

*Social, interpersonal and collaborative skills* are other aspects of capacity to learn. They refer to people working together cooperatively so when conflicts arise, they are recognized and dealt with directly. At the individual level, assessment of learning capacity can capture the strength of interpersonal skills, such as verbal and written skills and conflict resolution experience and behaviors. Team assessment can measure the demonstration of these interpersonal skills in the group context and evidence of cooperative behaviors and ways in which conflicts are resolved. Organizational assessment can examine organizational and systems structures and policies that facilitate communications. Also, sources of support for effective interpersonal interactions can be determined, such as facilitators or training.

Finally, knowing what is to be learned and how it will be evaluated is another component of learning capacity. The extent to which people accurately recognize the purpose and scope of the learning and subsequent measures for evaluation suggests that they understand and, therefore may be more likely to pay attention to, the learning process. They may be told before participating in learning experiences that they will be measured on recall of information or demonstration of knowledge, abilities, or skills. They may also be told how they will be measured—whether by online or paper-and-pencil tests, oral exams (questioning by one or more experts), or behaviors exhibited under controlled conditions, such as in a business simulation. Knowing expectations for the learning, the content, and measurement process may thereby affect learning capacity by focusing attention to the material and the importance of practice under different conditions.

In summary, a number of elements contribute to an individual's, group's, and organization's capacity for continuous learning. Goals, prior experiences, and actual participation are, of course, important to being a continuous learner. The motivation to learn, being ready to take action, and having the potential or aptitude for learning are also factors. The stage or complexity of development and an expectation that new knowledge can be generated in the learning process open the system (individual, team, or organization) to seeking learning opportunities. Relationships among individuals, including agreement in whether people see each other similarly and having collaborative skills, are additional factors that influence capacity. Finally, the "bottom line" is what is to be learned—the specific skills, areas of knowledge, and ideas—point to the possibilities for continuous learning.

### Evidence of Learning

Learning criteria can be reactions, evidence of acquired knowledge and skills, behaviors showing the new knowledge and skills, and/or results of the learning. Also, the assessment can measure learning processes such as behaviors in seeking learning experiences and feedback, participation in formal learning, and reflection about what can be learned from daily events and activities.

Criteria for assessing continuous learning include evaluation of professional growth and performance improvement. This requires longitudinal measurement in a way that examines the integration of past learning with new learning and determines how learning experiences contribute to later decisions and behaviors. The assessment needs to measure and control for various conditions that may affect growth, such as individual differences reflecting capability and motivation, changing demands of the situation, support for learning, and other factors that may and may not be under the individual's control. Assessing continuous learning needs to take into account formal and informal learning experiences over time. For instance, during a given period of time, an individual may attend a series of training programs and have a variety of key job experiences. Some of these experiences will be business as usual, but may still offer the chance to try new behaviors. Learning from these incidental experiences may not be obvious. Other experiences may be frame breaking, such as taking on a new assignment or position. Learning from these experiences may be more obvious to the learner than incremental learning, and indeed, such transitions are major opportunities for learning. Periodic assessment of learning should also capture sources of the learning, for instance, daily events that prompted insights as well as the major changes that led to considerable changes in perceptions, skills or knowledge, perceptions, and/or performance. Support factors should be examined, for instance, the availability and impact of a coach, trainer, or supervisor who monitors and rewards learned behavior and provides feedback; resources to attend training courses or workshops; a leader who champions new corporate strategies and behavioral strategies along with them.

Self-assessment can be a valuable guide to people in understanding their learning behavior. Table 4.2 lists assessment questions to help people consider their own continuous learning tendencies. People may be interested in learning

TABLE 4.2
Self-Assessment Questions for Continuous Learning

To what extent are you a continuous learner and in what directions?

**General Continuous Learning:**

In general, how much time do you spend enhancing your knowledge in your field of expertise? Are you constantly striving to learn more? Are you always on the look out for new ideas?

Do you tend to challenge conventional logic? Are you someone who is never satisfied with the way things are? Do you see opportunities that others do not see? Do you look for ways to apply new knowledge? Please explain and provide examples.

Would you describe yourself as a conformist or a nonconformist?

Each of the following items reflect an element of continuous learning. Circle the numbers next to the items that apply to you.

1. Making something new has always intrigued me.
2. I can't seem to leave well enough alone.
3. Nothing motivates me more than to hear someone say "it can't be done."
4. I plan incessantly.
5. There is something compelling about creating or discovering better ways to do things.
6. I strive to innovate.
7. I question, with irreverence, most traditional ways of doing things.
8. There is something about me that presses for expression in a large or bold way.
9. I would describe myself as a nonconformist.
10. Some would likely describe my focus on problem solving as obsessive.
11. New knowledge is important to me only if it can be applied.
12. I constantly see opportunities that others do not see.
13. I am always trying to understand the implications of advancements.
14. There is nothing more rewarding than doing more, doing it faster, and doing it better.
15. I like to influence the world around me.

**Technology-Focused Continuous Learning:**

Would you say you have a passion to learn about new technology? Are you continuously on the lookout for technological advancement? Do you enjoy putting new ideas into action? Explain.

Now, which of the following items apply to you?

1. I imagine a future centered on better, faster ways of doing all kinds of things thanks to technology.
2. The mechanics of gadgets fascinates me.
3. I am "beside myself" when I ponder the entrepreneurial possibilities that accompany technological innovation.
4. The real joy of technology lies in its ability to benefit from capital investments and grow exponentially.
5. I often think about how one application can lead to many sources of revenue as a result of technologies.
6. I think about the next generation of applications that I currently now work with or am developing.
7. It seems to me that technology will improve our quality of life.
8. People would describe me as a path breaker.
9. All progress is dependent on tinkering with gadgets and demanding that they do things they have never done before.
10. I am restless when people tell me a technology is not capable of performing up to my expectations.

*(Continued)*

TABLE 4.2 *(continued)*

11. I possess a driving passion for learning about new technology.
12. New technological advancements are typically fascinating to me.
13. It bothers me if others learn or use technologies before I am made aware of them.
14. I think about the evolution of new technologies or applications.
15. People tell me I am "too involved" in my work.

*Self and Other Focus:*

Would you say you are self-reflective? Do you ask others how you are doing? Are you well aware of your strengths and weaknesses? What do you do to learn more about yourself?

Do you try to learn about others' strengths and weaknesses? How?

Do you build close working relationships with your colleagues? Do you help others work together better? In what ways?

Which of the following items describe you?

1. I was never a person that sought feedback from others about my performance or interpersonal style.
2. I think about how others perceive situations frequently.
3. People that talk about feelings get on my nerves.
4. I try to avoid thinking about who I "truly" am.
5. I would say that I am a very good listener.
6. It is best to leave people alone so they can perform at their peak.
7. Clarifying the task is more important than managing relationships in a work team.
8. I develop interpersonal problems because others just don't understand me.
9. I often reflect on my past.
10. I don't try to analyze the motivations of others because I have better things to do.
11. I often compare myself to others.
12. Sometimes I evaluate myself against what I hope to become someday.
13. Building close relationships with others is too time consuming.
14. I am annoyed by management practices that make a big deal about "being sensitive" to others.
15. Human behavior is a fascinating topic.

*Support for Continuous Learning:*

Are people in your company rewarded for suggesting new ways of doing things?

Do you feel you work in an environment that welcomes new ideas, values learning, and encourages trying new ways of doing things?

Have you been successful has been successful in introducing change in your company? Have you introduced profitable new products and services?

Are you known for your cutting edge technical knowledge?

*Pressures to Be a Continuous Learner:*

How much uncertainty is there in your present role? Can you predict what will happen a year from now? Can you see what changes are on the horizon?

Are technological changes few and far between, or is technology affecting your business changing rapidly? Are your company's products or services of today likely to change dramatically a year from now? Is your company always on the look out for the latest market trends?

How much competition is there to implement the latest technologies? How hard is it to keep up with the competition in terms of having the latest technology?

*(Continued)*

TABLE 4.2 *(continued)*

*Support for Learning About Yourself and Others:*

Do you get enough feedback about how you are doing? Would you like more? . . . of what type? Please explain.

Do you feel that you have a job you can handle? Are you encouraged to set goals that are difficult, but possible to accomplish? Do you work for leaders who expect more than anyone can accomplish?

Do you get along with others at work? Do they know you—know your capabilities and what you can contribute? Do they want to know about you? Do they ask you to contribute in ways that draw on your strengths? Do they give you feedback about your performance?

*Outcomes of Continuous Learning:*

Have you overcome career barriers? Has being a continuous learner helped you?

Do you get frustrated when things get tough, or do you know where to turn?

Do you tend to see difficult tasks as surmountable? Do you maintain a positive attitude in the face of tough challenges?

How do you react when things change? Do you get flustered? Do you welcome change and want to find out everything you can about it?

Would you call yourself an entrepreneur? How so? Are you able to apply what you learn? Do you discover new uses for your knowledge?

Have you had success introducing new products or services?

How often do you take courses or participate in other activities to keep up with your field? What other activities (e.g., attend professional meeting, read professional journal, look for online information, talk to fellow experts)?

How do you think people, particularly your subordinates, react to you? Do they think you are overly analytic? . . . too picky? . . . expect too much?

Overall, how would you evaluate your job performance? . . . consistently exceed expectations . . . often exceed expectations . . . meet expectations . . . often fall below expectations . . . consistently falls below expectations.

*Note.* Based on London and Diamante (2002); items developed by Thomas Diamante, Manuel London, and Graham Millington.

in general, wanting to learn about something specific (for example, technology), and/or wanting to learn about themselves and the people with whom they interact. Answer the questions to determine your own continuous learning. Also, consider the questions that ask about support for continuous learning, and the need or pressures in the organization to be a continuous learner. In addition, consider the questions that ask about the outcomes/benefits of being a continuous learner in your organization.

## PULLING IT ALL TOGETHER

The following case demonstrates an example of putting theory and practice to use in successfully designing a learning environment that aids in the long-term learning of its individual learners.

**A Case Study: Learning at Alverno College**

For the last 30 years, Alverno College in Milwaukee, a 2,000-student, 4-year independent liberal arts college for women, has focused on preparing students for careers in the professions (Mentkowski & Associates, 2000). Alverno's philosophy of learning uses and extends the way corporations assess and educate employees. The school adopted assessment center methods from industry, assessing first-year students prior to the start of their studies using leaderless group discussions and information-processing exercises later coupled with reflective self-assessments and developmental feedback from faculty. The action-oriented, problem-centered, experiential learning methods and follow-up assessments were aimed at an educational experience to address what liberally educated women should be able to do with their knowledge.

At Alverno, learning is defined as an integrative activity. It involves thinking through the personal, disciplinary, or contextual frameworks that bear on a situation. It involves engaging in multiple experiences and performances to explore, demonstrate, and consolidate one's learning. It also means ongoing assessment that opens performance to observation, judgment, and insight. Learning integrates learning, development, and performance that demonstrates mastery and has the following characteristics (Mentkowski & Associates, 2000): They are:

*Integrative*—creating connections and new wholes out of multiple parts. Learners need to be able to learn to bring all the different pieces of what they are learning together into a coherent whole.

*Experiential*—connecting knowing with doing and theory with practice by experiencing and thinking or connecting during experiences. Learners need practice in relating abstract principles to concrete experiences that are meaningful in their lives.

*Self-aware and reflective, self-assessed and self-regarding*—increasing understanding of what learners are doing in relation to what they aim to do. They learn to monitor their own feelings, beliefs, values, decisions and actions and gain a deep self-awareness and realization of personal growth.

*Developmental and individual, transitional and transformative*—learning as an ongoing, advancing process. Learners build on what they already know and do, reconstructing their knowledge and ability with new learning, then carrying it forward to another level.

*Active and interactive, independent and collaborative*—learning as more than listening and reading. Learners test and develop their thinking by thinking aloud with others.

*Situated and transferable*—learning situated in the context of its ultimate use through practice settings, internships, apprenticeships, mentorships, and simulations. Learners ground their performances in a particular context. By also practicing across diverse settings, they can develop a framework that allows them to begin to transfer their learning from one context into others.

*Deep, expansive, purposeful, and responsible*—supporting habits of deep inquiry, delving into meaning, developing further levels of expertise, and letting imagination serve productive creativity.

***Assessment of Learning.*** At Alverno College, assessment is a key part of the learning process. For learning to be integrative and experiential, assessment is made to evaluate performance. For learning to be characterized by self-awareness, assessment examines students on expected outcomes on explicit criteria and also collects and helps students analyze self-assessment. For learning to be active and interactive, assessment includes feedback from others—that is, a variety of external perspectives, subjective and objective. For learning to be developmental, assessment is cumulative and broad. For learning to be transferable, assessment includes performance in multiple contexts. Active learners grow in reasoning, self-reflection, a deep sense of purpose and integrity, and performance. By connecting reasoning and performance, learners develop a sense of what they know and what they can do. These are metacognitive strategies. Learning centers on practicing increasing levels of each competency.

Alverno makes assessments on eight dimensions of performance, and these dimensions guide curriculum development. Each of the following eight abilities are evaluated on a six-level proficiency scale. To graduate, students must achieve Level 4 proficiency for each of the eight abilities. Each aspect of performance is examined on a variety of different simulated situations. In addition, graduates must also achieve Level 4 proficiency in their major. The abilities are as follows:

- *Communication abilities connecting people, ideas, texts, media, and technology;* Level 1: identify own strengths and weaknesses as a communicator; Level 4: communicate creatively in ways that show integration using disciplinary frameworks; Level 6: communicate with creativity and habitual effectiveness.
- *Analytical abilities;* Level 1: show observational skills; Level 4: analyze structure and organization; Level 6: master ability to employ independently the frameworks from an area of concentration.
- *Facility in using problem-solving processes;* Level 1: articulate own step-by-step problem-solving process; Level 4: independently examine, select, use, and evaluate different approach to solving problems; Level 6: solve problems in different professional settings and advanced applications.
- *Facility in making value judgments and independent decisions;* Level 1: identify own values; Level 4: engage in valuing decision making in different situations; Level 6: apply own theory of value.
- *Facility for social interaction;* Level 1: identify own interaction behaviors utilized in a group problem-solving situation; Level 4: demonstrate

effective social interaction behavior; Level 6: facilitate effective interpersonal and intergroup relationships.

- *Develop global perspectives;* Level 1: assess own knowledge and skills; Level 4: apply frameworks in formulating a response to global concerns and local issues; Level 6: develop responsibility toward the global environment.
- *Develop effective citizenship;* Level 1: assess own knowledge and skills in thinking about and acting on local issues; Level 4: apply own developing citizenship skills; Level 6: exercise leadership in addressing social or professional issues.
- *Develop aesthetic responsiveness;* Level 1: articulate a personal response to the arts; Level 4: take a position on the merits of specific works; Level 6: show the impact of the arts on one's life.

Alverno College has an advantage in creating learning. It is an educational institution whose mission *is* to educate, and "members" typically remain with the "organization" for 4 years. However, we believe that organizations that wish to instill learning with their employees can use many of the principles found to be successful by Alverno. The college put this system into place using methods already found in industry and has been using them for over 30 years. The methods are based on sound theory and research in learning (i.e., integrative, experiential, metacognitive, etc.). Also, learning is assessed according to objective criteria (competencies).

## CONCLUSION

The organizational environment sets the stage for individual learning in a variety of ways. All organizations provide learning resources, whether unwittingly or intentionally. The organizational context determines the skills, knowledge, and ways of behaving that are necessary for success in that environment. People learn the appropriate way to behave through the organizational environment, the way work is structured, the infrastructure, the management hierarchy, and the organizational culture—specifically the degree to which they are encouraged to learn and the degree to which they receive feedback. As examples, turbulent environments, complex (rather than simple) work structures, infrastructures that stretch individuals beyond their current development levels, and management structures that allow discovery, flow, and flexibility all encourage continuous learning beyond the adaptive level in individuals. An environment that empowers self-learning includes supervisors who offer learning resources, especially feedback and coaching on performance and time for training. Organizational cultures may promote performance feedback, encouraging managers and employees to talk about performance-related issues, develop plans for improvement, and participate in learning. Organizations create environments for learning by participating in solving real company problems that cross functional and hierarchical boundaries. Perhaps the most significant others in career- and job-related learning is the employee's immediate supervisor and other top executives who create a climate for learning. A key question is whether they *really* create such a climate and mean it or whether their prime attention is performance improvement and the organization's bottom line. The GE example demonstrated that an organization can be transformed by top executive commitment to a learning process that is based in solving actual problems and demonstrating increased corporate success measured in dollars and cents, market share, and other bottom-line indicators of performance.

Assessment is key to understanding whether learning has occurred. Continuous learning should not be taken for granted. Part of continuous learning is attaining information about the value and direction of learning. The feedback about processes and outcomes can redirect learning efforts to make them more worthwhile—fulfilling and enriching. Assessment can evaluate any one learning experience, provide evidence of development over time, and demonstrate the value of ongoing learning activities. Assessment can be viewed as an exploratory process, not a final exam. It should enhance self-awareness and provide evidence for personal reflection, group discussion, or organizational review. Assessment of learning shows the gap between accomplishments and desired goals and points the way for later actions and learning. Assessment of continuous learning shows the deepening and broadening of knowledge and capability. Measurement processes need to be reliable and valid for the specific purpose. Assessments can use a variety of measurement methods. Those selected should be realistic and cost effective. Indexes used should have clear meaning and be readily available for repeated use. Measurements and research designs should rule out rival alternative explanations for the results. Assessments should cover capacity to learn, learning processes, outcomes, and environmental support.

In learning, learners compare preconceptions to reality, acquire factual knowledge, and take control of their own learning by defining learning goals and monitoring their own progress. People develop their expertise by broadening and deepening their current skills and knowledge, new areas of application, or new disciplines. Learning has such characteristics as integrative, experiential, self-aware, reflective, developmental, interactive, collaborative, transferable to new situations, expansiveness, and purposeful. It encompasses such general skills as communications, analytic abilities, problem solving, decision making, social interaction, global perspectives, citizenship, and aesthetic responsiveness.

## QUESTIONS FOR THOUGHT AND DISCUSSION

1. Think of the jobs you have had. Did they provide opportunities to learn? In what ways? What factors in the environment promoted your learning? Consider the nature of the work you did, the structure of the organization, the

people you worked with, and the broader environment (your industry, economic conditions, or technology).

2. Have you encountered environmental conditions that hindered your learning—actually prevented it or made it more difficult?
3. As a supervisor, what would you do to help your employees learn?
4. What are the costs of supporting learning in an organization? What are the most cost-effective ways of promoting learning?
5. Sometimes learning is unplanned and unexpected. Do people (do you) recognize what you have learned from an experience? How can we help people understand and use what they are learning from activities in their daily lives? How can we help people learn from unusual activities, maybe handling crises or tough situations?
6. What are ways that supervisors can increase attention to performance improvement? What organizational systems, programs, or processes help them do that?
7. Consider you own career and professional development during the last 5 years. What were you doing 5 years ago? How many assignments or jobs have you had during this course of time? What do you do differently than you did then? Are you more effective? Are you a better performer? How do you know?
8. Have you participated in a multisource feeback survey? If so, how did you use the results? Did you look at them briefly and then file the report? Did you study the report to identify areas of strengths and weakness and ways you could improve? Did you follow up by setting goals for development and then participating in training or other opportunities to improve? Did your performance change over time?
9. Could you develop your own multisource feedback survey and send it out to your peers, subordinates, and supervisor? What items would you include? What would you say to encourage participation? What results would you expect?
10. Suppose multisource feedback was introduced in your organization. Would multisource feedback be a stimulus for adaptive, generative, or transformative learning? To ask the question in another way, would this process be a major shift in the way your organization operates? Would it fit into the culture? Would employees see the process as innovative or threatening? Would they expect the results to suggest ways for minor changes in behavior or major changes? Would they welcome the feedback and take it to heart or avoid or ignore it? How would you feel about the process and what would you do with the results?
11. What is an example of a reliable measurement of performance on your job? What is an example of a valid measurement?
12. Select an organizational change effort and develop a comprehensive assessment. How would you evaluate capacity to learn, learning processes, outcomes, and environmental support?

## TOPICS FOR RESEARCH

1. Design a study that measures how elements of work and organizational structure contribute to learning. What is the relationship between work conditions and participation in different developmental activities?
2. Develop a measure to identify communities of practice—teams in which members inform each other and reinforce each other's learning and performance improvement. Examine the experience of the members of such teams. Do people develop continuous learning habits as a result of being part of such communities?
3. Study the independent and joint effects of training, performance appraisal, and multisource feedback on subsequent participation in developmental activities, including engaging in discussions about performance management and ways to enhance performance. Determine aspects of these structures and systems that promote further learning.
4. Collect data in a variety of organizational units to distinguish between learner-centered and task-centered environments. What is the difference in terms of environmental conditions and learning behaviors?
5. Compare different modes of learning—distance versus classroom learning. Do they differ in learning outcomes? Are some people predisposed to learn better in one type of environment than another? What learning theories and styles of learning suggest that technology-based learning (i.e., the use of technology to deliver instruction and learning experiences) will be more effective? What individual difference and environmental factors determine the extent to which high-tech educational methods will be successful?
6. Assess employees' capacity to learn. Develop measures of readiness to set and act on learning goals.
7. Compare methods of learning on dimensions that predict that the learning will have lasting impact—characteristics such as integrative, experiential, encouragement of self-reflection, and transferability of skills. Determine the relationship between these characteristics of the learning environment and multiple learning outcomes, such as ability to be analytic, solve problems, recognize multicultural issues, and interact well with others.

CHAPTER

# 5

# Understanding Group Continuous Learning

This chapter begins the second iteration of our nested model of learning. Here we change our focus from the individual to the group. This adds a level of complexity to our thinking about continuous learning from a systems perspective. Individuals are whole systems themselves that are part of other wholes (teams or groups). Physiologically, we are an individual whole, whereas sociologically we are a part. Psychologically, we are both a whole and a part at the same time (or even a part in several instances as we are members of more than one group at work). Individually, we are endowed with reflective consciousness, but teams are not (Laszlo, 1996). This duality can lead to great confusion in understanding the concept of team learning. A key question in thinking about group learning is whether groups encourage and benefit from members' learning or whether groups learn as entities in and of themselves. We believe that the answer is both. Individual learning is important to the way groups do things. However, group learning is more than the sum of the individual members.

To add to the complexity, groups hold an intermediate position within the organization. They are intermediate in that they link individuals together and at the same time link to other groups to form organizations. Stated another way, groups link what might be thought of as lower order components of the organizational system (i.e., individuals, who are systems themselves) to higher order components (organizations). One of the functions of groups is to pull together the behavior of their members and integrate this joint behavior with other groups in the system (Laszlo, 1996). Therefore, teams are the linking pin between individual learning and organizational learning in our model.

In this chapter, we first explore what a group in an organization is and why groups are important to organizational learning. We then explore the concept of team learning, showing how groups, just as individuals, learn adaptively, generatively, and transformatively, and we discuss how learning lasts in a group, especially with changing membership.

## WHAT IS A GROUP OR TEAM?

A group or team is "two or more individuals who must interact and adapt to achieve specified, shared, and valued objectives" (Fiore et al., 2001, p. 310; see also Salas, Dickinson, Converse, & Tannenbaum, 1992). We are especially interested in groups within the context of an organization. As a note, individuals who are told they are a team do not automatically "make" a team. Often individuals are told they are a team, but continue to be managed as individuals; they do not interact, and they do not have mutual goals. Giving individuals specific assignments then coordinating the output can be effective. So can letting members take responsibility for the task. But the benefits of teamwork require actually working as a team. When we use the terms team or group we mean those who actually act in an interdependent manner to reach a goal.

Real groups provide a way for organizations to bring a range of expertise to bear on the organization's work, often with the expectation of getting the job done more effectively than would be possible relying on individual contributors who work in isolation.

How do we know if a group is being effective? Group effectiveness is commonly thought to depend on three factors (Hackman, 1990b, 2002): (a) the extent to which the group's outputs (products, services, or decisions) meet standards of quantity, quality, and timeliness as specified by the people who use them, (b) the extent to which the process of conducting the work increases the capability of members to work together interdependently later, and (c) the extent to which the team experience contributes to the growth and personal well-being of the group members. Criteria that are most important will vary from one situation to another. For example, temporary teams may worry more about outputs and less about working relationships between the members for the long term (Druskat & Kayes, 2000). Teams that are expected to exist over a long period of time may need to balance all three criteria of effectiveness.

## WHY GROUPS ARE IMPORTANT IN ORGANIZATIONS

In many of today's organizations, structures have shifted such that teams rather than individuals are the basic building blocks of organizations. More than 80% of medium-size to large organizations use teams in some fashion (Gordon, 1992). The purpose of a group in an organization is to "do something"—to create a product, perform a service, solve a problem, make a decision, and so on. And the group is expected to do a quality job, in a timely fashion, and on budget. Emphasis is primarily placed on that final project: namely some sort of outcome was produced by the deadline date. Little, if any attention is placed on the process by which the team reaches its goals. Thus, teams behave in a fashion that facilitates their goals of quality and efficiency—processes like reflecting on actions taken simply may not occur if the team is busy, accustomed to routine (Gersick & Hackman, 1990), and not held accountable for how it reaches its goals (Druskat & Kayes, 2000).

Thus, learning often rises to importance only when the group is unable to accomplish what it was mandated to do for whatever reason—otherwise learning falls by the wayside. Learning is not the goal of teams, it is a means to an end, and it may be the means to an end only when conditions are right (see next chapter).

Despite countervailing tendencies for groups to not learn in organizations—or at least not learn what we think they should learn—there is an increasing recognition that learning is a social process and teams (or communities) in organizations *are* where a lot of learning takes place (see Palincsar, 1998, for a fuller discussion of the social constructivist perspectives on learning). More than a decade ago Senge (1990) suggested that teams, not individuals, are the fundamental learning units in an organization. And recent theory on communities of practice (Wenger, 1999) and chaos theory (Harkema, 2003; van Eijnatten & Putnik, 2004) reiterate the relational properties of learning in organizations.

Finally, there is increasing recognition in the organizational learning literature that team learning is key to linking individual learning to organizational learning.

Groups may be the most important entities for "doing something" and for facilitating learning at all three levels: individual, group, and organizational. However, little is known about the relationship between group performance and group learning. On the one hand, because continuous improvement can be critical to sustained group effectiveness (Argote, Gruenfeld, & Naquin, 2001; Kozlowski, Gully, Nason, & Smith, 1999), whether a group learns or not should be related to its performance (see also Edmondson, 1999). On the other hand, learning efforts are not efficient—they consume resources and divert attention from existing initiatives. Therefore, learning may compromise performance if it is overemphasized or not necessary for performance. However, there is very little research that considers both group learning and group performance together. The research that exists is mixed, defines group learning differently, and uses different kinds of teams—making it difficult to draw any sort of conclusions on the relationship between performance and learning. For example, Druskat and Kayes (2000) did not find a relationship between learning and performance in short-term project teams. Some similar and some different group processes were associated with learning versus performance: interpersonal understanding and pro-activity in problem solving were associated with both learning and performance. Clear work procedures were negatively associated with learning. Confronting members who break norms was negatively associated with performance. However, in longer-term teams (e.g., product development teams, management teams, production teams, and surgical teams), Edmondson (1999, 2001) found relationships between learning and performance. The bottom line is that teams are paradoxically expected to produce a quality outcome in an efficient and timely manner yet take time to learn.

## DEFINING TEAM LEARNING

Learning at this level has been viewed in a variety of ways. These perspectives overlap and are not mutually exclusive. In fact, all may be viewed as a part of group learning.

*Team learning is a collectivity of individual learning* (Druskat & Kayes, 2000; Ellis et al., 2003). In this perspective, team learning occurs when individual team members create, acquire, and share unique knowledge and information. In this case, teams could focus on valuing, managing, and enhancing individual learning to enhance team functioning.

*Team learning is a process.* Here team learning is a process in which a team takes action, obtains and reflects upon feedback, and makes changes to adapt or improve. In this perspective, team learning is said to occur when the team engages in behaviors such as asking questions, seeking feedback, experimenting, reflecting, and discussing errors (Drach-Zahavy & Somech, 2001; Edmondson, 1999, 2001).

*Teams are systems that learn.* This definition encompasses the other definitions as team learning is seen as a dynamic process in which learning processes, the conditions that support them, and team "behaviors" change as the team learns (Argote, Gruenfeld, & Naquin, 2001; Kasl, Marsick, & Dechant, 1997). Changes in group "behavior" may be reflected in changes in the language, tools, documents, images, symbols, procedures, regulations, practices, and routines used by the group, all of which are explicit or observable, and/or rules of thumb, underlying assumptions, and shared worldviews, which are tacit or not easily observable.

Susan Jackson, Professor of Human Resource Management in the School of Management and Labor Relations at Rutgers University and one of the subject matter experts in our online discussion, offered the following about the meaning of group learning:

> Team learning is more than the aggregated learning of individuals in the team. Similarly, organizational learning is more than an aggregate of all organizational members' learning. One way to think about learning by social systems is to focus on changes/developments in behaviors and routines, rather than (or in addition to) cognitive changes/developments.
>
> A challenge for me is how to measure team learning. Measuring change/development is extremely difficult, so I am motivated to find something else to measure that may be presumed to be closely related. One thought is to focus on knowledge

seeking, knowledge sharing, and perhaps knowledge hoarding behaviors among team and organization members. Presumably, learning is grounded in such behaviors. Suppose a study identified the conditions that support or inhibit such behaviors. How big of a leap would it be to claim that those same behaviors support or constrain learning (even if learning per se was not measured)?

Jackson raises the question of how to measure learning constructs at the team level. Some researchers have used an aggregated measure to assess team learning. Her idea is to focus on changes in a team's or organization's routines rather than on individuals' cognitive changes. Changing team or organization structures, communication patterns, rituals, policies, or processes could be indications of team learning. Changes could be described along with the conditions that generated them and the extent to which the changes were intended to improve performance and actually did, and the extent to which the changes were maintained or developed further. Quantitative measures could assess the degree of change as well as other attributes such as their clarity, extent to which they are widely known and understood, permanency, degree of codification, and so forth. Furthermore, as Jackson suggests, assessment of learning may need to measure behaviors around the learning, such as knowledge-seeking, knowledge-sharing, and knowledge-hoarding behaviors. As with learning at the individual level, our primary concern is some sort of change in the group, be it changing structures, communication patterns, rituals, policies, or processes.

## GROUP FEEDBACK

As with individuals, group learning does not occur without feedback. Without the feedback loop, there is no way for the group to interpret whether the modified or new behavior that it engaged in "worked." Feedback allows groups to receive information about the impact of their behavior on the situation and add that information to their repertoire of possible behaviors. Without feedback, groups are unable to determine whether in another similar situation they should repeat that behavior, modify that behavior, or do something else entirely. Groups can receive feedback in a variety of ways: by determining how members feel to be a member of that team, by observing how others react to their outcomes, by noting whether rewards are forthcoming, or by tracking objective indicators of performance (e.g., goals are being met on time, outcomes are meeting quality standards, clients are returning for repeat business, etc.). In this chapter, as in chapter 2 for individuals, we discuss feedback groups receive from others.

Multisource feedback, which asks group members to rate themselves and each other and receive feedback from others outside the group, is growing in popularity at the group level (see chap. 4). Feedback can be provided to individual group members or, averaged across team members' or observers' (e.g., clients, supervisors) ratings, to the group as a whole. Interpersonal interactions in the group are opportunities for members to provide information about themselves to others. Over time, group members' feedback to each other can result in greater interpersonal congruence, that is, members seeing themselves in the way others see them (Bailey & Fletcher, 2002). The more team members interact with each other, the more likely they are to seek group-based feedback, perceive less cost from seeking feedback (e.g., the possibility of losing face), and be more likely to ask for feedback (Kung & Steelman, 2003).

Feedback in groups not only has the same challenges as those found in individual feedback, but also has a layer of complexity not inherent in feedback at the individual level. Group members receive feedback and modify their behavior toward their own individual goals at the same time that the group they are in receives feedback and modifies its behavior toward its goals. In order to understand feedback at the group level, it is necessary to take into account multilevel and multiple goals of individuals and groups. Addressing this issue, DeShon, Kozlowski, Schmidt, Milner, and Weichman (2004) found the following:

1. Group members who receive only individual feedback focus their attention and effort on their own individual performance and this results in the highest level of individual performance.
2. Group members who receive only group-level feedback are more likely to focus on group performance, and this results in the highest group performance.
3. Group members who receive both individual and group-level feedback are unable to optimally capitalize on the feedback.

Thus the highest levels of individual- and group-oriented performance occur when group members received a single-focused source of feedback. This study was conducted in the laboratory, and each individual was a member of one group. The complexity is greater with the realization that individuals at work are typically members of multiple groups as well as having individual responsibilities. This study suggests that individuals and groups are unable to capitalize fully on the feedback they receive in terms of performance. Very little is known regarding whether and what groups actually learn from feedback when it is multilevel and multigoal.

However, we contend that as with individual feedback, group feedback is necessary for learning to occur. Similarly, feedback is problematic at this level, particularly when that feedback is received from other people. It is difficult for groups to even receive feedback, much less the type of feedback they need to learn. As with individuals, groups must somehow purposefully contrive to get the feedback they need on their own.

## HOW GROUPS LEARN

When individuals are confronted with goals that require them to learn, they can learn about something—theories, concepts, and tools; or they can learn how to do something—practices. Groups can also learn about and learn how to. Most of what we think about in groups, though, is learning how to do something. That is, most groups learn by addressing and solving real problems as they go about their work. They learn how to configure and reconfigure themselves to best meet needs and they learn practices and policies.

Learning about can happen to individual members collectively, it can be learned by an individual and passed on to other members, or it can be learned by an individual and accessed by the group when needed. However, unless it is somehow captured in a communal memory by the group, the group as a whole cannot be said to have learned about. Learning about is captured is by language, tools, documents, images, symbols, procedures, regulations, prototypes, and rules of thumb. A relatively new way that groups are evolving to address this is through the use of group Weblogs (blogs) at work. Blogs let group members post information that can be seen by other group members (and others beyond) and mined for information at a later date.

Not surprisingly, technical companies already have sophisticated blogs. See, for example, Microsoft's publicly available channel 9 at http://channel9.msdn .com. However, less technical companies are using them successfully as well. For example, The Hartford Financial Services group is using blogs with its mobile groups. One team of 40 field technology managers who serve as links between The Hartford's network of insurance agents and the home office set up a blog. They use it to share information. Before, e-mail and voice mail sufficed, but e-mail threads die, voice mail is erased, and there is no way to search past share information (McGregor, 2004).

In addition, to learning about and learning how, there are three ways that groups acquire the behaviors, knowledge, and skills they need to achieve their goal. That is, in groups, learning can occur adaptively, generatively, or transformatively.

### Adaptive Learning

At the simplest level, a group can change in reaction to a stimulus in the external environment. Groups in organizations pick up clues from their organizational surroundings—clues about changes in the organization's climate, culture, norms, policies, procedures, and rules that inform members about the new way to negotiate and get their work done and thus change their behavior accordingly. As with individuals, adaptive learning in groups may occur automatically, without processing, as the group encounters unexpected demands, changes, or nonroutine situations. Unless the group is aware of how it is reacting to changing conditions, it can inadvertently adapt to situations that do not enhance its goals.

One way adaptive learning occurs is that the group changes its configuration or role structure in response to change. Early in a group's life, the members establish roles and a common notion of how they are to work together to accomplish the team's task. They develop routines—habitual patterns of behavior that allow members to predict other members' actions (LePine, 2003). Groups that repeat the same pattern of activity over time have an established role structure. This enhances group efficiency because the group does not have to invent ways of operating each time a new task arises. However, sometimes, if the task demands or the external environment changes (e.g., the team is asked to perform a task that is unfamiliar) or the internal environment shifts (e.g., a new member enters the group), the team may need to alter its original configuration and modify its habits, sometimes having to respond very quickly if the situation is unanticipated or an emergency. Adaptive performance is the capability of the team to maintain coordinated interdependence and performance by selecting an appropriate network (ways of interacting within the group and with other groups) from its repertoire or by inventing a new configuration (Kozlowski et al., 1999, p. 273).

These adjustments are reactive in the sense that the change is in response to something—an error, a problem, or new demand—as opposed to proactive behavior that anticipates the need for change. Also, these adjustments are typically not scripted in that the reactions are trial and error learning as the group deals with the problem at hand. A new configuration or role structure—the pattern of behavior within the group—emerges as the group transforms resources to address the need.

Adapting configuration or role structure is particularly important in groups that must integrate information to make a series of decisions during a designated time span because this requires adapting established role structure while actually performing the task. They don't have the time to stop and plan a rational response to an unexpected change (LePine, 2003). Consider flight crews, surgical teams, or command-and-control teams which must keep going in the face of, say, equipment failure. They have to adapt "on the fly" to be effective and avoid catastrophe. In decision-making groups, members share information with each other in order to make judgments about appropriate courses of action. Unexpected changes disrupt the smooth flow of information and could result in ineffective decisions. The ability of the group to adapt their role structures should enhance the team's ability to make timely and effective decisions.

Group adaptation is evident when members do the following after a disruption (LePine, 2003):

- Do not hesitate about changing the way they do the task.
- Adjust what they do to accommodate other members' needs.
- Coordinate the exchange of required information.
- Settle into a smooth pattern of communicating necessary information.

- Find a way to get information to the right member.
- Relearn how to perform their part of the team's task.
- Find a way to accomplish their responsibilities.

Another way of viewing adaptation is as the ability to cope with change and to transfer learning from one task to another as job demands vary (Han and Williams, 2003). Here, adaptive performance demonstrates creative, swift performance and learning (Johnson, 2001; LePine et al., 2000). Another way to view adaptation is in terms of the individual group members' ability to change. One study found that when team members were rated highly on level of adaptive performance on their jobs, their teams were also rated highly on adaptive performance (Han & Williams, 2003). The individual team members' adaptive performance seemed to benefit coordination and cooperation within the team. This allowed the team to function as a cohesive unit and to deal effectively with nonroutine tasks.

### Generative Learning

Generative learning is purposefully adding new behaviors, knowledge, and skills with a resulting change in group behavior. New behaviors, knowledge, skills, and competencies can be learned by groups in three ways. First, groups as a whole can learn or even create new knowledge, skills, and competencies. Second, individual group members can learn something new and incorporate it into the group. Third, group members can know "who knows what" and individually, without actually learning the new information, can know when the member with the needed knowledge, skill, or competency needs to be accessed.

Work groups as a whole can learn or even create new knowledge, skills, and competencies as they do their work. For example, Adam, a student in one of the first author's classes, revealed that the construction company he works for routinely conducts weekly "coordination" meetings:

> We were heading into the last quarter of the project that we were working on and the project manager asked during the meeting, "What past experiences can you reflect upon that could help us reduce problems that [typically] occur in the last quarter of projects?" Individuals were asked to think about the problems that they experienced in the last quarter of past projects and how they thought that these problems could be prevented.

In discussing what typically does not work in the final stages of the project, ahead of time, members can come up with typical problems to keep an eye open for and typical or new remedies that can be implemented currently, thereby incorporating their ideas and insights into the group process before a problem occurs.

Group members, individually, can learn something new and bring it into the group's practice. Individuals can have some sort of learning experience outside the boundaries of the group (in a training program, in another work group, etc.). Individuals in the team can attempt to change the team's activities so that it includes, or takes advantage of, their own learning experience. They communicate to the group what they learned, invite and engage the group in trying it out, add to or change the new learning to fit this particular group, and ultimately change the practice of the group—creating, not just adding, knowledge in the process.

Finally, group members know "who knows what" in the group. Individual members can learn new knowledge that is then used by the group as a whole without other members necessarily learning the new knowledge themselves. This is called *transactive memory* and is knowledge about the memory system of other group members.

***Transactive Memory.*** A *transactive memory system* (TMS) is "the cooperative division of labor for learning, remembering, and communicating relevant team knowledge" (Lewis, 2003, p. 587). Members retrieve information and expertise from each other through communications—that is, transactions. Group members expect each other to learn and remember new information. Transactive memory, therefore, consists of the beliefs group members have about each other's expertise and the accessibility of that knowledge (Lewis, 2003). For example, suppose Jim is a design engineer working on a new product. He knows that Sharon, a mechanical engineer on the project, has an extensive background in physics. Jim has learned that as issues of design that require a knowledge of physics arise, he can ask Sharon. Jim doesn't need to learn more physics himself. What Jim remembers and learns is affected by what he understands about Sharon's memory. This knowledge of Sharon's expertise, and Jim's confidence that Sharon will not only retain but continue to develop this expertise becomes part of Jim's "transactive" memory. Sharon understands this expectation, and conversely, relies on Jim for his knowledge of design. They cooperate to store, retrieve, and communicate information in their respective areas of expertise.

In a group, this transactive memory expands beyond dyads as members of the group develop knowledge of each other's expertise. They divide the cognitive labor. As a result, the group members working together are able to remember and draw on more knowledge than any of the members working alone or possibly in smaller groups. For groups to be effective, members must not only have the needed expertise. They must rely on each other to use and deepen their expertise. Also, each member needs to learn how to draw on each other's expertise. TMS may develop more quickly when members have complementary expertise. Keeping a core group of members together working on different tasks is one way to maintain the transactive memory that has already developed and maximize its value in the organization. As other group members are added, they will observe how the experienced members take responsibility for applying their expertise, and the new members will follow suit (Lewis, 2003).

Transactive memory has been found to be positively related to group performance (Austin, 2003; Moreland, 1999). TMS is especially important for knowledge-worker teams that are intended to leverage members' expertise to accomplish the group task. This applies to teams involved in consulting, product development, research, and other cross-functional and ad hoc project teams. The value of the team will be realized only when the differential expertise of its members is recognized and integrated (Lewis, 2003; Nonaka & Takeuchi, 1995). In these groups, members rely on each other to derive, consider, and relay information from different domains of knowledge (Wegner, 1987). Group members expect that those with specific expertise will be responsible for applying that expertise as needed by the task, and doing so in a way that is constructively interrelated with others' expertise. Members assume that all group members will apply their expertise appropriately, and so they don't have to monitor each person's contribution. This frees up members to concentrate on developing their expertise to benefit the group further while giving other members access to their knowledge. Such a cooperative memory system facilitates rapid and coordinated access to task-relevant expertise (Lewis, 2003). Group members who are trained together on a task develop differentiated and specialized knowledge and avoid redundancy—that is, individuals having to cover the same areas of expertise, as they would if they were each doing the task individually. Distributing responsibility for different areas of knowledge increases the relevant information available to the group (Wegner, 1987). Members feel mutually accountable for their area of knowledge. Group members know who in the group to go to when a particular area of expertise is needed, and they are encouraged to share their knowledge with other members of the group.

Lewis (2003) developed the following measure of transactive memory in groups. This can be administered as the group develops or at its completion. Groups may develop TMS at different rates as members learn about each other. TMS is a group-level variable; however, it exists as a function of individual members' knowledge. Each member responds to the following items, which are then averaged or summed across members to form a group-level score:

*Specialization:*

1. Each team member has specialized knowledge of some aspect of our project.
2. I have knowledge about an aspect of the project that no other team member has.
3. Different team members are responsible for expertise in different areas.
4. The specialized knowledge of several different team members was needed to complete the project deliverables.
5. I know which team members have expertise in specific areas.

*Credibility:*

1. I was comfortable accepting procedural suggestions from other team members.
2. I trusted that other members' knowledge about the project was credible.
3. I was confident relying on the information that other team members brought to the discussion.
4. When other members gave information, I wanted to double-check it for myself. (reversed)
5. I did not have much faith in other members' "expertise." (reversed)

*Coordination:*

1. Our team worked together in a well-coordinated fashion.
2. Our team had very few misunderstandings about what to do.
3. Our team needed to backtrack and start over a lot. (reversed)
4. We accomplished the task smoothly and efficiently.
5. There was much confusion about how we would accomplish the task. (reversed)

Measured by agreement: Items use a 5-point disagree–agree response format, in which 1 = strongly disagree, 2 = disagree, 3 = neutral, 4 = agree, and 5 = strongly agree.

### Transformative Learning

When groups engage in transformative learning, they undergo a dramatic and fundamental change in the way they see themselves and the world in which they live. Group transformation occurs through experiences and reflection (discussion) about these experiences. Next, we discuss two interventions that are used to help groups transform themselves: dialogue and appreciative inquiry. Then we discuss the underlying mechanism in these two interventions: reflection.

***Dialogue.*** Much of learning that occurs through experience emerges from interactions among people. In conversation, people are subjected to, and become familiar with, how different team members interpret their experiences (Baker et al., 2002). Bohm (1996) developed the process of dialogue in groups—which is aimed at the understanding of perceptions and consciousness as well as exploring the problematic nature of day-to-day relationships and communication. Bohm, Factor, and Garrett (1991) say that, in dialogue, a group of people can explore their individual and collective presuppositions, ideas, beliefs, and feelings that subtly control their interactions. Dialogue provides an opportunity to participate in a process that displays communication successes and failures. It can reveal the often puzzling patterns of incoherence that lead the group to avoid certain issues or insist, against all reason, on standing and defending opinions about particular issues.

Dialogue is a way of observing collectively how hidden values and intentions can control behavior, and how unnoticed cultural differences can clash without realizing what is occurring. It can therefore be seen as an arena in which collective learning takes place and out of which a sense of increased harmony, fellowship, and creativity can arise. Conversely, dialogue is not a discussion, a debate, a "salon," a new name for a sensitivity group of some sort. It is a means of exploring the way group members perceive and interpret their shared and individual experiences.

Dialogue involves the following steps (Bohm et al., 1991):

1. *Thoughts, impulses, and judgments are suspended.* Suspension involves exposing one's reactions, impulses, feelings and opinions in such a way that they can be seen and felt within one's own psyche and also be reflected back by others in the group. It does not mean repressing, suppressing, or even postponing them but simply giving them serious attention so that their structures can be noticed while they are actually taking place. Giving attention to reactions, impulses, feelings, and opinions, and especially sustaining that attention, tends to slow individuals down. It permits people to see the deeper meanings underlying their thought processes and to sense the often incoherent structure of any action they might otherwise carry out without thinking. Similarly, if a group is able to suspend such feelings and give its attention to them, then the overall process that flows from thoughts, to feelings, to acting-out within the group, can also slow down and reveal its deeper, more subtle meanings along with any of its implicit distortions. The result may be what might be described as a new kind of coherent, collective intelligence.

2. *The dialogue process requires a fairly large number of people, which may require combining groups for purposes of reflection.* Bohm and colleagues believe that dialogue works best with between 20 and 40 people seated facing one another in a single circle. A group of this size allows for the emergence and observation of different subgroups or subcultures that can help to reveal some of the ways in which thought operatives collectively. This is important because the differences between such subcultures are often an unrecognized cause of failed communication and conflict. Smaller groups lack the requisite diversity needed to reveal these tendencies and will generally emphasize more familiar personal and family roles and relationships.

3. *Dialogue needs some time to get going as it is an unusual way of participating with others.* Two hours is optimum per session. But deeper and more meaningful territory will be explored when the group can meet more regularly. There is no limit to how long a dialogue group may continue its exploration. But it would be contrary to the spirit of dialogue for it to become fixed or institutionalized.

This suggests openness to constantly shifting membership, changing schedules, or merely, the dissolving of a group after some period.

4. *Dialogue groups lack a controlling authority.* However, facilitators are useful, at least in the beginning. A dialogue is essentially a conversation between equals. Any controlling authority, no matter how carefully or sensitively applied, will tend to hinder and inhibit the free play of thought and the often delicate and subtle feelings that would otherwise be shared. Dialogue is vulnerable to being manipulated, but its spirit is not consistent with this. Hierarchy has no place in dialogue.

5. *Finally, dialogue can begin with any topic of interest to the participants.* If some members of the group feel that certain exchanges or subjects are disturbing or not fitting, they are encouraged to express these thoughts within the dialogue. No content should be excluded.

Can dialogue realistically be used in work groups? . . . in organizations? Members of an existing organization will have already developed a number of different sorts of relationship between one another and with their organization as a whole. There may be a preexisting hierarchy or a felt need to protect one's colleagues, team, or department. There may be a fear of expressing thoughts that might be seen as critical of those who are higher in the organization or of norms within the organizational culture. Careers or the social acceptance of individual members might appear to be threatened by participation in a process that emphasizes transparency, openness, honesty, spontaneity, and the sort of deep interest in others that can draw out areas of vulnerability that may long have been kept hidden. In an existing organization, the dialogue will probably begin with an exploration of all the doubts and fears that participation will certainly raise. Members may have to start with a fairly specific agenda from which they eventually can be encouraged to diverge. But, as we have mentioned, no content should be excluded because the impulse to exclude a subject is itself rich material for the inquiry. Most organizations have inherent, predetermined purposes and goals that are seldom questioned. At first this might also seem to be inconsistent with the free and open play of thought that is so intrinsic to the dialogue process. However, this too can be overcome if the participants are helped from the very beginning to realize that considerations of such subjects can prove essential to the well-being of the organization and can in turn help to increase the participants' self-esteem and the regard in which they hold each other.

***Appreciative Inquiry.*** Another transformative, experiential group learning process is appreciative inquiry (AI). One of the assumptions of AI is that systems grow in the direction of what they persistently ask questions about. Another assumption of AI is that every living system has many untapped and rich and inspiring accounts of the positive (Cooperrider & Whitney, 1999). AI is "the art and practice of asking questions that strengthen a system's capacity to apprehend, anticipate, and heighten positive potential" (Appreciative Inquiry Commons, 2003, p. 1). The method facilitates people discussing what helps them work together better. Rather than focus on conflict, group members learn to give each other positive feedback and rewards. They talk about the kind of relationships they want to have. In the process, a shared image of a desirable future emerges. Little attention is given to issues that prompt divisiveness.

There are four key stages in AI: (a) *Discovery*—mobilizing a whole system (in this case a group); (b) *Dream*—creating a clear results-oriented vision in relation to discovered potential and in relation to questions of higher purpose, that is, "What does the organization expect us to become?"; (c) *Design*—creating possibility propositions of the ideal group, a group design that people feel is capable of magnifying or eclipsing the positive core and realizing the articulated new dream; and (d) *Destiny*—strengthening the affirmative capability of the whole system, enabling it to build hope and momentum around a deep purpose and creating processes for learning, adjustment, and improvisation like a jazz group over time.

***Reflexivity.*** Reflection is at the heart of these transformative processes. Reflexivity is the extent to which team members collectively discuss the team's objectives, strategies, and processes and the environment in which they operate. Teams that act too quickly may jump the gun, implementing dysfunctional approaches or, if they are effective, burning out quickly.

Michael West, a member of our online discussion group, offered the topic of reflexivity as a basis for team learning:

> My thesis is that teams which operate in uncertain, challenging environments will be more effective to the extent that they attend to and reflect upon their objectives, strategies, processes and their organizational and wider environments; plan to adapt these aspects of their task functional worlds; and make changes accordingly. They will also facilitate creativity and skill development among team members. Moreover such "reflexive" teams will stimulate innovation or even revolution in their organizations by negotiating, challenging and influencing organizational goals, policies and practices.

Though few teams actually engage in such reflection, reflexivity together with a capacity to actually try out changes based on reflection are key ingredients for nurturing teams and realizing their potential (Edmondson, 2002). However, when they do engage in reflection, learning and the resulting behavior change occurs. For example, in cardiac surgery teams attempting to implement new surgery routines based on new technology, it was found that those teams that were able to implement new routines promoted shared meaning and process improvement through reflective practices (Edmondson, Bohmer, & Pisano, 2001).

West defines three stages of reflexivity: reflection, planning, and action:

1. *Reflection* involves questioning, planning, experimenting, analyzing, planning, and reviewing past events. This may be accomplished with various levels of

depth. Reflection may be shallow (involving only monitoring, questioning, and/or reviewing), a bit deeper (evaluating, generating alternatives, and learning by exploring), or deeper (using new knowledge explicitly, assimilating new awareness, and learning about how the group learns—"meta-learning").

2. *Planning* is how reflection is used to create action and adaptation. Plans vary in detail, inclusiveness of a range of alternatives, hierarchical ordering of subplans, and time horizon (long- or short-range). Planning creates a perceptual readiness to take action leading to goal-directed behavior (Gollwitzer, 1996). Teams that don't reflect and plan are unlikely to take action.

3. *Action* refers to the behaviors taken to accomplish the team's objectives. Actions vary in their magnitude, novelty, radicalness, and effectiveness (West & Anderson, 1998).

Reflexivity may result from a number of factors. The team leader may initiate it. It may arise from bringing new members into the team, recovering from a failure, or reveling in a success may stimulate reflection. Conflicts within the team, trouble synchronizing activities, interruptions, feedback, and organizational change may also cause team members to reflect, leading to planning and action.

West's concept of reflexivity raises a number of questions for reflection about group process. In particular:

- Reflection alone, even deep reflection, will not lead to planning and action. Implementation intentions or "mind-sets" need to evolve. How does this happen?
- Team learning requires doing, not just reflection.
- What prompts a group to move from one stage to another? Are there linking mechanisms? For instance, Michael says that teams need to have implementation intentions/mind-sets to move from reflection to planning and action. How do these mind-sets develop? Are there other linking mechanisms? What linking mechanisms move the team from planning to action?
- Teams don't have to be "right" the first time. Reflection, planning, and action are continuous processes that build on each other. How is the learning captured? What factors allow groups to build on their reflections and experiences rather than revert to lower forms of reflection (resting on their laurels or celebrating their successes but not learning from them)?
- Reflexivity, in its ultimate or ideal form, is a model to strive for. Do team members need to have a common image of this ideal state (a shared image of this meta-team performance, so to speak)? Do transformative leaders convey this image early in the team's life? Is it enough for the team leader or a few members to have this concept? Do any team members need to have it?

- Is getting to know each other part of team reflection? Does this help team process?
- How do early team experiences get the group started on a path to reflection?
- Does reflection always come before planning and planning before action? What happens when teams act before they are ready (shoot before they aim)? Is this a better learning experience—one that prompts, if not necessitates, reflection? In other words, is learning the hard way (i.e., through failure) better than deliberate planning?
- Do groups learn from serendipitous successes? We would think the answer is "yes," especially if the group reflects on their accomplishments.
- Task reflexivity doesn't arise naturally—it requires leadership—especially transformational leaders, that is, those who communicate a clear vision for the team. Also, it arises from other changes or dislocations, such as team member changes, failures, conflicts, difficulties of other sources (e.g., time allocation or synchronizing problems, interruption, crises/shocks, feedback). There must be something to reflect about. Do teams need issues that members may perceive differently?
- Reflection may be aversive—in other words, it's not fun. It may seem tedious to team members, a distraction from making progress, and/or demoralizing (from being forced to reflect on failure). Can reflection be engaging or stimulating? Does "no pain, no gain," always apply?
- Reflexivity is a manifestation of social cognition, and as such, can be viewed as individual and team-level phenomena. How do we conceptualize team-level phenomena—describing and measuring interactions and outcomes?

## Summary

Just as there are different degrees of individual learning, group learning can be adaptive, generative, or transformative. Groups adapt to changing expectations and conditions. They also purposefully seek new knowledge, take lessons from other groups, and experiment with new behaviors on their own. This generative learning allows the group to improve and be ready for new challenges as they emerge. As members acquire new skills and knowledge and as the group members draw on this expertise, the members learn who in the group is best at transacting different tasks. This becomes ingrained in the transactive memory of the group. Of course, this memory will evolve as new members enter the group, experienced members leave, and the group works on different tasks. Group learning is transformative when the group experiences a major shift in the way members view each other and interact. This can be prompted by methods for reflecting on group process, expressing views and feedback directly, sometimes giving voice to difficult or unpleasant issues, and being open to new ideas and experimentation.

## GROUP LEARNING THAT LASTS: SOCIALIZATION PROCESSES

Developing learning that lasts in practice combines "learning about" and "learning how" with adaptive, generative, and transformational learning, which together allow groups to learn by continually broadening and deepening their understanding. In terms of deepening skills, groups build on, expand, and transform their behaviors, knowledge, and skills. Some of this learning may be adaptive—the group may receive rewards for an innovative product, thus setting the stage for the group to want to create more innovative products. Learning may be generative such as when the group seeks information on new ideas to pursue to create another innovative product. Also, learning may be transformative as the group reflects on what it is actually doing that is successful in creating an innovative product and not only purposefully applies that learning, but expands upon it.

In terms of the broadening, groups learn to apply their learning to an increasing variety of contexts, for example, moving learning from a training program to the workplace and from project to project. And again, the learning can be adaptative (using the same behavior in a new situation and finding that it works), generative (purposefully trying a behavior learned in a training situation back on the group project), and transformative (realizing why a certain behavior, knowledge, or skill works across situations and deliberatively using that realization in a variety of novel ways).

Developing learning that lasts in groups, though, has an additional step. For example, in some cases, a group of employees is a unit for only a short amount of time. Do they even need learning that lasts? Alternatively, some groups are long-lasting and actually outlast the original members. Therefore, at the same time that the group itself is learning, it must also pass existing knowledge to newcomers. In these cases, groups need to be able to communicate and transfer information to new members. Being a newcomer to a group is an opportunity for learning both by the newcomer as they are brought into the team and by the team as they bring the newcomer into it.

Newcomers are likely to adjust faster when they enter the group with relevant preknowledge about the job and the group, have a proactive personality (i.e., they behave confidently, actively work to control their environment, and seek out information; cf. Crant, 2000), and have supportive supervisors, group members, and organizational experiences, such as an orientation program (Kammeyer-Mueller & Wanberg, 2003). These factors contribute to mastering the task, understanding one's role, feeling a part and contributing to the work group, and perceiving organizational politics, such as who seems to be powerful or influential. In the long run, these factors increase feelings of commitment to the group and increase the likelihood that the newcomer will remain in the group.

Ensuring new generations of group members can be approached from two points of view. First, based on Pygmalion and Galatea effects (cf. Eden, 1992), members and newcomers develop expectations based on newcomers' experiences and self-efficacy. The Pygmalion effect predicts that team leaders who have high expectations for new members will empower them with challenging work and develop positive working relationships with them. The new members, in turn, will internalize the leader's high expectations and be motivated to meet them. The Galatea effect occurs when the team member's own high performance expectations evoke a sense of confidence and intrinsic motivation. The new members with such high expectations then work harder, which helps them fulfill their own prophecy about their effectiveness. The Pygmalion effect is initiated by the team leader or others in the group, whereas the Galatea effect is self-initiated. Once the newcomer joins the group, characteristics of the task social exchanges and empowerment of the newcomer interact to predict newcomer role performance (how they fit into the group) (Chen & Klimoski, 2003).

Ways to socialize newcomers into the group include showing newcomers that other newcomers have been successful and setting challenging and specific goals for them soon after they join the team so that they can experience early success. Also, the leader and team members should be aware that they are models for newcomers, and that the behaviors they demonstrate, even during the recruitment process, are likely to influence newcomer perceptions and expectations. Team members should also be alert to how they can support and encourage the newcomer. However, instead of instructing team members to expect more of newcomers, Chen and Klimoski (2003) suggested that a less direct but possibly more potent way to raise team members' expectations may be to use factors that naturally increase their expectations by, for example, hiring more experienced employees and establishing a climate for productivity and achievement.

A second point of view for socializing newcomers into the group is the idea of legitimate peripheral participation (Wenger, 1999). Newcomers begin on the periphery of the group. There, they engage with low intensity, low risk, special assistance, low cost of error, closer supervision, or low performance pressures. From the periphery, newcomers learn how the group operates and begin to mutually engage with other members, understand their negotiation of the enterprise, and learn the repertoire in use.

In order to be taken in as a member of the group, the newcomers must be granted enough legitimacy to be treated as potential members. If the group rejects the newcomer for some reason, the newcomer will have a hard time learning what is needed to become a member of the group. Legitimacy may take many forms including being useful, being sponsored, or even being the right kind of person. Only with enough legitimacy can a newcomer's inevitable mistakes become opportunities for learning rather than cause for exclusion or dismissal.

At the same time that a group is bringing a newcomer into it, it continues to be goal oriented and thus to learn as a unit itself. Newcomers can act as instigators in this learning. They bring with them new perspectives, ideas, knowledge, skills, abilities, behaviors, and ways of doing things that can be beneficial for the group.

The extent to which the group can access these new approaches and use them in its own learning is beneficial.

In summary, maintaining group process—another way to say ensuring that group learning lasts—can be facilitated by deliberate socialization practices. Newcomers bring new ideas, but they also need to learn the transactive memory of the group. They can also instigate and invigorate group learning by prompting different modes of behavior made possible by the unique expertise and experience that they bring to the group.

## CONCLUSION

Group learning is a function of capturing the learning of its individual members for use by the group and the patterns of relationships and behavior that emerge among the group members. The group is at once the sum of its parts and greater than the sum of its parts—something whole and unique; an entity unto itself. As such, groups exhibit adaptive, generative, and transformative learning as they learn about learning. Groups can learn by trial and error. They can deliberately add new behaviors, knowledge, and skills. Discussion and reflection, in general, and more deliberate interventions, such as dialogue, appreciative inquiry, and reflexivity, have the potential to generate transformative group learning. In order to prepare for, create, and sustain these methods, team members must be open and willing to experiment. They must encourage partnership and imagination, allow for differences, take time for reflection, and use humility. Ways to pave the way include creating and sustaining a safe, receptive conversational space and context, listening reflectively, recognizing and valuing both cognitive and emotional dimensions of learning, and making a concerted effort to attend to these characteristics while maintaining a moderate pace that is appropriate to the situation.

However, learning that lasts in teams has an additional layer to the broadening and deepening of behaviors, knowledge, and skills. In some cases, learning that lasts is not even needed as the group is together for only a short amount of time. Other times, the group outlasts its members and needs mechanisms for passing information on to new members.

In the next chapter we discuss group characteristics that impact group learning. Where the group "is" in terms of its development, individual member characteristics, group-level characteristics, and organizational context influence what the group learns and how it learns.

## QUESTIONS FOR THOUGHT AND DISCUSSION

1. Does the idea of group learning, beyond the collective learning of individuals in the group, make sense to you? Do you think groups can be said to learn? Or do you think only individuals can learn?

2. Think of the "best" team you have ever been on. What made it so successful? Was learning a part of this? If so, what kinds of learning occurred? Did it seem to be adaptive, generative, or transformational? Was it learning about or learning how to? Did it build on what the group was already doing in some way or was it completely new?
3. Have you ever been on a team that did some sort of turnaround? That went from poor to successful? What sort of learning helped cause it to have the turnaround?
4. What has worked for groups you have been on to capture group knowledge about something? What has not worked?
5. Is the idea of group continuous learning a useful one for organizations?

## TOPICS FOR RESEARCH

1. Examine the feedback group members give to themselves at different stages of group development about each other's capabilities and contribution to the team and about the team's progress and performance. Do individuals in the team benefit from the feedback by increasing their self-understanding and ability to contribute to the group? Does the group as a whole benefit by knowing who is best at doing different tasks and thereby being able to respond more quickly and effectively when problems arise (using their transactive memory)?
2. Examine ways in which group members interact to form patterns of behaviors and utilization of knowledge and skills in order to achieve a goal. Identify ways this happens adaptively in reaction to events and conditions, generatively by group self-initiative to alter conditions by creating new patterns of interaction, and transformatively to radically switch patterns of interaction and design new modes of operating.
3. Study the development of transactive memory, its operation, and its stability or evolution in relation to adaptive, generative, and transformative learning.
4. Study the role of dialogues, appreciative inquiry, and reflexivity in group development.
5. Examine the match between individual and team readiness to learn. What happens to members who are not ready to engage with others in the group learning process?

# CHAPTER 6

# Facilitating Group Continuous Learning

In this chapter, we concentrate on group characteristics as well as the characteristics of group members and the environment to better understand how each affects group learning. We begin by tackling the meaning of group development. We consider how group members establish mutual respect and understanding, which they apply to support each other in the interest of accomplishing the group's task. Team development can be viewed as a developmental sequence of predictable stages or a series of transitions from equilibrium to adaptation as unexpected changes emerge or pressure arises to get the task done on time. Group member characteristics, group characteristics, and situational conditions set the stage and affect how the group learns. As we see, this suggests ways to compose a team, structure the task, and establish other situational conditions, such as rewards, to facilitate team learning and outcomes.

## WHAT IS GROUP DEVELOPMENT?

"Teamwork" is more than the group accomplishing a task or how members interact with each other. It is also the ability of the group to fully capitalize on all of its resources toward goals and objectives. Theoretically, as group members work together, they should experience process gains, meaning they should become increasingly effective and produce more than would be possible if individual team members worked alone and aggregated their production (cf. Steiner, 1972). That is, the collection of individuals begins to operate as a single well-oiled machine. Group development is the process of moving from a collection of individuals toward a well-organized, smoothly running system.

### Mutual Trust, a Shared Mental Model, and Cohesiveness

Over time, groups need to develop mutual trust, a shared mental model, and cohesiveness. These characteristics allow groups to act as single units rather than collections of individuals. Without mutual trust, individual group members will spend time and resources protecting, checking, and inspecting each other rather than working together (Cooper & Sawaf, 1996). Mutual trust is "the shared perception . . . that individuals in the team will perform particular actions important to its members and . . . protect the rights and interests of all team members engaged in their joint endeavor" (Webber, 2002, p. 205, as cited in Sims, Salas, & Burke, 2004). Trust is needed when group members rely on each other to meet deadlines, contribute to the task, and cooperate without subversive intentions (Sims et al., 2004).

Team member coordination requires that members establish knowledge structures that allow them to predict how each other will behave. This shared set of knowledge facilitates their interaction (Fiore et al., 2001). They need to maintain this shared understanding at a level that facilitates their working together. Part of this understanding is a shared conception of the situations they may encounter and how they are likely to react. A shared mental model is the convergence of knowledge structures possessed by the team members about the team's task and how group members operate together.

When a team is initiated, the members vary in their mental models of the system and environment in which they work. A shared mental model evolves as "transparency" grows—group members gain and store information about each other's strengths and weaknesses, each other's motivations, and how group members work together by sharing information, expressing disagreements and conflicts, and overcoming misunderstanding and perceptual distortions (Jassawalla & Sashittal, 1999). As members try to define themselves as a group, they openly express their likes and dislikes, their biases and behavior tendencies, along with their concerns about each other's ability to contribute. They learn to interpret what's going on in the environment and how they are likely to react to unexpected events. With shared mental models, group members are not likely to be confused or overwhelmed when the group confronts unforeseen or inexplicable events.

Cohesiveness is the glue that holds the group together. It occurs as group members develop a sense of task commitment, group pride, and interpersonal attraction (i.e., they enjoy being with the other members of the group). All three components are related to group performance (Beal, Cohen, Burke, & McLendon, 2003).

### Mutual Monitoring, Backup, and Mindfulness: Moving Toward Synergy

It is not until group members have a shared mental model, mutual trust, and cohesion in place that group members can perform both mutual performance monitoring and backup behaviors, demonstrate mindfulness, and produce synergy, so indeed they are doing more than any one individual could do alone. Mutual performance monitoring is "the ability to keep track of fellow team member's work while carrying out their own . . . to ensure that everything is running as expected . . . and to ensure that they are following procedures correctly" (McIntyre & Salas, 1995, p. 23, as cited in Sims et al., 2004). As groups develop, members learn to maintain an awareness of group functioning by monitoring other members' work in an effort to catch mistakes, slips, or lapses prior to, or shortly after, they have occurred.

Backup behaviors are "the discretionary provision of resources and task related effort to another . . . [when] there is recognition by potential back-up providers that there is a workload distribution problem in the group" (Porter et al., 2003, pp. 391–392. as cited in Sims et al., 2004). There are three purposes for backup behavior: (a) to provide feedback and coaching aimed at improving performance, (b) to assist the group member performing the task, and (c) to complete a task for a group member when an overload is detected (Marks, Mathieu, & Zaccaro, 2000). When one group member is overloaded (for any variety of reasons), the group can shift responsibilities to another member who can take them on for the time being. Backing up other members helps with stress, provides flexibility in how the work gets done, and increases group effectiveness.

***Mindfulness.*** In highly mindful groups, members recognize each person's potential contribution and who can back up whom. Members know each other's strengths—from either prior experience in the group, having observed each other in other work settings, or simply having been informed by each other about what they can and cannot do, what they are good at and bad at, and what they like to do and don't like to do. It is the cooperative division of labor in the group, for not only doing the task, but also learning, remembering, and communicating relevant team knowledge. Lewis (2003) called this *transactive memory*. Mindful groups have a strong transactive memory, which they pass on to others as newcomers enter the team.

Also, in highly mindful groups, members commit to decisions made by the team. They voice support for decisions made by the group and remind each other of this commitment (Jassawalla & Sashittal, 1999). They don't act unilaterally, but understand that they are "in this together." They act as a group, even when individual members are frustrated by lack of progress or disagreement with the direction the group is taking. Individual members may voice their frustration or disagreement, and try to influence the direction of the team to enhance its progress or redirect behaviors or decisions. But they understand the importance of the team acting as a unit, respecting each person's contribution and opinions and the group process for making decisions and taking action.

***Synergy.*** Synergy occurs when the combined efforts and product of the group are greater than the additive contributions of individual group members.

Synergy results from members voicing opinions and challenging each other's ideas, thereby giving the group members a sense of what they can accomplish together (Jassawalla & Sashittal, 1999).

In summary, group development refers to the establishment of mutual trust, a shared mental model of how the group will proceed, and, hopefully, a sense of cohesiveness. Once this occurs, members can monitor their performance, can establish ways to back each other up, and are mindful of each member's contribution and commitment to group decisions. Ultimately, successful groups develop synergy whereby they accomplish more than would be possible by summing what each member could do alone.

## STAGES OF DEVELOPMENT

The stages of group development are similar to stages of individual development. Groups may come to see the world quite differently as they mature, just as individuals change their perspective as they gain experience and shift goals. Here we review several stage theories that explain how groups develop. Each adds to our understanding of how groups operate and what can be done to make the group experience more effective and rewarding for the participants. In particular, we examine three types of models: (a) an integrative life cycle model, (b) the robust equilibrium/adaptive response model, and (c) the punctuated equilibrium model. These are fancy names but actually fairly simple concepts to grasp. As becomes apparent in the following sections, the life cycle model outlines stages of group development. The robust equilibrium/adaptive model suggests groups establish a way of working together fairly quickly. They may adapt to changes in the environment, but return to their established processes when they are able to do so. The punctuated equilibrium model suggests that groups don't make much progress until a deadline approaches (the sudden realization or "punctuation") and then the members get motivated and find a way of working together to achieve the goal. Now for a bit more explanation:

### Life Cycle Model of Group Development

The integrative, life cycle model argues that groups progress through the following five developmental stages, each reflecting a distinguishable pattern of behavior as group members become integrated into the team and the team accomplishes its task (Tuckman, 1965; Wheelan, 1994).

1. *Dependency and inclusion:* Members initially feel anxious and uncertain; they are polite and tentative, leader focused, and often defensive. (This stage is also known as "forming.")
2. *Counterdependency and fight:* The group members begin to feel that dependency on their leader is frustrating, and they try to clarify their own

roles, asserting independence from the leader. Members may form coalitions of like interests, and conflicts may occur between coalitions. (This stage is also known as "storming.")

3. *Trust and structure:* Conflicts are resolved, cohesiveness develops, and members become more confident about being accepted by the other group members. As a result, team members communicate more freely. Also, they begin to focus more directly on the task at hand. They engage in mature negotiations about team goals and their individual roles. Some members renegotiate their roles that initially emerged during the first stage but clearly were not working. (This stage is also known as "norming.")
4. *Engagement:* The group's work begins in earnest. Goals and structures have been set up and the group now works more effectively toward its goals. (This stage is also known as "performing.")
5. *Endgame:* Members of the team evaluate their work, give each other feedback, and state their feelings about each other and the group's performance. If the group is ongoing, this may occur as an annual or quarterly review or after the group has achieved a milestone, for instance, accomplishing an important goal. (This stage is also known as "adjourning.")

Group progress through these distinct stages is distinguished by patterns of structure and member behavior. The initial structure forms quickly—for instance, the members agreeing on who is the leader and the leader's role. Further structure may be determined as individuals assume, volunteer for, or are assigned to different roles, such as recording notes on a flip chart, summarizing progress, or taking minutes. Some members may be assigned to gather certain resources or perform particular elements of the group task. One member may become a facilitator to ask the group periodically questions about their group process or request and provide feedback from team members or others outside the team about the team's performance. Over time, members may contest the structure, suggesting different roles, and the structure may be adjusted. As the group concentrates on task performance, the structure solidifies. This structure changes when the group's bonds are broken, for instance, when members or the leader leave or when new members enter the team (Mennecke, Hoffer, & Wynne, 1992).

The pace at which these stages unfold, and the time needed for each stage, will vary from group to group. Some short-term groups may not be able to proceed through each stage and may be expected to "perform" immediately. Some groups will take longer for the initial stages and then act quickly once they reach engagement. Others will move through the early stages quickly but take longer to accomplish their task, perhaps because they did not devote enough energy to establishing trust and structure. Group leaders and facilitators who understand these stages can recognize their occurrence and focus the group on each of them, ensuring that the group doesn't move on prematurely. This includes ensuring that the group completes their work with a proper endgame, with feedback to individual group members and the team as a whole and a recognition of the team's degree of success and what might be done differently if given the chance. This will help members feel a sense of accomplishment and increase their readiness and willingness to serve on other teams.

### Robust Equilibrium/Adaptive Model

The robust equilibrium/adaptive model holds that groups establish a steady state of operation within the first few meetings. Members share their distinct experiences and knowledge bases to achieve this stable state (cf. Carley, 1991; Swann, 1996). They may face brief fluctuations due to unexpected demands or changes in conditions, for instance, a new group leader, the addition or subtraction of members, a new deadline, a new task. However, the group returns to a steady state. The group regulates itself to regain equilibrium, perhaps by informing the new leader or member about the history of the group, its performance, and procedures it followed in the past.

Although the equilibrium model can be applied to identify stages, these stages occur in an ebb and flow, not a continuously increasing development as in the life stage model. The element of adaptive response suggests that teams actively create and adjust their structure and behavioral modes in response to internal and external factors, such as the nature of the task and the abilities of the team members. If conditions change, the group adapts its structure in response. The environment will determine the extent to which the group's structure is stable, changes gradually, or changes abruptly. The group may even develop routines for adapting (a "meta-level habit") or detailed contingency plans. For instance, when members leave and new members come, they may develop standard methods for introducing new members to each other and the group, communicating expectations, hearing from and learning about the new members, and incorporating their ideas into the group's process. A group may have one set of methods for dealing with standard operating procedures and another set for dealing with emergencies.

### Punctuated Equilibrium Model

The punctuated equilibrium model suggests a two-stage phase developmental pattern. It posits that groups experience strong forces to generate a stable state that may be "punctuated" by periods of sudden, rapid change (cf. Gersick, 1989). The first is a period of inertia in which the direction is set, usually by the end of the first meeting. A structure will emerge early in a group's history and then remain stable, whether or not it is optimal or even satisfactory for performance. Even moderate changes in the environment will not affect the group structure. This lasts for half the group's allotted time.

However, a radical or abrupt change will jolt the group out of its stable pattern of interaction to form a new structure. This structure persists until the next radical, disruptive event occurs. This transition usually occurs at the midpoint when the group members realize their time is limited. The group undergoes a transition that sets a revised direction, which quickly evolves into another set pattern of inertia. The group's awareness of time and deadlines triggers the change more than the work that was completed (or wasn't) in the first stage. The sudden recognition that the group needs to make progress is a type of wake-up call that stuns the group into a new mode of operating.

For instance, a group that spent its first several meetings talking about, and debating, different courses of action—often failing to communicate or providing each other with incomplete information so time is spent correcting mistakes and redoing work—suddenly realizes that it must make create a product or devise a plan, even if it isn't optimal. The group members may then assign different tasks to different group members, or the leader may take action by drafting a plan and then sharing it with the others. The focus changes from debate to creating and fine-tuning document.

Other transitions that can "wake up" the team include suddenly being merged with another team, some longtime team members are forced to leave, or new team members suddenly appear. The team will quickly develop a new modus operandi. This may be very effective or it may be limited in its effectiveness in different ways from the previous team. Yet it will remain stable until the next environmental shift.

### Integration

Research on these models suggests that each model has merit in describing valid developmental patterns of groups and that these models are not mutually exclusive, with different models concentrating on different aspects of the group (Arrow, 1997; Chang, Bordia, & Duck, 2003). For example, the life cycle model describes a developmental pattern over time, and the punctuated equilibrium model describes a change in the way the group works on its task.

These theories are descriptive of the group's cycle of events and the tasks and accomplishments related to each stage. They suggest a developmental sequence that includes the group increasingly moving from a collection of individuals into a well-ordered system. Early stages and transition stages (depending on the model) suggest a focus on the group and group members—assigning roles, developing norms, planning goals, and so on. These are the times when the group establishes mutual trust, develops shared mental models, and becomes more cohesive. During later or stable stages, when roles, norms, and goals are clear, the group concentrates on the task at hand—practicing mutual performance monitoring, providing backup behaviors, demonstrating mindfulness, and benefiting from synergy.

## STAGES OF DEVELOPMENT AND READINESS FOR LEARNING

A group's capability of learning may depend on the stage of group development. We consider learning in transitional stages, and then in the more stable stages.

### Learning During Transitional Stages

During early stages and the last stage of the life cycle model and during transitional stages of the adaptive and punctuated equilibrium models, groups must learn how to alter their configuration, modify their habits, and reestablish roles and routines. This may be done adaptively, generatively, or transformatively. In adaptive learning, the adjustments are reactive as opposed to proactive. Group members try different patterns with little thought or plan. In generative learning, the group purposely learns how to develop and use contingency plans, perhaps through team training or facilitation. For instance, the group may establish a standard method for integrating new members. In transformative learning, dialogues, appreciative inquiry, and reflection are methods that may help members focus inwardly on group member relationships. However, until the group can (re)solve any internal issues and get itself into a stable state, members will probably have difficulty concentrating on the task at hand and performing optimally.

Kegan and Lahey (2001) build on their individual model of development (see chap. 3) to help groups develop during these developmental or formative phases. They outlined three steps, as follows.

***Mutual Regard.*** The first step is for the group members to develop ongoing regard for each other. Typically, when individuals voice their admiration for one another, they do so in indirect, nonspecific ways that confer attributes. For example, the first author of this book could say, "Manny is a great cowriter of this book. He is so patient, detailed, and smart." Although many group members would like to hear a little more of this from their teammates, Kegan and Lahey (2001) argued that groups will learn to work together even better if these comments are direct, specific, and nonattributive. To become more direct means to communicate specifically to the person. To be specific is to include detailed information, not global statements that give little if any ideas about what the speaker really values. To be nonattributive is to characterize the speaker's experience and not the person being attributed. This comes across as more sincere and authentic (especially if delivered in the halting voice). To improve the aforementioned statement, your first author could say:

> Manny, I am enjoying cowriting this book with you. I particularly appreciate the system we have set up where I write a messy first draft with no connections between parts and missing information and you take the time to fill in as you rewrite and add

> your own thoughts and ideas. It has really made a difference to my own thinking and writing, and I think will make this book a good contribution to our field's understanding of continuous learning.

***Public Agreement.*** The second step is to develop public agreement. At the beginning of new groups, there are often no troubled relationships, harbored resentments, or depreciative gossip. But this may not last. Once the group begins working together, in spite of the best intentions, individuals often get into hassles, annoy each other, and step on each other's toes. Developing public agreement on how to handle these, early on, helps group members to work though mishaps when they occur. The default mode is to talk behind people's backs. The value of public agreements is not to prevent violations of the agreement, but to create mechanisms to aid people during the violation. For example, team members can agree to go to teammates they are angry with and discuss the problem rather than talking behind their backs. Inevitably, they will not always do this and a violation occurs. However, if the public agreement has been made ahead of time, it can function in two ways when a violation occurs. First, "team integrity" can be created such that the person on the receiving end of the violation can say, "I am uncomfortable with this conversation. Didn't we agree that we would go to the person who irritated us first?". Second, violations can be used for surfacing further contradictions for learning (and enhancing team integrity). "Remember last time this happened? Let's do things differently this time and make things easier on all of us."

***Deconstructive Criticism.*** The third step is to move from destructive criticism through constructive criticism to deconstructive criticism. Destructive criticism tends to be vague (e.g., saying, "That was a lousy job."). It blames the person based on personality or some other unchangeable trait ("You're dumb."), or is threatening ("Next time you do that, you will be fired!"). It is pessimistic in that it offers no suggestion for doing things better. Many people know what we mean by "constructive criticism" and that it is preferred over destructive criticism, but they know being constructive is not easy. Constructive criticism is specific ("This is what I expect and why."), supportive, problem solving, and timely. Although constructive criticism seems perfectly reasonable, consider assumptions that underlie it. One assumption is that the perspective of the feedback giver (what he or she sees and thinks) is right or correct and that the feedback giver has the one and only correct view of the situation. The corollary to that is that the person receiving the feedback is wrong. A further assumption is that the feedback giver has the responsibility in this situation. He or she is the one who should do the saying, suggesting, and giving feedback, whereas the feedback receiver's responsibilities are to listen, accept, and receive the feedback. In some cases (as in when there indeed is a correct solution), this may be legitimate. But often, there is no one correct solution. Here's where deconstructive criticism comes in. The "I'm right, and you need to be corrected" teaching model can be modified into a source of deconstructive learning about differing viewpoints as varying viewpoints may hold some merit. In deconstructive criticism, the feedback giver must recognize and acknowledge the role of his or her own perspectives and assumptions in the feedback. This allows for more equal responsibility between the feedback giver and the feedback receiver and other alternative viewpoints can then be considered. Deconstructive criticism pulls apart the various elements of the feedback and acknowledges multiple perspectives that may apply to each element. So, for instance, a supervisor, in giving feedback to an employee about a particular incident, may explain how he (i.e., the supervisor) felt and why, how others might have reacted, and ask how the employee viewed the situation and what the employee was thinking and feeling. Together, they will deconstruct the incident, identifying key elements, interpreting them from multiple perspectives, and arriving at some suggestions for how the employee may behave differently in the future.

### Learning During Stable Stages

During the engagement or performing stage of the life cycle model and the stable stages of the equilibrium models, the group can really concentrate on learning how to do its task better. With trust, shared mental models, and cohesiveness in place, group members can perform mutual performance monitoring and provide backup behaviors. The group is mindful of its process and develops synergy. Again, learning can happen adaptively, generatively, or transformatively, but the focus is on the task, not on the group. In adaptive learning, groups can try out or update previous strategies they have used in the past. During generative learning, groups can learn new strategies and procedures for reaching their goals. During transformative learning, groups can attend to and reflect upon their objectives, strategies, processes, and the organizational and wider environment, stimulating innovation and even revolution.

During times of stability, mutual regard, public agreement on how to resolve conflicts, and deconstructive criticism work their magic. That is, groups that have established these elements of process are better able to reach synergy in accomplishing their goals than groups that have not. These process elements facilitate working on the task, just as they facilitate group process during transitional stages. Periods of stability are more likely to occur and be productive when the transitional stages have been used to establish mutual regard, reach and voice agreement on how to handle problems, and provide deconstructive criticism.

## GROUP AND SITUATIONAL CHARACTERISTICS

Now that we have covered ways that groups develop over time, we consider other variables that enhance or detract from group learning as well. First we examine individual member characteristics, and then we turn to characteristics of the team and the situation in which it is operating.

### Individual Member Characteristics

Although individuals are systems in their own rights, they are parts of groups. Thus, individual characteristics influence group learning. Here we consider cognitive ability and personality characteristics, functional background, motivation for joining the team, and orientation to be part of a team and see oneself as a team member.

***Cognitive Ability and Personality.*** Individual characteristics that enhance team effectiveness are similar to the ones that we suggested enhance individual learning and include cognitive ability (Ellis et al., 2003; LePine, 2003), openness to experience (Ellis et al., 2003; LePine, 2003; LePine et al., 2000), and task expertise (Burke, Fowlkes, Wilson, & Salas, 2003; Kendall, Stagl, Burke, & Salas, 2004). Holding all other factors constant, groups composed of individuals with high abilities and these positive personality characteristics will likely be more likely to learn and to outperform groups made up of individuals who are low on these abilities and characteristics (Tannenbaum, Beard, & Salas, 1992).

***Functional Background.*** Functional background is the distribution of a team member's work history across the different functional specializations in the organization, such as finance, marketing, and operations. People develop functional knowledge from the departments in which they work, the people with whom they work, and their education (college, graduate school, later workshops and courses). Functional background is a source of power in teams when other team members recognize that they need or value the expertise. On the other hand, team members are also likely to rely on people whose functional background or other characteristics are similar to them. People tend to trust, like, and identify with others who are similar to them.

Interestingly, one study found that team members with valued functional expertise were more likely to be involved in team decision making when power over decisions and workflow was decentralization while those with functional similarity were involved in decision making by top managers when power over decisions and work flow was centralized (Bunderson, 2003). Apparently, team members engaged each other to a greater extent when they were responsible for decisions and work flow and they recognized the value a given member brought to the team by virtue of his or her functional background. When power was centralized—that is, fewer people were involved in decisions—those who were involved in the decisions tended to be people who were similar to those making the decisions. That is, the key decision makers relied on people they trusted, liked, or identified with. Having functional expertise when decisions were centralized actually led to less involvement. Apparently decision makers felt that experts were different in some ways. Their presence may have threatened decision makers' esteem or the solidarity they felt with less expert, but more similar, members. Those with too little expertise may have been excluded as well, suggesting that when decisions were centralized, having too much or too little expertise was detrimental to being involved in the decision process. Centralized teams do not tolerate differences well.

***Motives for Joining the Team.*** Assuming people have some control over which work groups they join, they will tend to join groups that verify their self-concept. Moreover, they stay with a team, feel more committed to it, and make a more substantial contribution when fellow team members give them feedback that supports their self-concept—whether it be positive or negative (Polzer et al., 2002). Team members acquire this feedback after sharing information about themselves. In doing so, they support the development of the team in that members will have a better idea of each person's background, including their abilities, skills, and knowledge and how they can contribute to helping the team accomplish its task. This "identity negotiation" process is likely to occur very early in the group process. Without accurate information about the value each team member brings to the team, members may draw wrong conclusions or not draw members into the team process and take maximum advantage of their potential contributions. Information about others helps people predict their responses. Perceiving that others see you in the way you see yourself helps you predict how others will react to you. It also makes you feel comfortable that they will react in the manner you desire or at least expect.

Interestingly, people will actually withdraw from teams that don't support their self-concept. For instance, they may leave a relationship if other parties in the relationship have inaccurate views of them, even if they think more highly of them than they think of themselves (cf. Burke & Stets, 1999; De La Ronde & Swann, 1998). In other words, people don't appreciate others thinking they can do more than they actually can any more than they appreciate others thinking they can do less than they actually can.

Self-verification enhances people's perceptions of psychological coherence in that it signals that they are indeed the people they believe themselves to be and that things are as they should be (Swann, Polzer, Seyle, & Ko, 2004). It validates their *personal* self-views (individual characteristics that may have no relation to the group's task) and their *social* self-views (characteristics that are based on membership in particular social categories, such professor or African American) (Swann et al., in press). London (2003a) proposed that group members' motivation for self-verification and self-disclosure behaviors will be higher for people who are higher in their confidence in self–other relationships and the desire to enhance their own development. Also, the desire for self-verification will encourage individuals and groups to set learning goals and value differences among fellow group members.

A contrasting theory to self-verification argues that people are motivated for self-categorization. This is a sense of belonging to a group that helps them define their self-image and feel part of a group that distinguishes itself from others (Swann et al., in press). Membership in this group helps them enhance their social self-view. Whereas self-verification holds that individuals shape their perceived and actual experiences within the team reinforcing their personal self-view, self-categorization shapes the social self-views of its members. The process of confirming self-views also contributes to group development by helping members work together more effectively. However, Swann et al. point out that although self-verification may become the norm within the group, self-categorization may also occur if the group strives to separate itself from other groups.

***Members' Team Orientation.*** Intelligent individuals with all the "right" amount of intelligence, "right" personality characteristics, "right" functional background, and "right" motives for joining a group in the first place still do not necessarily join together to make an intelligent system. To turn a collection of individuals into a group, individuals must have a team orientation—that is, a preference for working with others and enhancing one's own performance through the coordination, evaluation, and utilization of task inputs from other members while performing group tasks (Driskell & Salas, 1992). Not only does team orientation improve individual effort and performance within a group, but it also has been found to facilitate overall group performance (Driskell & Salas, 1992; Shamir, 1990; Wagner, 1995).

The relationships among the group members, however, may still become dysfunctional, mirroring the way group members tend to relate to others. For instance, in therapy groups, maladaptive interpersonal patterns that were the reasons for clients to seek group therapy in the first place are eventually manifest in group members' interactions (Yalom, 1995). In general, one reason that dysfunctional relationships emerge in a group is that members' perceptions of themselves differ from the perceptions that the group members have of them (Corey & Corey, 2002). For example, group members who avoid, or are anxious about, forming attachments and/or have a distorted view of themselves or others are likely to have trouble developing an emotional bond/alliance with the group members (Chen & Mallinckrodt, 2002). Specifically, group members who are high in attachment avoidance and anxiety tend to overestimate interpersonal problems they and others are having compared to others' perceptions of interpersonal interactions in the group. Those high in attachment avoidance and anxiety may be hesitant to share their perceptions of themselves and others in the group during the early meetings. This may actually increase interpersonal conflicts as the group progresses, because members will not know each other well, thereby lessening or preventing group cohesion and decreasing interpersonal learning.

In summary, individual characteristics such as cognitive ability and personality, functional background, motivation for joining the team, and orientation to be part of a team are likely to influence group learning. Next, consider how these individual variables work together to comprise what we call team composition.

### Team Characteristics

Here we consider several characteristics of the team as a whole that influence whether and what a team learns: type of team, structure of team (power dynamics), its composition (diversity of members' demographics, abilities, and functions), social familiarity of members, group dynamics (such as conflict management), learning orientation, and situational conditions (such as reward structure and the degree to which the organizational culture supports teamwork).

***Type of Team.*** Many different types of groups or teams can occur in organizations. Groups may be nurse teams in intensive care units, the board of directors of a firm, engineers and managers charged with developing a new product, or faculty members developing a new curriculum. Groups vary in their mode of interaction and communications. Some always meet face-to-face; others never do. Some are in existence for long periods of time; others for very short time periods. Knowing the kind of group and the dimensions on which groups may differ can help with understanding different levels of group learning requirements. What is beneficial for learning in some groups may be different in others. For instance, a natural work team that has been together for many years may adapt to changing conditions differently than a newly formed project team that usually communicates electronically and may never meet face-to-face. And the nature of learning goals may differ across team—some may need to learn incrementally whereas others may need radical learning. All of these may occur in the same organization at the same time.

Devine (2002) offered an integrative taxonomy of teams classified by underlying contextual dimensions, such as work cycle, physical-ability requirements, duration, task structure, active resistance, hardware dependence, and health risk. For example, teams with a low task structure, indefinite temporary duration, high member anxiety, and high physical abilities (e.g., military infantry squads and tank crews) may require considerable learning time and sophisticated stages of development to be successful compared to short-duration groups with low member anxiety and low physical-ability requirements.

Fleishman and Zaccaro's (1992) taxonomy of team performance functions offers another way to classify the level of development necessary for the team to be effective. They identified seven team-level processes: orientation (information acquisition and exchange), resource distribution (allocation of members and resources to roles and balancing work roles), timing, response coordination (synchronization of members' actions), motivation, systems monitoring, and procedure maintenance (such as developing and maintaining performance standards).

Each of these components, and the different ways they are combined, affect what and how the group learns.

***Structure of Team: Power Dynamics and Psychological Safety.*** Individuals with less power in organizations are concerned about appearing incompetent in front of those with more power, thus losing out on such things as rewards (Lee, 1997; Winter, 1993). When the structure of the team is such that there is a wide range of power levels present, individuals with low power may not be willing to actively contribute their ideas, evaluations, or suggestions (Edmondson, 2001).

However, teams designed with team psychological safety in mind can mitigate the influence of power dynamics. Team psychological safety is the shared belief that the team is safe for interpersonal risk taking (Edmondson, 1996, 1999). Usually, there is a tacit (assumed, unstated) sense of confidence that the team will not embarrass, reject, or punish someone for speaking up. Psychological safety develops as the group builds mutual trust among team members. It facilitates group learning behaviors because it alleviates concern about other members' reactions to actions that have the potential for embarrassment. For example, in a psychologically unsafe environment, members who do not want to be seen as incompetent may not bring up errors that could help the group catch problems before they occur. In contrast, in a safe environment, individual members feel more confident that other members will not hold the error against them or that bringing up the error will not negatively impact promotions, raises, or other outcomes.

***Diversity.*** Group member diversity (or heterogeneity) can be measured in terms of demographics (e.g., gender, age, or tenure) and cognitions (e.g., knowledge, values, or skills) (cf. Kilduff, Angelmar, & Mehra, 2000). Team diversity may enhance learning because team members have diverse knowledge and information and different ways of thinking and expressing themselves, which they can share with their fellow team members. Team diversity encourages members to consider a range of information and different perspectives. Reflecting on the team's objectives, strategies, and processes, recognizing problems, scanning the environment, discussing alternative views, and generating creative solutions creates an intellectual atmosphere conducive to learning. However, demographic and cognitive diversity could have negative effects by increasing communication problems and conflict and decreasing cohesion and interpersonal attraction. So we would predict that extreme heterogeneity and extreme homogeneity are unlikely to be optimal for learning.

***Cross-Functional Groups.*** In a company, cross-functional teams may include representatives from departments of engineering, production, marketing, sales, distribution, and finance who have all been brought together to bring a product or service from an idea to reality. Multiple functions on a team can be thought of as a form of diversity. People do not collaborate naturally when they are thrown into a cross-functional team. For example, rather than developing a product in a linear fashion, moving from one department to the next, cross-functional teams organize functions concurrently. That is, each member works on his or her function at the same time. The intention of collaboration is for competing interests to achieve win-win solutions. Though teams of this nature are expected to engage in generative learning, they must spend a concerted effort during the transitional stages of group development to come together as a team. This may require members to renew their skills and adapt to challenges and changes in the environment. They need training, coaching, facilitation, liaisons, and matrix structures for reporting relationships (e.g., team members reporting to the team leader and to the manager of their functional department).

***Social Familiarity.*** The extent to which team members know one another and are used to performing a task are likely to affect their pacing in performing the task and the quality of their output. If team members know each other well and have worked with each other before, they may have learned how to coordinate work in relation to the demands of the task. Familiarity varies in the strength of the ties among members. Strong ties suggest friendships and long-term interactions, and these increase the likelihood of complex relationships. For instance, strong ties may entail relationships in which information and resources are shared, status differences arise, and members have, or develop, affection for each other. These relationship characteristics may affect the members' mutual respect, patience in dealing with each other's foibles, and expectations for behavior and contributions to the team. Weak ties are likely in short-term interactions. They suggest simpler relationships and little interpersonal knowledge.

*Familiar teams* are ones in which members have interpersonal experience with one another on a variety of activities and over a lengthy time frame (strong ties). *Continuing teams* have members who are may be unfamiliar with each other initially but develop some familiarity (weak ties) as they work with each other periodically over time. *One-shot teams* have members who have neither initial familiarity nor a chance to develop familiarity over time (no ties). Research demonstrates that familiar teams are faster and have higher-quality output, but continuing teams achieve speed and quality levels of the initially familiar teams over time. One-shot teams are consistently slower and have lower-quality output (Harrison, Mohammed, McGrath, Florey, & Vanderstoep, 2003). Teams learn performance rhythms related to the task. Teams benefit right from the start when they are composed of people who know each other. When members initially do not know each other, the benefits of familiarity arrive fairly quickly.

***Conflict and Controversy.*** Most if not all groups experience conflict and controversy to some degree. In fact, one of the functions of groups *is* conflict. The idea that "more heads are better than one" suggests that different viewpoints and conflicts are not only natural, but expected. Teams learn by a full and critical discussion of the available information and ideas (cf. Tjosvold & Deemer, 1980). Groups may benefit when conflicts are explicit and resolved. In the process, members learn to confront issues, take different perspectives, and be creative. However, in some groups, conflicts hurt relationships and have a dysfunctional effect on team effectiveness as a result of lingering antagonism, distrust, and tension (De Dreu & Weingart, 2003). Discussions that raise disagreements may facilitate group learning and decision making in the short term as long as the conflict does not become too intense (Carnevale & Probst, 1998). As conflicts becomes deeper, they impose "cognitive load," which interferes with cognitive flexibility and creativity.

Another perspective is that task conflicts (e.g., disagreements about the distribution of resources, procedures and policies, and judgments and interpretation of facts) can benefit work on nonroutine complex tasks that do not have standard solutions and therefore demand full scrutiny of issues and deeper, more deliberate processing (Jehn, 1997). However, relationship conflicts (disagreements about personal taste, political preferences, values, and interpersonal style) may get in the way of any type of task, complex or simple, by limiting information processing and focusing energy on nonproductive issues. As such, whereas task conflicts may be beneficial, relationship conflicts are not likely to be. A meta-analysis of research on the topic (a meta-analysis averages results across different studies) showed that relationship conflicts were negatively correlated with team performance and team member satisfaction (De Dreu & Weingart, 2003). However, there were strong and negative correlations between task conflict, team performance, and team member satisfaction, especially in complex tasks—those involving decision making and project management compared to less complex production tasks. Therefore, task conflicts don't necessarily produce positive results, although they may not have a deleterious effect when there are no relationship conflicts and when the task is fairly routine.

***Team Learning Orientation.*** Team learning orientation is the climate for proactive learning—a gauge for the team's overall learning propensity (Bunderson & Sutcliffe, 2003). Building on the concept of an individual's learning orientation (see chap. 3), the notion of team learning orientation is the extent to which the team "(a) looks for opportunities to develop new skills and knowledge, (b) likes challenging and difficult assignments that teach new things, (c) is willing to take risks on new ideas in order to find out what works, (d) likes to work on things that require a lot of skill and ability, and (e) sees learning and developing skills as very important" (Bunderson & Sutcliffe, 2003, p. 553; see also Bunderson & Sutcliffe, 2002; VandeWalle, 1997). Team learning orientation arises from situational cues from the team leaders and members that signal desired goals and behaviors. These cues may be embedded in the leader's and/or other members' statements and behaviors. They may also come from task characteristics, rewards, and expressions of openness and trust. These cues affect members' perceptions of how the climate balances performance goals with learning goals. These perceptions become stronger as the members are integrated into the group and feel a sense of identification with the group. Because team members experience the same situational cues and may talk to each other about the meaning of these cues, members are likely to agree on their perceptions of the team's climate and will come to a shared understanding around the balance for performance and learning goals are emphasized and rewarded. This shared understanding, whether for performance or learning goals, enhances group decision making, collaborative problem solving, and coordination, all of which help maintain the group's goal focus (Bunderson & Sutcliffe, 2003).

Most groups in organizations are expected to produce a product or outcome of some type. But the extent to which the group learns in the process can be beneficial as well. The stronger the team's learning orientation, the more the team will generate and pursue new ideas associated with a wide range of team activities, including ideas that go beyond current thinking and practice. However, though team learning orientation increases learning activities that contribute to increased performance, a strong focus on learning also limits the team's performance by overemphasizing learning, just as too little attention to learning may decrease the team's performance (Bunderson & Sutcliffe, 2003). Learning takes time, and experimentation incurs costs. Moreover, there is no assurance that the learning and experimentation will pay off (Edmondson, 1999; March, 1991). Teams that have been low performing may benefit more from active experimentation and exploration of new solutions because they may discover the variation that leads to a functional result. However, high-performing teams may discard practical solutions while they pursue untried solutions, lowering the current level of performance.

Team leaders, facilitators, and members need to assess the value of a learning activity relative to performance and promote learning accordingly. Teams that are not performing well can benefit from learning goals. Teams that are performing well can benefit up to a point. Leaders and facilitators need to recognize learning potential and help group members recognize that potential. Though a high-performing team may benefit from a learning climate, the attention to learning only goes so far. Some groups may achieve this point earlier than others. This requires considerable sensitivity and calibration on the part of the team leader and members as they value learning and experimentation but decide how much time to spend on it.

### Situational Characteristics

Though organizations are systems in their own right, they are also environments in which groups perform and learn. Here we consider two situational characteristics that affect team learning: the reward structure and the degree to which the organizational culture supports teamwork.

***Reward Structure.*** To move from an individually based organization to one that supports teams, much of the infrastructure may need to be changed. We concentrate on one component of the infrastructure: the reward structure. The way group members learn to interact may depend on rewards and how they are allocated. Beersma et al. (2003) studied 75 four-person work teams composed of students performing a laboratory task. The students earned class credit and were eligible for cash prizes based on their performance. In the cooperative condition, the teams with the best overall team performance would receive a $40 reward, which would be split evenly among the team members. In the competitive condition, the individuals with the best performance would receive $10, regardless of how well their teams performed. The task required a fair amount of interdependence. In the competitive condition, if one team member wanted to hog resources, other team members would have less opportunity to perform well. In the cooperative condition, if one team member was working slowly or ineffectively, the other team members would need to "clean up after" this person. Performance was a sum of the standardized scores for speed and accuracy measured at both the team and individual level. The results showed that reward structure had different effects on different performance criteria. The teams worked faster under the competitive condition, each team member wanting to work fast to be more productive. The teams produced more accurate results under the cooperative condition, team members wanting to carefully coordinate production to yield higher-quality outcomes. The composition of the team members affected how well they did under the different reward structures. Teams working under the cooperative structure performed better when the team members were extroverted and agreeable, whereas teams working under the competitive structure performed better when the team members were low in these personality characteristics.

The authors of this study pointed out that many tasks entail trade-offs between speed and accuracy. A single reward structure may not maximize both aspects of performance, and managers should consider which aspect of the task is most important. Also, the choice of most important performance criterion and the corresponding reward structure could be used to guide the selection of people for the team. If accurate team output is a priority and a cooperative reward structure is used, team members who likely to work well together (e.g., are extroverted and high in agreeableness) should be selected for the team. If speed is a priority and a competitive reward structure is used, team members who are more competitive by nature or who work better as individuals should be selected. Not surprisingly, from the standpoint of team learning, the modes of interaction teams learn will depend on the reward structure that is established.

An open question is whether teams can change how they interact if the priorities for performance shift and the reward structure is also changed to highlight the new performance priorities. This may depend on the composition of the team. If the team members were selected because of their personalities, then they may have a hard time adapting to a new reward structure. If the team members are heterogeneous in these characteristics, the team may do less well under a given reward structure, at least initially, but have an easier time adapting to change.

***Team Culture.*** Many leaders in organizations outwardly embrace the idea of structuring the organization around teams, but make few changes in the organization to actually allow groups to excel. In order for groups to be supported in an organization, not only is there a need for changes in the infrastructure (such as rewards discussed previously), but the organizational culture must also be modified to be supportive of teams and collaboration. Things to consider include:

- Is there a class structure in the organization—is there a strong hierarchy or a feeling of community?
- Is the culture participative—or are there a few exclusive star players who are given opportunities and everyone else?
- Who holds the information—is information held by a few or is it shared?
- Who makes the operational decisions—are they made by top managers or by the people most closely related to the decision?
- Is there a clear reason for teams to exist—teams must exist for a reason and they need the same sort of direction and accountability that we mentioned in the performance culture for individuals in chapter 4.

We have examined a number of team and situational conditions that affect group process. These include the diversity of the team, cross-functional representation, social familiarity, conflicts, psychological safety, learning orientation, and reward structure. A good question is how do these factors interact to affect team process and outcome? In the next section, we review a study that examined how individual and situational variables work together to affect group learning.

### The Interaction between Situational Conditions and Team Member Characteristics

Ellis et al. (2003) examined the extent to which personal and situational variables affect the acquisition of knowledge and skill within interactive project teams. Specifically, they studied the effects of cognitive ability, workload distribution, agreeableness, openness to experience, and structure on team learning.

They reasoned that three factors would affect team learning: (a) attentional capacity, (b) constructive controversy, and (c) truth-supported wins.

*Attentional capacity* refers to the ability of the team to focus on tasks and process more mental elements at a time as they do so. That is, the group processes incoming information, stores it for later use, retrieves information that has been stored, and, of course, uses that information to complete the task. The more cognitive ability team members bring to the task, the more the team overall is likely to be capable to acquire, process, and apply knowledge and skills needed to accomplish the work of the team.

How much attentional capacity is needed is likely to be a function of how the work is organized. Teams that are overloaded with information are not likely to learn as quickly as those that have a workload they can handle. Overloading some individuals but not others will interfere with learning. There, unevenly distributing the workload within a team will be likely to have a detrimental effect on learning.

*Constructive controversy* refers to discussing opposing perspectives. Teams learn by a full and critical discussion of the available information and ideas (cf. Tjosvold & Deemer, 1980). Some constructive conflict is likely when team members bring different sorts of information and expertise to the task. On the other hand, uncritical agreement within a team can result in "groupthink"—the idea that premature consensus has a negative effect on problem solving (Aldag & Fuller, 1993; Janis, 1982). Teams in which members are high in the personality variable agreeableness will have lower levels of learning, whereas those in which members are high in openness to experience will have higher levels of learning.

A *truth-supported wins* model of team problem solving suggests that if at least two team members share access to the same information, the group will attend to and acquire the information collectively (Hinsz, Tindale, & Vollrath, 1997). A team structure that allows two members to share expertise and information-processing responsibilities, called "role partners," is likely to be more effective in promoting team learning than a structure in which each team member represents a different function with unique expertise or information or a different division with unique responsibilities for performing a particular aspect of the task. When team members have unique functions or divisional responsibilities they are not likely to pay attention to their unique information because they cannot easily share it with the other team members. Even if they do, team members will have different frames of reference, limiting the value of the information. So the optimum, or most balanced, organizing framework for team learning is likely to be the role partners structure.

To test these predictions, Ellis et al. (2003) studied 109 four-person project teams of undergraduates students working on a simulated task. The task provided an index of effective and ineffective decisions of teach team member indicating the extent to which the team member learned and applied information as the team progressed. Team learning was the sum of each team member's score. Before performing the task, team members completed measures of cognitive ability and personality. Workload was unevenly distributed when one team member encountered the majority of situations with unknown information, whereas workload was evenly distributed when each team member encountered the same number of situations with unknown information. Structure was manipulated by giving each team member control over one type of function, each team member had all functions but represented a different division, or team members were paired so that two team members had the same function and represented the same division.

The results showed that teams learned more when composed of people who were high in cognitive ability and when the workload was distributed evenly. However, team learning was lower when the teams were composed of people who were high in agreeableness. Teams learned less when they were functionally or divisionally organized than when they were organized in a paired structure. The results showed that indeed attentional capacity is likely to affect information processing in teams, that constructive controversy is likely to be promoted when team members vary or are low in agreeableness than when all members are high (although openness to experience did not have the expected positive effect, suggesting that being disagreeable, rather than open to experience, prompts conflicting discussion, which in turn enhances learning).

Implications of these results for team learning include the following: First, group composition affects learning, and so who is selected for the team will influence its progress. Organizations that want to increase learning within project teams should include individuals who are high in cognitive ability. Also, teams should not be staffed with people who are all high in agreeableness—instead the group should be mixed on this factor. Whereas agreeableness would help promote group cohesion, too much agreeableness could hurt team learning.

Second, organizations can enhance the link between team member characteristics and team learning by paying attention to workload distribution and team structure. Workload should be distributed evenly among the team members, and several members of the team should have similar access to the same information. Although this will not guarantee maximum learning, it will reduce barriers to team progress as members acquire the needed knowledge and skills.

## ASSESSMENT OF GROUP LEARNING

Continuing our theme about the importance of assessment in understanding and fostering continuous learning, team-learning assessment may measure learning of each individual in a team and then average the results across the team members. Team members may be surveyed about their reactions and perceptions of learning, particularly, what they learned from participating in the group and how they contributed to educating other group members and to changing patterns of behavior in the group and improving group performance. In addition, assessors may observe group behaviors and conversations and document changing patterns of interaction. These patterns may then be correlated with events within the group and to group outcomes.

Assessors may follow the group over time as a task is completed or as new tasks are undertaken. Measures may examine the effects of groups within the organization as members are trained and gain more experience in the group process—for instance, as quality improvement teams are implemented throughout a hospital to improve patient services. Table 6.1 is an excerpt from a survey of hospital quality improvement team members. The survey questions ask the team members what they learned and how group interactions prompted members to learn about each other's potential to contribute to the group. Other measures may reflect the extent to which team members and leaders are trained, gain experience with the group process, become adept at moving from group to group, creating new groups, and moving a group to a successful conclusion. Assessors may observe and record organizational events, decisions, and outcomes over time, the amount of time devoted to group process discussions, and the time to task completion. The availability of support factors should also be taken into account in the assessment. These may include team facilitators, supportive supervisors who form teams or assign employees to teams, or other team resources.

Assessors may identify teams that can be classified as continuous learners. These may be teams that successfully move on to one task or project after another, teams that can lose old members and integrate new members with little loss of progress, teams that can easily merge or cooperate with other teams, teams in which the resolution of conflicts promote learning (e.g., the team doesn't repeat mistakes or repeat conflicts), and teams in which new routines are established and established routines are altered with little to no conflict or resistance.

## CONCLUSION

Group development refers to the process gains teams experience that allow them to be increasingly effective in accomplishing their goals. As a result, they can produce more than the sum of the individual members if they worked alone. The developmental process begins as team members establish mutual trust and develop a shared conception of the way they ought to operate and the goals they strive to achieve. In short, they become cohesive. Once this is in place, group members can monitor each other's behavior, essentially watching out for each other, giving each other feedback, and backing each other up when someone falls short. There is a mindfulness about the way the group operates. The members realize each other's abilities and potential contributions and smooth the way for each team member to do his or her "thing" in the interest of the group. They become synergistic in the integration of each other's efforts, ultimately accomplishing more than the sum of their parts.

Different theories have evolved to describe stages of group development. One approach holds that a group follows a life cycle—forming, norming, storming, performing, and finally, adjourning. Another approach holds that groups quickly reach a stage of equilibrium, but may have to adapt to environmental changes—members coming and going, changing goals and expectations, new technologies, and so forth. Yet another approach suggests that groups flounder in less than

TABLE 6.1

Excerpt From a Survey of Quality Improvement Team Members

To what extent did you learn the following from being a part of this team? (Fill in the circles for all that apply.)

1. ❍ Elements of quality improvement process
2. ❍ How to assess quality of service
3. ❍ How to collect data to determine problems
4. ❍ How to collect benchmarking data to compare our service to other organizations
5. ❍ Ways of cooperating with others in a team setting
6. ❍ Ways to express my emotions in a team setting
7. ❍ How my colleagues in different areas of medicine think about their fields
8. ❍ How to respect others' opinions regardless of their professional background
9. ❍ How to contribute my expertise to a group
10. ❍ When to speak up to have my views heard
11. ❍ How to influence a group
12. ❍ When to tell others what I think of them

Please indicate the extent to which the following questions apply to the quality improvement team and your role in the team, whether the team is currently working or whether the team has completed its work. For each item, rate the extent to which each of the following items applies to the team using a 7-point scale from 1 = low to 7 = high. Fill in the circle that best applies.

| | Low 1 | 2 | 3 | 4 | 5 | 6 | High 7 |
|---|---|---|---|---|---|---|---|
| 1. This team looks for opportunities to develop new skills and knowledge. | ❍ | ❍ | ❍ | ❍ | ❍ | ❍ | ❍ |
| 2. This team likes challenging and difficult problems that teach new things. | ❍ | ❍ | ❍ | ❍ | ❍ | ❍ | ❍ |
| 3. This team is willing to take risks on new ideas in order to find out what works. | ❍ | ❍ | ❍ | ❍ | ❍ | ❍ | ❍ |
| 4. This team likes to work on things that require a lot of skill and ability. | ❍ | ❍ | ❍ | ❍ | ❍ | ❍ | ❍ |
| 5. This team sees learning and developing skills as very important. | ❍ | ❍ | ❍ | ❍ | ❍ | ❍ | ❍ |
| 6. If you make a mistake on this team, it is often held against you. | ❍ | ❍ | ❍ | ❍ | ❍ | ❍ | ❍ |
| 7. Team members let each other know how their own knowledge and skills can contribute to the team's objectives. | ❍ | ❍ | ❍ | ❍ | ❍ | ❍ | ❍ |
| 8. I am open with others on the team about what I think of them. | ❍ | ❍ | ❍ | ❍ | ❍ | ❍ | ❍ |
| 9. I seek feedback from others on the team. | ❍ | ❍ | ❍ | ❍ | ❍ | ❍ | ❍ |
| 10. Team members educate each other about their own profession. | ❍ | ❍ | ❍ | ❍ | ❍ | ❍ | ❍ |
| 11. Team members are open with each other about their own limitations. | ❍ | ❍ | ❍ | ❍ | ❍ | ❍ | ❍ |
| 12. Team members tell each other how they feel about being on the team. | ❍ | ❍ | ❍ | ❍ | ❍ | ❍ | ❍ |
| 13. Team members ask each other about whether their ideas are understood. | ❍ | ❍ | ❍ | ❍ | ❍ | ❍ | ❍ |
| 14. Team members ask each other about what they think others expect of them. | ❍ | ❍ | ❍ | ❍ | ❍ | ❍ | ❍ |
| 15. Team members ask each other about the accuracy of their technical knowledge. | ❍ | ❍ | ❍ | ❍ | ❍ | ❍ | ❍ |
| 16. Team members ask each other about values and attitudes of the hospital. | ❍ | ❍ | ❍ | ❍ | ❍ | ❍ | ❍ |
| 17. Team members give each other feedback about their contributions to the group. | ❍ | ❍ | ❍ | ❍ | ❍ | ❍ | ❍ |

optimal ways until they reach the point where something must be done if the task is to be completed. Then the team members muster their experience and capabilities, build on the knowledge of each other acquired during the early meetings, and get the task done (punctuated equilibrium).

Different types of learning occur in transitional and stable stages. In both, this learning may be adaptive, generative, or transformative. In transitional stages, the group focuses on process issues. During these stages, group members need to develop a sense of mutual regard, publicly agree on how they will proceed when conflicts arise, and apply constructive criticism through specific, behavioral, and nonthreatening feedback. Only in periods of stability can the group fully concentrate on learning how to do the task better.

A variety of characteristics and conditions can also influence how learning unfolds. As individuals are parts of groups, their characteristics, such as cognitive ability, personality, background, motivation, and team orientation, determine how each person approaches the group. Together, these characteristics form characteristics of the team—its composition, members' familiarity with each other, their sense of psychological safety, and the group's readiness to learn. Organizational conditions, such as reward structure and overall support for teamwork, also influence group learning. Not surprisingly, organizational and individual conditions interact to affect team process and outcome. Variables such as attentional capacity, constructive controversy, and members (at least two) sharing expertise and information-processing responsibilities and acquiring information collectively affect learning. The group's learning capacity is likely to be higher when team members are high in cognitive ability. Members should also be high in agreeableness if the goal is to promote group cohesion. Workloads should be distributed evenly among team members, and team members should have equal access to the same information in order to reduce barriers to team progress and promote group learning.

In the next two chapters, we move from group to organization learning and development. In doing so, we find that individual and group learning and development is key to organization learning and development. Organizational learning and development occur as groups communicate their experiences and modus operandi. In this way, they spread the norms and processes they established within their group to other groups, broadly share their learning, and further the growth of the entire enterprise.

## QUESTIONS FOR THOUGHT AND DISCUSSION

1. Do group members influence what the group is interested in and capable of learning? How? In what ways?
2. Think about groups you have been in or that you observed. How long did it take them to make progress? What helped them move ahead? What prevented them from moving ahead?

3. Now think of groups you have been in that seemed to move very slowly. How did you feel as a member? . . . impatient? . . . frustrated? . . . angry? What was the reaction of the other members to this slow (or no) movement? What happened and why? Was the group successful in the end? What happened to make it so?
4. When a group starts, do the group members take the time to get to know one another? Do they share past experiences and inform each other of their expertise?
5. In your experience, what individual, group, and organization characteristics affect group learning?
6. Once again, consider groups you have been in. What stage model applied best and why? How much did the group's progress depend on the leader? . . . on particular members? . . . on the particular task or situation?
7. Can you give examples of groups that learned adaptively, generatively, and/or transformatively? Describe each type of group learning and factors that prompted it and helped it along.
8. Have you been part of a group that seemed to develop a rhythm for operating—a way of doing things that really worked? Describe the patterns of behavior that contributed to that rhythm.
9. What happened when someone left the group and/or a new person joined the group? What happened when the goal changed or some other unexpected event occurred, for instance, the group was given a tighter time line? Was the group able to adapt? Did this lead to new ways of operating, or did the group return to old patterns of behavior after the emergency ended?

## TOPICS FOR RESEARCH

1. Study team members' motivation to be on the team, seek self-verifying and self-enhancing feedback, and contribute to the group process. What factors increase member motivation to join and participate in a group?
2. Study the transition of teams from a collection of individuals to a cohesive system. Examine emergence of shared mental models, transactive memory, and group cohesiveness in heterogeneous and homogeneous groups with high and low task demands. How do group members monitor each other's contributions to the group, establish a sense of mindfulness about what they are doing, and develop synergy?
3. Determine the relationship between different models of group development (integrative life cycle, equilibrium/adaptive, and punctuated equilibrium) and group composition and purpose. How do time pressure, task difficulty, member competence, and member familiarity affect whether different stage models emerge?

4. What do groups have to know and what do they learn about their interaction (e.g., how to alter their configuration, modify their habits, and establish roles and routines)? What do they need to know at different stages of development?
5. Generate examples of adaptive, generative, and transformative learning. What factors (situational conditions, group member characteristics) determine which applies? Study the match between members' readiness for different types of learning and the needs of the group during transitional and stable stages of development. Replicate and extend Ellis et al.'s (2003) research on the extent to which personal and situational variables affect learning in interactive project teams.
6. Do groups establish learning goals? Develop assessment methods to determine group effectiveness and learning outcomes.
7. Study the differences in learning requirements between different types of groups and group tasks. Classify groups according to a taxonomy of teams (based on such contextual dimensions as work cycle and task structure) and predict the extent to which are able to learn at different stages of their development.

CHAPTER

# 7

# Understanding Organizational Continuous Learning

This chapter begins the third and final iteration of our nested model of individual, group, and organization learning as we focus on the organization as a whole. When we think of a business organization, we tend to think of large organizations employing hundreds, thousands, or tens of thousands of people. However, a single person can incorporate and become a "business," for example, a tailor or a business consultant. Small groups can also be organizations, for instance, a small grocery store, laundry, or a doctor's office. We define an *organization* as *a group of people intentionally organized to accomplish a particular goal or set of goals.* Similar to individuals and groups, organizations are goal-oriented systems involved in intention-bound work, with everyone in the organization sharing the same organizational goals. Of course, individuals may have personal goals, for instance, to make more money, advance to a position of power, or develop friendships. Work groups and business units may have their own goals, such as finishing a project on time and under budget. Yet the preeminent focus of the organization is on goals all employees—groups and the individuals in them—hold in common.

Organizational goals can be expressed as a vision, a set of values, and/or strategic goals. Members of the organization often have a shared vision or image in their minds about how the organization should be working and how it should appear when things are going well. Organizations operate according to tacit or explicit values that guide policies, procedures, behaviors, and decisions. These values are, in part, the culture of the organization. Organization members strive to achieve key or strategic goals directed toward the overall mission of the organization, for instance, manufacture and sell breakfast cereal.

Organizations possess certain characteristics that make them distinct from individuals. Organizations are systems developed and operated by people. Their structure is inseparable from the functioning of the system (Katz & Kahn, 1967). The "contrived-ness" and "event structured-ness" mean that organizations can be designed for a wide range of objectives. They do not necessarily follow the growth curves of humans, and they require control mechanisms of various kinds to keep their components functioning in the required interdependent fashion. All this is rather obvious, perhaps.

Organizations also possess certain characteristics that make them distinct from work groups, although a group, like an individual, can be an organization. For example, organizations have subsystems and processes that include *production* (the work that gets done), *support* (procurement, disposal, and institutional relations), *maintenance* (tying people into their roles), and *managerial* (controlling, coordinating, and directing the subsystems). Groups, as opposed to organizations, typically do not have such an elaborate structure of subsystems, although group members may take on different roles. Each organizational subsystem has a way of doing things, along with other subsystems, to achieve the overall goals of the organization. Often, these systems and processes are defined by plans, policies, and procedures. Of course, these are subject to change as the organization adapts to a changing environment and shifting goals, acquires new modes of operation, and sometimes transforms into one or more very different entities.

In this chapter, we describe what we mean by organizational learning, including the role of feedback. We then consider two ways that organizations learn. First, we connect individual, group, and organization learning through a variety of tacit and explicit knowledge management systems. Then we describe adaptive, generative, and transformative organization learning.

## DEFINING ORGANIZATIONAL LEARNING

The concept of organizational learning stems from developments that began in the 1930s and 1940s with John Dewey's work on experiential learning (1938/1997) and Elton Mayo (1946) and others' work on human relations in the workplace that led to understanding the value of participative management and action learning. Other background developments on organizational thought and practice were systems thinking and mental models in the 1940s and many perspectives of business and management such as strategy, culture, structure, and problem-solving ability (Society for Organizational Learning, 2003). These led to the popularization of the concept of organizational learning, which emerged with the publication of Argyris and Schön's (1978) book on the topic.

To date, organizational learning has been explored from five different perspectives (Wang & Ahmed, 2003). These perspectives overlap and are not mutually exclusive—in fact, they can be blended as we do in this book:

1. Organizational learning is a *collectivity of individual learning*. Organizational learning occurs when employees within the organization experience a problem and explore and try to solve it to better the organization. In this case, a learning organization would focus on valuing, managing, and enhancing the individual learning of its employees. This perspective is addressed in chapters 2, 3, and 4 of this book.

2. Organizational learning is the *development of culture*. An organizational culture is composed of the values, behaviors, and attitudes of employees ordered in a coherent, commonly understood way that allows them to make sense of unfamiliar events. Organizations can develop learning cultures by establishing mechanisms that support employees' continuous learning. Again, individuals do the learning whereas the organization makes this possible. We addressed this perspective in chapter 4.

3. Organizational learning is *continuous improvement*. From this perspective, a learning organization is continuously and incrementally moving forward by providing learning mechanisms and encouraging employees to take advantage of them. Employees continuously expand their capacity to accomplish the organization's goals. New and expansive ways of thinking are nurtured. Employees are continually learning how to learn together (Senge, 1990), and the organization's products and services continuously improve as a result. The organization develops "competencies" (new or better methods and procedures) as a result of individuals acquiring and generating new knowledge and developing new working relationships with each other (group learning).

4. Organizational learning is *innovation*. An organization strives for breakthroughs and quantum leaps forward in its products and services. The organization fosters individual and group creativity, encouraging employees to experiment with new and different products and services or methods for producing them. This allows the organization to maintain competitive edge in the marketplace or to enter new markets. Continuous and incremental improvement and innovation can be thought of as generative organizational learning.

5. Organizations are *systems that learn*. Organizations can be seen from a variety of different systems models, for instance, social systems (Crossan, Lane, & White, 1999; Katz & Kahn, 1967), living systems (Capra, 1997; Jaques, 2002), or natural systems (Laszlo, 1996). From the social-systems perspective, organizations are contrived collections of people (and therefore imperfect). From the living-systems perspective, organizations are constantly changing (learning) sets of individuals and groups. From the natural-systems perspective, organizations are organic, meaning an integration of functions and roles that are constantly interacting in accord with structured yet fluid relationships and hierarchies. Organizational learning involves monitoring and obtaining data about the environment (scanning), translating events and understanding consistent with prior conceptualizations of the environment (interpretation), and formulating knowledge about

the relationships between actions within the organization and the environment (learning) (Daft & Weick, 1984). Learning in this sense would mean some sort of change in the organization's "behavior." Changes in an organization's behavior may be reflected in changes in vision, strategies, language, tools, documents, images, symbols, procedures, regulations, practices, routines, and final products or services, all of which are explicit or observable, and rules of thumb, underlying assumptions, and shared worldviews, which are tacit or not easily observable. This is the perspective we focus on in this chapter.

In summary, organizational learning is the changing patterns of interactions, policies, and procedures that emerge from the collectivity of individual learning, continuous improvement, the development of culture, innovation, and systems operations. *Learning organizations* are systems of individuals and groups that do this well. They have the culture, structure, and resources to support and encourage continuous organizational learning.

Note that organization change does not necessarily mean that learning has occurred. Organizations may engage in frequent changes in response to shifting business conditions and emerging opportunities. Witness the mergers in the banking industry and altered corporate strategies in the telecommunications and cable industries. Organizations alter their direction, sometimes quite dramatically (e.g., recall AT&T, after a stream of failed ventures, withdrawing from the consumer market in July of 2004 after an 80% plunge in profits). However, this doesn't mean that change does not lead to learning. Indeed, groups and organizations may learn from tough experiences, just as individuals may learn from failure. Learning requires tracking and reflecting on results and experiences, interpreting their meaning, and using the information to change behavior and relationships. Feedback, our next topic, plays a major role in the process.

## ORGANIZATIONAL FEEDBACK

Feedback plays a crucial role in learning at the organizational level just as it does at the individual and group levels. Organizational learning does not occur without feedback. The organization uses feedback to determine whether a modified or new process, action, or policy "worked" and whether or not it should be refined and ultimately institutionalized or at least incorporated into the organization's repertoire of possible responses to similar situations. Without feedback, organization members are unable to determine whether in another similar situation they should repeat a behavior, modify it, or do something else entirely.

Feedback can come from a variety of sources, including employees who carry out processes in the organization, customers or clients who use the products and services, objective indicators of performance (e.g., sales data), or the larger environment, for instance, government, the public (society), the economy, or the competitive marketplace.

Another source of feedback is multisource or 360-degree feedback. Multisource ratings can be used at the organizational level by averaging data about individual employees. Data can also be gathered from different sources about groups or the organization as a whole. Such feedback can help organizations address the needs of strategically important populations inside and outside the organization. It can help bring everyone up to a standard, by defining and setting standards and providing data for comparison to the standards. It can be used as a tool to change the culture by communicating to employees and groups the skills needed to implement the business strategy or direction effectively. In addition, it can change organizational norms regarding giving and receiving feedback.

Ratings that are averaged across all people rated in an organization tell us about how the organization as a whole is operating. Average ratings at the organization level are less threatening to people than individual-level feedback. Still, organization-level data need to be interpreted to guide directions for development. This may mean new policies or procedures, or simply encouraging people to behave differently.

## HOW ORGANIZATIONS LEARN: LINKING INDIVIDUAL AND GROUP LEARNING TO ORGANIZATIONAL LEARNING

In some cases, organization learning depends on individuals and groups transferring their learning to others in the organization and in the process reformulating routines and standard operating procedures. Organizational learning can occur when individual and group learning become institutionalized—that is, embedded in routines, systems, structures, culture, and strategy of the organization as a whole (Crossan et al., 1999; Vera & Crossan, 2003). This happens as individuals intuit and interpret their experiences, groups integrate information and perceptions across individuals, and the organization institutionalizes new behaviors and policies. This is both a feed-forward process (e.g., integrating to institutionalizing) and a feed-back process (institutionalizing to intuiting). Crossan et al. (1999) defined each component as follows:

*Intuiting* is the preconscious realization of what has happened or what is possible (intuition by experts supports exploitation or use of existing modes of operation; intuition by entrepreneurs supports exploration and innovation).

*Interpreting* is the explanation in words or action of an insight or idea.

*Integrating* is the establishment a shared understanding and coordination of action by mutual adjustment (initially informal and tacit).

*Institutionalizing* is the formalization of coordinated actions that are recurring and significant; embedding learning by individuals and groups into the organization in the form of systems, structures, standard operating procedures, and strategies.

### Knowledge Transfer and Management

How does knowledge transfer from individual to group to organization and back again? This is the intersection of the concepts of organization learning and knowledge management. *Knowledge management* is the process of locating, organizing, transferring, and using the continually evolving set of behaviors, knowledge, and skills that resides in individuals, groups, and the organization.

One approach to knowledge management is through an attempt to control and manage the knowledge within an organization aimed at achieving the company's objectives. Unfortunately, trying to do this explicitly has proven difficult as companies experiment with such technologies as document tracking, warehousing, and building web pages and intranets. So far, these technologies have actually made people's jobs more, not less, difficult.

Another way knowledge is transferred is when an employee follows another's instructions. In the course of on-the-job training, employees are likely to consult others who are more knowledgeable and experienced than they are. However, experts may have difficulty instructing those who are less knowledgeable because the characteristics that constitute expertise may interfere with their ability to convey information to novices (Hinds, Patterson, & Pfeffer, 2001).

Experts differ from beginners in how they communicate information to others and promote others' learning. Experts organize their knowledge differently from beginners. Experts have acquired tacit knowledge that makes them adept at performing tasks. Hinds et al. (2001) found that experts use more abstract and advanced statements and fewer concrete statements than do beginners when providing task instructions to novices. Novices who are instructed by beginners perform better and report fewer problems with the instructions than those instructed by experts. However, novices working on another task (a different type of circuit) performed better—that is, were better able to transfer their learning when they had been instructed by an expert rather than a beginner. The expert's use of more abstract concepts helped the students form the abstractions needed to transfer the learning from one task to another.

Thus, the experience of beginners may be leveraged to bring novices up to a level where they can be productive. In fact, beginners may be better than experts in instructing novices. In general, transfer of knowledge can benefit from matching skill levels between the instructor and person being taught. Peer-to-peer learning may be quite beneficial. Workers discuss with each other details of their jobs. As such, employees become part of a learning community of peers. Still, experts have their place. Their ability to convey abstract, advanced knowledge may be especially important if novices are required to perform a variety of tasks in the same domain or the same task in different contexts or if they must adjust to a volatile environment or changing expectations for different aspects of task performance (Hinds et al., 2001).

A third approach to knowledge management is through emerging shared mental models (as we already discussed in chap. 6). Mental models are deeply held images of how things work, and, not surprisingly, these images influence what we do (Senge, 1990). Such models emerge in our minds as we experience and reflect and converse on what happens to us and what we observe and as we form abstract concepts to interpret our observations and ultimately test them by taking action and seeing what happens. Successful and unsuccessful actions are shared, typically informally, as insights to others. Over time, a shared understanding emerges and becomes a general map that guides reactions to similar situations in the future. Organizations as a whole learn through the shared experiences and actions of their employees, customers, suppliers, and others connected to them.

Cycles of individual learning through observation (experience), assessment (reflection), design (abstraction), and implementation (testing) influence the shared mental models that arise in the organization (Kim, 1993). The shared mental models make organizational memory usable. They incorporate the subtle interconnections between individuals and groups within the organization and between the organization and the world beyond it.

At the next level, group members share mental models, which become embedded in the routines and norms of acceptable behavior in the group. Groups, in turn, contribute to the organization's shared mental models as members share their mental models from one team that they are in with another team they are in.

The process can work in reverse as well, with organizational practices affecting group operations and individual mental images. Groups adopt practices by observing other groups and following standard procedures. Similarly, individuals learn about organizational and group practices by talking to others in the organization, observing them, imitating their behaviors, and adhering to standard practices and policies. These become the pathways by which individuals and groups implement strategies envisioned and communicated by top executives and others (peers and subordinates). They also dictate, or at least limit, how people respond in uncertain situations, perhaps emergencies. Not that people can't think for themselves. Indeed, common and accepted practices may include voicing concerns, divergent opinions, and new ideas. As such, there is a tension between the old and new. On the one hand, organizations have established behaviors that are expected and accepted. They have deeply held beliefs that are part of the organization's culture and are embedded in the mental images of the individuals within the organization. On the other hand, organizations have a need for novel, innovative responses to changed situations or the need to create change as a means to enhance the continued vitality of the organization (e.g., entering new markets or creating new products and services).

A fourth approach to understanding how knowledge is transferred from one part of an organization to another is through communities of practice. Communities of practice are groups of people who together cumulate and share their collective learning. An example would be the UPS workers who get together at lunch not just to eat, but to exchange information and even divide up the workload for the afternoon (Cohen & Prusak, 2001). Knowledge within communities of practice tends to be "leaky"—it passes freely from one member to another and evolves as members together interpret and add their own experiences. Communities of practice are also parts of larger networks. That is, individuals may be part of more than one. Or they may leave one and join another by changing jobs. Thus, communities of practice are linked together via these networks. Knowledge continues to transfer or leak along the networks built by these communities of practice. Knowledge "sticks" where practices are not shared across communities and networks do not exist.

### Summary

Organizational learning can be a function of individuals and groups transferring their learning to others in the organization. In the process, the organization "learns" in that new modes of interaction, policies, and procedures are adopted, new structures are designed, and new and improved outcomes emerge. Organizational learning itself can become institutionalized as part of the organization culture. For instance, members of the organization learn to share their knowledge and experiences as a matter of course so that other individuals and groups benefit. Knowledge transfer, and more generally, knowledge management, is a key ingredient to organizational learning. Control mechanisms and processes may be devised to promote communication of new knowledge. Giving instructions to others is another mode. In addition, employees may share their vision and conceptualization of how things should be, and they may establish communities of practice to delve into new ideas and learn together.

## ADAPTIVE, GENERATIVE, AND TRANSFORMATIVE ORGANIZATIONAL LEARNING

Organization learning can be adaptive, generative, or transformative, as can individual and group learning. Consider how these three types of learning apply to organizations.

### Adaptive Learning

Organizations need to ensure survival in a changing environment. In most formal organizations, structures are specifically designed to sense relevant changes in the outside world and translate the meaning of these changes for the organization. These structures include research and development, product research, market research, and long-range planning. They track changes and prompt the organization to make needed adaptations in response to consumer taste, cultural norms and values, competition, and economic and political power. Organizations can adapt by changing practices, policies, and procedures or relatively minor reconfigurations in structure, possibly some downsizing. The nature and purpose of the organization do not change much, however, and these changes are made with little turmoil, and sometimes with little thought (as in a "drive-by reorganization" where the reorganization is seen as the "medicine of choice" for problems faced, without thinking through the consequences and repercussions of the rearrangement; Albrecht, 2003).

***Single-Loop Learning.*** Argyris and Schön (1978) used the phrase, "single loop learning," to refer to adaptive learning. Errors are detected and corrected within the framework of existing organizational policies, procedures, structures, and practices. Single-loop learning is like a thermostat. When a thermostat in an air conditioner "senses" that it is too hot, the thermostat switches the air conditioner to "on." Similarly, organizations adjust rather automatically as they sense changes in the environment. Of course, how people in the organization interpret the environmental change will determine how the organization adapts.

Because environmental changes are often ambiguous and complex, the organization may not be able to distinguish between changes that are important and changes that are not. The organization must filter and interpret incoming information and make decisions based on those interpretations. One way that organizations interpret the environment is by categorizing changes as threats or opportunities (Dutton & S. Jackson, 1987). *Threats* are situations in which loss is likely and over which the organization has little control. *Opportunities* are situations in which gain is likely and over which the organization has a fair amount of control. Perceiving a situation as a threat that reduces control leads people to make conservative, internally directed actions (Chattopadhyay, Glick, & Huber, 2001). Organizational leaders are likely to be careful and slow to respond if they feel that they may lose control. In contrast, perceiving a situation as likely to generate losses leads to riskier, externally directed actions, perhaps because the possibility of gaining control is recognized as low and a "what the heck" attitude prevails. Opportunities are responded to in less predictable ways (Chattopadhyay et al., 2001). In any case, these threats and opportunities are conditions that generate adaptive responses, not cataclysmic transitions.

### Generative Learning

Generative learning is purposefully adding new knowledge and skills to change organizational actions. Generative change may take the form of continuous, incremental improvements or large, discontinuous changes. An example would be introducing a total quality management (TQM) program that calls for cross-functional teams to identify areas for improvement, implement their ideas, and track the gains. Participants learn how to work together to collect data about a problem, establish likely causes, create ways to change (improve) the situation or solve the problem, implement the change, and ensure that the change has the desired effect in the long run. Learning occurs about the problem at hand and about how to participate in such a process to bring about continuous improvement. Another example is introducing a competency model as a means for development planning and performance management. The competency model specifies behaviors, skills, and areas of knowledge that are important to the organization's performance. Human resource professionals develop the model by interviewing executives and studying excellent performers. The model communicates to employees what they should pay attention to in assessing themselves and establishing and carrying out a development plan. The competency model can be a way to increase the capability of the entire organization and sensitize managers and employees to the importance of development.

Discontinuous changes are major shifts that are infrequent, episodic, and intentional—for instance, the development and introduction of a major new data system or communication technology, a restructuring of the organizational hierarchy and with it changes in jobs and reporting relationships, a merger with another firm, or organizational strategies, such as entering global markets. These changes are planned, formal, and goal directed, and the organization tries to manage their introduction (Pettigrew, Woodman, & Cameron, 2001). They are in contrast to incremental changes, which are ongoing, evolving, and cumulative (Weick & Quinlan, 1999). Discontinuous changes require that employees alter their work tasks and routines, attend to different stimuli and criteria for effectiveness, and concentrate on what they need to do to accommodate these changing demands. The knowledge and routine interactions that were needed for error-free performance are likely to be disrupted. Employees find that ways of interacting that they learned well and that worked over long periods of time now don't fit new work structures and demands. Mutual understandings of how to get things done go by the wayside with no clear ways of filling these gaps. "By unsettling the entrenched relationships between people and technology, discontinuous change reduces access to this shared memory. Consequently, latent errors increase" (Ramanujam, 2003, p. 610).

Latent errors are deviations from well-structured, accepted procedures and policies that have negative consequences. Although the procedures and policies have been ingrained in the organization, for instance, in placing orders or handling customer complaints, frame-breaking change disrupts these routines, leaving the organization open to errors. Errors in judgment are also likely to occur as people analyze the changing situation and make choices about handling problems for which they have little experience. Discontinuous change makes previously routine activities prone to error (Ramanujam, 2003). Latent errors portend, and may even contribute to, organizational disasters or costly mistakes, such as product recalls, bankruptcies, or equipment malfunctions.

Discontinuous change is more likely to have negative effects in high-risk situations, which, by definition, are more prone to errors than routine operations. In high-risk work, many things can go wrong, and small errors can have major consequences (Perrow, 1984). Strategies to manage high-risk situations include formalization of safety and reliability goals, centralization, continuous training, constant monitoring, and redundancy (Roberts, 1993, as cited in Ramanujam, 2003). These factors constrain errors under standard conditions. However, these error control mechanisms may be disrupted in the face of discontinuous change when employees pay less attention to them. Ramanujam studied internal audit reports of the operations of the North American Financial Institution, which provides retail, private, and corporate banking services. Latent errors in a sample of audit reports included noncompliance with "know-your-customer" procedures, inadequate encryption of electronic transmission of sensitive customer information, significant delays in critical account reconcilements, and failure to test business continuity plan as required by corporate policy. As expected, the study found that disruptions resulting from changes were more likely to lead to latent errors in high-risk situations.

Ramanujam (2003) concluded that although change is a path to organizational learning and survival, it also increases the vulnerability of the organization to errors. In introducing major changes, organizations should create ways to protect and augment organizational attention and memory. For instance, the organization should select employees or teams to monitor routine operations, conduct operational audits, and establish criteria for assessing change initiatives, including standard criteria such as financial performance, speed, and costs. As such, managers will recognize the potential for errors and ways to prevent them.

### Transformative Learning

When organizations engage in transformative learning, managers and employees, and organizational structures and systems, undergo a dramatic and fundamental change in the way they see themselves and the world in which they function. Organizational transformation occurs through experiences and reflection (discussion) about these experiences.

Organizations may engage in transformative learning by learning from experience—either their own, or by observing the experiences of others in their industry (Chuang & Baum, 2003). Organizations, similar to individuals, may learn vicariously by observing other organizations' mistakes and avoiding them and by copying actions that seemed to work well for other organizations. Observation is a way to learn a variety of strategies, practices, and technologies (cf. Cyert & March, 1992; Levinthal & March, 1993). This is especially useful when organizations do not have the depth of experiences themselves to learn from their mistakes and successes. Observing the outcomes of other organizations' strategies and decisions can reduce the organization's uncertainty by providing clues about how to understand their own situation.

In addition, corporate executives (and thus the organizations they lead) do more than merely observe. They ask as well. Executives in firms that experience poor performance are likely to seek advice from fellow executives in other firms who are friends or similar to them (Hogg & Terry, 2000; McDonald & Westphal, 2003). Under some conditions, friendship ties can be beneficial, for instance, by increasing access to resources and enhance the exchange of valuable information. And links to suppliers and buyers can enhance the company's operations. But when performance declines and strategies need to change, CEOs turn to friends and others whom they can identify with to confirm their current strategies, not seek new directions (Hagg & Terry, 2000; Swann, 1996). Threat from poor performance and related performance-induced anxiety prompts rigidity, and executives reduce their feelings of uncertainty by seeking input from others with whom they are comfortable, have the same views as they have, and want to reduce their friend's feelings of uncertainty as well perhaps as bolstering their self-image. Unfortunately, advice in these cases usually doesn't result in much new insight because these outside colleagues are not likely to bring fresh perspectives. In fact, asking outside colleagues for advice tends to reduce the likelihood of strategic change in response to poor firm performance and indeed may have negative consequences for later performance.

Of course, organizations can learn from their own experiences. Indeed, organizational learning and change is stimulated by performance that falls short of aspirations or expectations. Good performance reinforces earlier actions, whereas poor performance calls earlier actions into question, disturbing the status quo and prompting search for solutions. "Failures are thus vital engines for change, initiating exploration of new practices, strategies, and courses of action, rather than reinforcing continued use and refinement of current ones" (Chuang & Baum, 2003, p. 37).

Chuang and Baum (2003) suggested the possibility of an interaction between an organization's own and others' experiences. Organizational momentum may bias decision makers' interpretation of failures in favor of their own prior choices. Whereas knowledge transfer and rapid diffusion may enhance learning, organizational momentum and competency traps may detract from the organization's ability to learn as the organization emphasizes replication of current strategies and processes.

Chuang and Baum (2003) studied nursing home chains deciding whether to maintain the use of local names of homes or adopt a single/common name for the entire chain as a means of establishing a reputation for quality and enhance recognition. They found evidence that highly visible negative outcomes caused chains with a common naming strategy to reduce the use of this strategy the next year. Similarly, chains with a local naming strategy that performed poorly increased their use of a common naming strategy the next year. However, interorganizational learning processes were more complex. Managers of chains with common naming strategies that performed poorly who observed other chains with common naming strategies performing poorly interpreted the other chains' difficulties as a competitive advantage. This, in turn, reduced the likelihood that their own relatively poor performance would induce them to change their naming strategy. That is, a chain's own negative outcomes seemed less dire when other chains experienced similar outcomes. Just as individuals compare their performance to others to evaluate how well they did, social comparison processes seem to influence organization's interpretations and reactions to their own performance.

In addition, momentum prevented the chains from initiating costly changes when the consequences were not well understood. Chuang and Baum (2003) explained that although failure may be an impetus for learning and change, organizations often resist change. They prefer to reemploy strategies they have used before, even when they failed. They may need to learn the hard way from repeated failures. Accumulating evidence that can no longer be ignored may be required before decision makers change their strategy. A single failure may be interpreted as idiosyncratic to the situation, whereas repeated failures become meaningful, making rationalization more difficult and encouraging serious consideration of alternatives.

Three types of transformative learning often associated with organizational learning are double-loop learning, triple-loop learning, and deutero learning.

***Double-Loop Learning and Beyond.*** In double-loop learning, error is detected and corrected in ways that involve determining why the error occurred in the first place and a resulting modification of an organization's underlying norms, policies, and objectives (Argyris & Schön, 1978). Triple-loop learning extends double-loop learning to include questioning all existing norms, policies, and objectives even beyond the organization and into society as a whole. Both double- and triple-loop learning occur when organization members reflect on and question the norms, policies, and objectives that are in place and change them. Deutero or second-order learning is when the members of the organization learn how to carry out single-, double-, and triple-loop learning (Argyris & Schön, 1978). They reflect on previous contexts for learning and inquire into previous episodes where learning occurred or did not occur and determine what went right or wrong.

***An Example of Transformative Organizational Learning.*** In chapter 4 on environments that support individual learning, we introduced North Shore–Long Island Jewish Health System's initiative to build a learning organization. Here we want to say more about why they started the effort, the components of the program, and how they assess its impact on the organization, as described by Kathleen Gallo, senior vice president and chief learning officer of the System (Gallo, 2004). The company recognized that the nature of work was changing, as it is in many other types of organizations. Increasingly, work was being done in teams. Employees faced challenging assignments, and there were continuous learning opportunities, including an abundance of feedback (Cappelli, 1999).

Within health care, the organizational (shared mental) model was changing as well. It was hierarchical, slow, inwardly focused, and reactive. The new organizational model was flat organizational structures and a mentality that is customer focused, adaptable, and proactive. Recognizing these trends, the key question for North Shore was how to effect a paradigm shift in the way the health care system was run. The goal was to create a world-class learning organization.

In 2001, representatives from General Electric, which pioneered this new approach, and Harvard University worked with North Shore to design the framework for a Leadership Institute that would support the health system's 2002–2006 strategic plan (Gallo, 2004). Typical leadership training is focused on short-term goals, led by external trainers, not linked to business results, and assumes relative stability. In contrast, the Institute's programs have a long-term perspective. They are lead by internal executives and managers, linked to improving results, and assume continuous change. The intention is to drive cultural change, align employees' behavior to organizational goals, and rapidly change the environment. People across organizational levels and functions are engaged in a way that helps them internalize learning and commit to life-long learning. Participants volunteer for the Institute's leadership program, but only those who are deemed to have the motivation and ability to advance in the organization are chosen. These are people who want to go the extra measure for the benefit of the System and their careers. They participate in leadership workshops, and in the process, learn to dialogue with each other—essentially to think together and challenge their own and others' assumptions. They learn to analyze situations in a way that identifies interrelationships and processes that unfold over time, not linear cause–effect chains and snapshots. This brings together individual visions to create a common, shared vision and foster commitment to learning and business improvement. Participants recognize that learning is a social encounter during which relationships are developed and best practices in the organization are shared.

The Center for Learning and Innovation was founded as North Shore's corporate university. The goal of the Center is to build "a first class organization of continuous learning" (Gallo, 2004). The company invests in a cadre of leaders at all levels and in all departments of the System. As employees and managers participate in the classes, the System is creating a culture dedicated to excellence, innovation, teamwork, and continuous change. The Center has four components: (a) a learning initiatives component, which includes the Leadership Institute and workshops in mentoring and a variety of other management topics, (b) an innovative solutions component, which includes human resource programs such as orientation, recruitment and retention, performance management, employee assistance (for those needing referrals for mental health problems), and employee recognition, (c) a think tank component, with professionals in organization development and human resources who keep tabs on latest developments in the field, commission views from outside experts, and assess the learning programs, and (d) a Six Sigma component, which is a continuous quality improvement initiative used in a number of other companies to apply data and statistical analysis to measure and eliminate errors and improve service-related processes (Chowdhury, 2001).

The System identifies employees with potential to advance, rotates them into developmental assignments, sends them through a series of core management classes, involves them in "capstone" projects, and encourages them to teach others. The capstone teams consist of people who have been through the core management development workshops and Six Sigma methods. They work together on a project that needs to be addressed. Examples of projects are improving patient flow across ambulatory care sites, increasing compliance with smoking cessation education for cardiac patients, and decreasing acute discharges within 14 days of admission for long-term-care patients. For each project, the effect is documented and the annual revenue increased or saved is measured.

Overall, these various programs are a way to change the "DNA" of the company—that is, shift the shared mental model and transform the organization. They do so as current and emerging leaders intuit, interpret, and institutionize (to apply Crossan et al.'s, 1999, 4-I model) or observe, assess, design, and implement (Kim's 1993 OADI model) ideas for continuous improvement. They, in turn, show others in the organization how to implement new approaches and behaviors, and ensure that the next generation of top management is ready to personify this new approach. The process is self-generative and transformative in that new insights are continuously emerging and applied such that the organization of today and the near-term future, affected by these changes, will look very different from the organization of the long-term future. Of course, the procedure for getting there (the Center's activities including the Leadership Institute's activities) are likely to change as well in ways that are unforeseen today.

As can be gathered from this chapter, organizational learning is dynamic, moving from continuity to change as standard methods are utilized and improved incrementally, new ideas are explored and implemented, individuals gain insight and understanding, groups form new ways of interacting, and the organization formalizes procedures and responds to emerging demands in a changing environment. Learning involves a tension between assimilating new learning (exploration) and using what is already learned (exploitation, or realization, for continuity; Rogers, Wellins, & Conner, 2002). That is, there is a tension between continuity and change or renewal (Jelinek, 2003). This tension must be dealt with across levels—that is, by individuals, groups, and organizations. Organizational learning processes facilitate strategic renewal at each level and this can take a long time. A very long time . . .

Business as usual with small incremental changes trumps innovation as long as critical knowledge remains principally within individuals or limited small groups (Jelinek, 2003). What a few see as a strategic change effort is merely seen as an irritating distraction to others. Until the organization embraces a proposed change at multiple levels with enough buy-in to create sustainable momentum, innovative efforts are little more than ephemeral visions easily dissolved. In this case, repeated efforts and outside events drove the action.

Our online panelists (Appendix A) recognized the value of generative and transformative learning but questioned whether organizations really reflected on needed changes and understood change processes with a focus on the long term, or merely responded with knee-jerk reactions by adopting fads in the hope of positive results in the short term. Our panelists realized that generative and transformative organizational learning are not easy and certainly not automatic.

## CONCLUSION

Organizational learning can be viewed as the aggregate of individual learning, the development of culture, continuous improvement, innovation, and the evolution of a living (organic) learning system. Methods such as multisource feedback, averaged across respondents in groups and the entire organization, can lead to insights into the degree to which the organization has changed and directions for further development. Organizational learning can occur as individual and groups learn. Individuals and groups communicate their knowledge and experiences and translate them into new ways of behaving that become institutionalized, at least until the next change occurs. Organizational learning is a dynamic, continuously evolving process of intuiting, interpreting, integrating, and institutionalizing changes. Individuals and groups transfer knowledge using technology, instruction, shared mental models, and communities of experience based on their experiences, creating new and better (more efficient and effective) ways of doing things. Organizations, as a whole, can learn adaptively, generatively, and transformationally. All this suggests that an organization is never "still"; it is constantly adapting, changing, developing, evolving, and re-creating itself.

The case of North Shore University Hospital was an example of transformative organizational learning. Up-and-coming leaders engaged in collaborative learning. They participated in joint learning projects that focused on real problems and issues, and in so doing established and disseminated new mental models that provided a vehicle for continuous organizational learning.

As Robert Mintz stated (see Appendix A), people need to be "awake"—open to new ideas and behaviors, ready to learn and not merely adopt trends mindlessly. They need patience and reflection. This is all the more important because organizations are complex and chaotic systems confronted by the rapid pace of globalization, technological evolution, and shifting economic conditions. There is no single solution, and old methods may work as well as new. The challenge for leaders is to learn mindfully and resist the temptation to jump on the latest bandwagon. Organization development initiatives, such as the hospital's Leadership Institute, can establish new ways of thinking and learning. However, the process is not easy, and the learning rests in sharing ideas and experiences, collaborating, and reflecting on the process and results. This, not the training techniques themselves, creates new mental models that comprise organizational learning.

In the next chapter we discuss organizational characteristics that affect organizational learning. Where the organization "is" in terms of its development, individual member characteristics, group-level characteristics, organizational characteristics, and organizational context influence what the organization learns and how it learns.

## QUESTIONS FOR THOUGHT AND DISCUSSION

1. Do you think organizations can learn? If yes, why? Can you give an example of organizational learning? Have you experienced this in an organization with which you have been affiliated?
2. What is the difference between organizational learning and learning organizations?
3. How do individual and group learning contribute to organizational learning? Give an example of when individual learning affected the entire organization. Give an example of when one group changed and in turn changed the entire organization.
4. What are ways in which organizations adapt to changing conditions? Give an example of adaptive organizational learning.
5. What do organizations do to prepare for an uncertain future? Do they consider likely events and how they may affect the organization and then develop contingency plans?
6. Have you seen organizations that persist with old ways of doing things even when conditions change dramatically? Why does this happen?
7. Have you seen organizational changes that failed? Why did they fail? To what extent was the failure due to internal factors, such as employee resistance or group intransigence? To what extent was the failure due to external factors beyond the control of the organization? Could anything be done to pick up the pieces? Was the end result the demise of the organization, a return to the former status quo, or eventually renewal and reinvention? How long did this outcome take to emerge—a matter of months or of years?
8. Think of an organization that successfully underwent a major transformation—for instance, introduced an entirely new product or established an entirely new direction (product, service, or mode of operation). What stimulated the change? To what extent was the change initiated by the organization itself rather than a reaction to conditions?

## TOPICS FOR RESEARCH

1. Develop a taxonomy of individual, group, and organizational feedback, examining different sources, modes of delivery, performance measures (objective

and subjective, financial and nonfinancial), and reactions. Who receives organizational-level feedback, or, stated another way, how do people in different roles and different organizational levels perceive organizational-level data? How are organizational-level data used to alter organizational-level policies, decisions, and structures? What impact do organizational-level results have on individuals and teams?

2. What are different models for knowledge management (ways to identify, organize, and communicate data), and what are the pros and cons of each model? Study the effects of these different models across a large sample of organizations.
3. Measure organizations' shared mental models (images of how things work). Study how they are transferred from group to group and individual to individual. Study how newcomers are socialized into the organization and the effects of different socialization strategies.
4. Trace how groups develop new procedures and structures and "teach" them to other groups in the organization, thereby transferring and spreading new modes of interaction.
5. Study adaptive, generative, and transformative organizational learning. What characterizes these different types of learning, and what affects their impact on organizational-level performance? Study the relationship between leadership vision and employee and work group readiness to follow that vision. What happens when there is a mismatch between the organization's readiness to change and the leader's expectations or the demands of the environment?
6. Identify cases of single- and double-loop learning (e.g., where errors are ignored vs. detected and corrected in ways that involve determining why the error occurred in the first place). Study the effects of degree of learning on changes in organizational norms, policies, and objectives.

CHAPTER

# 8

# Facilitating Organizational Continuous Learning

This chapter covers internal and external factors affecting organizational learning including organizational development, organizational capabilities (such as individual-, group-, and organizational-level characteristics), and factors external to the organization such as changes to the environment, changes to the marketplace, and competition.

## WHAT IS ORGANIZATIONAL DEVELOPMENT?

Organizations, like individuals and groups, can be said to develop. Organizational development is the progression of the organization over time. Organizations are not static, although some change faster than others. Applying the term "development" to organizations implies progress or growth—that is, change for the better in one or more ways. The change may refer to organizational processes, for instance, policies, reporting relationships (hierarchy), structure (business unit configuration), communications patterns, and strategies and methods. Alternatively, it may refer to products, goals (e.g., for sales or return on investment), and markets (domestic, international) as well as outcomes. Organizational development can be looked at from a variety of perspectives (see Van de Ven & Poole, 1995). The organization can be viewed as a single entity or as multiple entities and their interactions. Development can be seen as movement through stages that occur according to plan or prescription (the way things are supposed to happen). Development can also be viewed as movement through a set of stages that are constructed as they evolve—not by happenstance exactly, but by hard work that occurs as organization members, top management in particular, design and redesign the organization as events unfold and opportunities emerge.

### Models of Organizational Change

Here, we consider four simple models of organizational change and development. These may be combined into more complex models. Also, different parts of the organization may develop in different ways

***A Life Cycle Model.*** Life cycle models propose that organizations move through a predetermined set of changes from a primitive, simple state to more mature and complex states. Life cycle models typically contain stages that move from birth or start up through youth or growth and adulthood or maturity (this might also be called harvest) to termination or decline. Sometimes, before reaching the termination stage, organizations experience a revival, reinventing themselves and their products or services (Cameron & Whetten, 1981).

Similar to life stage models of individual development, the stage of organization development determines what an organization is learning. When the organization is in the start-up phase, it develops and implements a business plan, obtains initial financing, and enters the marketplace. Organizational learning focuses on how to turn the original vision into a reality, survive, and become a sustainable entity. In the growth stage, the firm has achieved a degree of success. Now the organization can actively seek and engage in expansion opportunities. In this stage, the organization learns to stabilize production and product (and/or service) reliability, meet increases in demand, maintain cash flow, and formalize organizational structure. In these two early stages, learning is often generative and purposeful. In the mature stage, despite a slowing growth curve, the organization often sees itself as successful. Learning is centered on efficiency and how to do better. At this stage, learning is often adaptive. The nature and purpose of the organization is set and is "working"; minor adaptations are enacted with little turmoil. In this stage, organizations have trouble engaging in generative or transformative learning because there is little perceived need for it (even if individuals in the organization see the need for learning at the organization level). In the final stage, the demand for an organization's traditional products and/or services is reduced, prompting management to consider such strategies as mergers, downsizing, and layoffs to ensure organizational survival. Organizations that consider restructuring strategies may learn adaptively (e.g., trying out the latest management ideas) or generatively (e.g., changing goals). Alternatively, the organization may elect to build a new market or rejuvenate market share. Those organizations need to learn generatively by adding new knowledge and skills or transformatively by undergoing a dramatic and fundamental shift. In either case, learning of some sort must occur or the organization may fail to prosper and possibly fail to sustain itself altogether.

***A Teleological Model.*** In teleological models (after teleology—the philosophical study of purpose in natural phenomena), goals or purpose guide an organization through development and change. The organization constructs an envisioned "end" state (for example, in 5 years, we would like to have facilities up and running in China). It then takes action to reach the goal, and monitors progress, making adjustments as necessary. Here the process might be: goal formulation, implementation, evaluation, and modification (of goal or process). Development is purposeful and constructed as the organization moves forward, unlike the life cycle approach, which suggests a fixed set of stages.

Again, learning depends on organizational stage. During goal formulation, learning may focus inward on the workings of the organization (changing and clarifying goals, policies, practices, improving communication systems, etc.) with less of an emphasis on the product or service. The organization and the people in it need to work in a new manner, and thus learning is likely to be generative. During the implementation phase, attention may shift to the product or service and is likely to be adaptive or corrective. During the evaluation stage, attention shifts back to the workings of the organization. Learning is likely to focus on measuring and gaining an understanding of how well the organization is accomplishing its goals. Finally, during the modification stage, the organization will vary in terms of whether it needs to modify its goal or process or even start the process over again. Depending on the organizational need, different types of learning can occur, from adaptation when the process is working, to complete transformation.

***An Evolutionary Model.*** In evolutionary models, change proceeds through a continuous cycle of variation, selection, and retention. Competition for scarce resources between entities whether within the organization or between organizations begins the evolutionary cycle. Change can either be gradual or sudden. However, unless the cycle has been started (and the organization remains in the retention stage), there is little need for organizational learning. Additionally, from an evolutionary standpoint, most learning will be adaptive. Variations are often viewed as just happening—they emerge by random chance (Van de Ven & Poole, 1995).

***A Dialectic Model.*** Finally, in dialectic models, conflicts emerge between entities within organizations. Using Hegelian logic, a thesis is countered with an antithesis, which leads to conflict and eventually to a synthesis (which itself may become the new thesis). Change occurs when those holding the antithesis viewpoint gain enough power to confront the status quo. Stability occurs as long as the status quo is maintained. During periods of stability, there is little need for learning beyond adapting. During times of change, adaptive, generative, or transformative learning may occur, depending on the antithesis and what is needed for synthesis.

***Summary.*** Organization development may be thought of as an orderly process through a series of predetermined stages (life cycle model), goal directed and purposeful (teleological model), an ongoing struggle for scarce resources (evolutionary model), or a continuous give and take between entities within the organization and with other organizations (dialectic model). Each of these approaches to understanding organization development may be useful, and, as mentioned earlier, they are not mutually exclusive. Goal direction, resource drive, and conflict resolution can occur as the organization passes through fairly predictable, life cycle experiences. The nature of learning depends on the stage of development within each model. Learning will be adaptive when there is little incentive or need for change. It will be generative when there is motivation to seek new experiences and knowledge to promote growth. It will be transformative when there is a recognized need and the motivation for renewal.

Note that the term organization development (OD) is also used to refer to the facilitation of organizational change and growth. A field of specialization, OD experts may be industrial and organizational psychologists or people with advanced degrees from business schools in the fields of organizational behavior or organizational development. OD interventions in organizations include analyzing team and organization performance, structures (e.g., departments, hierarchical levels), and relationships between organizational units and individuals within them. An OD intervention might be designing and implementing a continuous quality improvement program or a 360-degree survey feedback process. Individuals learn about themselves and their relationships to others. Teams learn more effective group processes. Organizations learn to confront issues directly, improve communications channels, and be flexible in response to changing conditions.

OD interventions vary in the model of development used to analyze the organization's situation. Each model suggests different ways to encourage organization learning depending on the stage of development. Life cycle, goal, fitness for survival, and conflicts with other organizational entities—these models all provide ways to diagnose organizational conditions and suggest ways for the organization to learn to deal with the current situation.

## ORGANIZATIONAL CAPABILITIES

Now that we have covered ways that organizations develop over time and how this affects learning, we consider other variables that enhance or detract from learning. First we examine individual and group characteristics and then we turn to characteristics of the organization and the environment in which it is operating. In terms of our nested model, it is necessary to understand what the parts (individuals and groups) bring to the whole of the organization. And it is necessary to understand the environment that contains the goals and obstacles of the organization as it engages in its work.

### Individual and Group Characteristics

The individual characteristics needed for individual learning (discussed in chap. 3) and the individual and group characteristics needed for group learning (discussed in chap. 6) are also beneficial for organizational learning. Here we review an approach that was developed specifically to understand characteristics that affect organization learning. In particular, Peter Senge (1990), author of *The Fifth Discipline: The Art and Practice of the Learning Organization,* distinguished between five characteristics—he called them "disciplines"—that create the possibility of organizational learning. The five disciplines are personal mastery, managing mental models of processes and relationships, building shared visions of what can be, learning how to work effectively as a team, and systems thinking.

***Personal Mastery.*** This is a culmination of many of the characteristics that we discussed in chapter 3. It is the discipline of personal growth and mastery—people with high levels of personal mastery are continually trying to create the results in life they seek. Dweck (1986) called this *learning orientation,* and London and Diamante (2002) referred to this as *expansiveness.* To us, this is very much the essence of *continuous learning* at the individual level.

***Mental Models.*** These are deeply held internal images of how the world works. These models limit people to familiar ways of thinking and acting. They don't need to think much before acting. Their mental models guide them in analyzing situations and responding. What worked in the past is likely to work in the future. However, this may not always be the case, and people are sometimes brought up short when what they expected to happen doesn't. This causes them to think more deeply about their actions and to surface the mental models that guide their behavior. Reflecting on these models, testing them, and changing habits, essentially improving the model(s), may be a useful exercise. But this is not an easy process. People don't necessarily have insight into the models that guide their behavior. This is because for many people, what they say they believe (their espoused theory) and what others see them do (their theory in use) are not one in the same (Argyris & Schön, 1978). In other words, individuals have a tendency to say one thing and do another. People don't always behave in a manner that is consistent with what they say they believe. For example, saying that you encourage innovative thinking and putting it into action are two different things. David Garvin, a Harvard Business School professor, wrote in his book, *Learning in Action: A Guide to Putting the Learning Organization to Work,* that few managers understand how to direct innovative thinking into practice (Garvin, 2000; for a summary, see Aron, 2000). Garvin gave the example of the Nike Corporation, which made the mistake of sticking to its reputation for high-quality, high-performance footwear for competitive athletes whereas Reebok introduced softer, more comfortable athletic footwear. Nike missed the market trend, not because it didn't have data, but because managers did not recognize the market signals or that these signals applied to them. Sales lagged until the company changed its strategy.

In *learning organizations,* values and beliefs are clearly articulated as outcomes of the visioning process. Time is allocated to examining the gap between vision and reality, and top managers model the values—allowing time and space to invite feedback on how they are doing (Laiken, 2003).

Argyris and Schön (1978) distinguished between two mental models of individual efforts during organizational interventions aimed at bringing about change. They called these Model I and Model II. Model I behavior is the "It's my way or the highway" approach. People exert control over a situation and how it is interpreted, not allowing for alternative viewpoints and different ways of doing things. This establishes competitive or win–lose situations. Model I leaders don't want to hear they are wrong. Therefore, they create inhibitory loops that maintain the status quo. As a result, they probably won't receive or perceive information that disconfirms their current views of themselves, the situation, or the effects of their actions and decisions. The hallmark of Model I behavior is defensive reasoning or rationalization—explaining exceptions or unexpected events by blaming them on factors outside of their control. Employees engaging in Model I behaviors inhibit their own and the organization's learning.

Model II behavior is being open to others, not attempting to control the situation unilaterally, evaluating outcomes, being aware of errors, considering reasons for errors, and examining and trying alternative actions. The hallmark of Model II behavior is productive reasoning from an open mind-set that welcomes and encourages feedback and change. Employees engaging in Model II behaviors learn through adaptation, generation, or transformation.

Unfortunately, managers who are good at Model I are often thought to be effective. And why not? After all, this is what they are taught to do from childhood on. "Under Model I, we win, don't lose, don't encourage inquiry. . . . We educate youngsters early in life about Model I. We educate them in defensive routines in adolescent groups, college groups, and in organizations. They become skillful at it—the business of withholding information, spinning, and so on. It is tacit. Taken for granted, and, indeed, they are rewarded for doing it" (Crossan, 2003, p. 44).

Individuals are bounded by another kind of mental model that evolves throughout their lives—their psychological development level (Kegan, 1994). As we discussed in chapter 3, development level, both in terms of life stage and in terms of how individuals make meaning, guides what motivates people to learn, what kinds of learning are attractive to them, what they are capable of learning, and the kinds of transformations that they might make. This has an impact on organizational learning because many of the characteristics needed for organizational learning assume that individuals have achieved high levels of development. Understanding of the organization as a "learning place" that promotes Model II behaviors is at Kegan's fourth order of consciousness. However, a majority of the adults in the United States are *between* the third and fourth orders of consciousness and thus not able to fully understand these terms and how to enact them. Given that organizations will continuously have employees across a range of orders of consciousness at all times, the majority of the people in the organization are not able to fully comprehend organizational learning and why it is important in the first place. They are not able to move the organization forward in terms of its learning without mechanisms (pacers of transformation or organization development facilitation) that help them do so.

***Shared Vision.*** Shared mental models are as important at the organization level as they are at the group level. Senge's (1990) shared vision is a specific kind of shared mental model. Individual or personal visions are pictures or images people carry in their heads and hearts. When people truly share the same vision, they are connected and bound by common aspirations. Jennifer Deal, a research scientist at the Center for Creative Leadership in response to the muse of "How do you herd cats?" suggested simply, "Open a can of tuna." One can easily imagine cats gathering—some sitting, some aloof, and some more actively trying to get to the tuna. But they are all looking at the same can with the same vision in mind. Shared vision is vital for organizational generative and transformational learning because it provides the direction and motivation for individual learning. The trick is how to develop it. Leadership is a vital key here. Generative and transformational leaders communicate a clear vision that organizational members can comprehend, perceive the value in for themselves and the organization, and exert energy to accomplish.

***Team Learning.*** Senge's fourth discipline, team learning, is similar to what we covered in chapters 5 and 6. It is a group of people learning to function as a unit, as a whole. Team members have mutual trust, shared mental models, and cohesiveness. Mutual monitoring, backup behaviors, and mindfulness move the group toward synergy. Group learning is important because in many of today's organizations important decisions are made in teams. In addition, group learning acts as a microcosm for learning throughout the organization. Insights or decisions gained by the group are put into action. Skills learned by groups can propagate through communities of practice and networks. A team's accomplishments can set the standard for learning in the organization as a whole, via systems, structures, standard operating procedures, and strategies.

***Systems Thinking.*** The fifth discipline is systems thinking. Organization members get in trouble when they think they can act in isolation and they don't realize that they are part of a larger system. Systems thinking consists of the tools, knowledge, and conceptual framework that demonstrate patterns. These help us see that simple changes in one area have often unexpected pervasive effects on behaviors and outcomes. Senge (1990) emphasized systems thinking because it binds the other disciplines together and allows them to work as levers, such that a small change can make a major difference. He articulated "laws" of systems thinking. For instance, "today's problems come from yesterday's 'solutions,'" "the harder you push, the harder the system pushes back," "behavior grows better before it grows worse," and "faster is slower." He pointed out that cause and effect may not be related in time and space, and there is no one to blame. Another law is "dividing an elephant in half does not produce two small elephants."

Feedback is important to systems thinking. A feedback loop indicates that any occurrence can be both cause and effect. Organization members learn how to distinguish between positive feedback that reinforces behavior and negative feedback that balances behavior, causing moderation, reverses direction, or invokes a new direction entirely. Systems thinkers learn to recognize dynamic interrelationships rather than simple linear cause–effect chains. They see patterns, not independent events, and understand how small changes, often those that are least obvious, can have the biggest impact.

***Employee Organizational Orientation.*** Intelligent individuals with all the "right" characteristics, with personal mastery, understanding of their mental models (and the strengths and liabilities associated with those models), a shared vision, commitment to the team, and skill in systems thinking do not necessarily make an intelligent system at the organizational level. To turn a collection of individuals into a coherent organization, people must act in a way that moves the organization as a whole toward its goals while enhancing their own performance through the coordination, evaluation, and utilization of task inputs from other organization members. They have developed what we call "organizational orientation." They understand and are committed to the organization as individuals, they act cooperatively and cohesively as team members, and they exhibit loyalty and dedication as organizational members. They care about organization-wide goals. They "see the forest for the trees," meaning that they understand the organization's objectives and how they contribute to them. They are responsive to people in other departments, and they comprehend how their actions affect constituents outside the organization, for instance, how their actions affect the organization's customers or clients.

To the best of our knowledge, "organizational orientation" is a new concept, but it is close to a number of other characteristics. Individuals who have an organizational orientation may be high in organizational citizenship behaviors (OCBs). OCBs, such as going the extra mile to help out a colleague who is late in delivering a project, enhance and maintain the social and psychological environment in the organization and support task performance (Borman & Motowidlo, 1993). Other related concepts include prosocial organizational behavior (Brief

& Motowidlo, 1986), and extrarole behavior (Van Dyne, Cummings, & McLean Parks, 1995). OCBs can be directed toward other individuals and includes such things as helping others who have heavy workloads, going out of one's way to help new people, and taking a personal interest in other employees. OCBs can also be directed to the organization as a whole and can include attendance above the norm, conserving organizational resources, and not complaining at work (Williams & Anderson, 1991).

***Summary.*** Organization development is fostered by the developmental level and orientation of the individuals and groups within it. Organizations strive to encourage personal mastery, recognition of mental models, the development of shared mental models, team learning, and systems thinking. Together, these form an organization orientation that promotes individual, group, and organization learning.

### Organizational Characteristics

Most organizations do not exist to learn; they exist to produce some sort of outcome, and to do so on a larger scale and more economically than is possible for one person or group to do alone. Learning is a by-product that occurs when the organization shifts goals or discovers obstacles in its path as it does its work. In addition, organizations (and the people in them) may actively resist learning because they have a considerable investment in appearing to know everything they need to know. Leaders fear that acknowledging their limitations, uncertainties, and limited control will undermine their credibility and reduce their prospects for career advancement (Argyris, 1991; Senge, 2003). In this framework, competition to keep operational costs as low as possible, standardized products and services, structured jobs, and a heavy reliance on the advantages of economies of scale all make sense. Predictability, order, and control are good things to ensure that the organization is able to repeat what has been successful in the past (or at least to maintain that illusion). However, again predictability, order, and control are not typically conducive to learning beyond adaptation. Sometimes, when situations change or when the route forward no longer works, organizational learning is needed. Organizations are both empowered and imprisoned by policies, procedures, structures, and standard operating procedures that govern their operations (Albrecht, 2003). Paradoxically, organizations and the people in them need to have predictability, order, and control *and* the capability to know when learning is needed and how to let go of standard procedures so that disorganization, discovery, flexibility, and variety needed for learning can occur.

There are many inhibitors of learning in organizations that serve useful purposes in moving an organization toward its goals. These same characteristics can be turned into promoters of learning in organizations. Here we consider several characteristics of the organization such as beliefs about workers, leadership, culture, strategy, structure, routines, integrating mechanisms, and standard operating procedures. We also consider situational conditions that provide the "switch" to let organizations know that learning needs to occur, including changing regulations, changes in the marketplace, competition, and the possibility of organizational failure.

***Beliefs About Workers.*** Assumptions about "workers" in the organization, particularly assumptions held by top management, have a powerful impact on whether organizational learning can and will occur. In the early 1900s, the common belief was that the fundamental motivation of all hired workers was to do the least amount of work possible (see Albrecht, 2003) and that workers were in general incompetent (Handy, 1995). These beliefs were codified into and permeated the organization—seen in strategies, structures, language, subsystems, practices, policies, and so on. Albrecht still sees evidence of these beliefs in his own consulting practices to this day. He has noted that sometimes the vocabulary of management betrays contempt for employees—a sense that they are an entity separate from and apart from the real company, like cattle to be herded around, negotiated with, or bought off when they act up. This belief has an impact on controls and directives, rules and procedures, layers of management, and pyramids of power (Handy, 1995). For example, organizations were structured so that workers were treated as interchangeable parts of a production machine. No matter what learning mechanisms are put into place in these organizations, it will be difficult for these organizations to learn.

The situation is very different when employees are seen as competent adults who want to master their jobs, continuously update their skills, develop new skills that are valuable to the organization, and disseminate their information to others within the organization. Their continuous learning helps the organization adapt, generate, and transform its own learning (James, 2003). For example, at Starbucks, full-time employees are treated as associates of the company, and all employees are listened to and valued. "Baristas" (those who make the coffee) attain a level of mastery and knowledge that customers value. Regular customers are greeted by name and their coffee is ready before they pay for it. The explicit, guiding assumption is that all employees are capable and critical to the success of the enterprise.

Kerka (1995) provided an example of how educational institutions teaching vocational special-needs students became learning organizations. Teachers, support staff, and parents are included as fully competent individuals. In one case, a school system implemented a program called the "Restructuring Through Interdisciplinary Team Effort." Teams composed of teachers, support staff, and parents attended a summer program focused on building team-driven, collaborative procedures in their schools (Smith & Stodden, 1994). In another example, an elementary school, teachers, administrators, and staff transformed the school around quality principles and a set of core values that included treating teachers as professionals and parents as partners and sharing decision making (Duden, 1993).

***Leadership.*** Another powerful inhibitor and promoter of an organization's ability to function in its environment and learn when needed is top management. Executives need to provide leadership while at the same time allowing freedom and autonomy (Laiken, 2003). Ideally, senior executives are continuous learners in their own right and have the desire and ability to drive their top-management team and the organization as a whole toward a learning orientation. However, top management can also be incompetent, misguided, or even malfeasant. There is evidence that the major factor in a person moving into a position of high authority is not demonstrating the skills and potential for excellent performance (or learning) but instead an intense desire to have control (Albrecht, 2003).

Leaders can focus the organization on maintaining the status quo, improving the efficiency of transactions adaptively, or on learning, teaching, and changing the organization. Again, ideally, leaders can interpret (or encourage the interpretation of) the environment and help the organization in deciding what is needed. Often, maintaining the status quo with adaptations is exactly what the organization needs. Change is not necessarily needed and too much might actually hurt the organization. Other times, change is desirable, and employees need considerable autonomy to make it happen, and leaders at all organizational levels have key roles in the process. Of course, top-level managers need to be aware of trends in their industry, the needs of their customer or client populations, and the context in which their organization is functioning. They need a strategic, visionary focus that they communicate clearly (Laiken, 2003).

This implies a fundamental reframing of the concept of leadership, from director, monitor, and decision maker to designer, teacher, coach, and steward (Senge, 1990). Organizations that learn need effective leaders who share decision making and who realize that their leadership must be learned and earned (Gratton, 1993; Kerka, 1995; Murrell & Walsh, 1993). Leaders in organizations that learn force inquiry and dialogue and help employees through the feelings of threat and disruption that result (Gratton, 1993). For example, Lou Gerstner aided IBM in changing its mission from being product oriented to service oriented—indeed servicing all products used by clients, not just IBM products.

***Culture.*** Beliefs about workers pervade the culture of organizations. Argyris and Schön (1978) demonstrated this by extending their models of individual learning to organizational learning. Models O-I and O-II are Models I and II at the organizational level and refer to the culture of the organization. In Model O-I organizations, Model I behavior is pervasive and self-reinforcing. Leaders' espoused theories and theories in use may be different, but no one is going to point out this inconsistency. In Model O-II organizations, leaders are more egalitarian. That is, they are more open to feedback, they give feedback to others and help them interpret it, and they are willing to experiment with new ways of doing things. They create a set of norms and beliefs that exemplify egalitarian values and facilitate and promote organizational learning.

For example, in Model O-I, meetings, especially those that contain exploratory conversations, are often experienced as time away from the real work and therefore time is wasted. In Model O-II learning organizations, organization members understand that reflective time is an important component of learning from experience. They see how it increases their productive capability and individual knowledge and skill. Learning organizations try to legitimize and make space for this informal learning during meetings, recognizing the paradox of slowing down in order to speed up. They help establish (or simply not prevent) supportive mentoring relationships in which the mentor acts as a coach, or peer partners (team members) act as coaches for one another. They encourage "communities of practice" that enable informal dialogue on work-related issues of concern. They provide skill development in the process-oriented and facilitative skills necessary to support reflective practice. And they develop a shared set of values that reinforce and make public the organization's commitment to creating an environment for learning (Laiken, 2003). For example, Southwest Airlines views all employees as leaders in a culture that puts employees first so that they in turn can put customers first.

Another cultural aspect that we have not yet touched upon is that organizations tend to be conflict averse. Controversial issues are difficult to raise because organization members fear repercussions. Organizations that learn discourage, if not prohibit, the use of threat, punishment, or blame. Instead mistakes or problems are viewed as opportunities for learning. Organizations that learn may offer special training in needed interpersonal skills. They design opportunities to reflect and address issues into work systems and processes. And they use multirater feedback for developmental purposes (Laiken, 2003).

In a learning culture, the shared mind-set is that individual, team, and organizational learning is a necessary part of the work of the organization. A learning culture can be seen in signs at three different levels:

1. Are individuals able and willing to learn? Do they seek feedback, even when uncomfortable, approach problems in a learning mode, adapt to organizational transitions and change, and monitor learning?
2. Are groups able and willing to learn together as a collective? Do they seek and share information, discuss and interpret the information together, and take unified action?
3. Do organizational processes and systems evolve and change (learn) as situations change? Do organizational systems and managers generate data and information, provide opportunities to learn, and hold individuals, groups, and the organization as a whole accountable for learning?

Organizational functions can reflect a learning culture. For instance, hiring, performance management, and reward systems can hire learners, measure learning, and reward learning. Multisource feedback (and other processes that can be connected to it, such as coaching) can (a) provide feedback to the individual learner, (b) empower individuals to seek the kind of feedback they need when they need it, (c) encourage collective learning and sharing about individual strengths and weaknesses, (d) allow groups or the organization itself to gain multiple perspectives on strengths and weaknesses as collectives, and (e) use performance ratings to link individual and group learning to the organization's learning needs and the resources needed to direct and support learning throughout the organization.

***Strategy.*** Clearly articulated strategies are simple tools that can lead to shared vision within the organization. In organizations that learn, strategies can emerge from anywhere in the organization, not just senior management. They may come from knowledge workers and team members who are trained in strategic decision making and who can be champions of ideas (James, 2003). For instance, at General Electric's Crotonville training center, managers participate in solving real business problems and in the process learn to make strategic decisions as they challenge and enhance decision-making processes. At Stony Brook University, where the second author works, students and staff from any department may initiate new programs that have strategic value for recruiting higher-achieving students, improving students' academic success, and enhancing student involvement and satisfaction (e.g., the grassroots emergence of a new freshman honor society and the development of undergraduate colleges to enhance the first-year experience).

***Structure.*** Organization structure needs to follow strategy and objectives and mission. The mission defines the purpose of the organization. Objectives are the goals that need to be accomplished to carry out the mission. Strategy is how the goals will be accomplished. Organizational structure is a part of strategy. It refers how employees are organized—for example, into function-specific departments, such as product development, sales, manufacturing, finance, and human resources. It also refers to the organizational hierarchy—numbers of organizational levels within departments, how departments are interconnected, and related roles and responsibilities of executives, managers, functional specialists, and support staff. Structure is explicit on organizational charts. However, the structure may be flexible, with people and departments realigned to meet specific needs, for instance, the formation of temporary, cross-functional product teams to design and bring new products or services to market (matrix organizational structures with people from one unit also reporting to another team). Also, the structure may change as departments and reporting relationships are adjusted to meet changing goals.

Misinterpretations and misuses of the concepts of scientific management, bureaucracy, and administrative theory have left a legacy of organizational forms that are tenaciously hierarchical and inflexible, unresponsive to turbulent environments, and notoriously inhospitable to human creativity and learning. However, since the advent of the behavioral school of management (1930s–1960s), through the growth of the field of organizational development (1970s–1980s), to the current exploration of organizational learning, attempts have been made to change organizational forms. Learning is the common element in ensuring successful functioning of organizations that are experimenting with new forms (Laiken, 2003). A learning structure may appear as a small, loose federation or network of people or departments. This may take the form of weblike configurations that are not limited by vertical chains of command. Teams bring together core competencies and transfer knowledge to others (James, 2003).

One interesting new idea about structure is *organizational ambidexterity*. This is the capacity to achieve alignment and adaptability simultaneously (Gibson & Birkinshaw, 2004). Alignment is the coherence among all patterns of activities in the business unit—they are working together toward the same goals. Adaptibility is the capacity to reconfigure activities in the business unit quickly to meet changing demands in the task environment. Gibson and Birkinshaw suggested the following for understanding how organizations can achieve ambidexterity: Context characteristics (the capacity that encourages individuals to make their own judgments as to how best divide their time between the conflicting demands for alignment and adaptability) facilitate contextual ambidexterity, which then mediates the relationship between context characteristics and performance. Context characteristics include stretch, discipline, support, and trust. Stretch is an attribute of the context that induces members to voluntarily strive for more, rather than fewer, ambitious objectives. Shared ambition, collective identity, and having personal meaning in contributing toward the overall purpose of the organization all contribute to stretch. Discipline induces members to voluntarily strive to meet all expectations generated by their commitments. Clear standards of performance and behavior, a system of open, candid, and rapid feedback, and consistency of sanctions contribute to the establishment of discipline. Support induces members to lend assistance to others. Mechanisms allowing employees to access resources, freedom of initiative at lower levels, and senior responsibilities of giving priority to providing guidance and help rather than exercising authority contribute to support. Finally, trust induces members to rely on the commitments of each other. Perceptions of fairness and equity, involvement in making decisions and activities, and staffing positions with people who possess and are seen to possess required capabilities contribute to the establishment of trust.

***Routines.*** Organizational routines are "repetitive, recognizable patterns of interdependent actions, carried out by multiple actors" (Feldman & Pentland, 2003, p. 95). We usually think of routines as a source of organizational stability. After all, routines reduce variability, enhance standardization, and avoid failure (cf. March, 1991, p. 83). However, routines provide an opportunity for improvisation and adaptation to situational conditions. The people who carry out routines are influenced by their subjective perceptions. Though routines are a means of these individuals' cognitive efficiency, they are also a source for self-reflection and reflection of others' behavior. These individuals selectively perceive their experiences and what they retain from them. This is filtered by their biases and their desire for control. For instance, routines are a basis of the power managers hold over labor. However, individuals who enact routines perform them in their own way, just as actors in a play bring spontaneity and improvisation to the script and direction. The subjectivity, power, and selective perception that individuals bring to routines make them a source of change as well as stability (Feldman & Pentland, 2003).

Generative learning happens when inferences that stem from experiences are encoded into routines that guide behavior (Levitt & March, 1988; Miner, 2002). Conventional wisdom is questioned, and routines are altered (Garvin, 2000). Organizations must be open and be able to acquire information, interpret it, and apply it—translating the ideas that emerge from the interpretation into action. It's easy to miss, ignore, or distort relevant data, especially if the data are not consistent with expectations and there are subtle differences between data points. Garvin (2003) described examples of companies that have questioned convention and altered routines successfully. For instance, L. L. Bean assesses goods by using them in the field. That is, employees actually use the products, giving them a test run, so to speak. Corporate officials evaluate the employees' observations, using their in-the-field reactions to suggest directions for product improvements. At Boeing, a top-executive team developed a "lessons learned" manual from their work on the 737 and 747 aircraft to apply to future models. Corporate leaders created a supportive environment in which they tolerate dissent and listen to new viewpoints. Leaders needed to learn how to ask open-ended questions, listen carefully to the responses, and facilitate a productive discussion without being evaluative. American Express's CEO encourages managers not merely to come up with the right answer but to think about issues the right way, which means recognizing why they think the way they do, examining alternatives and the reason for them, and recognizing the premises that underlie their thinking. Effective leaders don't accept or reject employees' ideas but rather help employees make decisions about their ideas. Experimentation is okay. Once something is learned, whether as a result of a success or failure, the knowledge is shared with others in the organization.

These routines are maintained even when there is considerable turnover of employees. They are communicated to newcomers from others in the organization who explain and model "how things are done around here." The routines can change in response to subsequent successful events. On the downside, this can result inadvertently in a *competency trap* of less-than-optimal routines. This happens when current routines are repeated, thereby limiting opportunities to experience better processes and procedures. Also, current routines may be more a matter of interpretation than actual successful behaviors. Recollection and repetition of behaviors may be inconsistent and ambiguous or adapted in relation to beliefs about the organization's culture. Problems such as complex, ambiguous, or too little information may limit the historical memory and lead to distortions, which become embedded in routines.

The likelihood that organizational learning will lead to improved routines is greater when more time is spent reflecting on experiences. Organizational members can collect more observations and interpretations and consider events that almost happened or that might have happened under different conditions. In addition to reflection, two more reliable approaches are *exploration* and *exploitation* (March, 1991). Exploration involves experimenting with new approaches. This may be costly and have few benefits, especially if ideas are undeveloped. Exploitation entails refining and extending existing competencies that have worked well in the past. But this can lead to being trapped in the status quo and applying behaviors that do not fit changing conditions and circumstances. A balance of both exploration and exploitation may be the best strategy for organizational learning.

***Integrating Mechanisms.*** How an organization's employees, systems, and processes are linked affects whether information flow is "sticky" or "leaky." Companies that require that information flow through formal channels of authority, up one hierarchy and across to another to an organizational level that is too high to appreciate its significance are too sticky. That is, information does not flow freely to where it is needed. Organizations that provide (or allow) both horizontal and vertical links enhance sharing of knowledge and learning across business units. Information doesn't get stuck in one department because formal channels must be used to convey knowledge between units or departments. Such formal channels may not even exist, or occur rarely (e.g., at a company-wide meeting that happens only once a year).

Some organizations are too leaky when it comes to information transmission. That is, there is too much information, and the right data do not necessarily get to the people who need it. Companies that promote the flow of information so it can be used efficiently use a variety of techniques. For instance, they use internal benchmarking, which means identifying and describing best practices used in one department so other departments can be aware of them and apply them in their own way (James, 2003). Another is technology transfer, which is taking technology used in one area (e.g., computer software to schedule appointments in the service department that may be revised and applied to the function of registering employees for classes in the training department).

***Standard Operating Procedures.*** Though standard operating procedures are important for consistency and training newcomers, they may also prevent mistakes from being unearthed and discussed. For instance, data on outcome failures (e.g., poor sales in a particular region) may not be reported up the line until it is too late to do anything about it. Memos about problems may be passed through a large bureaucracy so that by the time the information crosses departmental lines and moves up the organizational hierarchy, it is sanitized or hidden. These *inhibitory loops* are self-sealing and nontestable, to use Argyris and Schön's (1978) terms. We avoid conflict and dilemmas at the cost of continuing errors—sometimes with damaging results, as in the Columbia Shuttle or the collapse of Enron. Too often, organizational members are silent. Indeed, "silence is not only ubiquitous and expected in organizations but extremely costly to both the firm and the individual" (Perlow, 2003, p. 1). Pressures for unanimity prevent team members from exploring their differences in opinion. This is likely even when they are of the same rank in the organization.

Another standard operating procedure is concentrating on the installation of new solutions (learning) rather than realizing the anticipated benefits (application of the learning) (Rogers et al., 2002). *Installation* is the process of introducing a new solution (e.g., a succession management initiative, a recruiting process, a global training program, etc.) into the organization. During installation, attention is focused primarily on the logistics—how to physically introduce the solution into the work environment and how to orient and train people in its use. Actions associated with installation would include announcing the new program or process, integrating the necessary software, allocating resources, and a host of other related activities. As important as installation is, however, it can become dysfunctional if it is treated as the end state. Business solutions that are merely "installed" may achieve physical, resource, and training milestones, but these milestones typically do not represent the true intent of the effort.

In contrast, *realization* of the outcome is possible only when an organization goes beyond simply deploying a new process or system and steadfastly pursues the actions necessary to see the results that were originally anticipated (Rogers et al., 2002). When installation becomes the terminal objective, only the appearance of change is accomplished; when realization is the objective, the intended change materializes and the organization benefits by having a true competitive differentiator.

Unfortunately, managers who champion changes are often rewarded for installation rather than realization. Upon successful installation, managers are promoted or moved with high accolades. When the champion of the change moves on, the energy, will, and funding have a tendency to disappear and the change is never realized.

***Situations That Drive the Need for Organizational Learning.*** A number of common situations may demand that the organization learn and drive their readiness for change. Here are a few:

• One situation is changing governmental regulations. An example of this is the banking deregulation that occurred in the 1990s. Federal laws enacted during the Great Depression blocked banks, brokerage houses, and insurance companies from entering each other's line of business. The three industries for years lobbied Congress to streamline regulatory hurdles that bar such operations. One outcome of deregulation is that banks are now permitted to offer checking accounts, insurance, and stocks under one roof. In order to learn how to do this successfully, banks were called on to change the inner workings of almost their entire systems.

• A second situation is a change in the economy, for example, an economic downturn leading to a sharp downturn in the use of a company's products or services. The company may find that long-term clients are canceling contracts—not due to any error or problem on the part of the company but because the client has been forced to cancel important projects. Fewer new clients may be found. For example, during the recent business downturn in the early 2000s, the computer maker Dell "played judo with the competition" by developing a strategy for capturing market share through efficiency and lower prices. It deliberately drove down the prices of its computers to knock competitors out of business.

• A third situation is when an organization decides to move from a local business to a national one, or from a national company into a multinational corporation. Laws and business practices vary state by state in the United States. This is compounded when a company moves into the international arena. In addition to differing laws and regulations, companies that "go global" also need to learn how to work with local cultures, customs, and currencies, manage people who are different from anyone they have managed before, and manage in a geographically dispersed manner, sometimes by long distance, to mention a few of the changes.

• A fourth situation is when the competition or marketplace changes. Perhaps the company has never had a major competitor to contend with before, or the field has been limited in number, or even the product moves from being a specialized service to being a commodity.

• Finally, the environment may change so drastically that without a major transformation, the company has the potential to wither. An example of this is the typewriter industry. One company that successfully survived is Rand Typewriter, albeit in a very different form. The origins of Remington Products Company LLC date back to the formation of E. Remington & Son, a firearms maker founded in 1816. E. Remington & Son occasionally branched out into other ventures such as sewing machines and farm implements—and typewriters. Typewriter inventor Christopher Sholes persuaded the company to develop the typewriter with the "QWERTY" keyboard, which is still the standard today. E. Remington & Son sold the typewriter company in 1886 when it became Remington Typewriter Co. (the gun company became Remington Arms Company, still a leading firearms maker). Remington Typewriter merged with Rand Kardex Corporation in 1927 and became Remington Rand Inc. Remington Rand branched into office equipment, making such things as adding machines, filing cabinets, and punch card tabulating machines to become a leading office equipment company. Still later, they moved into electric shavers. In 1950, the company bought the Eckert-Mauchly Computer Company and delivered the first Univac computer to the U.S. Census Bureau the following year. Remington Rand merged with Sperry Corp. in 1955. The combined company became Sperry Rand Corp. In 1979, Sperry Rand sold off its office machines business and electric shaver company. This left Sperry Corporation, with the computer business and related operations. Burroughs Corp., another computer company, bought Sperry in 1986. The merged company became Unisys Corporation. In contrast, SCM Corporation, once a leading American producer of typewriters, went into bankruptcy in 1995 and never came out. In the midst of the demand for computers and computer-related products, it never changed and eventually died (see Albrecht, 2003, p. 26).

***Summary.*** We examined characteristics of organizations and changing situations that affect organizational learning. Assumptions about workers, as pawns or free thinkers, affect the contribution of employees and the extent to which they can influence directions for learning and development. Other variables are leadership, culture, strategy, and structure—organizational conditions that influence the ease and direction for change. The nature of the organization's routines, integrating mechanisms, and standard operating procedures are other conditions that may facilitate or inhibit organizational learning. Rather than following standard procedures routinely, organizations are more likely to learn when they focus on realizing the full benefit of new procedures or systems. The nature of the situation also drives organizational learning, such as government regulations, the economy, or international conditions.

## ASSESSMENT OF ORGANIZATION LEARNING

Just as we have emphasized the importance of assessment of learning outcomes for individual and group learning, consider how to assess organization learning. Because organizations are, after all, composed of individuals, organizational learning may be measured by measuring individual learning and then averaging across team members and then across teams, for instance, to examine how much employees in an organization have learned from participating in quality improvement efforts. The assessment may examine the extent to which the organization has altered organizational structure, work processes, or relationships within and between departments. Other factors that may be measured may be changes in the leader's objectives and strategies, or other organizational changes, such as a merger with another organization.

Assessment should include the extent to which the organization has adopted new processes and methods, such as quality improvement, self-managing teams, or a participative management philosophy. The assessment would tract the implementation and evolution of the process or method over time. Tracking data may include attitude survey results to assess employee morale across the organization and a variety of performance measures averaged across individuals or teams or reflecting bottom-line performance of the organization as a whole. Support factors that need to be taken into account may include leaders who champion causes or communicate a strategic vision and/or facilitators who work with departments or teams to transform the organization in different ways.

Evidence of a continuous learning organization may include the extent to which an organization attracts continuous learners, makes frequent shifts in ways of doing business to match changing conditions and opportunities, and shows that employees react positively to such shifts (i.e., morale remains high).

***Environmental Audit.*** The group and the organization are both learning systems and learning environments at the same time. From an individual's point of view, groups and organizations are environments in which the individual interacts. Of course, the organization is an environment for groups.

Support for continuous learning may be assessed by determining the availability of training, opportunities for practice, role models, expectations, reinforcement, goals, coaching, communication of competencies (explicit, implicit), feedback, pressure to learn, and the social context for learning. The climate for learning in the organization is also an important indicator of learning capacity. Elements of a supportive learning climate to assess would include employees recognizing a shared purpose, a sense of mutual trust, encouragement for change, and expectations that people will engage in learning activities.

We could also assess characteristics of the learning setting itself. A learning setting may be a workshop, business simulation, or online training course. Important dimensions of capacity for effective learning include the setting's similarity to the environment and demands on the job; opportunities for practice, feedback, and reinforcement; and varied contexts for practice so that participants can try new behaviors in settings or situations they may face at some point in time but not in daily job activities, such as handling emergencies or working with people in other cultures.

## CONCLUSION

Organizational learning is like turning a large ocean liner. It is slow and takes a great deal of effort, but once the turn is made, the ocean liner and the organization can stay the course. Organizational learning is a serious undertaking that should not be viewed lightly. In this chapter, we examined models of organizational development and suggested that learning depends on the stage of development. Different ways of describing development—including life cycle, goal focused, evolutionary, and dialectic—affect when adaptive, generative, and transformational learning are likely to occur. Generally speaking, and at the risk of oversimplification, when conditions are static and the status quo is acceptable, learning is likely to be limited to minor adaptations. Organizations are stimulated to grow and sometimes transform when conditions drive the need for renewal and individuals are motivated to reinvent organizational directions and strategies. We reviewed Senge's (1990) dimensions of personal mastery, mental models, shared models, team learning, and systems thinking as important individual and group conditions for learning. We also covered a host of organizational and situational conditions.

This leaves us with a neat parallel between individual, group, and organizational learning. At each level, we can identify stages of development and conditions that are ripe for learning, or on the other hand, conditions that prevent learning. Individual, group, and organizational characteristics and situational conditions affect learning at each level of analysis. As we discovered in the last chapter, organizational learning, similar to individual and group learning, is a continuous process. Sometimes it advances at a slow, and possibly painstaking pace (like moving an ocean liner). Other times, organizations learn at an amazing pace, reinventing themselves rapidly because the alternative is a rapid demise. Of course, not all organizations survive, and some collapse faster than anyone could have foreseen. Organizations are organic, living systems, and as such change, and with it learning, are continuous. This is an evolving process of intuiting, interpreting, integrating, and institutionalizing changes. Some organizations are learning cultures that foster individual and group learning and welcome change for the organization itself. They are flexible, responsive to environmental conditions, and creators of their own environments. They develop and share mental models of operations that thrive on learning. Over time, they take different shapes (structures), adopt different goals, and demonstrate new behaviors and strategies. They experiment, and in the process, encourage individual and group learning. They can be exciting environments, at least for people who themselves are continuous learners. Alternatively, they can be stick-in-the-muds, slow to adjust, and a source of frustration to people who desire lively interaction and are open to change. So the question is, which is it? Readiness to change or resistance to change? We have shown here that this depends on situational conditions, characteristics of the parties and organizational entities involved, and stage of development.

Change is not synonymous with learning. We occasionally use the terms as if they are—that change means the organization must have learned. But this is not necessarily the case. Change may happen to an organization or to an individual. But for learning to take place, that is, for the change to prepare the organization to apply new behaviors or systems to new conditions, the individuals involved must be aware of what has happened and why and how they can use their new insights, knowledge, or skills. Organizations too need to "recognize"—which may mean institutionalize or formalize—new systems and processes. One way to enhance recognition of learning is to assess what is learned—to evaluate the effects of a change or an intervention that is intended to promote change and learning. Did it have the desired effect? If it wasn't a deliberate intervention to educate, what was gleaned from the experience and what value did it have to the individuals, teams, and the organization as a whole? Assessment or evaluation becomes an integral part of understanding organizational learning and development. We consider this issue next as we conclude our treatise on continuous learning.

## QUESTIONS FOR THOUGHT AND DISCUSSION

1. Think of an organization you know something about—maybe a university or public school system, or perhaps a company you have worked for or a company in the news. Or take a company and investigate its history. Describe how it changed over time using life cycle, goal-focused, evolutionary, and dialectic models. Can you use each of these models to describe its history? Does one model seem to be most descriptive at a particular period of time—for instance, when conditions were calm and static or uncertain and volatile?
2. Can you think of an organization that reinvented itself, similar to the earlier example of Rand?
3. Can you think of an organization that experience a major shift, failed to change, and as a result went out of business? How about Woolworths or W. T. Grant? What happened to People Express—once an upstart airline that valued employees' contributions and ownership? (If you're not familiar with these companies, look them up.) What effect did the emergence of Blockbuster Video or Home Depot have on its competitors? What types of companies were driven out of business? What new competitors emerged? What did these companies (both those that succeeded and those that did not) learn (or fail to learn) in the process?
4. How does systems thinking promote organization learning? Give examples of how other disciplines of organizational learning (personal mastery, mental models, shared models, and team learning) are the foundation for systems thinking.
5. Think of an organization you know well. Does it encourage employees to learn? If so, how? If not, are there factors that prevent or discourage employees from learning?
6. What is the role of leaders in promoting learning?
7. If you were to start your own organization, how would you create an environment that is responsive to change? That is, what would you do to ensure that the structure and systems you establish to run the organization are flexible and able to adjust to changing circumstances?
8. Let's say you have just been appointed CEO of a large organization with a long history. It has many employees who have been in their jobs for years.

There are many established procedures. However, the industry is changing dramatically. There are fierce competitors and uncertain economic conditions. What do you do? How would you promote generative and transformative learning?

9. Now, suppose you have just become CEO of a company that had very few rules and structures. It had started as a fast-paced, high-technology company and the CEO deliberately kept things simple and flexible. There were no job descriptions and pay structures or only loose departmental structures. This was fine when the company was young and small. As the company grew, shareholders claimed mismanagement and the CEO was fired. (Do you know of a company that had this experience? If not, do some research.) So let's say you are on board as the new CEO. Do you impose structures and systems? How do you get employees to accept new ways of doing business? How do you ensure that new processes are aligned with corporate goals? How do you create a balance between clear rules and regulations, on the one hand, and laissez-faire business practices, on the other?

## TOPICS FOR RESEARCH

1. Collect a sample of organizational histories and track the development of these organizations. Classify organizations according to models of organizational development (predictable/life cycle model, goal-directed/teleological model, resource scarce/evolutionary model, and conflict/dialectic model). Do different models apply to the same organization at different times? What factors predict which model applies? What is the relationship between the different models and types of learning (adaptive, generative, and transformative)? What is the long-term impact of each model on measures of organizational change and performance? Develop a contingency model to indicate interventions for enhancing organization development under each model and stage of development within models.
2. Examine the longitudinal effects of organizations trying to encourage personal mastery and develop shared mental models on team and organizational learning and organizational performance.
3. Develop measures of individual, group, and organizational learning orientation (i.e., the degree to which the system strives to learn and fosters learning) and explore relationships between levels. Determine the effects of a mismatch of learning orientation between levels, for instance, how individuals react when they are high in learning orientation and the organization provides little support for learning.
4. Study characteristics of organizations and changing situations that affect organizational learning. Determine the effects of leadership vision, culture, strategy, and structure on organization change.

5. Examine the extent to which evidence of organizational continuous learning (e.g., attracting continuous learners, making dramatic shifts in organization strategy) is related to support for continuous learning (e.g., availability of training, opportunities for practice, role models, expectations, reinforcement, goals, coaching) and to organization change and performance.

CHAPTER

# 9

# Future Directions

Our goal in this book has been to help readers get their arms around the concept of continuous learning and its application at the individual, group, and organization levels. In chapter 1, we described the field as *nested* (individual learning is embedded in group learning, group in organization, organization in environment), *iterative* (learning mechanisms are similar at each level), *integrated* (to understand learning at one level it is necessary to take into account the other levels), and *systemic* (input, throughput, and output components with feedback loops and open to the environment). Our goal in this final chapter is to pull together the themes of the book and offer ideas for strengthening continuous learning in organizations. The themes are the following:

1. Learning occurs at individual, group, and organization levels, and to understand learning at one level, you need to understand learning at the other levels. This sometimes imposes challenges and dilemmas because forces for learning at one level are influenced, and may even be contradictory to, forces at other levels.
2. Learning is adaptive, generative, or transformational.
3. Learning depends on capacity and readiness to learn (stage of learning and development) and environmental conditions.
4. Continuous learners are self-directed; learning cannot be forced, it may only be triggered and supported (or not). Using these themes, we suggest general ideas for incorporating learning into organizations at the individual, group, and organizational levels. Specifically, we suggest analyzing current practices that are in place in organizations from a learning perspective and "evolutionizing" (to coin a term) those practices to be more learning oriented.

## RELATIONSHIPS BETWEEN LEVELS PRESENT CHALLENGES FOR LEARNING

Individual, group, and organizational learning are intertwined, and understanding how learning occurs at one level requires understanding how it happens at the other levels. To fully understand learning, we must study how people make sense of the situations they face and how they feel about them (their cognitions and emotions) as well as their readily observable behaviors and decisions. Similarly, we must understand the internal workings of groups—their culture and values. We must understand the exterior of the group—"behavior," practices, procedures, policies, structures, strategies, and visions. Finally, we must understand the internal and external workings of the organization. Each of these is related to, and affects, the other.

### Nested and Iterative Learning Systems

Whether learning takes place, how learning takes place, and what kind of learning takes place are also dependent on systems dynamics. Individual employees are whole "systems" in and of themselves. However, they are also the basic building blocks of other systems—groups and organizations—which themselves need to be understood as whole systems. Similarly, groups are systems in and of themselves, and they are networked (linked) together to form organizations, which are also whole systems. This forms an increasingly complex hierarchy of nested, networked systems. In addition, as we have shown in this book, it is useful to think in an iterative fashion. Organizational learning builds upon group learning, which is dependent on individual learning. Yet group learning is more than the learning of the individuals in the group, and organizational learning is more than the patterns of behavior established by individuals and groups within the organization. Finally groups and organizations comprise the learning environment for individuals and their learning. And organizations are environments that impact group learning.

### Challenges and Dilemmas of Learning

We must address a number of complex challenges in order to understand learning at all three levels. Complex challenges look like they may be easily solved using current assumptions, measures, and tools, but upon closer scrutiny, at least an element of the challenge requires profound and fundamental change (Drath, 2003; Heifetz, 1994; McCauley, 2004). A force at one level affects learning at the other levels.

A first example is that at the individual level, humans like predictability, order, and control. That is, we like to repeat what we have done before—behaviors that feel comfortable and that have worked for us in the past (Bellman, 2000). This continues at the organization level in the drive to be efficient, to optimize, to simplify. Repetition, order, and control simplify work—it is easier and takes less effort. The dilemma is that we may forfeit discovery, flow, and flexibility—all needed for learning at the individual, group, and organization levels—in favor of predictability. Learning at the individual level takes a great deal of effort. Thus, there are strong countervailing tendencies *not* to learn at any level unless there is a need. The challenge is to learn to balance predictability, order, and control with discovery, flow, and flexibility.

Second, forces at one or more levels may thwart learning at another level. As an example, individuals like to achieve something. And in order to "achieve," that something must be recognizable as an achievement (Bellman, 2000). Combined with this need for achievement is a countervailing organization-level force. Employees can no longer expect to stay at a single employer for a lifetime in the United States—or even more than a few years. In fact, in the past decade, many middle and upper-level managers have experienced "serial unemployment" where they are laid off for perfectly good business reasons at one employer, unemployed for a long period of time before finding a comparable position in another organization, only to be laid off again for perfectly good business reasons. Given this human propensity for achievement and in this environment where they need to achieve something fast to look good for their next employer, why should an employee engage in activities that serve to allow the group or organization to learn, unless there is direct benefit (i.e., accomplishment) that can be directly attributable to the individual employee? For example, it is more beneficial to an employee to institute a change (and claim responsibility for it on their résumé) than to follow through or "realize" a perfectly reasonable and beneficial change instituted by someone else. The challenge here is to help individuals identify their achievements in aiding in group and organizational learning so that they will both help their current organization's learning and have accomplishments that will be beneficial in finding another job.

Here's another dilemma: Many people are attracted to and rely on organizational hierarchy to confer status. Those who are attracted to status are inclined to focus more on what will elevate them and less on what's best for the larger organization (Bellman, 2000). In this need for status, individuals want to draw attention to their individual accomplishment and draw attention away from, or take credit for, the group's accomplishments. The challenge here is to ensure that those individuals who focus on group and organizational learning and accomplishment as well as their own learning and accomplishment are recognized and afforded the opportunity to higher-status opportunities.

Fourth, today's organizations focus on short-term results. Related to this emphasis is the need for performance, performance, performance. Individuals feel that their bosses are constantly asking, "What have you done for me lately?" The complex challenge here is how to allow the time needed for learning in this short-term environment as learning takes a long time—especially given that initial learning often causes a short decrement in performance before a major improvement (the "J" curve; Albrecht, 2003).

Finally, many organizations have a conflict-averse culture. Controversial issues are difficult to raise because organization members fear repercussions. However, learned employees have opinions—lots of them. The challenge here (combined with the need for short-term performance results) is how to encourage and allow time for the conflict that needs to and will emerge when learned employees differ in what they know and what they think is the best way for themselves, their groups, and the organization to proceed.

In summary, the interrelationships between individual, group, and organizational learning are not necessarily mutually supportive. Indeed, learning at one level may be thwarted by another. Demands for change and growth at one level may actually prevent learning, or make it more difficult, at another. Individuals, groups, and organizations experiment and practice setting goals, trying new behaviors, seeking feedback, and finding ways of interaction that work best for them. Sometimes they change the environment in the process, making it more welcoming and beneficent—a greater source of enrichment and support. Sometimes they give up, especially when goals are unclear or unattainable, when obstacles are too great, or when the environment is not conducive to experimenting.

## ADAPTIVE, GENERATIVE, AND TRANSFORMATIONAL LEARNING

At its simplest, learning is adaptive. Adaptive learning is an unconscious behavior change where the learner *reacts* to a new stimulus—an obstacle or uncertainty that gets in the way of attaining a goal. Learners may try a solution they have used with other unexpected stimulus, modify a familiar solution, or maybe try a wholly new behavior. Learners pick up information from their environment on how they should act, and they change their behavior accordingly. For instance, employees may "learn" that the only thing that counts toward their yearly bonus is bottom-line performance. Thus, although they might attend a training program on managing diversity or read a book on emotional intelligence, the majority of their energy at work will be directed toward getting the best bottom-line performance, no matter what it takes. Now if the diversity-training or emotional-intelligence guidelines they acquire suggest applications that produce results, then fine. But making these connections takes time and is not so direct. They may not realize that there can be a connection. Their automatic pilot is on behaviors that result in tangible reinforcement.

However, people are endowed with reflective consciousness—the capacity to know and monitor their own mental states. As a result, humans, and systems made of humans, can engage in generative learning. This is purposefully adding new knowledge and skills in the expectation that the new knowledge or skill will aid in goal attainment.

Also, learners can undergo a dramatic and fundamental shift in the way that they interact with the environment in order to achieve their goal. This is transformative learning. Some people have a proclivity or talent for transformation. Others are resistant. After all, sticking with the status quo or making minor adaptations is easier and more comfortable than major change. Sometimes, learners (individuals, groups, or organizations) are forced into transformational change, or at least trying to transform. They must re-create themselves or cease to exist. They develop a new understanding of themselves through reflective practice and experiential learning. A project team that is not meeting its performance objectives may purposely restructure itself and its practices and processes into a high-performing team that has a clear direction and goal and the means to reach that goal in order to keep from being disbanded in an organization.

## LEARNING CAPACITY AND READINESS

Whether learning takes place, how learning takes place, and what kind of learning takes place are, in part, dependent on characteristics of the learner—the capacity and readiness to learn and the environment. At the individual level, the life stages perspective of adult development suggests that younger employees will be more interested in learning deeper competence in their area of expertise and chosen career path than in other areas. Once on a career trajectory, adults will be interested in learning whatever it takes to advance, including continued skill development for increased productivity, mastery, and credentials as well as learning the "right stuff" to play the corporate game for promotion and recognition purposes. Later, individuals may switch from deepening to broadening their skills as they move up in the organization, start their own organization, or change careers. Still later, they may become less interested in "doing" and more interested in molding the next generation and creating their legacy. Moreover, they may become less interested in organizational learning and more interested in accomplishing their own goals.

From the perspective of orders of consciousness, where people "are" in terms of their ability to construct meaning influences how they perceive and experience the world. In the interpersonal stage, adults define themselves through their relationships with others; they want to be seen as "competent," as skilled, or as an expert by others. They want to learn how to do their job better. However, they may wait to be told what to learn. Others may perceive them as needing to be more assertive and confident in taking control of their own learning. During the institutional stage, individuals define themselves by their work and employer. They define their goals and what is important to learn. Also, they may be attracted to learning that exposes them to a bigger picture of the organization, perspectives of others, taking different perspectives and examining alternatives from those perspectives, empowerment, creativity, taking initiative, self-management, and dialogue. In the interindividual stage, learners realize that they are not defined by their work roles, career, or duties. Their goal is to help the organization learn and develop simultaneously. They realize that what they and others choose to learn creates the situation.

Many characteristics influence whether individuals will engage in continuous learning on their own. We discussed personality, including characteristics that demonstrate a readiness for learning, such as beliefs about the self, openness to experience, conscientiousness, expansiveness, a learning/mastery orientation, motivation, and learning style, all affecting whether an individual will engage in continuous learning on their own or whether they need more encouragement from their environment.

Finally, the organizational environment influences individual learning. We need to understand the environment and the messages it sends in order to recognize what individuals are learning and why they are behaving the way they do. We gave examples about how individuals learn from how work is done in the organization, the structure of the organization (e.g., its management roles, functions; and hierarchy), the communities within the organization, the culture of the organization, and the broader environment (e.g., the industry, economic conditions, advancing technology). This learning may be unexpected, unintentional, and sometimes even conflicting, as when employees receive conflicting messages from different managers about what to do.

At the group level, we suggested that teams experience a developmental sequence that includes the group moving from a collection of individuals to become a well-ordered system. Early stages suggest a focus on the group and group members—assigning roles, developing norms, setting goals, planning work processes, and so forth. During this stage, the group establishes deepening levels of mutual trust, shared mental models, and cohesiveness. During later or stable stages, when roles, norms, and goals are clearer, the group concentrates on the task at hand—monitoring each other's performance, helping each other, and being mindful about what needs to get done when and by whom. During transitional stages of development, groups learn how to alter their configuration, modify their habits, and reestablish roles and routines.

Both individual and group characteristics affect group continuous learning. At the individual level, characteristics including cognitive ability, personality characteristics, functional background, motivation for joining the team, and team orientation are important to learning. Team characteristics that impact learning include type of team, structure (in terms of power and psychological safety), composition (diversity of members' demographics, abilities, and functions), social familiarity (how well team members know each other), conflicts and experience with conflict resolution, and learning orientation (the group's experience with trying new ways of interacting and work processes). The degree to which the organization supports groups and the corresponding reward structure are two environmental characteristics that affect group learning. Not only does the structure of the organization, such the way rewards are given, need to change, but so does the culture. In terms of structure and rewards, the extent to which all group members share the benefits of group productivity and/or whether individuals within the group are rewarded for their performance impacts group learning. In terms of culture, the degree to which there is a clear need for groups to exist at all impacts group learning.

At the organizational level, development can be approached from a variety of perspectives depending on what is being "developed." In terms of organizational "life stage," when the organization is in the start-up phase, organizational learning focuses on how to turn the original vision into a reality, survive, and become a sustainable entity. In the growth stage, the firm learns to stabilize production and product (and/or service) reliability, meet increases in demand, maintain cash flow, and formalize organizational structure. In the mature stage, learning is centered on efficiency or how to do better. In the final stage, management may consider restructuring activities to ensure organizational survival. Alternatively, the organization may elect to build a new market or rejuvenate market share. In this last stage, learning of some sort must occur or the organization may not survive, let alone grow.

From a teleological approach, learning depends on organizational stage. During goal formulation, learning may focus inward on the workings of the organization (changing and clarifying goals, policies, practices, improving communication systems, etc.) with less of an emphasis on the product or service. During the implementation phase, attention may shift to the product or service. During the evaluation stage, learning is likely to focus on measuring and gaining an understanding of how well the organization is accomplishing its goals. Finally, during the modification stage, the organization will vary in terms of whether it needs to modify its goal or process or even start the process over again.

From the evolutionary perspective, change can be either gradual or sudden. However, unless the cycle has been started (and the organization remains in the retention stage), there is little need for organizational learning. In addition, changes are often viewed as just happening—emerging by chance. From the dialectic perspective, change occurs when entities representing the antithesis viewpoint gain enough power to confront the status quo. Stability occurs as long as the status quo is maintained. During periods of stability, there is little need for learning beyond adapting.

Individual, group, and organizational characteristics affect organization learning. Individual and group characteristics include personal mastery motives, shared mental models, shared vision, team learning, systems thinking, and employee organizational orientation. Organizational characteristics that impact learning include assumptions about workers' motivation, leadership, culture, strategy, structure, routines, integrating mechanisms, and standard operating procedures. Environmental conditions that provide the "switch" to let organizations know that learning needs to occur, include changing regulations, changes in the marketplace, competition, and the possibility of organizational failure.

In summary, individual, group, and organizational capacity and readiness to engage in continuous learning can be viewed from multiple developmental perspectives and the effects of multiple characteristics. There is no single perspective or single characteristic that dominates in explaining learning. Rather, we can benefit from these different ways of understanding learning processes, understand the interrelationships between levels of analysis, and find ways to support continuous learning.

## LEARNING CANNOT BE FORCED, BUT IT CAN BE TRIGGERED AND SUPPORTED

Our final theme is that learning is self-determined. Outsiders cannot direct a living system to learn, they can only "disturb" it and support it. The living system not only specifies its structural changes, it also specifies which disturbances from the environment trigger them. Individuals, groups, and organizations will learn only what they need or want to learn, and will use that learning only if they perceive they need it. We find that this may require a frame shift for many people—from a "teaching" perspective to a learning perspective that includes providing learning triggers and opportunities, resources, and support for learning. Teaching or training is something that is done to someone. Learning is something that an individual, group, or organization does in order to reach a goal or overcome an obstacle. Teachers, consultants, facilitators, and mentors can provide stimuli, opportunities, needed resources, and encouragement or support.

There are four ways to help learners learn. First is to help them set goals that require a stretch—that is, goals that are challenging but can be accomplished (Locke & Latham, 1990). Second is to assess the learner's current capabilities and reassess periodically to track learning. Third is to create an environment that allows the organization to operate at a fairly sophisticated level while providing a safe holding environment and drawing learners forward through pacers of transformation (Kegan, 1994). This allows the organization to operate at higher levels and helps individuals and groups towards higher levels of development at the same time. The policies, procedures, practices, structure, and culture in an organization can be designed to provide encouragement and resources for learning and communicate that experimentation is okay.

Fourth is to take into account the zone of proximal development (ZPD) of the learner, which is the distance between the learner's level of actual development and potential development (Vygotsky, 1978). We elaborate on how recognition of the ZPD can support learning next.

The ZPD encompasses functions (behaviors, work processes) that are not yet mature but are in the process of maturation. The essential feature of learning is that it creates the ZPD—it awakens a variety of internal development processes that are able to operate only with a more capable person or peers. Once these processes are internalized, they become developed and developable. For example, unless adults have exposure to more complex ways of thinking by interacting with others who exhibit this, they may not continue to develop into the more advanced stages of cognitive complexity.

For individuals, social interaction creates, extends, and utilizes ZPDs to foster skills and capacities. The learner observes others, emulates them with support (e.g., the help of a supervisor or coach), then internalizes new behaviors as part of their own repertoire of skills for independent use. Learning assistance can occur in a number of different ways. These include modeling, coaching, questioning, exploration, reflection, structuring, instruction, and scaffolding. For example, scaffolding provides the learner with support and assistance to complete a task or solve a problem that couldn't have been mastered without help through such methods as hinting, elaborating, leading, linking, requesting, reworking, suggesting, commenting, prompting, probing, simplifying, and providing emotional support. Modeling provides the learner with a prime example of appropriate or desired behavior then gradually gives control of the situation over to the learner. This learning can occur during some sort of formal learning or can occur "naturally" in a community of practice, such as a work group.

These zones can be extended to the group and organizational levels. Groups and organizations may benchmark (collect information about best practice) and emulate other teams and organizations that are performing well in the organization. They may also benefit from a team coach who aids the team through scaffolding techniques. If top management of organizations are made aware of ZPDs, they can more knowledgeably pick which techniques to benchmark and emulate with less of a need to try out every management fad. Coaches, trainers, and top management should be selected based, in part, on their level of development. Individuals operating at lower orders of consciousness à la Kegan (1994) need to be paired with mentors, coaches, managers, and peers operating at higher orders of consciousness. This requires a long-term commitment on the part of the organization because development cannot be rushed. Also, the developmental level of all parties must be known to the organization with a deliberate pairing of individuals at lower orders of consciousness with those at higher orders. This requires that those at higher orders of consciousness be equal to or higher in the organizational hierarchy than those in lower orders of consciousness, and that they learn, use, and be rewarded for using appropriate techniques for learning assistance such as modeling. However, people at higher levels of the organization are not necessarily at higher orders of consciousness than those at lower organizational levels, which won't help learning.

In summary, there are many ways to support learning at the individual, group, and organization levels. Goal setting, assessment, a safe and supportive environment, and a recognition of capabilities and potential provide a context for ongoing learning and development. At this point, we have reviewed the four major themes of the book: (a) Learning occurs at multiple levels—individual, group, and organizational; (b) learning is adaptive, generative, and/or transformational; (c) various characteristics and conditions indicate and shape learning capacity and readiness; and (d) learning is self-directed but can (and needs to be) supported. Next, we consider ways that organizations can analyze current learning practices and transform or "evolutionize" practices to promote continuous learning at all levels.

## INCORPORATING LEARNING THROUGHOUT THE ORGANIZATION: AN EVOLUTIONARY PROCESS

We suggest moving continuous learning forward in any organization using an evolutionary perspective (as proposed by Colarelli, 1998). Interventions in organizations rarely meet expectations. That does not mean that they have failed. Many organizations don't even follow methods that would be deemed by management and organizational psychologists as standard practice, such as training needs analyses and evaluation of training programs, so it is no wonder they are disappointed when interventions don't work. Instead, organizations institute changes and then select and retain variations that happen to work, not interventions that are planned based on theory and formally introduced (Weick, 1979). Thus, an evolutionary approach to the criteria for evaluating an organization intervention, say multisource feedback, training, or goal setting, should focus on what elements of the process work well, not just whether the intervention overall achieved the intended goal.

For instance, for managers receiving multisource feedback, instead of assessing whether the feedback resulted in improvement in long-term, bottom-line performance or even performance ratings 1 year later, we might examine how the feedback process was implemented, who benefited, and whether it focused attention on learning needs. Managers may benefit merely by participating in the development of the performance dimensions that were rated in the survey and debating what behaviors are needed now. Indeed, later iterations of the multisource instrument may change (i.e., new performance dimensions may be substituted for others that are less important) because the needs of the organization are different. This precludes comparing performance ratings over time, to researchers' dismay, but adds value to what the organization needs now.

In addition, different interventions may be needed at different times depending on what is happening in the organization. Organizations experience periods of calm during which incremental changes are made. They also experience periods of major transition or turmoil during which frame-breaking changes are made (Gersick, 1991). For instance, an employee attitude survey may be valuable during steady-state periods, but not times of disruption (e.g., downsizing). "Interventions that focus on specific outcomes and make incremental improvements are most appropriate during stable periods; those that focus on more general outcomes and probably adaptive consequences are more appropriate during revolutionary periods" (Colarelli, 1998, p. 1050).

Furthermore, because the future is always uncertain, interventions might be selected based on their relevance to the immediate situation. There is no point trying to anticipate which interventions will work over a long time period (Mintzberg, 1994). The principal criterion of success may be producing a specific outcome within a specific period of time. The value of an intervention may take considerably more time to be evident and occur in unintended or unforeseen ways. Learning occurs as the intervention percolates through the organization. The organization "assesses" the net effects of the intervention. If its effects are positive, the intervention is likely to become integrated within the organization as routine; if the effects are negative, the organization will probably reject it (Colarelli, 1998; Levitt & March, 1988). The intervention may actually enhance variation in the organization, that is, shake things up, leading the organization into new directions, and perhaps creating new ideas giving rise to new ways of working or new products and services. Instead of focusing on theory testing and ideal outcomes, the evolutionary approach enriches the organization's capabilities and options: "The usefulness of an intervention has as much to do with understanding the conditions under which it is adaptive as it does with its capacity to produce intended effects" (Colarelli, 1998, p. 1054).

### Evolution of Training Programs

A first example for improving training programs is simply to evaluate them on whether or not they incorporate basic learning principles. One set of principles is incorporated in what Marsick, Cederholm, Turner, and Pearson (1992) called action-reflection learning (ARL). ARL is learning by doing rather than learning by lecture. The basic characteristics of ARL include working in small groups to solve problems and building skills to meet the training needs that emerge during the project. Some of the assumptions emerging from the work include:

- We increase our learning when we reflect on what we did; by relying on experts, we may become immobilized and not seek our own solutions.
- We are most challenged when we work on unfamiliar problems in unfamiliar settings. (As a result, nonhierarchical, cross-functional teams enhance learning through exposure to new perspectives.)
- Facilitators can help by helping people think critically (perhaps forcing the process to slow down).
- Learning should accommodate and challenge different learning style preferences.
- Whether in individual or group learning, we should examine the organizational system as a whole.

ARL applies when problems are complex and there are no obvious solutions in sight; when managers need to develop a cross-functional overview; when learning is closely tied to cultural change; when the participants need to develop judgment and to think strategically; and when participants prefer to learn by doing while getting work done. If these conditions apply, existing training methods can be evaluated (or new methods can be designed) using ARL principles.

Another example of this evolutionary approach is to create training programs using the learning principles we have discussed in this book as a guide. For example, Gilleard (1996) describes a training program on improving communication in her organization. She applied learning theories to the training program and showed how the theories actually work! The training was delivered by e-mail and was "just in time," meaning available to participants when they felt they needed it. The program worked as follows:

1. The responsibility for driving the training was at the behest of the worker as suggested by Knowles' (1990) concept of the self-directed learner. This was possible because the training could start whenever the worker was ready and continue at the worker's convenience, rather than traditional face-to-face, classroom training that occurs at a certain time for a specific duration of time, whether the worker is ready or not.

2. Participants were highly motivated because there was a close correspondence between the training and their job-related performance. Participants did not attend the training as a reward for good behavior or merely at the behest of their supervisor—rather, it stemmed from their own desire to improve their performance.

3. Due to the technology used, the training was able to be one-to-one and personalized, rather than having a trainer trying to "speak to" a variety of people at the same time.

4. Participants were expected to take personal responsibility for their own performance enhancement. They were given sample reports and began submitting their own reports (behavioral modeling).

5. Using Vygotsky's (1978) zone of proximal development, participants did not have their mistakes automatically corrected by the trainer but were helped to recognize and correct their own errors. They were encouraged to solve their own problems and seek confirmation or further support only after they attempted the solution themselves.

Another way to evolutionize training is through the use of blended learning solutions (Pulley, 2003). That is, simply take advantage of multiple modes of training and learning. As we have made clear throughout the book, learning occurs outside of formal training programs more often than it occurs inside training programs. Face-to-face training, technology-based training, and learning on the job can be combined as needed with support from mentors, coaches, group facilitators, and organization development experts.

### Recognizing Learning Potential of Practices Beyond Formal Training

As we have made clear throughout the book, learning occurs outside of training programs more often than it occurs inside training programs at the individual level. Group and organizational learning rarely occur in the classroom. A second evolutionary step is to examine current practices already in use (or recent past use) in the organization for their learning potential. There are quite a few practices that have emerged in the past two decades that include elements of learning in them including: benchmarking, business process reengineering, continuous improvement, total quality management and ISO9000, competency models, balanced scorecards, knowledge management, and talent management. Rather than concentrating on whether or not these "worked," emphasis could be on which parts of each practice have been incorporated into the organization or somehow changed practices, whether at the individual, group, or organization levels. In analyzing these parts of practices, it may become clear how a particular organization learns best. Some examples might be that one particular organization reacts best from trickle-down practices, another from trickle-up practices, another from trickle-across (learning moves from department to department), and another from concentrated organization change efforts at all levels. Another example might be that simpler feedback measurements work best in one organization whereas another needs more sophisticated feedback measures. Once the learning in and by a particular organization is understood, the environment can be deliberately designed for more learning to occur.

### Organization-Wide Evolution Toward Continuous Learning: A Case Example

A major evolutionary step is to implement a transformational organizational learning process where multiple organizational systems, practices, policies, and procedures are used at once to deliver the same messages about learning as based on organization needs, mission, and strategy. Here, we describe a case originally presented by Barriere, Anson, Ording, and Rogers (2002). They centered their intervention around a leadership development program as a way to turn a standard bureaucratic organization into one that can more easily respond to change. They started with the belief that leaders are role models and sources of reinforcement for change in an organization, and leadership development can be a way to help leaders acquire the skills they need to be effective models for change and bring about a cultural transformation in their organizations. In this intervention, assessment (using climate surveys), training programs, feedback, selection, performance appraisals, and compensation were all aligned around areas of learning.

This is the case of a health care organization, similar to the case of the North Shore–Long Island Jewish Health System that we described in chapters 4 and 7. In health care, organization change needs to be accomplished while maintaining a failure-free environment, at least as much as possible. In health care organizations faced by high costs, demands for improved efficiencies and quality, and increased competition, managers must foster teamwork and align representatives from diverse backgrounds, departmental affiliations, and disciplines to work on common goals.

Barriere et al. (2002) gave the example of a hospital that needed to transition from a bureaucratic institution that operated efficiently in a stable environment to a highly adaptive organization operating under conditions of uncertainty, pressure, and competition. The hope was to start at the top of the organization with commitment to change from the CEO and then cascade actions for innovation and strategy development down into lower levels of the organization. Previously, the most senior managers conveyed all plans and strategies to department managers. However, demands for expedient and diverse solutions meant that department managers needed to make decisions guided by a keen understanding of the overall goals of the hospital. Previously, interpersonal competencies such as coaching, providing constructive feedback, and inspiring initiatives were given little attention. This needed to change. Moreover, managers needed to understand that the status quo was not good enough. Although the hospital was reasonably successful, managers needed to be forward thinking and recognize the changing environment. A climate survey was administered before and after the training programs to assess perceptions of role clarity, standards, personal responsibility, recognition, support, and commitment. Initial measures characterized the organization as having high staff commitment and role clarity but lacking in innovation, individual initiative, communication, and teamwork.

Two leadership development programs were implemented during the course of 4 years. (Change doesn't happen overnight.) The first focused on leaders' skills in coaching subordinates and inspiring them to take more initiative. This intervention was aimed at changing six dimensions of leadership (Barriere et al., 2002, p. 122):

1. Communicating the hospital's values (e.g., effectively balancing the hospital's business and patient care priorities; setting challenging performance goals and standards).
2. Encouraging individual initiative (e.g., clarifying who is responsible for what within the group, encouraging people to initiate tasks or projects they think are important).
3. Providing constructive feedback and coaching (e.g., giving people candid feedback on how they are doing on their jobs, providing feedback that is even-handed and fair).

4. Creating a climate of openness and trust (e.g., conducting meetings in a way that builds trust and mutual respect, behaving in a way that leads others to trust you).
5. Demonstrating personal leadership (e.g., selecting and promoting the best people for the organization; managing change in a thoughtful and well-planned rather than a reactive manner).
6. Leveraging the entire hospital team (e.g., putting hospital objectives ahead of personal, unit, or departmental agendas; collaborating effectively with people in other departments or units).

A multisource feedback performance survey with self- and subordinate ratings provided feedback to managers so they could track the extent to which their behavior changed. The results identified the leadership practices managers needed to improve most. Feedback on the survey was incorporated into a 2-day workshop and several follow-up activities, such as one-on-one coaching and supervisor–staff meetings to discuss the implications of the feedback. The workshop itself helped the participating managers interpret their feedback results and identify developmental needs. The managers also participated in training on critical leadership skills that the climate survey indicated that most managers needed to develop, in particular, how to provide effective coaching, inspire employees to take more initiative, and facilitate teamwork. Activities included discussions of case studies, videotaped role-play exercises, and individual coaching. These materials had been developed from in-depth interviews and focus groups with hospital employees to ensure their relevance.

Other human resource initiatives supported these efforts, for instance, formal performance appraisals that included evaluation of support for innovation and change, revised selection procedures to hire managers who already possessed strong interpersonal skills, and compensation linked to interpersonal performance as well as technical performance.

Posttraining discussions with senior managers indicated that teamwork within departments had improved. However, a recent merger called attention to the need for cross-departmental teamwork. So a second leadership development program implemented 2 years after the first focused mainly on this topic. This was a 1-day workshop that focused on an intensive role-play exercise on a staff allocation problem. It incorporated a negotiation process for meeting both department and overall organization goals. The workshop was preceded by another multisource feedback survey, and participants in the workshop received their feedback results and updated their action plan for development during a coaching session.

Data from the two multisource feedback surveys averaged across individuals showed improvements in management style and support for teamwork. Specifically, managers improved in demonstrating personal concern for the well-being and success of employees and encouraging them to design new ways of saving money, increasing productivity, and improving the quality of patient care. Large increases were found in managers encouraging employees to initiate tasks they thought were important do, thereby empowering them to do what was necessary to deliver high-quality care. In addition, there was considerable improvement in being supportive and providing fair and even-handed feedback.

Overall, the case shows that over time, interventions can change leaders' support for organizational and individual learning. The initiatives had several key characteristics for organizational change: They were customized to the specific context of the organization. Employees were involved in defining strategic initiatives. A sense of urgency was created, and there was ongoing commitment from senior staff. Current conditions were assessed and changes in behavior were tracked. Managers received feedback on their performance on competencies related to the intended change, and the organization aggregated the individual results to examine change across the hospital. External consultants helped throughout the process to provide unbiased views and lend their specific expertise to needs assessment, program design and implementation, and evaluation.

In terms of the themes of our book, the case demonstrated learning at the individual, group, and organizational level. Some changes were adaptive, but generally, this was a generative, and indeed, transformational change. Conditions were created to support the learning. These included the demands in the health care environment and the policies, training programs, and norms that were established, modeled by top management. These conditions empowered managers and employees to make their own decisions for learning and on-the-job performance improvement.

### Consulting as a Learning Process

Finally, we would be remiss if we did not focus our learning lens on human resource and training professionals, group facilitators, and organization development specialists. So we end this book as we began it, by holding ourselves, your authors, accountable for continuous learning. Coaches, trainers, and organization development consultants facilitate learning in organizations. Indeed, learning can be thought of as the bedrock of the consulting profession. Just as consultants promulgate continuous learning in organizations, they need to be continuous learners themselves. Some may be tempted to assume that once they master a body of knowledge they can stop learning and apply their craft. They may have fixed ideas about what to do under certain circumstances and how to use a set of process assessment tools and methods. They may assess, impart their knowledge, and transplant their model of effective organizational processes. However, learning is a process that the consultants need to both teach and apply to themselves. Webb (1995) studied how consultants learn from their experiences. "Being an effective learner is connected to understanding and strategically deploying and developing one's self in new and different situations" (Webb, 1995, p. 123). She recognized that how one learns depends on one's personality, drive, or preferences and to early learning experiences (Bunker & Webb, 1992). Learners tie their experiences to their needs, values, and self-perceptions. Consultants are driven by their technical competence, need for autonomy, service value, creativity, and desire to make a difference. The consulting practice provides a basis for learning if consultants are ready to reflect on what they are driven to learn and if they are open to examining their successes and mistakes.

Webb (1995, p. 125) offered the following questions consultants can ask themselves to assess their capacity for active learning. These questions may be useful to managers, employees, and members of almost any profession as they consider their continuous learning motivation, ability, and behavior:

1. Do I view my practice as an ongoing learning opportunity? Do I ask myself regularly what I am learning? Do I keep a journal of my insights?
2. Am I willing to confront significant learning challenges? Do I invite myself into new and different situations rather than seeking the familiar? Can I confront those aspects of myself and my practice that need to be changed?
3. Do I analyze my successes and failures? Do I know the "why" behind what works and what doesn't?
4. Do I know what drives me in my work? Can I match this to my strengths and weaknesses? Can I assess where I am susceptible to overdoing my strengths?
5. Do I seek and use feedback to improve?

Participants in our online discussion had some thoughts about challenges professionals face in fostering continuous learning. Their comments are in Appendix A. Some themes that emerged from their final discussion were the following: Training and other human resource interventions are not magic pills. We need research on cultural differences in learning or conditions that foster learning. We need to assess readiness to learn before designing an intervention to promote learning. Those who design interventions need to understand how systems operate.

## Summary

Training, coaching, supervision, group facilitation, and consulting can be enhanced to support learning, development, and continuous learning at individual, group, and organization levels. This is an evolutionary process, not a one-time event. The themes of this book can be infused in organization change effort. Sometimes these efforts focus on the design of specific programs, for instance, a workshop to help supervisors support adaptation to change. Other efforts are more generative and transformational in nature, such as the health care organization example in which leadership development was supported by commitment from top executives and employees were empowered to analyze situations and make decisions. The environment demands an organization that responds quickly and accurately. The organization provides the learning resources and support. Managers and employees need to recognize the need for change and be willing, indeed motivated, to learn. People learn new behaviors that affect their job performance, work group processes and performance, and the organization as a whole. Finally, we pointed out that professionals in the field of human resource development need to be continuous learners just as they support continuous learning.

## ASSESSMENT RESEARCH

Assessments track the process and outcome of continuous learning. The idea is to understand what is happening in the individual, group, and organization to engage in, and benefit from, continuous learning. If people are participating in learning, what are they doing? What is the quality of the learning process? Is the breadth and depth appropriate for the situation or the goals of the learning? Is the purpose mastery and professional growth, or is it aimed at accomplishing specific objectives, the success of which is an indicator of the value of learning? What is actually learned? For instance, did participants in a class learn the facts and use them on the job? How does the current learning build on past learning and pave the way for future learning? Is the environment conducive for learning? These questions can be asked at the individual, group, and organizational level to make assessment a continuous process. Methods for assessment of process include observation, self-report surveys, observer surveys, and records of events and interactions, perhaps minutes at meetings. Methods for assessment of continuous learning outcomes include tests that demonstrate knowledge and skills at increasingly higher levels of complexity. Simulations might be used in the learning process and the assessment process to examine application of new knowledge and skills on the job. Surveys can measure support for learning as well as what needs to be learned.

Assessments can be combined with basic research about continuous learning. For instance, research can study people who are continuous learners (expansive) with case studies and critical-incident techniques. Research can capture patterns of behavior and outcomes. Participation in continuous learning can be measured and used to predict later outcomes. Multiple measures should be made at different points in time, especially at key times in the individual's, team's, or organization's life. Research can study how continuous learners learn and how style of learning may change over time with age or experience. Research can also examine self-reflection that results from self-assessment and feedback.

Another direction for research is to examine the conditions under which continuous learning is more likely to lead to positive outcomes. Potential moderators of this relationship may include job complexity, age, personality (e.g., internal control), social context, functional background (experiences in different functions), intelligence, eclecticism (range of interests), expertise, and experience in relation to goals (match between goals and experience—fit with the organization, department, group, and task). For example, continuous learning may be more valuable for people whose jobs are complex, people who are older and have accumulated more experiences and expertise, people who feel they control the positive things that happen to them, people who work in a positive, friendly social environment, and so on.

### Assessing the Effectiveness of Training Programs

One area of assessment that has received a great deal of attention is assessing training program effectiveness. Training is a pervasive method organizations use to enhance employees' and managers' productivity and interpersonal skills. As such, training typically focuses on individual learning, although it has implications for team and organizational capabilities and performance. In 2000, U.S. companies with 1,000 or more employees budgeted $54 billion for formal training ("Industry Report," 2000, as cited in Arthur, Bennett, Edens, & Bell, 2003, p. 234). In addition, corporate universities have grown quickly. In 1988, there were 400. In 1998, there were 1,000. Forty percent of these granted, or were interested in granting, an accredited degree, often working with universities in their local areas to provide undergraduate and graduate programs and instructors (Meister, 1998; as cited in Miner, 2002, p. 834.).

In a recent meta-analysis (a compiling of research from a wide range of sources) on the relationship between characteristics of training design and evaluation and the effectiveness of training, Arthur et al. (2003) found medium to large effect sizes for organizational training on outcomes such as reactions to the training, learning (knowledge and skills acquired), behaviors applied on the job, and bottom-line results, such as financial performance—the range of training criteria suggested by Kirkpatrick (1959, 1976, 1996). This indicates that training is indeed effective in producing positive reactions, demonstrated learning, behavioral change, and performance improvement at the individual level of analysis. Arthur et al. pointed out that this is equivalent to, or better than, effect sizes of other organizational interventions, such as appraisal and feedback, management by objectives, and goal setting found in earlier meta-analyses (Guzzo, Jette, & Katzell, 1985; Kluger & DeNisi, 1996; Neuman, Edwards, & Raju, 1989).

### Comprehensive Assessment of Learning From an Organizational Change

Consider the case of the implementation of a quality improvement program supported by the Robert Wood Johnson Foundation and Institute for Health Care Improvement at seven hospitals around the country. The program is called "Pursuing Perfection." Although this may sound overly ambitious if not unrealistic, it connotes the need for hospitals to improve continuously to reach the highest levels of performance. This is what the public expects in the United States from its health care system, even if it is not fully achieved. One, the Hackensack University Medical Center in Hackensack, New Jersey, is implementing the program in several ways (Gross, 2003). They established multidisciplinary coordination of care teams. Rather than the MD being the principal driver in a patient's care, the team makes rounds together and takes joint responsibility for the patient. The members include the attending physician, the patient's staff nurse, the advanced practice nurse, and representatives of social service, discharge planning, nutrition, and pharmacy. Their goals are to:

- Collaboratively and concurrently review and facilitate the patient's plan of care.
- Ensure the appropriate plan of care is in place for the most current and acute problems.
- Assist the physician in providing appropriate services in a timely manner.
- Collect trend and report data related to delays in the patient care.

These components are sensitive to hospital standards of excellence, patient safety, and the flow of patient care. Important off-shoots are staff education and mentoring and the assurance of implementing protocols for excellent practice.

In implementing such a new procedure, the following questions were addressed:

***Individual learning capacity:***

• *Readiness:* Are employees aware of the need and willing to act now to take on the challenge? Are teams able to coalesce quickly? Do members revert to old roles (e.g., nurses' subservience to the physician)? Has the hospital invested in briefing meetings and training for staff members? Does a functional organizational structure (e.g., departments of nursing, nutrition, etc.) impede or facilitate team members? Do members feel they are serving two masters—their functional department head or the team?

• *Potential to learn:* Are employees too immersed in their field of expertise to understand how they work with other specialties? Have teams existed before in the organization? Were employees and team responsive to change in the past? Does the organization have proper measurement tools and equipment for tracking changes in patient outcomes?

• *Desire:* Do employees care about the hospital? Do they feel they have a stake in the hospital's reputation, or are they there temporarily, ready to move on at a moment's notice to another hospital that will pay more? Do they feel valued? Are they adequately compensated? Are teams overworked (too high a caseload)? Do employees feel that the hospital is serious about this change? Do they see it as a fad that will pass when the grant funds run out? Do they see the change in relation to the reputation of the hospital in the community? Do they care about the hospital's reputation?

• *Prior experience:* Have the employees, teams, and organization had prior experience with quality improvement programs in the past? Were they well received? Have employees worked in teams before, and have they been successful? Is this new program viewed as building on this foundation of past improvement or it is viewed as just the latest change in an effort to satisfy regulatory bodies or grab on to a trend?

• *What has to be learned:* Do employees understand the demands of working in a team, sharing their experience, contributing on an equal basis with others regardless of their training or discipline, and raising questions and alternative viewpoints in self-managing teams? Do team members understand group process dynamics, ways of communicating clearly and efficiently as multiple patients are covered in a day, and ways of raising and resolving disagreements? Is the hospital willing to adjust its structures to give teams authority? Can the hospital administration be responsive to teams' requests for equipment, data systems, and data on results? Is the hospital willing to share such information publicly?

• *Mutual perceptions:* Do employees understand each other's discipline and respect each other's training? Do team members take the time to get to know one another as they begin their work as a team? When new members are added to the team does the team take the time to acquaint the new members with its modes of communication and operation? Is the team able/willing to adjust to new ideas and behaviors of new member? Is the hospital cognizant of factors that enhance team interaction? Is the administration willing to listen to team members when they have suggestions for improved operations?

• *Feedback:* Do employees talk about performance issues? Do team members take time to give each other feedback in a respectful and constructive way? Does the team take the time to talk about the team's overall functioning and performance and ways they can improve? Does the hospital have facilitators to help the teams work more effectively?

• *Goal Setting:* Do employees set goals for the career development? Is this part of the hospital's performance management process? Do teams set goals for improved patient care and track their results, making improvements along the way to enhance performance further?

• *Participation in Learning:* Are individuals committed; do they feel forced? Are team members dragged along or does each person on the team feel equally empowered? Have MDs given up sole authority and responsibility or do they still see themselves as the center of attention? Do top officers of the hospital participate on care teams? Do they demonstrate the intended behaviors?

Learning and continuous learning outcomes should be assessed over time in several ways at each level of analysis:

1. *Individual:*

   *Learning:* This includes surveys of reactions to the team process, performance in behavioral exercises that demonstrate collaborative skills covered in workshops, and performance evaluations from fellow team members and functional supervisor.

   *Development:* Repeated measures of collaborative skills indicate improvement over time and the ability to move into new groups smoothly.

   *Continuous learning:* This includes observations and records of the individual's participation in development, seeking feedback, and search for new information. The individual demonstrates inquisitiveness and working with others to explore uncharted territory (e.g., formulate experiments to test new ideas).

2. *Team:*

   *Learning:* Observations and interviews indicate that team members become proficient in communicating information to each other, processing information, raising alternative viewpoints, making decisions by consensus, and reviewing outcomes.

   *Development:* Team outcomes and member attitudes improve over time. Teams that initially were bogged down in disagreements, had trouble making decisions, or were not listening to everyone equally learn to raise divergent opinions, involve all members, and reach agreement quickly.

   *Continuous learning:* Teams track their own outcomes, discuss their group dynamics, and make changes in the way they interact.

3. *Hospital:*

   *Learning:* Teams have been formed; methods for tracking performance have been established; organizational systems (data and performance management systems), facilitators, and training programs are available and used. Protocols are followed. Mistakes are noted and communicated so they can be avoided in the future.

   *Development:* Levels of patient care have been improved.

   *Continuous learning:* The hospital supports ongoing training, brings experts for Grand Rounds presentations, and expands teams to additional areas of patient care.

## CONCLUSION

We started this book by saying that continuous learning is risky and end the same way. By that we meant that it opens doors to new ideas, experiences, experimentation, and change. The status quo that is welcoming and comforting goes out the window. Uncertainty, trial and error, and risk taking come in. We conclude this book by reminding our readers that continuous learning naturally occurs at multiple, interacting levels—individual, group, and organization. It is to our benefit to understand learning and capitalize on it. Learning can be adaptive, generative, and/or transformative. People, groups, and organizations learn when they are good and ready. Continuous learners, especially, are self-directed. Organizations provide resources that enable continuous learning. There are a number of challenges to learning at all levels, such as the natural tendency by many to resist change. Organizational changes may demand learning but not reward it. Some people discover that the "reward" for learning is being downsized out of a job, although learning prepares the individual to be competitive for whatever may lie ahead. Readiness to learn depends on such factors as career and life stage, developmental complexity, and openness to change. Goal setting, assessment, feedback, and organizational policies, programs, and resources help individuals, groups, and organizations move closer to their potential capabilities. This is an evolutionary process. Support systems can be made continuously better as they are designed and refined to encourage continuous learning and in the process improve performance at all levels. Our panel of experts reminded us that the challenges of today, whether they be natural tendencies to maintain the status quo, or fast-paced pressures, such as those facing a multinational organizational operating in diverse cultures, are not dangers to be avoided by exciting opportunities for continuous learning.

We gave an example of a comprehensive organizational change effort that affected individuals, teams, and the organization as a whole. An assessment plan was needed to capture learning over time at all three levels of analyses. Multiple methods were designed (e.g., surveys of participant perceptions, measures of team behaviors and decisions, and records of organizational actions and events) to track continuous learning and evaluate and fine-tune the change effort.

## QUESTIONS FOR THOUGHT AND DISCUSSION

1. What does continuous learning mean to you at the individual, group, and organization level? How is continuous learning at these different levels connected? Give an example of how individual learning affects group learning and vice versa. How does group learning affect organization learning? How does organization learning affect individual learning?
2. Summarize the meaning of adaptive, generative, and transformative at individual, group, and organization levels. What are ways to stimulate and encourage adaptive, generative, and transformative learning?
3. What conditions make people, groups, and organizations ready to learn? Give an example of when learning is needed but the learner (individual, group, or organization) is not.
4. What can you do to facilitate readiness to learn at the individual, group, and organization level?

5. How do goal setting and assessment affect readiness to learn?
6. Does feedback increase or decrease learning readiness? Does feedback motivate you to learn? If so, why? If not, why not?
7. What challenges do individuals, groups, and organizations face today that encourage, if not require, continuous learning?
8. As you think about your future, what will make you a continuous learner? What can you do to ensure you are competitive and your career does not come to a premature ending? How ready would you be to change careers? What learning would be required?
9. What can you do to ensure your work group is ready for new challenges? How can you influence your organization's readiness to learn?

## TOPICS FOR RESEARCH

1. Study how forces and learning at one level of analysis (individual, group, or organization) affect other levels. Identify, measure, and track the impact of these forces. Explore consistencies and inconsistencies between levels (e.g., individuals' significant contributions to work teams are not reinforced or recognized by the supervisor or others in the organization; team members' task motivation does not match the needs of the task; organizational culture thwarts disagreements that may raise important issues). Can a team learn new patterns of behavior without individual members or the organization as a whole benefiting?
2. Study environmental factors that create barriers to change and learning. What interventions can help overcome these barriers?
3. Understand how individuals, groups, and organizations take responsibility for their learning. What sparks and reinforces their self-initiative and enhances their drive for learning?
4. Find examples of continuously learning individuals, groups, and organizations. Study their characteristics. How do they differ from organizations that fail to change or change too slowly so they can't catch up with competitors?
5. Do goal setting, training, feedback, assessment, recognition, and resources predict continuous learning? Are they more strongly related to transformative and generative learning than adaptive learning?
6. How do continuous learning systems (individual, group, or organization) enact and move from adaptive to generative to transformative learning?
7. What is the role of leaders, facilitators, coaches, and human resource development managers in promoting learning over time?
8. Develop and implement a plan for assessing the impact of a major organizational change effort. Identify and measure elements of the change and its effects on behavior and outcomes at the individual, group, and organizational levels.

APPENDIX

# A

# Online Discussion of Continuous Learning With Subject Matter Experts: Excerpts

## PARTICIPANTS*

*William Byham* is the CEO and cofounder of Development Dimensions International (DDI). DDI is an internationally renowned human resource training and consulting company specializing in assessment centers, behavioral-based interviewing, behavioral job analysis, results-based training and development, and acceleration pools (a method of succession management). These technologies have been described in 21 books and more than 200 articles.

*David Day* is a professor of industrial/organizational (I/O) psychology at Pennsylvania State University. His primary research interests are in leadership and leadership development. Prior to attending graduate school he was employed for 8 years as an hourly worker at the Ford Motor Company's Cleveland Casting Plant (i.e., Satan's private little bakery). No continuous learning there!

*Phillip Doesschate* is a computer systems designer who specializes in systems development (programming and testing) and implementation. Over the course of his career, he has taken half a dozen major systems and many minor systems from a conceptual level through implementation. He takes great pains to see that the

*Valerie Sessa and Manuel London also participated, as did Susan Jackson, whom we quote in chapter 5.

systems are not "still born" and that they not collapse under their own weight. His experience has made him an advocate of evolutionary change rather than revolutionary change.

*Cynthia McCauley* has worked at the Center for Creative Leadership (CCL) for almost 20 years in various research and management positions. Individual learning and development have been at the core of practically all of her research and applied work (e.g., learning from job experiences, developmental relationships, 360-degree feedback). And as a manager at CCL, she became more familiar with the exhilaration and frustration of organizational learning. Her latest project was the revision of the CCL *Handbook of Leadership Development* (with coeditor Ellen Van Velsor).

*Robert Mintz* is a "recovering Corporate type"—25 years in top human resource jobs at corporations like Revlon, PepsiCo, Time Warner, and Electronic Data Systems. He left it all 4 years ago and completed a PhD in Human & Organizational Systems. He is writing his first book from research that he did with 25 CEOs who came to a place in *their* lives when they felt that what they were doing either was total bullshit or was in the process of killing them and thus went out and reinvented themselves. Thus, life transformation is his "sweet spot" and he is in the process of building a portfolio life that includes continued research, writing, and teaching.

*Michael West* is a Professor of Organizational Psychology and Director of Research at Aston Business School and a member of the Centre for Economic Performance at the London School of Economics. He has authored, edited, or coedited such books as *Effective Top Management Teams* (2001, Blackhall) and the *Handbook of Workgroup Psychology* (1996, Wiley) and has written numerous articles for scientific and practitioner publications. His areas of research interest are team and organizational innovation and effectiveness, particularly in relation to the organization of health services.

## INITIAL CONVERSATION (CHAPTER 1)

### Stimulus Questions

How do you define individual, group, and organization continuous learning?

How can you tell whether learning has occurred at each level?

Do you feel that learning is similar or different at each level?

Is learning different from development?

Do you believe that continuous learning is more important today than ever before?

*From Robert Mintz*

I will speak from organizational practice more than theory. My career focus was primarily group and organizational in nature . . . my focus has shifted (for a number of reasons) to the personal . . . and my recent experience has changed much of what I used to believe about individual learning.

***Individual Learning.*** It is my current belief that individual learning is developmentally linked based on life scripts imparted at the earliest of ages. These "truths," socially constructed by the birth family, get tested as one begins to experience other "truths." Thus, if one spends most of one's life in a rural, remote farming town, one is less likely to experience any narrative disruptions that challenge the "truths" proffered by those in their lives. The child of an international relocating executive will have quite a different experience as they will constantly be confronting "truths" that are different from theirs. It is my contention that learning (and, therefore development) occurs when there is sufficient narrative disruption that creates enough internal conflict for the individual that they must face the "new truth," try it on (so to speak) and then decide if it has a place in their belief system. At the same time, the individual must revisit "old truths" and decide what no longer holds for them.

These narrative disruptions are occurring in people's lives much more frequently than in the past due to globalization and technology advances. This leaves the individual with three choices: hunker down and hold onto current beliefs despite the discomfort, seek comfort in some form of fundamentalism, or reshape their belief system through introspection, expanding one's network, etc. I do believe that people have a need to continually make coherent sense of their life stories and thus, are prompted to conduct these reviews fairly frequently. Often, this requires validation from new "scripter" or mentors/teachers who support the new world view. I also believe that it is our developmental journey to complete individuation as Jung suggests . . . and I believe script confrontation not only supports individuation (making more and more authentic choices) but also helps an individual shift from external validation to having more of an internal compass. Interestingly enough, the greater the individuation, the greater the personal Proteanism (in my experience)—not greater isolation.

I believe that there are certain life stage triggers that influence quantum leaps in learning/development: first significant script challenges of adolescence when one typically encounters new beliefs about the world where new heroes replace old ones; first significant life choices (education, career, significant other, and defining "the good life); first significant mistakes or successes . . . and finally midlife review. I would also proffer that the more ongoing script/narrative disruption that occurs over the life span, the greater the learning and the less painful the midlife review. Once someone experiences the process of using learning to resolve conflict, create mastery, build self-sufficiency and independence, change power relationships and ultimately increase their sense of power and autonomy, I believe an internal compass guides them to continuous learning.

### *From Cynthia McCauley*

I'm personally feeling some resistance to putting "continuous" in front of learning and am trying to understand why. Maybe because I've been more influenced in recent years by the constructivist tradition which tends to see learning as going on all the time because human interaction is going on all the time (although the quantity and quality of the learning might often be low). So "learning" and "continuous learning" would not be a needed distinction in that framework. I think that understanding which of these traditions we are operating out of is important because my hunch is that some of the reactions that Bob [Mintz] had was because of his constructivist perspective.

### *From William Byham*

To me, individual and group learning mean just what they say. It implies people learning as individuals or learning as a group. Organizational learning gets into sharing of organizational knowledge, etc. I see it as being quite different; it's more in the area of institutional learning.

It's one thing to be concerned whether learning has occurred and another to be concerned about whether the learning is applied. I think that is the more important issue and that gets in to the whole area of realization. People don't go through a training program for the sake of being in a training program; they go to change behavior or to have knowledge when it's needed, etc. Organizations should focus on realization of training, which then, of course, depends on what learning has occurred.

The world is changing and business and job requirements are changing—all requiring people to adapt. It takes much more sophisticated leadership today than it used to. The requirements are higher for "acceptable/unacceptable" performance. Organizations that are not filled with continuous learners will inevitably fall behind, not meet their strategic goals, etc.

There are many academic differentiations between learning and development. Some people would say that learning means acquiring knowledge or skill and development is broader to encompass the early applications of the knowledge or skill and continuous improvement. Personally I would see development being a better word because it is less associated with training and more associated with on-the-job experiences.

One sure relationship is the need to coordinate the acquisition of skills at various levels [individual, group, and organization] so that an initiative can be implemented. For example, if you train managers to be empowering, you need to give their subordinates the skills to be empowered. If you don't, then the managers won't use their newly acquired empowering skills because they know they won't work. Similarly, we all know that learning at one level is much enhanced if the boss has the same learning and is available to encourage application and reinforce efforts. This requires multiple levels of learning.

The world of work is full of examples of organizations that may teach one skill but reinforce another. Again, empowerment would be an example. Organizations may be running training programs to make their leaders empowering while surrounding the leader and his or her subordinates with high control measures, which inhibit decision-making at lower levels. Also with empowerment, very often you'll train leaders at one level to give up authority and responsibility to leaders at a lower level without making the organizational changes to give the leaders who are giving up power and authority something new to do. It's very unlikely that they will then take the step to actually give up power and authority because they fear becoming redundant.

My big current research interest is "realization." The following is the definition of realization that I use: Realization is a sustainable, positive change in people's performance that dramatically increases the ability of an enterprise to achieve its business goals. I'm doing research on realization of 360° and assessment center feedback (less than 10 percent of the people who get feedback do anything with it), and realization of training and development applications at various levels in the organization.

#### *London Responded to Byham*

I agree with you that we need to examine how learning is coordinated in groups and organizations so that people can interact better, have a common vocabulary, etc. This will help us understand organization learning processes. An example is how leaders can call for attention to reflection.

You used the word, "adapt," as a key to responding in today's world of rapid change. As you indicate, continuous learning is a necessity. Those who are not continuous learners "will inevitably fall behind."

### Doesschate's Models

One of our online participants offered his own view of relationships between individual, team, and organization learning and development. Phil Doesschate, a systems analyst, designer, and executive, considered the meaning of continuous development at individual, group, and organization levels and developed the models for learning and development outlined in Tables A1 and A2. In Table A1, he provides examples of learning at different levels of depth, meaning complexity, cognitive requirements, interactions, and/or organizational systems and processes. A given individual, group, or organization may engage at learning at a given level at any time. In Table A2, Phil gives examples of increasing developmental stages. Here too he suggests parallel processes for individual, group, and organization learning and development. The notion of stages of development connotes the cumulative and evolutionary nature of learning and that earlier stages

TABLE A1
Deepening Learning Processes

| *Order* | *Defining Characteristic* | *Individual* | *Group* | *Organization* |
|---|---|---|---|---|
| Low | Rote learning. How to do something. | How to tie shoes.<br>How to drive a car.<br>Survival techniques.<br>Rote memorization. | How to get something done.<br>Aural history.<br>Tribal rites. Orientation. | Corporate training programs (e.g., how to hire, how to use computer systems).<br>Induction/initiation rites.<br>Corporate standards. |
| Medium | Learning something with the intent that it be able to be applied as a tool. | Learning of a foreign language.<br>Learning a computer language.<br>Learning of algebra, calculus, topology, etc. | Software engineering projects working out solutions to problems.<br>Engineering project.<br>Congressional inquiry/legislation. | Leader-initiated organizational redirection.<br>Common vocabulary. |
| High | Enable to define new principles. Independent thought. | Abstraction.<br>Figuring out new laws/principles.<br>Self-motivated learning. | Research projects. | Microsoft embracing the Web in its software line in 1995.<br>Six Sigma quality initiative. |
| Extraordinary | Major break-through in understand-ing. Paradigm changes. | Einstein's general and special relativity.<br>Descarte's *Meditations.*<br>Euclid: *The Elements of Geometry* | Bardeen's group at Bell Labs that invented the transistor.<br>Watson, Crick, Franklin, and Wilkins' effort to define structure and function of DNA.<br>Effort to write the U.S. Constitution. | NASA man on the moon effort (i.e., Mercury, Apollo missions).<br>Manhattan project. |

*Note.* From P. Doesschate, personal communication. Used by permission.

are necessary before an individual, group, or organization can move to the next level in the stage hierarchy.

### *London's Response*

Phil Doesschate proposed an organization of learning and development that calls attention to (a) the difference between the two, (b) their variation in complexity, and (c) their application to individuals, groups, and organizations. Phil

TABLE A2
Stages of Development

| *Order* | *Defining Characteristic* | *Individual* | *Group* | *Organization* |
|---|---|---|---|---|
| Primal | Basic connection to one's environment | Survival<br>Language acquisition | Socialization<br>Family dynamics<br>Childhood play | Tribal identity |
| Identity formation | Capable of defining and holding one's place in the world | Literacy<br>Control bodily functions<br>Self-preservation | Team building | Branding<br>State building<br>Feudal organization |
| Self-interest actuated | Capable of shaping the environment in interests of the self | Control emotions<br>Design<br>Literacy | Winning team | Cartel/trusts/slavery<br>Shapes market<br>Intellectual domination<br>Empire building |
| Self-fulfillment | Mastery of environment | Leadership<br>Ethics<br>Conceptualized knowledge | Collaboration | Democracy<br>Six Sigma quality initiatives<br>Free market |
| Enlightenment | Sustainable development view of good of society, environment, world | Good of society<br>Good of environment | Good of society's children's children | Sustainable development<br>Long-term good<br>Equality of all humans above the law |

*Note.* From P. Doesschate, personal communication. Used by permission.

challenged us to revise the defining characteristics of each level of learning and development and to add to the tasks that reflect each level of individual, group, and organization learning and development.

Perhaps one way to categorize levels of learning requirements is to draw on task and group taxonomies. For instance, Ed Fleishman and colleagues distinguished between cognitive and perceptual-motor ability requirements and their relationship to the probability of error (Buffardi, Fleishman, Morath, & McCarthy, 2000). We might postulate that the more a task component has error potential, the more difficult it is to learn, and the more such task components are combined, the more the difficult the overall task it to learn. Cognitive ability requirements include written communications, problem sensitivity, oral expression, deductive reasoning, visualization, and number facility. An example of an ability scale for understanding written communications would include the following learning requirements:

Low—requires understanding short, simple written information containing common words and phrases (e.g., reading a road map).

High—requires understanding complex or detailed written information containing unusual words and phrases and involving fine distinction in meaning among words (e.g., understanding an instruction book on repairing a missile guidance system).

## DEFINING CONTINUOUS LEARNING (CHAPTER 2)

***Phil Doesschate***

A polymath is said to be one who is of "encyclopedic learning" (*Webster's New Collegiate Dictionary*) or "A person of much or varied learning; one acquainted with various subjects of study" (*Oxford English Dictionary*). The polymath represents the extreme case of attainment of individual learning. These aren't just "Jacks of all trades" and "masters of none," but people who have the abilities and motivations to devour new areas of interest. When we think of historical figures who were polymaths, we may think of a Thomas Jefferson, a Benjamin Franklin, or a John von Neumann.

I came across the autobiographical statement of one James Murray in the *New York Times Review of Books* (Buckley, 2003, p. 13):

> "I possess," the schoolteacher had written straightforwardly, "that general lexical & structural knowledge which makes the intimate knowledge" of any language "only a matter of a little application. With several I have a more intimate acquaintance as with the Romance tongues, Italian, French, Catalan, Spanish, Latin & in a less degree Portuguese, Vaudois, Provençal & various dialects. In the Teutonic branch, I am tolerably familiar with Dutch (having at my place of business correspondence to read in Dutch, German, French & occasionally other languages), Flemish, German

> and Danish. In Anglo-Saxon and Moeso-Gothic my studies have been much closer, I having prepared some works for publication upon these languages. I know a little of the Celtic, and am at present engaged with the Sclavonic, having obtained a useful knowledge of Russian. In the Persian, Achaemenian Cuneiform, & Sanscrit branches, I know for the purposes of Comparative Philology. I have sufficient knowledge of Hebrew & Syriac to read at sight the Old Testament and Peshito; to a less degree I know Aramaic Arabic, Coptic and Phenecian to the point where it was left by Gesenius."

James was hired to head the effort to put the "Oxford English Dictionary" together some 10 years after he had written this statement (in 1875), and he went on to master several other subjects. He would seem to fit the description of the polymath. He would also seem to fit the ideal of being someone who was engaged in continuous learning. What allowed him to master these languages? What allowed him to develop such a level of mastery on such a wide range of subjects?

***Phil Continued***

Humans are hardwired to learn. So learning is, by definition, continuous for the species. The ability to learn and absorb is almost infinite in one's early years and drops off as the brain's wiring becomes optimized for certain tasks. The drop off can be accelerated due to emotional or physical traumas. It can also be closed off because one learns a particular way of doing something or viewing the world, because of anger, hatred, hubris, or complacency. What we're looking at here is really keeping up the diversity and quality of the learning experience through life. It is keeping oneself engaged and interested throughout one's life.

I like to believe that continuous learning has to do with not losing the ability to look at the world with a child's open eyes. I think that continuous learners enjoy trying something new, experiencing something old in a new way, identifying and fully experiencing the unexpected. It's diving in headfirst and experiencing and knowing things fully. To me, it is delving into something at considerable depth, turning something over, looking at it a new way, and coming up with a new perspective and a new foundation with which to step into a new level of experience and sometimes a new level of development.

I sometimes expect others to be as passionate about learning new technologies and skills in their professional life as I. But there are many people I have known who don't manifest the drive for continuous learning in the workplace, they do their work by the book and don't seem to have any passion for continuous learning. But, then one day, I've turned around, taken another look at them in a new light, and found that they have a whole set of other facets of their life and experience that just glow (and don't have anything to do with work) that I haven't even had a minor clue about. Joseph Campbell spoke about "following one's passion". He said that the ideal in life is that one's joy becomes one's work. These people haven't followed that advice, they've branched off and found other avenues. . . . They work to live and to learn. They don't live to work.

I think you have seen these people in your own life. There's the person who works as a programmer by day, but takes joy in dance at night. There's the person who works as an accountant by day, and is fully engaged in sports at night. Then there's the electrician whose driving interest is in politics. There are the people who are passionate about their hobbies, family or religion. Are any of these less valid than those who drive themselves into their work?

There are also the people who have figured out how to do what Joseph Campbell has suggested. Their work and their passion are one. These are probably the ones that have the most developed forms of development and experience continuous learning to its fullest.

My passion is in understanding the world around me. I like understanding how things work, why they are done and how to make them better. I think that man was placed on earth to figure out why we are here and to figure out life's mysteries. There are many mysteries. When you think you've gotten a handle on something, it unveils itself to show you something different. If there is a God, he placed us here just to understand those things.

Continuous learning is just a part of my persona. It is what makes each day interesting. It is what makes life fun. It is a form of protection against boredom. Understanding what happens and why it happens makes me feel secure.

To be honest, I think I have helped others become continuous learners, but I think that the people I am around most of the time happen to be just that sort. I think for the most part my role has been to be a spark that ignites a new level of continuous learning or maybe just taking it in another direction.

In the workplace, I tend to look for people who just have it. In interviews, I like to ask people the nebulous question "What is your biggest accomplishment in life." It's kind of the open-ended question that allows you to see whether they have know accomplishment, known something at depth, and know what is important to them. I'm very disinterested in someone who tells me that back in 1965 he programmed the first payroll system on a CDC 6600 computer. That type of response says to me that the person didn't get the spark of continuous interest. That they did the one deed that made life worthwhile and that was that.

What I do like to do is to give a young new hire something to work on that gives her a perspective on things. The task is one of those doable things that can lead to something else that leads to something else, etc. That's one technique that gets the spark going.

In a broad form it is a combination of asking the right question and then being willing to mentor someone through their learning experience. The ideal question is one that can be answered in the context of their stage in their life experience. It may be a question that they can answer, but come back to and answer a different way in the filter of life's experience. The child's "where do we come from?" question is one such question. The mentoring side is important because, invariably, people can fall into the trap of learning the wrong things from their life experiences. Sometimes such learning experiences are dead end traps. It is sometimes imparting that sense that the answers we gave to the questions yesterday are not valid today. . . . The next step is developing an understanding of why, so that we come closer to the truth.

### *Cynthia McCauley*

I find myself agreeing with Phil's perspective that learning by definition is continuous, i.e., humans can't help but learn if they are having experiences and interacting with others. So, yes, I'm a continuous learner, but how often do I approach the maximum amount of learning from my experiences? Probably not often. To really be in the intentional learning mode, I have to be paying close attention, experimenting (i.e., taking action), and reflecting. I also experience a difference in (a) learning that is primarily assimilating new knowledge, ideas, and behaviors into my existing way of making sense of the world (or that requires only a little accommodating of my existing worldview) and (b) learning that requires me to go "against the grain" (a phrase we use at the Center for Creative Leadership to denote learning new behaviors that seem to go against our very nature) or learning that is developmental (i.e., my world view is transformed). The first type of learning experience is easiest for me to label "continuous learning" because it happens all the time (although, as noted above, not necessarily at a maximum level). In some ways, trying to go against the grain or to grasp some new way of making sense of the world feels more like "discontinuous learning" . . . e.g., it happens in fits and starts. I gain ground then I lose ground. I think I've changed my behavior, but then in a stressful situation I regress, I think I'm grasping some new insight only to have it evaporate.

### *Michael West*

I think when we stop continuously learning we stop living. I took up meditation practice when I was 19, and it was the beginning of a process of learning about consciousness and human experience that never stopped, even though my practice of meditation lapsed after about 20 years. I like to think (fool myself) that I learn and meditate throughout rather than during special sessions now. But I have come to believe that continuous learning for me as an individual is rooted in awareness and consciousness of here and now and the fact of life itself. It seems such a miracle and so precious to have this life (with suffering as well as pleasure and monotony as well as excitement) that being aware of it inevitably promotes continuous learning and a hunger for more learning. Perhaps, promoting continuous learning is also about promoting awareness and consciousness and demoting all the stuff that gets in the way of that.

### *Robert Mintz*

Continuous Learning means . . . to me . . . to be AWAKE! To have the humility to recognize that something or someone who is right around the corner could change your life totally. It means to me what proteanism meant to Lifton . . . an inability to hold to only one set of beliefs . . . ability to live with paradox . . . an obsession with all things new, particularly as they relate to self. It's about questioning the best use of every moment . . . if time is my wealth . . . how do I choose to spend it? Helping others to become continuous learners is my life's work. Getting people to wake up, let go of their fear, stare down their dogma(s), question their "truths" and gain an ability to accept that there are many "truths" . . . to follow their heart's desire, not the expectations of their societal programming. To find those in their lives that feed them . . . and to identify and eliminate the toxic . . . that continuous growth is not only possible but necessary. That the good news is anyone can do it . . . and the bad news is we must CONTINUE to do it . . . we're never done.

## REFLECTIONS ON LEARNING ENVIRONMENTS (CHAPTER 4)

Our online discussion produced some pointed remarks about learning environments. Recall that we began with the example of organizations establishing competencies or dimensions of performance that are valued, trained, measured, and rewarded. These competencies are a means of communicating to managers and employees what the organization cares about. They serve as a basis for learning as well as performance appraisal.

### *From David Day—On Environments That Focus on Performance Versus Learning*

Something that I believe is very important to establishing a learning culture, learning organization, or even just a stronger learning orientation at the individual level is enhancing the intentionality of learning. We tend to let learning fall off the radar screen, individually and collectively, by not paying much attention to it. We allow ourselves to get wrapped up in performance and overlook learning. This is only natural because it is the performance that gets rewarded, rarely the learning. Doing things that make our learning intentional or explicit can help to overcome these apparently natural tendencies to overlook our learning. I doubt that we will ever replace a performance orientation with a completely learning one, but there are things that can be done to balance these presses. Someone who I had the pleasure to work with in the past always asked at the end of a work session, "So what have we learned from this?" And there was (is) always something to be learned, regardless of how mundane the work. Not only did this question prompt the reflection that drives individual learning, sharing one's learning with others helped to create collective learning. I would often have a new insight into our shared work by hearing what someone else had learned from their experiences that day.

Making learning intentional does not originate in organizational policies, structures, HR practices, or the like. But it can cross hierarchical levels in an organization. Having a boss or someone else in a visible, powerful position who models an espoused learning norm by making learning intentional (by asking others about their learning) contributes to a continuous learning environment. But I wonder why there seem to be so few role models that emphasize learning in most organizations—even (especially?) academic organizations

## ON ROLES AND SUPPORT FOR LEARNING

***From Robert Mintz***

My favorite model for thinking about the systematic issues of learning comes from Blair Sheppard at Duke. It details a simple model of organizational learning with three roles:

Architects = Top Management

Translators = Middle Management

Doers = Workers

thus, creating a simple, hierarchical model of not only planning and doing, but also of learning and development.

In "real life," too few CEOs REALLY know how to be architects. Often they are translators of Board needs, marketplace demands, etc. Even if they have the gift of architecture, do they have the right kinds of managers to translate that architectural vision to the rest of the organization? In doing so, do these translators understand what learning gaps are implied by each of their translations? And how often have we been shown (e.g. "Work Out") that it's the doers who really make the best architects and translators.

Thus the essential systemic questions for me are:

Are we teaching everyone to be all three?

Are there vibrant communication channels in place to allow the system to function and transmit feedback freely, constantly educating and improving the system?

***Reactions from Phillip Doesschate***

The model of Architects, Translators and Doers certainly makes sense. I agree with Robert that "too few CEOs really know how to be architects," but I don't necessarily believe that current business culture expects that from them.

In my experience in various types of organizations, new insights come from special people who are scattered around in an organization. I'm sure you've seen them. They are in a position that is not a leadership position, but they have the knowledge, skills, abilities and have a driving interest to find new ways of doing things. These people are vital and critical resources to an organization. If they are mentored they will turn into architects, if they aren't they'll be stuffed into some back office staff position and turn into professional malcontents.

Some of the reasons for the demise of middle management in organizations is due to the fact that there is less need for translators.

*Reactions from Bob Mintz*

Alas . . . a comrade in arms! And even a tad more cynical than I! But I have to say, real life examples fit your model and nomenclature better than they do mine. Sad, but true. It's a governance and institutional shareholder problem . . . and you're right, they put into place what they think will fix the problem, not take on the big, tough issues.

*Phil Doesschate Responds*

Bob may have just shattered my view of myself as a pragmatist and realist. . . . In any case, I want to come back to the "architect, translator, doer" model for a moment and suggest that a higher level is missing. The level that is missing is the architect's sponsor. The sponsor is the one who give the broad statement of direction and need to the architect. The sponsor is the one who places the general bounds on what can and should be delivered.

Just as architects don't design buildings without a sponsor and an abstract, but bounded, statement of direction, organizations don't launch into new directions without some broad conceptualization of desire and need (e.g. market).

The sponsor can either be internal or external to the organization. Sometimes the sponsor is external, as an example in the founding of the Institute for Advanced Study in Princeton, NJ, by the Bambergers back in the 1930s who were dry goods retailers. Other times they are internal. In an ideal world the architect and sponsor are one in the same, there are many examples from private industry but a few that come to my mind is Jim Goodnight of the SAS Institute, Charles Wang of Computer Associates, and Bill Gates of MicroSoft.

*Reactions from Bob*

I have a big problem with your "higher than architect" proposition. You and I BOTH know that Boards of Directors don't care about what goes on in a company as long as the stats are right. They don't care HOW you make the numbers as long as you make the numbers. They don't care if you're written about in the *Harvard Business Review.* They don't care if everyone loves or hates you . . . did you meet or exceed the targets YOU said (NOT WE SAID) you could make. Get a grip, Phil. The sponsor . . . like the producer of a movie or play . . . takes the word of the author and director that they can make this WORK. They hold them accountable . . . they don't care what they have to do or produce to make or exceed a number.

Our on-line discussants focused on the importance of people in the organization as creators and supporters of learning environments. One viewpoint is that managers, particularly "real world" top executives, care about the bottom line above all else. Another viewpoint is that managers are keys to learning environments.

We saw this earlier in the GE example with Jack Welch as principal architect of a transformation in corporate culture.

## ON REFLEXIVITY (CHAPTER 5)

### *From David Day*

Asking "what have we learned," may be a principal way to capture the learning. Without this reflection, learning may go unnoticed by the learner as well as others who could benefit from the learning. As a consequence, the performance impact may be minimized and the extent to which learning lasts may be diminished. This suggests that, to a large extent, learning is a team process—that is, it helps to have at least one other person with whom to share it. Sharing is itself part of the learning process. As Michael West suggests, a supervisor or coach can model learning and facilitate the reflection process.

### *From Michael West*

Implementation intentions often are made because of external demands; we do something because we have to. Necessity is the mother of invention *and* implementation intentions. It's the "burning bridges" situation. We learn and apply learning because otherwise we'll go down with the bridge. Of course, there are many other mechanisms for learning, but demands and threats are important.

Yes, team learning requires doing, not just reflection. Even at the simplest level, we know that proprioceptive feedback encourages learning about physiological responses. We have to apply what we learn and see if it works.

Trained facilitators can encourage reflexivity successfully in their teams during just one day sessions. At its simplest, reflection is about encouraging team members to ask "What can we learn from this?" at the end of meetings, successes, problems, failures. It's about having an explicit intention to reflect and learn. That, for example, is what effective sports teams do all the time in viewing videoplaybacks, at half time, in strategy meetings, etc.

### *London Responds*

I agree with that necessity (e.g., critical events or crises) can motivate learning. Michael West's ideas about prompting reflexivity agree with David Day's thoughts about the value in asking, "What have I (we) learned?" I can see how a group facilitator or leader can learn to do this quite simply at the end of meetings or events.

## REFLECTIONS ON ORGANIZATIONAL LEARNING (CHAPTER 7)

Methods for generative learning, stimulated quite a bit of discussion among our online panelists.

***Robert Mintz***

I must take issue about the value of competency models. HR professionals set them up in organizations . . . but did the organization actually DO anything with them over time . . . or were they dumped, like Total Quality Management (TQM), as a fad we don't have time for . . . because they created TOO much staff work and were ANTIQUATED as soon as they were defined because the business had moved on. The only use I've seen marginally—and it's making a comeback . . . is very broad definitions of leadership competencies for high potential managers taught in corporate universities. But these are very generic across organizations . . . are almost timeless in their nature . . . not the unique picture of success for "this" company. I seriously would like to know if someone can name more than a half dozen companies that even use the phrase, "competency model." But let me be clear . . . just because this is my observation of practice, I believe in my head and heart that organizations need to STOP—DEFINE THOSE COMPETENCIES—AND USE THEM AS YOU SAY.

My broad experience with 360 feedback is that it is positioned positively but is truly meant as a collective view of what's broken. Signature strengths and building on them are hardly discussed in my experience.

I studied 25 CEOs who discovered that their "competencies" were not providing them with a life—and walked away. They learned through their lives (I used narrative life story interviewing) by embracing dissonant myths of self and success . . . and the triggers for learning were widely varied . . . and they were not highly measurable claps of thunder . . . rather they were quiet unfoldings . . . a completion of a gestalt if you will . . . they measured their learning by positioning/evaluating NOW in light of their life stories. . . . The ways in which they made their life stories coherent demonstrated the integration of major turning points . . . AFTER the fact.

***London Responds***

Bob: Sure, competency models are not long lived. Yet, in my view, they move the organization forward. They communicate expectations, provide directions for self-evaluation, not to mention evaluation by others, and ideas for development. I have seen organizations build on prior competency models, refining them, sometimes unveiling a new set of competencies and performance management programs in relation to changing organization needs. This does not mean that the earlier iterations had no effect.

I would say the same about other human resource programs, such as TQM. These programs had their pluses and minuses, clearly, but they educated many employees about the nature of quality improvement and ways of encouraging people to participate in the process. Some employees don't benefit, and some departments don't, but others do. Unfortunately, we rarely track the evolution of these programs, how human resource initiatives build on each other, and whether they increase the organization's effectiveness and adaptability with each iteration.

***Later, Robert Mintz Writes***

Manny: You are entitled to your delusions. But not a SINGLE one of the "isms" you preach made a measurable difference in ANY corporation [in] America . . . and I challenge you to prove me wrong with just ONE example. Competency models . . . at best . . . describe what an organization HISTORICALLY has wanted . . . it has NO relevance to what it is . . . nor to what it thinks it can become. They don't clarify expectations . . . you HIGHLY underestimate the intelligence of most workers . . . everyone knows it's the flavor of the month. Get a grip! Did they have an effect? SURE . . . they distracted HOURS of worker time . . . during which awake people could have practically solved the problems of the day. Same challenge on TQM . . . Rubbermaid was an icon and now . . . ? You academics had better start spending a WHOLE lot more time LIVING in real organizations. You're dreaming. Actually, and more accurately, hallucinating.

***London Responds***

I spent 12 years as a corporate human resource manager. Of course that proves your point, not mine. I'm just not as cynical by nature. But I'm not pollyannish either. I agree that the value of organizational learning and development programs is largely unknown, weak, and possibly detrimental in distracting from the "real" business at hand. There has been some research to indicate their limited effectiveness under certain conditions, but many forces beyond the corporation's human resource operations influence success and failure.

***From Valerie Sessa***

I've learned quite a bit through my work at the Center for Creative Leadership, my consulting work, and my experience within large organizations, and I've run into folks like those Bob suggests (such as being sexually harassed by a man being groomed as the next CEO of a VERY large financial institution, and sitting gape-mouthed as I listened to top executives make inappropriate comments about gays, etc.). I've also run into people at all organizational levels who really believe they can make a positive difference in themselves and their organizations. And they are looking for new and old models to help them, and they are willing to try. I've seen mediocre stuff by well meaning employees or consultants. I've seen some terrible stuff instituted by snake oil salesmen-type consultants who earn their bread and butter through "guerilla warfare" and care not whether they truly help the organization. And I've seen great (old?) ideas instituted across organizations that really seem to "work." I have watched teams who had received some of the best team training I've encountered (developed by organizational psychologists, incidentally) actually using tools and doing great teamwork Xerox during their Malcom Baldridge quality improvement turnaround era, and I've seen wonderful leadership development work with high potential managers at Bristol Meyers Squibb. These programs don't last forever, but they have their place and effect.

And given that I deliberately went into an applied psychology field with the hopes that I could do a little to move science and practice forward, I guess I'm more optimistic. And I hope not in a "Candidian sense."

I agree our old models don't work . . . not because they can't work, but because of the way we try to institute them and because of all the unforseen and unintended consequences of pushing levers in a largely piece meal manner in complex systems. I guess what I see us as needing and am hoping to add through our exploration of continuous learning is a more complex understanding of change (learning) in individuals, teams, and organizations and how these levels interact. Rather than all revolutionary new models, maybe a new layer that helps us pull together our knowledge and practice.

The following discussion relates to organizational learning in general.

***From Robert Mintz***

Having worked in large ones for 25 years, I'm not convinced there is such a thing as organizational learning. The most powerful form of organizational learning that I witnessed early on was compliance to cultural norms. These norms served as a backdrop against which interventions could be devised by level. Cultures have all but been obliterated in most organizations . . . and today, most organizations seem incapable of even articulating a cogent business strategy, let alone building any kind of meaningful organizational learning plan.

I think group learning occurs on some level. I also believe that the recent literature about gender differences in team building is informative. Net net, men quickly build weak teams; women are slow to build, but once the team is built, it's virtually indestructible. Men focus on the task; women focus on the relationship and the worthiness of the objective.

What I see today is a vacuum created by the loss of corporate culture and a compelling vision-myth-belief system that engages workers and makes them want to be a part of something larger than they. Organizations are currently so chaotic and toxic principally because they ARE systems but are not being lead by systems thinkers. There are actors acting out locally, creating tremendous global reactions that they neither expected nor planned for. With few exceptions, organizations are simply no longer "safe" enough for people to explore their own creativity. In contrast, the European CEOs that I've worked with have managed to retain some view of the end game. This (with albeit arcane labor laws and practices) provides a much higher level of engagement on the part of workers than I see in the US. For me, the broad issue is: how are American multinationals going to move past their sole obsession with near-term results . . . so they can meaningfully reengage their people to invent approaches and solutions that are new and appropriate? We've pretty much demonstrated our ability to overuse the old tools and virtually beat our businesses into the ground as a result. Compounding the problem in the US is the cynicism at all levels with too many years of consultants selling silver bullets . . . and with CEOs who dump an idea on a dime for the next one that looks sexier. I think there is a prevailing sense out there (most painfully at the highest levels of corporate governance)—that people haven't a clue what to do. They've burned out themselves and their key people do the old stuff "bigger, better and faster." What they need are new approaches, but are creating environments that stifle any creativity. Thus, it's hard for me to think about this from a tactical perspective when I see so much systemic disease.

### *From Cynthia McCauley*

I wonder, do knowledge-based organizations pose any truly new challenges for people interested in understanding and managing organizations? I have heard two themes from managers in more knowledge-intensive organizations: (1) An increased awareness that their competitive advantage is in their human capital, and thus increased worries about the knowledge walking out the door. This gives knowledge workers more power in an organization. Does the shift in power among organizational constituency groups bring new challenges for managing organizations? (2) More lateral interaction within organizations at lower hierarchical levels. To meet customer needs or to work on organizational challenges, knowledge-intensive organizations seem to be more likely to bring people together who not only have different knowledge bases and knowledge structures, but also different perspectives on what's most valuable or important for the organization. I'm not sure this is a brand new challenge for organizations. Organizations have traditionally used the management hierarchy to resolve perspective differences, but in the knowledge-intensive organizations, perhaps there's more expectation for the integration and coordination of perspectives to occur among the knowledge workers themselves as they work on customer or organizational issues.

In response to Bob Mintz, I find myself not as seemingly pessimistic as I interpreted your comments about "learning organizations." I agree that there is likely not an organization out there that has achieved the ideal processes and outcomes that are often associated with this concept, but I have read about and talked to people who have been members of organizations when they felt the organization had gone through a period of useful learning. Again this might all be definitional. That is, by *useful* learning, I mean that there have been collective changes in know-how, behavior, and practices that made the organization more successful. Perhaps organizations are better able to engage in Mezirow's (1991) "instrumental learning" and what many need is more "transformative learning" which is less likely when short-term gains are the only focus.

Definitional perspectives aside, I totally agree that there are great pressures to increase the speed of learning (at the individual, team, and organizational levels). We hear about it all the time at think tanks and training institutes like the Center for Creative Leadership, and it is a perplexing problem. A number of tactics have been utilized to speed up learning at one or more of these levels, for example, pairing experts and novices in work projects, using action learning projects to integrate learning into work, creating and supporting communities of practice (that allow experts to more quickly connect with one another to solve problems), and rapid prototyping of new products and services. Do you believe the pressure for speed is so great that even these types of tactics don't help? Are the expectations for speed unrealistic or are we just experiencing the "in over our heads" feeling because we haven't developed adequate ways of understanding this problem?

***From David Day***

As you likely know, I am also interested in how to enhance organizational cultures/systems/practices so that more learning, and in particular, more transformative learning (à la Mezirow, 1990, 1991) happens as a regular part of life in work settings. I agree that intentionality is a key construct or dimension—one that could be operationalized at individual, team, and organizational levels. What might be other dimensions? What about interaction? The hypothesis would be that organizational systems/practices that increase interaction among individuals, among teams, or among organizations would enhance learning.

Why do we have so few role models? Maybe in our individualistic culture, we expect individuals to be effective at their own learning, but don't expect or reward them for creating a context for others to learn.

I believe that team and organizational learning is more than the aggregate learning of individual members of the team or organization I'm not sure how to articulate the "more than." As you say, changes in collective routines may be one indicator. What about being able to work in more complex and interconnected ways?

***Robert Mintz***

I feel that SOME organizations are (more than they used to) asking "what did we learn" from specific experiences. I see/hear about momentary reflection . . . my issue is the lack of real analysis and integration of learning. I've seen organizations try to use Senge's (1990) concepts of dialogue and reflection work . . . with people throwing their hands up at the "wasted time" failing to utilize yet another tool. My sense is that "useful learning" as you describe it is more cathartic and emotional than an agent for real change. That said, I do think there are pockets of "useful learning" all over corporations that do just what you suggest, using the tools you describe. My question is . . . does their management have a clue? Do they get rewarded for using these tools, or are they penalized for taking too much time? Also, staff "right-sizing" has all but eliminated the experts from a huge numbers of organizations, leaving contract "experts" (workers or consultants) to fill the gap. They may add some content knowledge, but they lack the old mentoring qualities of contextual understanding linked to content knowledge. I agree that action learning is popular, but it isn't processed unless something goes wrong . . . and then the person is shot, not the process. I saw more communities of practice within companies in the 1980s . . . more of what today we would call blogs and virtual communities created because of the LACK of them inside organizations.

I definitely feel that we are experiencing the "in over our heads" phenomena because our first inclination is adrenalin, not reflection. And, we still think the old tools will work . . . if we just bang them hard enough . . . when what we really need is time to think about what totally new approaches are required.

I totally agree with your assessment that our individualistic culture says, "Hey, learning agility/ability is YOUR problem and a competence we expect you to walk in the door with."

### *Later, Robert Mintz Added*

I think we have to teach people to be awake . . . all day . . . every day . . . that around the next corner may come their greatest insight. And to teach them they will find genius in the most unlikely of spots . . . and to stop looking at the traditional bearers of power . . . because they have demonstrated to the world that they are actually powerless. And we have to teach them that, through their exchanges with strangers, they will come upon the new "truths." The alternative is total arrogance. What will fix the emerging . . . will come from the emerging ideas of lots of people in dialogue . . . venerating "holders of knowledge" Didn't the crap of the 20th century teach anyone anything? Ladies and gentlemen, flush your "models" — it's a new day.

## SOME FINAL WORDS FROM OUR ONLINE DISCUSSION PARTICIPANTS (CHAPTER 9)

We asked our panelists about pressures, trends, and opportunities in learning and development today.

### *From Bill Byham*

We have the same old pressures for more quality with less time and expense. It's just exacerbated by the current economic situation. Many companies are jumping on a Web-delivered, self-learning paradigm for which there is no good evidence of effectiveness in leadership training. In fact, there's little evidence people even take the training. There's no question that a lot of traditional training and development is wasted, but on the other hand, there's no magic pill, people still have to be taught, they still have to practice and get feedback, etc.

Of course there are interesting cultural differences around the world, but we find that our training programs work everywhere in the world with basically the same content, in basically the same format, and set up. We find that in certain countries in Europe, for instance, you have to provide more theory before you get into skill building. We find that the skills that are important for interpersonal effectiveness vary slightly among organizations and among cultures. But in general, we've been impressed how universal are the needs for training and development. I think they'll even get more common as the world becomes more inter-related.

We often comment that in dealing with big multi-national companies, the differences between companies are greater than the differences between countries. While saying the above, there certainly is a need for more research on cultural differences. There are many important differences. One example is that if you factor analyze 360° data on exactly the same competencies, but administered in different countries, you get different factor structures for the different countries. This has meaning in comparing people from one country to another, and more importantly, it tells you something about the nature of work within those countries.

***Valerie Sessa***

There are some things that inhibit people's learning and development. A person's current development level may affect many behaviors we typically think of as "skills" (Kegan, 1982). One easy example is that perspective-taking might mean something wholly different to people in different stages of development. Systems thinking may not even be possible at certain levels of development. A person's Zone of Proximal Development also has an impact on what can be learned and developed (Vygotsky, 1978). Today's organizational complexity calls for more than the what current employees at many levels of capable of. Systems thinking? That's an understatement in what's needed in today's organizations. Double/triple loop learning may sound nice to employees in the abstract, but do they really "get it" (do I really get it?).

Karakowsky and McBey (1999) suggested two other variables that may affect readiness to learn in addition to developmental stage. First is *psychological presence,* which they define as the extent to which individuals are tuned in to their performance or behavior at work. People with low psychological presence in the workplace can not accomplish developmental tasks of intimacy or self-reflection, nor can they learn about or change ineffective patterns of behavior. Second, is *schemas about work,* which reduce the need to continually question and confront what's really going on at work. I once heard the term "velvet rut," which I pretty much think summarizes these two in lay terms!

Some things at the organization level that inhibit individual learning and development: At a broad level, I think that most organization policies, procedures, systems affect individual learning and development. The most obvious is the reward system. Individuals learn to do what is rewarded. Work overload and job stress (due to downsizing/right sizing, mergers and acquisitions, emphasis on short term goals, the current economy, etc.) have left employees happy to have jobs but wanting to keep their heads down and not be noticed. Many employees are in survival mode, and this influences the organization's performance.

Karakowsky and McBey (1999) mentioned several other workplace factors that affect learning and development. *Reliance on routinized work* (while good and useful at saving time and energy to the organization) does not provide sufficient challenge for individuals to think beyond the immediate requirements of their jobs. Also, in organizations in which *institutionalized structures* (the processes by which shared beliefs take on a rule-like status) are deeply entrenched, employees are less likely to question or push the status quo or take risks and thus learn and develop. In addition, encouraging/rewarding employees to submit heavily to their *role expectations* at work without considering the appropriateness of these duties to the self outside the role inhibits learning and development. Bellman (2000) suggested that largely people's desire for predictability leads to stagnation.

***Robert Mintz Replies***

Ahhh . . . ALL of us are trying to find ways to link our worlds and experience to Kegan's because we REALLY want to, but there is so little evidence. Yes, you DO get double and triple loop learning. My problem with both you and Manny is that you are clearly operating at this level DAILY . . . while the rest of the world . . . you're right, doesn't get you.

And I think your nailing of Bellman is ABSOLUTELY right . . . it is the deviants who create learning environments. I seriously question if humans like "predictability, order and control" REALLY . . . but absent a useful and meaningful alternative, what are they to choose? Your point about hierarchy is my BIGGEST issue with what's going on in institutions . . . the "young" are looking up to "the toxic" and deciding that's what they need to emulate . . . and it IS a natural inclination on their part. Ladies and gentlemen . . . it is the alpha males and females that the rest model themselves after . . . and it is THOSE PEOPLE that are most toxic and are putting our organizations at most risk. They are NOT learners, in my humble opinion.

Upon reflection, a point that I didn't make as clear as I wanted was the lack of systems understanding of those who attempt organizational interventions. The key elements of the intervention/education are great, but the problem is that designers and implementers don't understand the systemic consequences of these huge initiatives. They are literally too much for the system to focus on, and entropy occurs QUICKLY. So you lose the baby AND the bath water . . . and worse . . . set up a thicker defensive shield in the organization for the next time you want to do something. Those in charge of learning have this annoying habit of forgetting that line people have day jobs.

APPENDIX

# B

# Personal Reflections on the Meaning of Continuous Learning

The following are personal reflections on the meaning of continuous learning. We asked a selected group of acquaintances who seemed to us to be continuous learners whether they thought of themselves this way and to express what continuous learning meant to them. In particular, we asked whether they considered themselves to be continuous learners and about the importance of continuous learning in their lives. We also asked whether they believed they had helped others to become continuous learners.

This is a convenience sample of people we happened to know. Other individuals who are less highly educated or come from different walks of life may have different ideas. Nevertheless, the responses shed light on the meaning of continuous learning and how it has a defining impact on the lives of these people. Here's what they had to say:

### *Ann Helfgott—Judaic Scholar and Educator, Artist, and Hebrew Calligrapher*

Yes, I consider myself to be a continuous learner! Although I am not taking any formal courses at the moment, I am constantly researching various topics, usually in order to teach, but sometimes in order to paint them on a ketubbah [a Jewish wedding contract]. I find that at this time in my life, I more easily remember what I learn if I use my new knowledge right away. To me continuous learning means many things: adding to my fund of information; acquiring a new skill or polishing an old skill; learning to see something in a different way; and making new connections between facts or ideas that I have previously mastered. There are probably many other activities which I would consider to be continuous learning, but these are my main ideas on the subject.

The importance of continuous learning? It makes me feel alive, and I plan to do it until I die. I hope to take some more formal courses when I am less busy. Right now I'm teaching a college course on the Holocaust, and I find that I'm constantly learning in order to be a better teacher—I'm learning more about my subject, I'm learning about resources to use to get my point across, and I'm constantly evaluating and re-evaluating what works and what doesn't. I also try to give my students several different ways to think about the events which we discuss. I think that one of the most exciting things about teaching is figuring out how to organize the material. I'm also teaching Hebrew to a group of nine senior citizens, several of whom are well into their eighties. They are great! They have eased my fears of growing old.

***Richard Bronson, MD—Infertility Specialist***

Yes, I am a continuous learner, for better or worse. I can only speculate how I became one. Was I born with the personality that desires to continually acquire knowledge? I do feel uneasy about "doing nothing" during the day. I keep my time quite filled, on a moment to moment basis. I like to read, and there is a lot to know. I'm curious about most things as well. Learning also helps one to understand life's many aspects. This occurs not only through reading, but doing. Learning can encompass music, art, poetry. It also includes acquisition of physical skills used in sports. It's all a lot of fun, too. Do I feel anxiety at times, when I have placed too many burdens on myself? Yes, but most of the time, I do value the varied experiences and obligations I set for myself or that are required of me.

In high school, I was inculcated with the values of "citizenship" in America, and the need to be informed and politically active. The pursuit of knowledge and awareness of current events was emphasized as important to maintain democracy. Staying informed was the first rule of the active life. Then, in medicine, I feel an obligation to keep up with the advance of knowledge, which has been particularly rapid . . . though I'm not sure it is any more rapid than in some other fields. In medical school, my mentors taught me, through their example, the value system of continuous education. CME [continuing medical education] credits, post graduate courses, conferences are all part of the medical "scene," though how much of these activities involve socializing and traveling versus true acquisition of knowledge can be debated. Am I a compulsive learner?

I have not discussed this philosophy with my children, though two of them seem to have followed my path. Nor have I discussed these thoughts with medical students with whom I interact. There has been no opportunity, which is a sad thing. . . . Something bad has happened to medical education, and I am not sure the students actually desire it or know how to find mentors. This sense of uneasiness goes beyond curricular review, to more basic issues of medical education that have not yet been addressed. I see this, having the advantage of a longer perspective.

***Richard Gerrig, PhD—Professor of Experimental Psychology***

The term suggests an on-going curiosity that transcends the particular requirements of one's job. In the way I just defined the concept, I believe that I do qualify as a continuous learner. Still, as I've grown older the breadth of my curiosity has narrowed. That is, I read all the time, but in a smaller number of areas than I did 20 years ago. I consider continuous learning to be absolutely critical. As much as I enjoy my major areas (experimental psychology), I'd grow fatally bored if I didn't continue to acquire new knowledge in other fields. I encourage my students to expand their horizons and to lay the groundwork for a lifetime of reading.

***Br. Clark Berge, SSF—Protestant Campus Ministry Chaplain***

I have long considered myself a continuous learner. I think I came to that realization after seminary. Preparing one or two weekly sermons has required me to read, talk with others, challenge my pre-conceptions and get honest about my assumptions.

Being a continuous learner means more than just reading or studying books. It has meant looking at my life and the life of the people around me and trying to be open to the text of Life. As a Christian I ask myself: what is God trying to teach me about myself? About the world? Sometimes the insight has come as a welcome gift. Other times I have felt sorely burdened and upset, especially when the new insight into myself or others has meant I need to change my life. So far, even the difficult times have proved, in retrospect, to be blessings. This then is the importance of continuous learning: that I grow into greater maturity, learn to appreciate the complexity of life and accept the parts I have no idea what to do with just yet.

I believe very strongly that when a person gives up on life, when they stop asking questions of themselves and others, their life begins to diminish. So I try very hard to provoke others to question, to open themselves up to the surprise of life. I do this in my teaching, preaching, and informally whenever I am struck by a different perspective, a new idea, a different insight, or see something really beautiful.

***Stella Lee—Web Designer***

I am always in the process of acquiring new knowledge (including but not limiting to new skills, technique, information, hobbies, etc), new perspectives on things. Yes, I'm definitely a continuous learner. I always can find something interesting and new to learn. Just not enough time!

I think I just have this urge to learn; I'm just very curious about things I don't know and also to keep up with professional knowledge. I can't imagine anyone not being a continuous learner. It is almost required in this day and age for one to keep on learning. Besides, what else is there to do if you don't watch TV?

I always encourage people to go back to school, pick up a new hobby, etc.

***Sr. Margaret Ann Landry, RSHM—Chaplain, Catholic Campus Ministry/Interfaith Center***

I see continuous learning as equivalent to *lifelong learning,* a process that goes on throughout all stages of one's life. Education begins in the family, carries through structured education outside the home and continues with *all* our life experiences beyond the classroom. All of these comprise both "formal" and "informal" education, i.e.: education of the mind and heart. A motto I use in my own life is "The glory of God is a person fully alive!" (St. Irenaeus) I believe one remains "fully alive" by always trying to learn from *life experiences* and being attuned to all the events, circumstances and especially the people with whom one journeys through life.

Yes, I definitely consider myself to be a continuous learner. Fortunately, I was born into a family with strong religious values and one that believed strongly in the value of education. As a result, I went to excellent schools before joining a religious community. I graduated from college with a major in Philosophy and a minor in French, then pursued an M.A. in History. Throughout my life I have studied Theology, Spirituality and Worship, Economics, Latin and Chinese history. Beyond these formal educational experiences, I have had the opportunity to learn by my experiences in travel throughout the United States, Europe and Africa. One cannot help but learn through these experiences about diverse cultures, traditions, languages and religions. I believe in the importance of athletics in my life and their importance in the lives of others. Through sports we learn about the "game" of life . . . how to be a leader, a team player and a good sportsman (woman). Another important learning experience is that of realizing the significance of transferable skills. In my life it has been invaluable to realize this significance in positions I have held as an educator at the secondary school level and in administrative positions at the college level. I have been Director for Transfer Students and was fortunate to be the first Director of Academic Advising at Marymount Manhattan College. At Marymount I established a Peer Advising Program. In this program I utilized the same skill sets that I do in working with college age students as Chaplain in Catholic Campus Ministry at Stony Brook University where I established the Peer Minister Program.

Continuous learning is vital to my personal spiritual religious life. There is a necessity to learn more about and develop my relationship with God and it's meaning in my own life and its relationship to the wider world community.

I believe I need to keep growing as a spiritual person so that I can *connect* with and be of assistance to others. This is especially important when relating to students who look to me for guidance and counsel. When one stops learning, one becomes static with regard to world views and approaches to people. Keeping au courant of current articles, books, etc. is essential. For several summers, my religious community has sponsored a program called "Festival of Learning" at which we do in-depth study on such issues as eco-spirituality, ecology, post-modernism, etc. I am also a member of our "On-Going Spiritual and Theological Renewal Committee" which plans and sponsors programs in these and many more far-reaching topic areas that enhance spiritual growth and development.

I am a person who assists others to be continuous learners . . . with staff and students especially.

The staff in the Interfaith Center encourages one another in the area of professional development devoting our meeting time every other week to a topic related to effectiveness in our ministries. We learn about each other's religions and discuss scriptural passages, etc. Currently, we are reading and discussing a very timely book: *Abraham: A Journey to the Heart of Three Faiths* by Bruce Feiler. Last year, we presented a very effective series of programs entitled "Candid Conversations," which provided students and staff the opportunity to ask questions about each others' faiths.

Students indicate that I assist them in becoming continuous learners in both the religious/spiritual context and in their own personal growth and development. Through programs we offer in Catholic Campus Ministry students learn about various cultures, spiritual and religious traditions, ethnic foods, etc. I endeavor to provide opportunities to learn about and appreciate the wealth of diversity on the campus. I encourage students to participate in "education beyond the classroom" experiences by participating in campus activities and engaging in leadership roles. My mission is to assist students to achieve their highest potential both spiritually and academically, as well as giving them the opportunity to raise their awareness and consciousness about justice and peace.

I believe strongly in the concept of valuing one's *work* experience—recognizing that what one does in the workplace can be invaluable as an aspect of "continuous learning." At Marymount Manhattan College, I was the Coordinator for the Life Experience for Credit Program. In this program the adult learners developed a *Life Experience Portfolio* demonstrating what they had learned as a result of their experiences with specific references to courses in the college catalogue for which academic credit was being requested. The process was very demanding but well worth the effort the students made in presenting their portfolios. It gave them an appreciation of what they had accomplished. We always indicated that no matter how many or how few credits they received, they should give credit to themselves for all they had achieved in their lives. The program was a model for other colleges and universities.

# References


Ackerman, P. L. (1996). A theory of adult intellectual development: Process, personality, interests, and knowledge. *Intelligence, 22,* 227–257.

Ackerman, P. L., & Rolfhus, E. L. (1999). The locus of adult intelligence: Knowledge, abilities, and nonability traits. *Psychology and Aging, 14,* 314–330.

Albert, R. D. (1996). A framework and model for understanding Latin American and Latino/Hispanic cultural patterns. In D. Landis & R. S. Bhagat (Eds.), *Handbook of intercultural training* (2nd ed., pp. 327–348). Thousand Oaks, CA: Sage.

Albrecht, K. (2003). *The power of minds at work: Organizational intelligence in action.* New York: AMACOM.

Aldag, R. J., & Fuller, S. R. (1993). Beyond fiasco: A reappraisal of the group think phenomenon and a new model of group decision processes. *Psychological Bulletin, 113,* 533–552.

Anderson, W. T. (1997). *The future of self: Inventing the postmodern person.* New York: Putnam.

Antonioni, D. (1996). Designing an effective 360-degree appraisal feedback process. *Organizational Dynamics, 25,* 24–38.

Appreciative Inquiry Commons. (2003). Retrieved May 19, 2003, from http://appreciativeinquiry.cwru.edu/intro/whatisai.cfm

Argote, L., Gruenfeld, D., & Naquin, C. (2001). Group learning in organizations. In M. E. Turner (Ed.), *Groups at work: Theory and research* (pp. 369–412). Mahwah, NJ: Lawrence Erlbaum Associates.

Argyris, C. (1991, May–June). Teaching smart people how to learn. *Harvard Business Review,* pp. 99–109 (Reprint No. 9130).

Argyris, C., & Schön, D. A. (1978). *Organizational learning: A theory of action perspective.* San Francisco: Jossey-Bass.

Aron, L. J. (2000). Managing to learn: How companies can turn knowledge into action. In *Working Knowledge.* Boston, MA: Harvard Business School. Retrieved November 13, 2004, from http://www.hbsworkingknowledge.hbs.edu

Aronson, D. (1999). *Thinking page.* Retrieved June 23, 2003, from http://www.thniking.net/index.html

Arrow, H. (1997). Stability, bistability, and instability in small group influence patterns. *Journal of Personality and Social Psychology, 72*(1), 75–85.

Arthur, W., Jr., Bennett, W., Jr., Edens, P. S., & Bell, S. T. (2003). Effectiveness of training in organizations: A meta-analysis of design and evaluation features. *Journal of Applied Psychology, 88*(2), 234–245.

Atwater, L. E., Waldman, D. A., Atwater, D., & Cartier, P. (2000). An upward feedback field experiment: Supervisors' cynicism, reactions, and commitment to subordinates. *Personnel Psychology, 53,* 275–297.

Austin, J. R. (2003). Transactive memory in organizational groups: The effects of content, consensus, specialization, and accuracy on group performance. *Journal of Applied Psychology, 88*(5), 866–878.

Ausubel, D. P. (1968). *Educational psychology: A cognitive view.* New York: Holt, Rinehart & Winston.

Bailey, C., & Fletcher, C. (2002). The impact of multiple source feedback on management development: Findings from a longitudinal study. *Journal of Organizational Behavior, 23*(7), 853–867.

Baker, A. C., Jensen, P. J., & Kolb, D. A. (2002). Conversational learning: An experiential approach to knowledge creation. Westport, CT: Quorum Books.

Bandura, A. (1986). *Social foundations of thought and action: A social cognitive theory.* Englewood Cliffs, NJ: Prentice-Hall.

Barrick, M. R., & Mount, M. K. (1991). The big five personality dimensions and job performance: A meta-analysis. *Personnel Psychology, 44,* 1–26.

Barriere, M. T., Anson, B. R., Ording, R. S., & Rogers, E. (2002). Culture transformation in a health care organization: A process of building adaptive capabilities through leadership development. *Consulting Psychology Journal: Practice and Research, 54*(2), 116–130.

Baumeister, R. (1998). The self. In D. Gilbert, S. Fiske, & G. Lindzey (Eds.), *The handbook of social psychology* (Vol. 1, pp. 680–740). Boston: McGraw-Hill.

Beal, D. J., Cohen, R. R., Burke, M. J., & McLendon, C. L. (2003). Cohesion and performance in groups: A meta-analytic clarification of construct relations. *Journal of Applied Psychology, 88*(6), 989–1004.

Beersma, B., Hollenbeck, J. R., Humphrey, S. E., Moon, H., Conlon, D. E., & Ilgen, D. R. (2003). Cooperation, competition, and team performance: Toward a contingency approach. *The Academy of Management Journal, 46*(3), 572–590.

Bell, B. S., & Kozlowski, W. J. (2002). Goal orientation and ability: Interactive effects on self-efficacy, performance, and knowledge. *Journal of Applied Psychology, 87*(3), 497–505.

Bellman, G. (2000). *The beauty of the beast.* San Francisco: Berrett-Koehler.

Ben-Peretz, M. (2002). Retired teachers reflect on learning from experience. *Teachers and teaching: Theory and Practice 8*(3–4), 313–323.

Berry, D. C., & Dienes, Z. (1993). *Implicit learning: Theoretical and empirical issues.* Hove, England: Lawrence Erlbaum Associates.

Bohm, D. (1996). *On dialogue.* New York: Routledge.

Bohm, D., Factor, D., & Garrett, P. (1991). Dialogue—A proposal. Retrieved April 27, 2005, from http://www.david-bohm.net/dialogue/dialogue_proposal.html#1

Bonk, C. J., & Kim, K. A. (1998). Extending sociocultural theory to adult learning. In M. C. Smith & T. Pourchot (Eds.), *Adult learning and development: Perspectives from educational psychology* (pp. 67–88). Mahwah, NJ: Lawrence Erlbaum Associates.

Borman, W. C., & Motowidlo, S. J. (1993). Expanding the criterion domain to include elements of contextual performance. In N. Schmitt, W. C. Borman, & Associates (Eds.), *Personnel selection in organizations* (pp. 71–98). San Francisco: Jossey-Bass.

Bransford, J. D., Brown, A. L. & Cocking, R. R. (2000). *How people learn: Brain, mind, experience, and school.* Washington, DC: National Academy Press.

Brass, D. J., Galaskiewicz, J., Greve, H. R., & Tsai, W. (2004). Taking stock of networks and organizations: A multilevel perspective. *Academy of Management Journal, 47,* 795–819.

Brief, A. P., & Motowidlo, S. J. (1986). Prosocial organizational behaviors. *Academy of Management Review, 11,* 710–725.

Bronfenbrenner, U. (1979). *The ecology of human development: Experiments by nature and design.* Cambridge, MA: Harvard University Press.

Brown, D. J., Ganesan, S., & Challagalla, G. (2001). Self-efficacy as a moderator of information seeking effectiveness. *Journal of Applied Psychology, 86*(5), 1043–1051.

Bruner, J. S. (1960). *The process of education.* New York: Vintage.

Buckley, W. F. (2003, October 12). You could look it up. *New York Times Review of Books,* p. 13.

Buffardi, L. C., Fleishman, E. A., Morath, R. A., & McCarthy, P. M. (2000). Relationships between ability requirements and human errors in job tasks. *Journal of Applied Psychology, 85*(4), 551–564.

Bunderson, J. S. (2003). Team member functional background and involvement in management teams: Direct effects and the moderating role of power centralization. *Academy of Management Journal, 46*(4), 458–474.

Bunderson, J. S., & Sutcliffe, K. M. (2002). Why some teams emphasize learning more than others: Evidence from business unit management teams. In H. Sondak (Vol. Ed.), E. A. Mannix, & M. A. Neale (Series Eds.), *Research on managing groups and teams: Vol. 4. Toward phenomenology of groups and group membership* (pp. 49–84). Oxford, England: Elsevier Science.

Bunderson, J. S., & Sutcliffe, K. M. (2003). Management team learning orientation and business unit performance. *Journal of Applied Psychology, 88*(3), 552–560.

Bunker, K. A., & Webb, A. D. (1992). *Learning how to learn from experience: Impact on stress and coping* (Report No. 154). Greensboro, NC: Center for Creative Leadership.

Burke, C. S., Fowlkes, J. E. Wilson, K. A., & Salas, E. (2003). A concept of soldier adaptability: Implications for design and training. In R. Hoffman & L. Tocarcik (Co-Chairs), Innovative Design Concepts for the Objective Force, *Proceedings of the Army Research Laboratory Collaborative Technology Alliance Annual Symposium.* College Park, MD: .

Burke, P. J., & Stets, J. E. (1999). Trust and commitment through self-verification. *Social Psychological Quarterly, 62,* 347–360.

Button, S. B., Mathieu, J. E., & Zajac, D. M. (1996). Goal orientation in organizational research: A conceptual and empirical foundation. *Organizational Behavior and Human Decision Processes, 67,* 26–48.

Cameron, K. S., & Whetten, D. A. (1981). Perceptions of organizational effectiveness over organizational lifecycles. *Administrative Science Quarterly, 26,* 525–545.

Cappelli, P. (1999). *The new deal at work.* Boston: Harvard Business School Press.

Capra, F. (1997). *The web of life: A new scientific understanding of living systems.* New York: Anchor Books.

Capra, F. (2002). *The hidden connections: Integrating the biological, cognitive, and social dimensions of life into a science of sustainability.* New York: Doubleday.

Carley, K. (1991). A theory of group stability. *American Sociological Review, 56,* 331–354.

Carnevale, P. J., & Probst, T. M. (1998). Social values and social conflict in creative problem solving and categorization. *Journal of Personality and Social Psychology, 74,* 1300–1309.

Cattell, R. B. (1943). The measurement of adult intelligence. *Psychological Bulletin, 40,* 153–193.

Chang, A., Bordia, P, & Duck, J. (2003). Punctuated equilibrium and linear progression: Toward a new understanding of group development. *Academy of Management Journal, 46*(1), 106–117.

Chattopadhyay, P., Glick, W. H., & Huber, G. P. (2001). Organizational actions in response to threats and opportunities. *Academy of Management Journal, 44,* 937–955.

Chen, E. C., & Mallinckrodt, B. (2002). Attachment, group attraction, and self–other agreement in interpersonal circumplex problems and perceptions of group members. *Group Dynamics: Theory, Research, and Practice, 6*(4), 311–324.

Chen, G., & Klimoski, R. J. (2003). The impact of expectations on newcomer performance in teams as mediated by work characteristics, social exchanges, and empowerment. *The Academy of Management Journal, 46*(5), 591–607.

Chonko, L. B., Jones, E., Roberts, J. A., & Dubinsky, A. J. (2002). The role of environmental turbulence, readiness for change, and salesperson learning in the success of sales force change. *Journal of Personal Selling & Sales Management, 22,* 227–245.

Chowdhury, S. (2001). *The power of Six Sigma: An inspiring tale of how Six Sigma is transforming the way we work.* Chicago: Dearborn Trade.

Chuang, Y. T., & Baum, J. A. C. (2003). It's all in the name: Failure-induced learning by multiunit chains. *Administrative Science Quarterly, 48*(1), 33–59.

Cochran, C. C., Lammlein, S. E., Logan, K. K., & Bennett, W., Jr. (2003, April). *Improving the effectiveness of training: Toward a model of skill retention.* Paper presented at the 18th annual meeting of the Society for Industrial and Organizational Psychology, Orlando, FL.

Cohen, D., & Prusak, L. (2001). *In good company: How social capital makes organizations work.* Boston: Harvard Business School Press.

Colarelli, S. M. (1998). Psychological interventions in organizations: An evolutionary perspective. *American Psychologist, 53*(9), 1044–1056.

Cole, M., Sharp, D., & Lave, C. (1976). The cognitive consequences of education: Some empirical evidence and theoretical misgivings. *Urban Review, 9,* 218–233.

Colquitt, J. A., LePine, J. A., & Noe, R. A. (2000). Toward an integrative theory of training motivation: A meta-analytic path analysis of 20 years of research. *Journal of Applied Research, 85,* 678–707.

Colquitt, J. A., & Simmering, M. J. (1998). Conscientiousness, goal orientation, and motivation to learn during the learning process: A longitudinal study. *Journal of Applied Psychology, 83,* 654–665.

Cooper, R., & Sawaf, A. (1996). *Executive EQ: Emotional intelligence in leadership and organizations.* New York: Grosset/Putnam.

Cooperrider, D. L., & Whitney, D. (1999). *A positive revolution in change: Appreciative inquiry.* Manuscript in preparation (Available at http://appreciativeinquiry.cwru.edu/uploads/whatisai.pdf). Accessed April 27, 2005.

Corey, M. S., & Corey, G. (2002). *Groups: Process and practice* (6th ed.). Pacific Grove, CA: Brooks/Cole.

Crant, J. M. (2000). Proactive behavior in organizations. *Journal of Management, 26,* 435–462.

Crossan, M. (2003). Altering theories of learning and action: An interview with Chris Argyris. *The Academy of Management Executive, 17*(2), 40–46.

Crossan, M. M., Lane, H. W., & White, R. E. (1999). An organizational learning framework: From intuition to institution. *Academy of Management Review, 24*(3), 522–537.

Csikszentmihalyi, M. K. R., & Rathunde, K. R. (1998). The development of the person: An experiential perspective on the ontogenesis of psychological complexity. In W. Damon (Ed.) *Handbook of child psychology* (5th ed., Vol. 1, pp. 635–664). New York: Wiley.

Cyert, R. M., & March, J. G. (1992). *A behavioral theory of the firm* (2nd ed.). Malden, MA: Blackwell.

Daft, R. L., & Weick, K. E. (1984). Toward a model of organizations as interpretation systems. *Academy of Management Review, 9,* 284–295.

De Dreu, Ca. K. W., & Weingart, L. R. (2003). Task versus relationships conflict, team performance, and team member satisfaction: A meta-analysis. *Journal of Applied Psychology,* 88(4), 741–749.

De La Ronde, C., & Swann, W. B., Jr. (1998). Partner verification: Restoring shattered images of our intimates. *Journal of Personality and Social Psychology, 75,* 374–382.

Deci, E. L., Egharari, H., Patrick, B. C., & Leone, D. R. (1994). Facilitating internalization: The self-determination theory perspective. *Journal of Personality, 62,* 119–142.

Deci, E. L., & Ryan, R. M. (1991). A motivational approach to self: Integration in personality. In R. Dienstbier (Ed.), *Nebraska Symposium on Motivation: Vol. 38. Perspectives on motivation* (pp. 237–288). Lincoln: University of Nebraska Press.

DeNisi, A. S., & Kluger, A. N. (2000). Feedback effectiveness: Can 360-degree appraisals be improved? *The Academy of Management Executive, 14,* 129–139.

DeShon, R. P., Kozlowski, S. W., Schmidt, A. M., Milner, K. R., & Weichmann, D. (2004). A multiple goal, multilevel model of feedback effects on the regulation of individual and team performance in training. *Journal of Applied Psychology, 89,* 1035–1056.

Devine, D. J. (2002). A review and integration of classification systems relevant to teams in organizations. *Group Dynamics: Theory, Research, and Practice, 6*(4), 291–310.

Dewey, J. (1900). Psychology and social practice. *Psychological Review, 7,* 105–124.

Dewey, J. (1986). *How we think: A restatement of the relation of reflective thinking to the educative process.* Boston: Heath. (Original work published 1933)

Dewey, J. (1997). *Experience and education.* New York: Simon & Schuster. (Original work published 1938)

Diener, C. I., & Dweck, C. S. (1980). An analysis of learned helplessness: II. The processing of success. *Journal of Personality and Social Psychology, 39,* 940–952.

Drach-Zahavy, A., & Somech, A. (2001). Understanding team innovation: The role of team processes and structures. *Group Dynamics: Theory, Research, and Practice, 5*(2), 111–123.

Drath, W. H. (2003). Leading together: Complex challenges require a new approach. *Leadership in Action, 23*(1), 1–5.

Driskell, J. E., & Salas, E. (1992). Collective behavior and team performance. *Human Factors, 34,* 277–288.

Druskat, V. U., & Kayes, D. C. (2000). Learning versus performance in short-term project teams. *Small Group Research, 31,* 328–353.

Duden, N. (1993). A move from effective to quality. *School Administrator, 50*(6), 18–21.

Dunbar, E. (1996). Sociocultural and contextual challenges of organizational life in Eastern Europe. In D. Landis & R. S. Bhagat (Eds.), *Handbook of intercultural training* (2nd ed., pp. 349–365). Thousand Oaks, CA: Sage.

Dutton, J., & Jackson, S. (1987). Categorizing strategic issues: Links to organizational actions. *Academy of Management Review, 12,* 76–90.

Dweck, C. S. (1986). Motivational processes affecting learning. *American Psychologist, 41,* 1040–1048.

Dweck, C. S. (1989). Motivation. In A. Lesgold & R. Glaser (Eds.), *Foundations for a psychology of education* (pp. 87–136). Hillsdale, NJ: Lawrence Erlbaum Associates.

Dweck, C. S., & Leggett, E. L. (1988). A social-cognitive approach to motivation and personality. *Psychological Review, 95,* 256–273.

Eden, D. (1992). Leadership and expectations: Pygmalion effects and other self-fulfilling prophecies in organizations. *Leadership Quarterly, 3,* 271–305.

Edmondson, A. (1996). Learning from mistakes is easier said than done: Group and organizational influences on the detection and correction of human error. *Journal of Applied Behavioral Science, 32,* 5–28.

Edmondson, A. (1999). Psychological safety and learning behavior in work teams. *Administrative Science Quarterly, 44,* 350–383.

Edmondson, A. (2001). Disrupted routines: Team learning and new technology implementation in hospitals. *Administrative Science Quarterly, 46,* 685–716.

Edmondson, A. (2002). The local and variegated nature of learning in organizations: A group-level perspective. *Organization Science, 13,* 128–146.

Edmondson, A. C., Bohmer, R. M., & Pisano, G. P. (2001). Disrupted routines: Team learning and new technology implementation in hospitals. *Administrative Science Quarterly, 46,* 685–716.

Efimova, L. (2003). Blogs: The stickiness factor. In *Proceedings of "BlogTalk: A European conference on Weblogs,"* Vienna, Austria. Retrieved November 23, 2003, from: https://doc.telin.nl/dscgi/ds.py/ViewProps/File-34088

Efimova, L., & Fiedler, S. (2004). *Learning webs: Learning in weblog networks.* In P. Kommers, P. Isaias, & M. B. Nunes (Eds.), *Proceedings of the IADIS International Conference Web Based Communities 2004* (pp. 490–494). Lisbon, Portugal: IADIS Press.

Ellis, A. P. J., Hollenbeck, J. R., Ilgen, D. R., Porter, C. O. L. H., West, B. J., & Moon, H. (2003). Team learning: Collectively connecting the dots. *Journal of Applied Psychology, 88*(5), 821–835.

Evans, K., Hodkinson, L., & Unwin, L. (Eds.). (2002). *Working to learn: Transforming learning in the workplace.* London: Kogan Page.

Evans, K., & Rainbird, H. (2002). The significance of workplace learning for a "learning society." In K. Evans, P. Hodkinson, & L. Unwin (Eds.), *Working to learn: Transforming learning in the workplace* (pp. 7–28). London: Kogan Page.

Farr, J. L., Hofmann, D. A., & Ringenbach, K. L. (1993). Goal orientation and action control theory: Implications for industrial and organizational psychology. In C. L. Cooper & I. T. Robertson (Eds.), *International review of industrial and organizational psychology* (pp. 193–232). New York: Wiley.

Fedor, D. B., Rensvold, R. B., & Adams, S. M. (1992). An investigation of factors expected to affect feedback seeking: A longitudinal field study. *Personnel Psychology, 45,* 779–805.

Feldman, M. S., & Pentland, B. T. (2003). Reconceptualizing organizational routines as a source of flexibility and change. *Administrative Science Quarterly, 48*(1), 94–118.

Fiedler, S. (2003). Personal Webpublishing as a reflective conversational tool for self-organized learning. In *Proceedings of "BlogTalk: A European conference on Weblogs."* Vienna, Austria.

Fiore, S. M., Salas, E., & Cannon-Bowers, J. A. (2001). Group dynamics and shared mental model development. In M. London (Ed.). *How people evaluate others in organizations* (pp. 309–336). Mahwah, NJ: Lawrence Erlbaum Associates.

Fisher, D., Rooke, D., & Torbert, B. (2000). *Personal and organizational transformations through action inquiry.* Boston: Edge\Work Press.

Fleishman, E. A., & Zaccaro, S. J. (1992). Toward a taxonomy of team performance functions. In R. W. Sweezey & E. Salas (Eds.), *Teams: Their training and performance* (pp. 31–56). Norwood, NJ: Ablex.

Fletcher, C., Baldry, C., & Cunningham-Snell, N. (1998). The psychometric properties of multisource feedback: An empirical study and a cautionary tale. *International Journal of Selection and Assessment, 6*(1), 19–34.

Gagné, N. L. (1978). *The scientific basis of the art of teaching.* New York: Teachers College Press.

Gallo, K. (2004, March 19). *Building a learning organization.* Unpublished manuscript presented at Hofstra Department of Psychology, Hofstra University, New York.

Gardner, H. (1993). *Multiple intelligences.* New York: Basic Books.

Garrison, D. R. (1992). Critical thinking and self-directed learning in adult education: An analysis of responsibility and control issues. *Adult Education Quarterly, 42*(3), 136–148.

Garvin, D. (2000, April 18). Learning in action. In *Working knowledge.* Boston: Harvard Business School. Retrieved April 27, 2005, from http://hbswk.hbs.edu/item.jhtml?id=1450&t=organizations.

Garvin, D. (2003). *Managing to learn: How companies can turn knowledge into action.* Boston: Harvard Business School.

Gary, L. (2003, December 1). The smarter way toward self-development. In *Working knowledge.* Boston: Harvard Business School. Retrieved April 27, 2005, from http://hbswk.hbs.edu/item .jhtml?id=3806&t=career_effectiveness.

Gergen, J. J. (1991). *The saturated self: Dilemmas of identity in contemporary life.* New York: Basic Books.

Gersick, C. J. G. (1989). Marking time: Predictable transitions in task groups. *Academy of Management Journal, 32,* 274–309.

Gersick, C. J. G. (1991). Revolutionary change theories: A multilevel exploration of the punctuated equilibrium paradigm. *Academy of Management Review, 16,* 10–36.

Gersick, C. J. G., & Hackman, J. R. (1990). Habitual routines in task-performing groups. *Organizational Behavior and Human Decision Processes, 47,* 65–97.

Gibson, C. B., & Birkinshaw, J. (2004). The antecedents, consequences, and mediating role of organizational ambidexterity. *Academy of Management Journal, 47,* 209–226.

Gilleard, J. (1996). Delivering training and development down the line. *Industrial and Commercial Training, 28,* 22–27.

Goldsmith, M., Beverly, K., & Shelton, K. (2000). *Learning journeys: Top management experts share hard-earned lessons on becoming great mentors and leaders.* Palo Alto, CA: Davies-Black.

Gollwitzer, P. M. (1996). The volitional benefits of planning. In P. M. Gollwitzer & J. A. Bargh (Eds.), *The psychology of action: Linking cognition and motivation to behavior* (pp. 287–312). New York: Guilford.

Goodstone, M. S., & Diamante, T. (1998). Organizational use of therapeutic change: Strengthening multisource feedback systems through interdisciplinary coaching. *Consulting Psychology Journal: Practice and Research, 50,* 152–163.

Gordon, J. (1992, October). Workteams: How far have they come? *Training,* 59–65.

Gordon, L., & Stomski, L. (2003, April). *Successful virtual coaching program.* Paper presented at the 18th annual meeting of the Society for Industrial and Organizational Psychology, Orlando, FL.

Gratton, M. (1993). Leadership in the learning organization. *New Directions for Community College, 21*(4), 93–103.

Gross, P. A. (2003, November 24). *The art and science of implementation in health care.* Unpublished manuscript presented at the Health Sciences Center, State University of New York at Stony Brook.

Guile, D., & Griffiths, T. (2001). Learning through work experience. *School of Education and Work, 14,*113–131.

Guthrie, E. R. (1940). Association and the law of effect. *Psychological Review, 47,* 127–148.

Guthrie, E. R. (1952). *The psychology of learning* (Rev. ed.). New York: Harper & Brothers.

Guzzo, R. A., Jette, R. D., & Katzell, R. A. (1985). The effects of psychologically based intervention programs on worker productivity: A meta-analysis. *Personnel Psychology, 38,* 275–291.

Hackman, J. R. (1990). Work teams in organizations: An orienting framework. In J. R. Hackman (Ed.), *Groups that work (and those that don't)* (pp. 1–14). San Francisco: Jossey-Bass.

Hackman, J. R. (2002). *Leading teams: Setting the stage for great performances.* Boston: Harvard Business School Press.

Hackman, M. Z., Ellis, K., Johnson, C. E., & Staley, C. (1999). Self-construal orientation: Validation of an instrument and a study of the relationship to leadership communication style. *Communication Quarterly, 47,* 183–194.

Han, T., & Williams, K. J. (2003, April). *Multilevel approach to individual and team adaptive performance.* Paper presented at the 18th annual meeting of the Society for Industrial and Organizational Psychology, Orlando, FL.

Handy, C. (1995). Managing the dream. In S. Chawla & J. Renesch (Eds.), *Learning organizations: Developing cultures for tomorrow's workplace* (pp. 44–55). Portland, OR: Productivity Press.

Harkema, S. (2003). A complex adaptive perspective on learning within innovation projects. *The Learning Organization, 10,* 340–346.

Harrison, D. A., Mohammed, S., McGrath, J. E., Florey, A. T., & Vanderstoep, S. Q. (2003). Time matters in team performance: Effects of member familiarity, entrainment, and task discontinuity on speed and quality. *Personnel Psychology, 56*(3), 633–669.

Hebb, D. O. (1941). Clinical evidence concerning the nature of normal adult test performance. *Psychological Bulletin, 38,* 593.

Heifetz, R. A. (1994). *Leadership without easy answers.* Boston: Harvard University Press.

Hinds, P. J., Patterson, M., & Pfeffer, J. (2001). Bothered by abstraction: The effect of expertise on knowledge transfer and subsequent novice performance. *Journal of Applied Psychology, 86*(6), 1232–1243.

Hinsz, V. B., Tindale, R. S., & Vollrath, D. A. (1997). The emerging conceptualization of groups as information processors. *Psychological Bulletin, 121,* 43–64.

Hodkinson, P., & Bloomer, M. (2002). Learning careers: Conceptualizing lifelong work-based learning. In K. Evans, P. Hodkinson, & L. Unwin (Eds.), *Working to learn: Transforming learning in the workplace* (pp. 29–43). London: Kogan Page.

Hogg, M. A., & Terry, D. J. (2000). Social identify and self-categorization processes in organizational contexts. *Academy of Management Review, 25,* 121–140.

Hui, C. H., & Triandis, H. C. (1989). Effects of cultural and response format on extreme response style. *Journal of Cross-Cultural Psychology, 20,* 296–309.

Huselid, M. A., Jackson, S. E., & Schuler, R. S. (1997). Technical and strategic human resource management effectiveness as determinants of firm performance. *Academy of Management Journal, 40,* 171–188.

Ilgen, D. R., Fisher, C. D., & Taylor, M. S. (1979). Consequences of individual feedback on behavior in organizations. *Journal of Applied Psychology, 64,* 349–371.

Jackson, W. H. (1996). *Androgogical stages of development.* Retrieved April 26, 2005, from http://internet.cybermesa.com/~bjackson/Papers/AndroStage.htm

James, C. R. (2003). Designing learning organizations. *Organizational Dynamics, 32*(1), 46–61.

Janis, I. L. (1982). *Victims of groupthink* (2nd ed.). Boston: Houghton Mifflin.

Jaques, E. (2001). *The life and behavior of living organisms: A general theory.* Westport, CT: Praeger.

Jarvis, P., & Tosey, P. (2001). Corporations and professions. In P. Jarvfis (Ed.), *The age of learning: Education and the knowledge society* (pp. 147–156). London: Kogan Page.

Jassawalla, A. R., & Sashittal, H. C. (1999). Building collaborative cross-functional new product teams. *Academy of Management Executive, 13*(3), 50–62.

Jehn, K. (1997). Affective and cognitive conflict in work groups: Increasing performance through value-based intragroup conflict. In C. K. W. De Dreu & E. Van de Vliert (Eds.), *Using conflict in organizations* (pp. 87–100). London: Sage.

Jelinek, M. (2003). Enacting the future: A time and levels-based view of strategic change. *Multi-Level Issues in Organizational Behavior and Strategy: Research in Multi-Level Issues, 2,* 303–349.

Johnson, J. W. (2001). The relative importance of task and contextual performance dimensions to supervisor judgments of overall performance. *Journal of Applied Psychology, 86,* 984–996.

Judge, T. A., Erez, A., Bono, J. E., & Thoresen, C. J. (2002). Are measures of self-esteem, neuroticism, locus of control, and generalized self-efficacy indicators of a common core construct? *Journal of Personality and Social Psychology, 83*(3), 693–710.

Judge, T. A., Locke, E. A., Durham, C. C., & Kluger, A. N. (1998). Dispositional effects on job and life satisfaction: The role of core evaluations. *Journal of Applied Psychology, 83,* 17–34.

Judge, T. A., Thoreson, C. J., Pucik, V., & Welbourne, T. M. (1999). Manegerial coping with organizational change: A dispositional perspective. *Journal of Applied Psychology, 84,* 107–122.

Kammeyer-Mueller, J. D., & Wanberg, C. R. (2003). Unwrapping the organizational entry process: Disentangling multiple antecedents and their pathways to adjustment. *Journal of Applied Psychology, 88*(5), 779–794.

Karakowsky, L., & McBey, K. (1999). The lessons of work: Toward an understanding of the implications of the workplace for adult learning and development. *Journal of Workplace Learning, 11,* 192–201.

Kasl, E., Masick, V. J., & Dechant, K. (1997). Teams as learners: A research-based model of team learning. *The Jounral of Applied Behavioral Science, 33,* 227–246.

Katz, D., & Kahn, R. L. (1967). *The social psychology of organizations.* New York: Wiley.

Keep, E., & Rainbird, H. (2000). Towards the learning organization? In S. Bach & K. Sisson (Eds.), *Personnel management: A comprehensive guide to theory and practice* (pp. 64–90). Oxford, England: Blackwell.

Kegan, R. (1982). *The evolving self: Problem and process in human development.* Cambridge, MA: Harvard University Press.

Kegan, R. (1994). *In over our heads: The mental demands of modern life.* Cambridge, MA: Harvard University Press.

Kegan, R., & Lahey, L. L. (2001). *How the way we talk can change the way we work: Seven languages for transformation.* San Francisco: Jossey Bass.

Kelly, S. W., Burton, A. M., Kato, T., & Akamatsu, S. (2001). Incidental learning of real-world regularities. *Psychological Science, 12*(1), 86–89.

Kendall, D. L., Stagl, K. C., Burke, S., & Salas, E. (2004, April). *Understanding team adaptability: A conceptual framework.* Paper presented at the 19th annual meeting of the Society for Industrial and Organizational Psychology, Chicago.

Kerka, S. (1995). The learning organization: Myths and realities. In *ERIC Clearinghouse: Adult, career, and vocational education.* Retrieved June 3, 2003, from http://ericacve.org/docs/mr00004.htm

Kerr, S. (1997). On the folly of rewarding A, while hoping for B. *Academy of Management Journal, 18*(4), 769–775, 779–783. Reprinted in R. P. Vecchio (Ed.), *Leadership: Understanding the dynamics of power and influence in organizations* (pp. 246–256). Notre Dame, IN: Notre Dame University Press. (Original work published 1975)

Kilduff, M., Angelmar, R., & Mehra, A. (2000). Top management-team diversity and firm performance: Examining the role of cognitions. *Organizational Science, 11,* 21–34.

Kim, D. H. (1993). The link between individual and organizational learning. *Sloan Management Review, 35*(1), 37–51.

Kirkpatrick, D. L. (1959). Techniques for evaluating training programs. *Journal of the American Society of Training and Development, 13,* 3–9.

Kirkpatrick, D. L. (1976). Evaluation of training. In R. L. Craig (Ed.), *Training and development handbook: A guide to human resource development* (2nd ed., pp. 301–319). New York: McGraw-Hill.

Kirkpatrick, D. L. (1996). Invited reaction: Reaction to Holton article. *Human Resource Development Quarterly, 7,* 23–25.

Kluger, A. N., & DeNisi, A. (1996). The effects of feedback interventions on performance: A historical review, meta-analysis, and a preliminary feedback intervention theory. *Psychological Bulletin, 119,* 254–284.

Kluger, A. N., & DeNisi, A. (1998). Feedback interventions: Toward the understanding of a double-edged sword. *Current Directions in Psychological Science, 7*(3), 67–72.

Knowles, M. S. (1975). *Self-directed learning.* River Gove, IL: Follett.

Knowles, M. (1990). *The adult learner: A neglected species* (4th ed.). Houston, TX: Gulf Publishing.

Koffka, K. (1924). *The growth of the mind* (R. M. Ogden, Trans.). London: Kegan Paul, Trench, Trubner.

Kohler, W. (1947). *Gestalt psychology: An introduction to new concepts in modern psychology.* New York: Liveright. (Reprinted 1959, New American Library, New York)

Kolb, D. A. (1984). *Experiential learning: Experience as the source of learning and development.* Englewood Cliffs, NJ: Prentice-Hall.

Kotelnikov, V. (2004). Case study: General Electric: Creating an extraordinary organization. Retrieved March 29, 2004, from http://www.1000ventures.com/business_guide/cs/Index_ge.html

Kozlowski, S. W. J., Gully, S. M., Nason, E. R., & Smith, E. M. (1999). Developing adaptive teams: A theory of compilation and performance across levels of time. In D. R. Ilgen & E. D. Pulakos (Eds.), *The changing nature of work and peformance: Implications for staffing personnel actions and development* (pp. 1–20). San Francisco: Jossey-Bass.

Kozlowski, S. W. J., & Salas, E. (1997). A multilevel organizational systems approach for the implementation and transfer of training. In J. K. Ford, S. W. J. Kozlowski, K. Kraiger, E. Salas, & M. Teachout (Eds.), *Improving training effectiveness in work organizations* (pp. 247–290). Mahwah, NJ: Lawrence Erlbaum Associates.

Kroth, M., & Boverie, P. (2000). Life mission and adult learning. *Adult Education Quarterly, 50*(2), 134–149.

Kruglanski, A. W., & Mayseless, O. (1990). Classic and current social comparison research: Expanding the perspective. *Psychological Bulletin, 108,* 195–208.

Kulik, C. T., Oldham, G. R., & Hackman, J. R. (1987). Work design as an approach to person-environment fit. *Journal of Vocational Behavior, 31,* 278–296.

Kung, M. C., & Steelman, L. A. (2003, April). *A cross-cultural study in feedback seeking.* Paper presented at the 18th annual conference of the Society for Industrial and Organizational Psychology, Orlando, FL.

LaBier, D. (1986). *Modern madness: The end and fallout of success.* New York: Simon & Schuster.

Labouvie-Vief, G., & Diehl, M. (2000). Cognitive complexity and cognitive-affective integration: Related or separate domains of adult development. *Psychology and Aging, 15,* 490-509.

Labouvie-Vief, G., Chiodo, L. M., Goguen, L. A., Diehl, H., & Orwell, L. (1995). Representations of self across the life span. *Psychology and Aging, 10,* 409-415.

Laforge, R. G., Velicer, W. F., Richmond, R., & Owen, N. (1999). Stage distributions for five health behaviors in the USA and Australia. *Preventive Medicine, 28,* 61–74.

Laiken, M. E. (2003). Models of organizational learning: Paradoxes and best practices in the post industrial workplace. *Organizational Development Journal, 21,* 8–19.

Larson, J. R., Jr. (1984). The performance feedback process: A preliminary model. *Organizational Behavior and Human Performance, 33,* 42–76.

Laszlo, E. (1996). *The systems view of the world: A holistic vision for out time* (Advances in systems theory, complexity, and the human sciences). Cresskill, NJ: Hampton Press.

Lee, D. Y. (1997). The impact of poor performance on risk-taking attitudes: A longitudinal study with a PLS causal modeling approach. *Decision Science, 28,* 59–80.

LePine, J. A. (2003). Team adaptation and postchange performance: Effects of team composition in terms of members' cognitive ability and personality. *Journal of Applied Psychology, 88*(1), 27–39.

LePine, J. A., Colquitt, J. A., & Erez, A. (2000). Adaptability to changing task contexts: Effects of general cognitive ability, conscientiousness, and openness. *Personnel Psychology, 53,* 563–594.

Leslie, J. B., Gryskiewicz, N. D., & Dalton, M. A. (1998). Understanding cultural influences on the 360-degree feedback process. In W. W. Tornow & M. London (Eds.), *Maximizing the value of 360-degree feedback* (pp. 196–216). San Francisco: Jossey Bass.

Levesque, D. A., Prochaska, J. M., & Prochaska, J. O. (1999). Stages of change and integrated service delivery. *Consulting Psychology Journal: Practice and Research, 51*(4), 226–241.

Levine, D. P. (2002). Thinking about doing: On learning from experience and the flight from thinking. *Human Relations, 55,* 1251–1268.

Levinson, D. J. (1978). *The seasons of a man's life.* New York: Knopf.

Levinson, D. J. (1996). *The seasons of a woman's life.* New York: Alfred A. Knopf.

Levinthal, D. A., & March, J. G. (1993). The myopia of learning. *Strategic Management Journal, 14,* 95–112.

Levitt, B., & March, J. G. (1988). Organizational learning. *Annual Review of Sociology, 14,* 319–340.

Lewis, K. (2003). Measuring transactive memory systems in the field: Scale development and validation. *Journal of Applied Psychology, 88*(4), 587–604.

Lindsey, E. H., Homes, V., & McCall, M. W. (1987). *Key events in executives' lives.* Greensboro, NC: Center for Creative Leadership.

Locke, E. A., & Latham, G. P. (1990). *A theory of goal setting and task performance.* Englewood Cliffs, NJ: Prentice-Hall.

London, M. (1983). Toward a theory of career motivation. *Academy of Management Review, 8,* 620–630. Reprinted in *The Art and Science of Successful Business Management* (Vol. 1). Emerson, NJ: Kent, in press. Also reprinted in L. W. Porter & R. Steers (Eds.), (1987). *Motivation and work behavior.* New York: McGraw-Hill.

London, M. (1985). *Developing managers: A guide to motivating and preparing people for successful careers.* San Francisco: Jossey-Bass.

London, M. (2003a). Antecedents and consequences of self-verification: Implications for individual and group development. *Human Resource Development Review, 2,* 273–293.

London, M. (2003b). *Job feedback* (2nd ed.). Mahwah, NJ: Lawrence Erlbaum Associates.

London, M., & Diamante, T. (2002). Technology-focused expansive professionals: Developing continuous learning in the high-technology sector. *Human Resource Development Review, 1*(4), 500–524.

London, M., & Mone, E. M. (1999). Continuous learning. In D. R. Ilgen & E. D. Pulakos (Eds.), *The changing nature of performance: Implications for staffing, motivation, and development* (pp. 119–153). San Francisco: Jossey-Bass.

London, M., & Noe, R. A. (1997). London's career motivation theory: An update on measurement and research. *Journal of Career Assessment, 5*(1), 61–80.

London, M., & Smither, J. (1995). Can multisource feedback change perceptions of goal accomplishment, self-evaluations, and performance-related outcomes? Theory-based applications and directions for research. *Personnel Psychology, 48,* 803–840.

London, M., & Smither, J. (1999a). Career-related continuous learning. Defining the construct and mapping the process. In G. R. Ferris (Ed.), *Research in personnel and human resources management* (Vol. 17, pp. 81–121). Stamford, CT: JAI.

London, M., & Smither, J. (1999b). Empowered self-development and continuous learning. *Human Resource Management, 38*(1), 3–15.

London, M., & Smither, J. (2002). Feedback orientation, feedback culture, and the longitudinal performance management process. *Human Resource Management Review, 12,* 81–100.

London, M., Smither, J., & Reilly, R. R. (2003). *Assessment of multisource feedback. Update and prognosis for theory, research, and practice.* Unpublished working paper, State University of New York at Stony Brook.

March, J. G. (1991). Exploration and exploitation in organizational learning. *Organization Science, 2,* 71–87.

Marin, G., Gamba, R. J., & Marin, G. V. (1992). Extreme response style and acquiescence among Hispanics. *Journal of Cross-Cultural Psychology, 23,* 498–509.

Marks, H. A., Mathieu, J. E., & Zaccaro, S. J. (2000). A temporally based framework and taxonomy of team processes. *Academy of Management Review, 26,* 356–376.

Marsick, V. J., Cederholm, L., Turner, E., & Pearson, T. (1992). Action-reflection learning. *Training and development, 46,* 63.

Martocchio, J. J., & Judge, T. A. (1997). Relationship between conscientiousness and learning in employee training: Mediating influences of self-deception and self-efficacy. *Journal of Applied Psychology, 82,* 764–773.

Maslow, A. H. (1970). *Motivation and personality* (2nd ed.). New York: Van Nostrand Reinhold.

Mathews, R. C., Buss, R. R., Stanley, W. B., Blanchard-Fields, F., Cho, J. R., & Druhan, B. (1989). Role of implicit and explicit processes in learning from examples: A synergistic effect. *Journal of Experimental Psychology: Learning, Memory, and Cognition, 15,* 1083–1100.

Mathieu, J. E., & Martineau, J. W. (1997). Individual and situational influences on training motivation. In J. K. Ford (Ed.), *Improving training effectiveness in work organizations* (pp. 193–223). Mahwah, NJ: Lawrence Erlbaum Associates.

Matthews, G., Zeidner, M., & Roberts, R. (2003). *Emotional intelligence: Science and myth.* Cambridge, MA: MIT Press.

Maurer, T. J., Weiss, E. M., & Barbeite, F. G. (2003). A model of involvement in work-related learning and development activity: The effects of individual, situational, motivational, and age variables. *Journal of Applied Psychology, 88*(4), 707–724.

Mayo, E. (1946). *The human problems of industrial civilization.* Boston: Division of Research, Graduate School of Business Administration, Harvard University.

McCall, M. (1994). Identifying leadership potential in future international executives: Developing a concept. *Consulting Psychololgy Journal, 46*(1), 49–63.

McCall, M., & Lombardo, M. (1983). What makes a top executive. *Psychology Today, 17*(2), 26–31.

McCauley, C. D. (2004, April). *Leading together: An approach to complex organizational challenges.* Paper presented at the 19th annual conference of the Society for Industrial and Organizational Psychology, Chicago.

McCrae, R. R., & Costa, P. T., Jr. (1986). Personality, coping, and coping effectiveness in an adult sample. *Journal of Personality, 54,* 385–405.

McCrae, R. R., & Costa, P. T., Jr. (1987). Validation of the five-factor model of personality across instruments and observers. *Journal of Personality and Social Psychology, 52,* 81–90.

McDonald, M. L., & Westphal, J. D. (2003). Getting by with the advice of their friends: CEOs' advice networks and firms' strategic responses to poor performance. *Administrative Science Quarterly, 48*(1), 1–32.

McGregor, J. (2004). It's a blog world after all. *Fast Company, 81,* 84.b.

Mennecke, B., Hoffer, J., & Wyne, B. (1992). The implications of group development and history for group support system theory and practice. *Small Group Research, 23,* 524–572.

Mentkowski, M., & Associates. (2000). *Learning that lasts: Integrating learning, development, and performance in college and beyond.* San Franscisco: Jossey-Bass.

Mezirow, J. (Ed.). (1990). *Fostering critical reflection in adulthood: A guide to transformative and emancipatory learning.* San Francisco: Jossey-Bass.

Mezirow, J. (1991). Tranformative dimensions of adult learning. San Francisco: Jossey-Bass.

Mezirow, J. (1994). Understanding transformation theory. *Adult Education Quarterly, 44*(4), 222–232.

Miller, R. B. (1978). The information system designer. In W. T. Singleton (Ed.), *The analysis of practical skills* (pp. 278–291), Baltimore: University Park Press.

Miner, J. B. (2002). *Organizational behavior: Foundations, theories, and analyses.* New York: Oxford University Press.

Mintzberg, H. (1994). *The rise and fall of strategic planning.* New York: The Free Press.

Moreland, R. L. (1999). Transactive memory: Learning who knows what in work groups and organizations. In L. L. Thompson, J. M. Levine, & D. M. Messick (Eds.), *Shared cognition in organizations: The management of knowledge* (pp. 3–31). Mahwah, NJ: Lawrence Erlbaum Associates.

Murrell, P. H., & Walsh, J. P. (1993). Leadership development at Federal Express Corporation. *Human Resource Development Quarterly, 4*(3), 295–302.

Nadler, D. A. (1979). The effectsof feedback on task group behavior: A review of the experimental research. *Organizational Behavior and Human Performance, 23,* 309–338.

National Research Council (1999). *How people learn: Brain, mind, experience, and school.* Washington, DC: National Academy Press.

Neuman, G. A., Edwards, J. E., & Raju, N. S. (1989). Organizational development interventions: A meta-analysis of their effects on satisfaction and other attitudes. *Personnel Psychology, 42,* 461–489.

Noe, R. A. (1999). *Employee training and development.* Burr Ridge, IL: Irwin/McGraw-Hill.

Noe, R. A., Wilk, S. L., Mullen, E. J., & Wanek, J. E. (1997). Employee development: Issues in construct definition and investigation of antecedents. In J. K. Ford (Ed.), *Improving training effectiveness in work organizations* (pp. 153–192). Mahwah, NJ: Lawrence Erlbaum Associates.

Nonaka, I., & Takeuchi, H. (1995). *The knowledge-creating company: How Japanese companies create the dynamics of innovation.* New York: Oxford University Press.

Palincsar, A. S. (1998). Social constructivist perspectives on teaching and learning. *Annual Review of Psychology, 49,* 345–375.

Pavlov, I. P. (1927). *Conditioned reflex* (G. V. Anrep, Trans.). London: Oxford University Press.

Perlow, L. A. (2003). When silence spells trouble at work. In *Working Knowledge.* Boston: Harvard Business School. Retrieved April 27, 2005, from http://www.hbsworkingknowledge.hbs.edu

Perrow, C. (1984). *Normal accidents: Living with high risk systems.* New York: Basic Books.

Pettigrew, A. M., Woodman, R. W., & Cameron, K. S. (2001). Studying organizational change and development: Challenges for future research. *Academy of Management Journal, 44,* 697–713.

Piaget, J. (1952). *The origins of intelligence in children.* New York: International Universities Press.

Polzer, J. T., Milton, L. P., & Swann, W. B., Jr. (2002). Capitalizing on diversity: Interpersonal congruence in small work groups. *Administrative Science Quarterly, 47,* 296–324.

Pratt, M. W., Diessner, R., Hunsberger, B., Pancer, S. M., & Savoy, K.(1991). Four pathways in the analysis of adult development and aging: Comparing analyses of reasoning about personal-life dilemmas. *Psychology and Aging, 6,* 666–675.

Prochaska, J. H., Prochaska, J. O., & Levesque, D. A. (2001). A transtheoretical approach to changing organizations. *Administration and Policy in Mental Health, 28*(4), 247–261.

Prochaska, J. O., DiClemente, C. C., & Norcross, J. C. (1992). In search of how people change: Applications to addictive behaviors. *American Psychologist, 47,* 1102–1114.

Pulley, M. L. (2003, June). Blended learning solutions: The future of leadership development. Greensboro, NC: Center for Creative Leaderhsip. Retrieved April 27, 2005, from http://www.ccl.org/CCL Commerce/news/newsletters/enewsletter/2003/JUNEmaypollresults.aspx?CatalogueID=News &CategoryID=ENewsletter(Newsletters)

Purdie, N., Hattie, J., & Douglas, G. (1996). Student conceptions of learning and their use of self-regulated learning strategies: A cross-cultural comparison. *Journal of Educational Psychology, 88*(1), 87–100.

Ramanujam, R. (2003). The effects of discontinuous change on latent errors in organizations: The moderating role of risk. *The Academy of Management Journal, 46*(3), 608–617.

Reber, A. S. (1993). *Implicit learning and tacit knowledge.* Oxford, England: Oxford University Press.

Reeve, C. L., & Hakel, M. D. (2000). Toward an understanding of adult intellectual development: Investigating within-individual convergence of interest and knowledge profiles. *Journal of Applied Psychology, 85,* 897–908.

Revans, R. (1980). *Action learning.* London: Blond & Biggs.

Rogers, C. R. (1969). *Freedom to learn.* Columbus, OH: Merrill.

Rogers, R. W., Wellins, R. S., & Conner, D. R. (2002). *The power of realization: Building competitive advantage by maximizing human resource initiatives* (White paper). Pittsburgh, PA: Development Dimensions International.

Rogoff, B. (1990). *Apprenticeship in thinking: Cognitive development in the social context.* New York: Oxford University Press.

Rotter, J. B. (1966). Generalized expectancies for internal versus external control of reinforcement. *Psychological Mongoraphs, 80*(1, Whole No. 609).

Ruderman, M. N, Hannum, K., Leslie, J. B. & Steed, J. L. (2001). Making the connection: Leadership skills and emotional intelligence. *Leadership in Action, 21*(5), 3–7.

Salas, E., Dickinson, T. L., Converse, S. A., & Tanenbaum, S. I. (1992). Toward an understanding of team performance and training. In R. W. Swezey & E. Salas (Eds.), *Teams: Their training and performance* (pp. 3–29). Norwood, NJ: Ablex.

Salovey, P., & Mayer, J. D. (1990). Emotional intelligence. *Imagination, Cognition, and Personality, 9,* 185–211.

Schaie, K. W. (1994). The course of adult intellectual development. *American Psychologist, 49,* 304–313.

Senge, P. M. (1990). *The fifth discipline: The art and practice of the learning organization.* New York: Doubleday.

Senge, P. M. (2003). Taking personal change seriously: The impact of organizational learning on management practice. *The Academy of Management Executive, 17*(2), 47–50.

Shamir, B. (1990). Calculations, values and entities: The sources of collectivistic work motivation. *Human Relations, 43,* 313–332.

Simmering, M. J., Colquitt, J. A., Noe, R. A., & Porter, C. O. L. H. (2003). Conscientiousness, autonomy fit, and development: A longitudinal study. *Journal of Applied Psychology, 88*(5), 954–963.

Sims, D., & McAulay, L. (1995). Management learning as a learning process: An invitation. *Management Learning, 26*(1), 5–20.

Sims, D., Salas, E., & Burke, C. S. (2004, April). Is there a "big five" in teamwork? Paper presented at the 19th annual conference of the Society for Industrial and Organizational Psychology, Chicago.

Skinner, B. F. (1971). *Beyond freedom and dignity.* New York: Knopf.

Smith, G. J., & Stodden, R. A. (1994). Restructuring vocational special needs education through interdisciplinary team effort. *Journal for Vocational Special Needs Education, 16*(3), 16–23.

Smither, J. W., M. London, & Reilly, R. R. (2005). Does performance improve following multisource feedback? A theoretical model, meta-analysis, and review of empirical findings. *Personnel Psychology, 58*(1), 33–66.

Snyder, H. (1974). Self-monitoring of expressive behavior. *Journal of Personality and Social Psychology, 30,* 526–537.

Society for Organizational Learning. (2003). Retrieved May 19, 2003, from http://www.solonline.org

Squires, P., & Adler, S. (1998). Linking appraisals to individual development and training. In J. W. Smither (Ed.), *Performance appraisal: State-of-the-art in practice* (pp. 445–495). San Francisco: Jossey-Bass.

Steelman, L. A., Levy, P. E., & Snell, A. F. (2004). The feedback environment scale (FES): Construct definition, measurement and validation. *Educational and Psychological Measurement, 64,* 165–184.

Steiner, I. D. (1972). *Group processes and productivity.* New York: Academic Press.

Swann, W. B., Jr. (1996). *Self-traps: The elusive quest for higher self-esteem.* New York: Freeman.

Swann, W. B., Jr., Polzer, J. T., Seyle, D. C., & Ko, S. J. (2004). Finding value in diversity: Verification of personal and social self-views in diverse groups. *Academy of Management Review, 29,* 9–27.

Tannenbaum, S. I., Beard, R. L., & Salas, E. (1992). Team building and its influence on team effectiveness: An examination of conceptual and empirical developments. In K. Kelly (Ed.), *Issues, theory, and research in industrial and organizational psychology* (pp. 117–153). New York: Elsevier Science.

Tennant, M., & Pogson, P. (1995). *Learning and change in the adult years: A developmental perspective.* San Francisco: Jossey-Bass.

Thorndike, E. L. (1932). *The fundamentals of learning.* New York: Teachers College Press.

Thornton, J. E. (2003). Life-span learning: A developmental perspective. *International Journal of Aging and Human Development, 57,* 55–76.

3-D Group. (2003). *Benchmark study of North American 360-degree feedback practices: 2002 study.* Berkeley, CA: Data Driven Decisions.

Tjosvold, D., & Deemer, D. K. (1980). Effects of controversy within a cooperative or competitive context on organizational decision-making. *Journal of Applied Psychology, 65,* 590–595.

Toegel, G., & Conger, J. A. (2003). 360-degree assessment: Time for reinvention. *Academy of Management Learning & Education, 2*(3), 297–311.

Tolman, E. C. (1932). *Purposive behavior in animals and men.* New York: Appleton–Century–Crofts.

Torff, B., & Sternberg, R. J. (1998). Changing mind, changing world: Practical intelligence and tacit knowledge in adult learning. In M. C. Smith & T. Pourchot (Eds.), Adult learning and development: Perspectives from educational psychology (pp. 109–126). Mahwah, NJ: Lawrence Erlbaum Associates.

Tosey, P., & McNair, S. (2001). Work-related learning. In P. Jarvis (Ed.), *The age of learning: Education and the knowledge society* (pp. 95–108). London: Kogan Page.

Tuckman, B. W. (1965). Developmental sequence in small groups. *Psychological Bulletin, 63*(6), 384–399.

Ulrich, D., Kerr, S., & Ashkenas, R. (2002). *The GE Work-Out: How to implement GE's revolutionary method for busting bureaucracy and attacking organizational problems—Fast!* New York: McGraw-Hill.

Van de Ven, A. H., & Poole, M. S. (1995). Explaining development and change in organizations. *Academy of Management Review, 20,* 510–540.

Van Dyne, L., Cummings, L. L., & McLean Parks, J. (1995). Extra-role behaviors: In pursuit of construct and definitional clarity (a bridge over muddied waters). In B. M. Staw & L. L. Cummings (Eds.), *Research in organizational behavior* (Vol. 17, pp. 215–285). Greenwich, CT: JAI.

Van Eijnatten, F. M., & Putnik, G. D. (2004). Chaos, complexity, learning, and the learning organization: Towards a chaordic enterprise. *The Learning Organization, 11,* 418–429.

VandeWalle, D. (1997). Development and validation of a work domain goal orientation instrument. *Educational and Psychological Measurement, 57,* 995–1015.

VandeWalle, D., Cron, W. L., & Slocum, J. W., Jr. (2001). The role of goal orientation following performance feedback. *Journal of Applied Psychology, 86*(4), 629–640.

VandeWalle, D., & Cummings, L. L. (1997). A test of the influence of goal orientation on the feed-back-seeking process. *Journal of Applied Psychology, 82*(3), 390–400.

Van Velsor, E., & Guthrie, V. A. (1998). Enhancing the ability to learn from experience. In C. D. McCauley, R. S. Morely, & E. Van Velsor (Eds.), *The Center for Creative Leadership handbook of leadership development.* San Francisco: Jossey-Bass.

Velicer, W. F., Fava, J. L., Prochaska, J. O., Abrams, D. B., Emmons, K. M., & Pierce, J. (1995). Distribution of smokers by stage in three representative samples. *Preventive Medicine, 24,* 401–411.

Vera, D., & Crossan, M. (2003). Organizational learning and knowledge management: Toward an integrative framework. In M. Easterby-Smith & M. A. Lyles (Eds.), *The Blackwell handbook of organizational learning and knowledge management* (pp. 122–141). Malden, MA: Blackwell.

von Bertalanffy, L. (1976). *General system theory* (rev. ed.). New York: George Braziller.

von Glaserfeld, E. (1996). Introduction: Aspects of constructivism. *Constructivism: Theory, perspectives, and practice* (pp. 3–7). New York: Teachers College Press.

Vroom, V. (1964). *Work and motivation.* New York: Wiley.

Vygotsky, L. (1978). *Mind in society: The development of higher psychological process.* Cambridge, MA: Harvard University Press.

Wagner, J. A. (1995). Studies of individualism-collectivism: Effects on cooperation in groups. Academy of Management Journal, 38, 152–172.

Walker, A. G., Wang, M., & Lodato, M. A. (2003, April). *Incremental validity of peer and leader ratings in a multisource feedback application.* Paper presented at the 18th annual meeting of the Society for Industrial and Organizational Psychology, Orlando, FL.

Wang, C. L., & Ahmed, P. K. (2003). Organizational learning: A critical review. *The Learning Organization, 10,* 8–18.

Watson, J. B. (1924). *Behaviorism.* New York: Norton.

Webb, A. D. (1995). A consulting practice is a learning process. *Consulting Psychology Journal: Practice and Research, 47*(2), 122–125.

Wegner, D. M. (1987). Transactive memory: A contemporty analysis of the group mind. In B. Mullen & G. R. Goethals (Eds.), *Theories of group behavior* (pp. 185–208). New York: Springer-Verlag.

Weick, K. E. (1979). *The social psychology of organizing* (2nd ed.). Reading, MA: Addison-Wesley.

Weick, K. E., & Quinlan, R. E. (1999). Organization change and development. In J. T. Spence, J. M. Darley, & J. Foss (Eds.), *Annual review of psychology* (Vol. 50, pp. 361–386). Palo Alto, CA: Annual Reviews.

Wenger, E. (1999). *Communities of practice: Learning, meaning, and identity.* New York: Cambridge University Press.

West, M. A., & Anderson, N. (1998). Measuring climate for work group innovation: Development and validation of the team climate inventory. *Journal of Organizational Behavior, 19,* 235–258.

Wheelan, S. (1994). *Group processes: A developmental perspective.* Boston: Allyn & Bacon.

Whitbourne, S. K. (1986). *The me I know: A study of adult identity.* New York: Springer-Verlag.

Wilbur, K. (2001a). *A brief history of everything.* Boston: Shambhala.

Wilbur, K. (2001b). *A theory of everything: An integral vision for business, politics, science, and spirituality.* Boston: Shambhala.

Williams, L. J., & Anderson, S. E. (1991). Job satisfaction and organizational commitment as predictors of organizational citizenship and in-role behaviors. *Journal of Management, 17,* 601–617.

Winter, D. G. (1993). Power, affiliation, and war: Three tests of a motivational model. *Journal of Personality and Social Psychology, 65,* 532–545.

Wlodkowski, R. J. (1998). *Enhancing adult motivation to learn: A comprehensive guide for teaching all adults* (rev. ed.). San Francisco: Jossey-Bass.

Wonderlic. (1992). *Wonderlic Personnel Test user's manual.* Libertyville, IL: Author.

Wortley, D. B., & Amatea, E. S. (1982, April). Mapping adult life changes: A conceptual framework for organizing adult development theory. *Personnel and Guidance Journal,* pp. 476–482.

Yalom, I. D. (1995). *The theory and practice of group psychotherapy* (4th ed.). New York: Basic Books.

# Author Index

## S



## T



## U



## V



## W

**Y**



**Z**

# Subject Index

## P



## Q



## R



## S



## T



## Z

Made in the USA
Lexington, KY
17 March 2014